New Hope
for People with
Bipolar Disorder

REVISED SECOND EDITION

NEW HOPE
for People with
BIPOLAR DISORDER

REVISED SECOND EDITION

Your Friendly, Authoritative Guide to the Latest in Traditional and Complementary Solutions

JAN FAWCETT, M.D.,

BERNARD GOLDEN, PH.D.,

NANCY ROSENFELD

THREE RIVERS PRESS • NEW YORK

Published in the United States by Three Rivers Press, an imprint of the Crown
Publishing Group, a division of Random House, Inc., New York.
www.crownpublishing.com

Three Rivers Press and the Tugboat design are registered trademarks
of Random House, Inc.

Originally published in slightly different form by Prima Publishing, Roseville,
California, in 2000.

Library of Congress Cataloging-in-Publication Data
Fawcett, Jan
   New hope for people with bipolar disorder : your friendly, authoritative guide
to the latest in traditional and complementary solutions / Jan Fawcett, Bernard Golden,
and Nancy Rosenfeld.
      p. cm.
   Includes bibliographical references and index.
   1. Manic-depressive illness.   2. Depression, Mental.   I. Golden, Bernard.
II. Rosenfeld, Nancy.   III. Title.
   RC516.F39   2007
   616.89'5—dc22   2007006690

ISBN 978-0-307-35300-9

Printed in the United States of America

Design by Meryl Sussman Levavi

10 9 8 7 6 5 4 3 2 1

First Edition

I dedicate this effort to my family—to my wife, Katie, and my children, Robin, Holly, Marc, Andrea, and especially my son Craig, who struggled to have a meaningful life despite experiencing much of what this book is about, and who died in his sleep on July 29, 2007. I am grateful to his wife, Shauna, and his daughters, Brittany and Amber, for the love and moments of pride and joy they gave him during the last years of his life.

—DR. JAN FAWCETT

Contents

Acknowledgments

This book was Nancy Rosenfeld's idea. The first time I met Nancy, she outlined her idea for a book about coping with bipolar disorder and asked me to write a chapter on diagnosis. I supported the idea of a book by someone who had experienced this illness, and agreed. The next thing I realized, I had written this and three more chapters.

Somehow Nancy had convinced me to become a coauthor along with Bernie Golden, whom I met and enjoyed working with in the course of producing the book. How did this happen? Nancy, the person who carries the "stigmatized" diagnosis, brought together, cajoled, and motivated two other people, with somewhat different perspectives but a common interest in reducing stigma and increasing awareness and hope with regard to bipolar disorder, to write this book.

Perhaps this is an example of the creative energy and determination that goes way beyond the concept of bipolar illness (this book wouldn't have happened without it). This is the lesson behind the message of the book. A person can become so much more than their illness. I've made two new friends and I hope our work will help people with bipolar illness and their families become informed consumers of services and see the possibilities for productive and meaningful lives.

—JAN FAWCETT

Completing this book marks the end of an extremely rewarding journey and collaboration. I am extremely grateful to Nancy Rosenfeld for inviting me to participate in this project. I thank her for her vision and courage. I am appreciative of her determination, commitment to quality, and for the many moments of personal joy I experienced as part of this team. Nancy started with a story and finished with a true message of hope. My deepest appreciation goes to Dr. Patricia Robin for her thoughtful consideration and confidence in recommending me to Nancy.

A special thanks to Jan Fawcett for his enthusiasm, knowledge, energy, and sense of calmness and centeredness that he brought to this endeavor. Frederick K. Goodwin, who spent countless hours reading and rereading our manuscript, also offered invaluable feedback, encouragement, and support.

Martha Hellander, executive director of Child and Adolescent Bipolar Foundation (CABF) provided us with parent interviews. This proved to be an invaluable source of material for chapter 11, "A Special Concern: Childhood/Adolescent Bipolar Illness."

My friends and colleagues listened to my ideas and offered critical feedback and encouragement. I also want to express my gratitude to Three Rivers Press for their enthusiastic confidence in the value of this book.

Finally, my sincere appreciation to all the clients who have shared their journeys with me.

—BERNIE GOLDEN

From first conception, the writing of this book was a team effort and could not have been achieved without everyone's total commitment. I wish to thank my coauthors, Jan Fawcett and Bernie Golden, for their dedicated help, abiding loyalty, and steadfast willingness to go that extra mile. The strength of our teamwork could best be compared to a healthy and successful marriage. I recall a comment that I made to my coauthors at one meeting, "If this is work, who needs entertainment?"

A book of this nature, one that touches every aspect of the human soul, would have been impossible for me to author had it not been for the love and understanding of my husband, Marty. His patience was tested on many occasions, but each time he responded with unwavering loyalty and support.

I am deeply grateful to Frederick K. Goodwin for his substantial contribution. Besides providing the foreword, Dr. Goodwin offered indispensable critical feedback and guidance. It was his intention from the very beginning that this book meet all standards of professional excellence. His tome, *Manic-Depressive Illness* (Goodwin/Jamison), reached ultimate acclaim by the Association of American Publishers: "Most Outstanding Book, Bio- and Medical Sciences, 1990."

Deborah Bullwinkel, former program director of National Depressive and Manic-Depressive Association (DMDA), now the Depression and Bipolar Support Alliance (DBSA), introduced me to several key people when I first began this book venture. National DMDA became an invaluable source of research material and information throughout the writing of this book. A special thanks to the staff!

Finally, my most sincere appreciation to Three Rivers Press / Random House for giving us the opportunity to move forward with this revised second edition. The suggestion originated from Carrie Thornton, publishing manager, whose proposal was based on the success of the book's 2000 release, and Brandi M. Bowles, our editor, who carefully checked and rechecked all revisions and additions. Thank you both!

—NANCY ROSENFELD

Foreword

Bipolar illness has long been a source of fascination in the mental health field. The fascination stems from the dramatically different states of mania and depression, which are alternating components of the same illness yet often occur simultaneously; the sudden and dramatic processes by which intense depression becomes mania literally overnight, as if a switch had been turned on; the challenge to understand how the same drug (lithium) can bring mania down and lift depression up; and, finally, the paradox that in bipolar disorder, arguably the most genetic and therefore the most biological of all mental illnesses, the psychosocial environment appears to activate the genetic vulnerability, converting it into a lifelong illness.

These features are ample reason for the growing interest among mental health professionals and brain scientists, but what of the recent surge in interest among the general public? To understand this, we might turn to another fascinating character of the illness: For many bipolar patients, the dark cloud of the illness is leavened by silver linings—creativity, intelligence, and drive. As a result, the bipolar spectrum is a more prevalent phenomenon among those in the public eye: artists, performers, writers, composers, and charismatic leaders.

Of course, this has long been true, but public opinion has also been bolstered of late by decades of research investment, principally by the National Institute of Mental Health and the pharmaceutical industry, which have yielded effective treatment for the illness. Today there are hundreds of thousands of bipolar patients leading successful and productive lives. In so doing, each of them sends a powerful and destigmatizing message, especially if they are in the public eye.

Not surprisingly, books have been the major vehicle increasing public knowledge. So far, what's out there falls into one of two categories: books by professionals and books by a patient or a family member. With the appearance of this book, a new genre has been established—a close collaboration between a bipolar patient and Dr. Jan Fawcett, one of the world's leading authorities on depression and bipolar disorder. The result of this unique collaboration? First, it is a book that vibrates with the flesh and blood of real people—principally, coauthor Nancy Rosenfeld and her story, supplemented by detailed stories and quotes from others with the illness. Nancy at moments seems to jump off the pages, right into your heart. At the same time, the reader is treated to a scientifically sophisticated discussion of bipolar illness—its genetics, biology, and psychology, along with its psychosocial impact and various pharmacological and psychotherapeutic treatments.

There is no wall between the author/patient and her two coauthors/doctors. Her story and her reflections are woven in the scientific and professional material, painting a compelling portrait of the patient as a full collaborator in advancing the understanding and treatment of her own illness. This itself is an important message for the public to absorb.

The book delivers another powerful message, both explicitly and implicitly, that patients need not be defined by their illness. Each one is a unique person with their own personality, life experience, strengths, and weaknesses. The authors send this message by using bipolar illness as a springboard to examine various aspects of the human condition—from suggestions for managing stress and advice about sexual happiness and optimum experience ("flow," or total involvement in life), to strategies for enhancing self-awareness and achieving job satisfaction, to a nicely accessible explanation of how cognitive psychotherapy works.

While venturing into these broader areas, the book remains true to its primary focus on the key issues in bipolar disorder: its genetic and biological basis; how psychosocial stress can alter its course; the problems of substance abuse, self-stigmatization, and compliance; the impact of the illness on family, friends, and career; and, of course, state-of-the-art treatment strategies.

The authors are especially to be commended for giving particular emphasis to childhood bipolar disorder and to the issue of suicide, each of which is assigned its own chapter. Only recently has it begun to dawn on our field that the conventional wisdom that bipolar disorder rarely occurs in childhood is a myth. Likewise, for decades, the field of suicidology, spearheaded predominantly by sociologists, overlooked the fact that the great majority of suicides occur in the context of a major psychiatric disorder, principally major depression and bipolar illness. In my opinion, Jan Fawcett is our field's leading authority on suicide and the author of the most definitive study of the clinical features of depression that can predict this tragic outcome. Having this information greatly increases the chance of preventing suicide. In addition, new hope that this ultimate tragedy can be averted comes from a recent review of twenty-eight separate reports involving more than sixteen thousand patients. The review concludes that the suicide rate among bipolar patients treated with lithium is six to eight times lower than it is among bipolar patients not on lithium. This is the first large-scale demonstration in psychiatry that a specific treatment can actually save lives, and it's appropriately noted in this book.

A final note. It's fair to ask how this unique collaborative effort came about and how it so clearly succeeded. I have a one-word answer: Nancy. Her boundless, almost hypomanic energy and enthusiasm were the engines, and her vision was the glue. So Nancy's own "silver linings" made it happen. What better way to teach the public about what's possible for people with bipolar disorder who have the courage to get into treatment and stick with it, working to improve their physical and emotional health every day.

—FREDERICK K. GOODWIN, M.D.
Director of the Psychopharmacology
Research Center
George Washington University Medical Center
Washington, D.C.

Introduction

This book is the collaborative effort of three people, each of whom approaches the subject of bipolar disorder from a distinct vantage point: Jan Fawcett, a renowned psychiatrist and psychopharmacologist; Bernard Golden, a psychologist and associate professor of psychology; and Nancy Rosenfeld, a woman who lives with bipolar disorder.

The uniqueness of this book is its multidimensional approach to bipolar illness rather than a concentration on a single perspective. We address the subject clinically, personally, and with an educational emphasis. Our main purpose is to bridge the gap between those of us who are afflicted and those who live around us by opening new areas of communication and thereby increasing each other's awareness and understanding.

Dr. Jan Fawcett, who is eminently qualified as a forerunner in the field of depression and manic depression, details the diagnosis, biology, and treatment of bipolar disorder as well as medical strategies and risk factors for suicide. Dr. Fawcett includes the latest psychiatric findings and treatment models.

Dr. Bernard Golden focuses on the stigma of mental illness; cognitive therapy; and optimism, hope, and transcendence. In addition, Dr. Golden offers a professional analysis of Nancy's probing questions: How do we, who live with bipolar disorder, appear to others and how do we affect people who live around us? Dr. Golden also addresses the family, which is too often the forgotten link in the wellness plan. While everyone's attention is focused on the one who is ill, the rest of the family is frequently left to survive on its own.

Readers who have bipolar disorder can identify with Nancy, whose experiences are threaded throughout the book. We also cite other cases, some interesting vignettes of people whose stories illustrate points that are emphasized in each chapter.

A MESSAGE FROM DR. FAWCETT

The fact that you are reading this book suggests you are looking for answers to your own dilemma or to a problem from which someone you care about is suffering from—either directly affecting you or out of pure caring for them. I hope something in this book is helpful to you. Before you search for answers to your dilemma, I will present some caveats that might make the material to follow more helpful.

My teachers taught me that if I did not expect too much in life then I would be more likely to be happy or, at least, less likely to be unhappy. Let's examine three very difficult concepts regarding mood disorders in general and bipolar disorder in particular:

1. Acceptance of the diagnosis of bipolar disorder
2. Acceptance of the number of treatment trials and medication combinations often necessary to stabilize bipolar disorder and the limitations of partial responses to treatment
3. Acceptance of the changes in lifestyle necessary to keep bipolar disorder or mood disorders from dominating your life or the life of your loved ones

Accepting the Diagnosis

Nobody is happy to be told they have a medical illness. Even less acceptable is to receive a psychiatric diagnosis. Furthermore, psychiatric diagnoses are easily disputed. First, no diagnostic medical test exists for proving a psychiatric diagnosis. My own hypertension diagnosis hit me in the face at a medical staff meeting. At thirty-eight years old I was nearly at the top of my game after being appointed department chair of a medical school at a large prestigious hospital. When I say "nearly" at the top of my game, I must confess that my successful career and the devotion it required had precipitated some serious marital problems. So when I sauntered over to a couple of nurses at the

"Mr. Fit" high blood pressure screening desk, with martini in one hand while cavalierly holding out my other arm for a blood pressure reading, the result gave me pause: 200/100. Nonsense, I thought, those nurses probably aren't so great at taking blood pressure. At my internist's office two weeks later I was confident about receiving a substantially lower reading. I felt very healthy, so I knew it must be a mistake since I was much too young for that. The internist personally took my pressure and repeated it a second time with a look of concern. "Jan," he said, "you have significant hypertension and need treatment. You also need to make some lifestyle changes." What changes? What's wrong with sixty- to eighty-hour workweeks and being just slightly overweight? After all, I was helping people. Not until my working hours stretched to a hundred per week and I collapsed from fatigue and out-of-control blood pressure did it dawn on me that I was running a high risk of something much worse than a short career. You know, "Live fast, die young, and leave a good-looking corpse." I was in jeopardy of a debilitating stroke, which meant no more running, no more work, no more lovemaking, no more fine red wine—a life devoid of all meaning. This realization got through to me, and I restructured my life and reduced the risk. I've learned to follow the advice of the eminent legislator Everett Dirksen: "Live as if you're going to die tomorrow; but plan as if you're going to live forever."

Although this may seem a long way from bipolar disorder, it is a fundamentally parallel scenario in that both prognoses are subject to initial doubt and resistance from the patient. However, as we have neither measures nor tests to make a definitive diagnosis of bipolar disorder, that natural skepticism is increased threefold. A diagnosis of bipolar disorder is based on symptoms reported over time by patients and available significant others and signs or symptoms noted at the time of evaluation by the examining clinician. It is more subjective than the sequential blood pressure readings used to diagnose hypertension or a fasting blood sugar test followed by a glucose tolerance test to diagnose diabetes, so it is much easier to question—or even doubt—the diagnosis.

Furthermore, nobody feels shame with a diagnosis of hypertension or diabetes, but the diagnosis of bipolar disorder often makes people feel "labeled." Society traditionally has regarded any mental disorder a sign of personal weakness more so than any other medical disorder. By this reasoning the patient is deemed responsible for his or her symptoms and frequently hears such comments as "You should try harder, or control your feelings or take a jog. Count your blessings, and by all means do not take happy pills or drugs that will zone you out. That's an escape from life." Years ago we considered mental disorders the result of "devil possession," implying the patient got what they deserved for consorting with the devil. Consider Job's suffering—his "friends" all agreed that he must have done something to deserve the pain. We have made some advances in medical and psychiatric science, but attitudes based on fear, ignorance, and prejudice still exist in modern guise. If people think this way, how can we expect patients to readily accept a diagnosis marked with stigma?

It is not unusual for a patient who is diagnosed with bipolar disorder to have witnessed a parent or close relative with the illness and suffered from their behavior. Receiving the same diagnosis can be difficult in this case. It is also hard to grasp the fact that the same diagnosis does not necessarily imply the same behavior or outcome, especially with more recently available treatments.

Young people in particular resist any diagnosis, especially the diagnosis of bipolar disorder. They often refuse to accept it and the treatment that goes with it at a time in life when any flaw is a disaster, and the mere idea of a mental illness and taking medication is anathema. *What would my friends think? I won't have any friends. People will think I'm nuts. Who would want to be my friend if they found out?* Friendships are more conditional at this stage of life.

A very common response is the denial of the diagnosis and/or "feeling over it" once symptoms abate, resulting in a range from refusal to discuss it to poor adherence to medication schedules. Many patients who go into this sort of denial suffer several episodes and even multiple hospitalizations while enduring a lot of pain. Some also experience severe life setbacks, such as the loss of their job and the disintegration of their marriage and family before they finally come to accept the treatment. This huge amount of loss and suffering can be avoided merely by seeking and sustaining early effective treatment.

Adhering to the following four components is the most effective way to prevent bipolar disorder from defining your life:

1. Accept a well-supported diagnosis
2. Learn as much as possible about bipolar disorder and its treatment
3. Establish a working alliance with a competent psychiatrist (and therapist) who understands bipolar disorder
4. Establish necessary support and healthy living patterns

Accepting Treatment with Limitations

You have been handed a diagnosis and have decided that if medication and therapy will help, it is a small price to pay for the symptoms from which you've been suffering. This is only the beginning.

First, medication is useless if it is not taken regularly, as prescribed. This used to be called compliance, a term that became politically incorrect, and is now referred to as adherence. Regardless of terminology, if you want benefit from treatment, you must strictly adhere to whatever regimen your doctor prescribes.

Now the bad news: Adherence to a medication regimen does not guarantee relief unless the medication or, more likely, the combination of medications works in your situation.

Unfortunately, no universal panacea for bipolar disorder has yet been established. Where there is suffering, always beware of people who, with no good evidence, promise you miracle cures. Internet sites will tell you, "Forget those toxic medications and take a natural cure that gets results, like J. K. Everyguy from Catalousa, Tennessee."

The truth: No panacea exists for bipolar disorder. No panacea exists for any medical illness. Penicillin perhaps came closest as a cure for pneumonia, but treatment-resistant organisms appeared almost instantly to complicate the picture. Every successful treatment is about finding the correct medication (or combination of medications) for the individual patient. For the fortunate few, this will happen on the first try, but for most patients it will take two or more tries to find the most effective and best-tolerated treatment.

New hope lies in learning about the illness, getting the best treatment available, forming an alliance with your doctor against the illness, and being patient while trying different medications until you find the combination that works for you. Never change the formula unless some negative side effects make it worth the chance.

Another fact that can be difficult to accept: Fewer than 20 percent of all successfully treated bipolar patients are well controlled with a single medication. Medicine has developed an aversion for "polypharmacy" too frequently undeserved. For the treatment of many conditions—including hypertension, diabetes, and mood disorders—it usually takes two to four medications, simultaneously administered, to control the illness. For example,

I take four medications for hypertension, another medication to reduce cholesterol (one of the causes and results of hypertension), and a third type of medication to control a diabetic tendency that "appeared" and—if left uncontrolled—can aggravate my hypertension. Although I hate doing it, I'm very glad I can stave off a debilitating stroke with these wonderful new medications. I'm an avid skier and, at seventy-two years-old, am able to walk the golf course instead of sitting in a wheelchair in front of the television set. It's the same with bipolar disorder and mood disorders, except you suffer directly from the mood state even though your physical health is not obviously impaired. The odds of cardiac and stroke problems are significantly higher with an untreated mood disorder.

Please note that you may need to try several medications before finding one that has no significant side effects, that you can comfortably take (keep in mind some side effects diminish or wear off over time), and that is truly effective in controlling your mood cycles and your depression. Notice I put "controlling your mood cycles" in first priority, because if you don't have mood stability, you are bound to have depression. However, it is possible to have mood stability in terms of manic, hypomanic, or mixed manic cycles and still have depression. Stabilization is the key to a good result.

You may need two, three, four, or even five medications to control your illness unless you are extremely "lucky." In a large study of bipolar disorder funded by the National Institute of Mental Health (NIMH), fewer than 20 percent of patients were able to achieve remission on one medication. At first glance this seems like a disappointing result—it's scary when medications don't do the job. However, as so many combinations exist, you will eventually find the solution for you—it may not be perfect, but it will help. Our message: Never give up! If your doctor gives up, get another opinion. It is important that you keep trying because something will ultimately help. How long will it take? This varies from case to case, but inevitably you *will* find the right formula to free you from the pain and limitations imposed by bipolar disorder.

Anything worth attaining requires time and sustained effort, despite what we hear from mass media and quick-fix marketing schemes that advertise alternative treatments with sketchy success stories. When expansive claims are made, always inquire about published results in a peer-reviewed journal. Facts found in someone's book or on an Internet site should be discounted until verified. If you keep at it and enlist the most knowledgeable and supportive help you can find, you will get the help you need—but don't expect it overnight.

Every patient responds differently to various treatments. One patient may get a great result from lithium while another may not find it tolerable or even beneficial. When people are desperate to get better, they often are susceptible to success stories, no matter the source. On the other hand, if a parent or sibling has bipolar disorder and has found a medication or combination of medications that are helpful, you might also respond to the same regimen. Family history will be helpful to your psychiatrist in choosing the best medication regimen for you.

Making Life Modifications to Control Bipolar Disorder

Difficulty in accepting a diagnosis of bipolar disorder was discussed above, but true acceptance of the diagnosis implies a willingness to make necessary life changes to control the disorder. The first change, as we discussed, requires vigilance to a prescribed medication regime on a regular basis. For many people this can entail a lifestyle change.

The next step involves learning to live within the limits of the vulnerability for bipolar disorder. Buddhist teachers sometimes say that true freedom is being able to live fully within the limits of your reality. It is imperative to abstain from street drugs such as cocaine, other stimulant drugs, cannabis, opiates, and excessive amounts of alcoholic beverages. All of these substances can provoke mood cycling and worsen the bipolar condition.

Third, establishing a routine of adequate sleep, adequate amounts of rest, and stress reduction is helpful in maintaining mood stability. Going to bed at the same time every night is a good way to do this. It is a good idea to keep a daily chart of your moods as well as the medication you are taking, and any major changes or stresses that are occurring in your life. This record will help you and your doctor assess the benefit you are getting from your medication regimen.

Finally, attending a self-help group can teach you a lot about bipolar disorder, including how to manage medication side effects. You can receive necessary support at little cost by availing yourself of these community support groups. Chapter 10 discusses the availability of such groups and how they can be helpful to individuals with bipolar disorder.

Attention to the areas discussed above can make a huge difference in how far you let your bipolar condition define your life.

A MESSAGE FROM DR. GOLDEN

We have experienced deep gratification for the very positive response to this book since its first publication six years ago. Those living with bipolar illness, their friends and family, and the greater professional community have each voiced appreciation both for the content as well as the unique blend of perspectives that are presented It is based on this reaction that we have decided to once again join efforts and further elucidate on new directions in the areas of treatment, attitudes, actions, and resources regarding the effective management of bipolar disorder.

Hope is not a static state of mind. Rather, it reflects an ongoing process, an optimistic attitude that hinges on a belief that things can get better. For anyone dealing with bipolar disorder, it is easy to understand moments when the road seems especially challenging. Yet we truly believe that the ideas presented here can only strengthen the evolving hope of all who read them.

A MESSAGE FROM NANCY ROSENFELD

As an author and researcher, I have devoted more than seventeen years to studying bipolar disorder in order to more fully understand and resolve my own issues. The opportunity to write a book on bipolar disorder became both my ultimate challenge and my biggest reward. After taking charge of the illness that nearly destroyed my life, I can finally reach out to others with insight and hope. I have struggled with some of the same problems that you, the reader, may face. One of the biggest impediments to overcome was stigma, and it is one of the focuses of this book. Since knowledge influences public opinion, education is the key to the elimination of stigma. It is our hope that people who suffer from mental disorders will no longer feel deviant or somehow flawed. The "feeble-minded madman" is a stereotype of the past!

I wrote this book to provide you with the answers and tools that have proven most valuable in my personal journey to wellness. Together, with my team of experts, we hope to help you achieve a smoother journey to health and well-being.

CHAPTER 1

Living with Bipolar Disorder

s it possible to turn suffering into genuine human achievement? Nancy Rosenfeld now answers yes to this question, but it took her many years of struggling before she arrived at that answer. She was well into adulthood—married, with two grown children and a grandchild—before she truly understood the positive aspects of her illness.

Over the years Nancy often asked herself why life is unfair to people who don't deserve to suffer. In her search for an answer, she was introduced to Rabbi Harold Kushner, whose son Aaron had died from progeria, a condition that produces rapid aging, just two days after his fourteenth birthday. After Aaron's death, Kushner explored this very question in his book *When Bad Things Happen to Good People*. The rabbi wrote, "God gave me the strength and wisdom to take my personal sorrow and forge it into an instrument of redemption which would help others." In the wake of a personal tragedy, he discovered the resiliency of the human soul. Through strength and courage, Kushner rebuilt his life. Rabbi Kushner became an inspiration to Nancy.

Nobody is promised a life free of pain and disappointment, but our capacity for strength and courage enables us to survive even the greatest of life's tragedies. Although bad things *don't* happen for a good reason, Rabbi Kushner found meaning in the very experience of them. If life was free of pain and sorrow, we would have no way to measure and test our strength and to explore the outer limits of our capabilities. We live in an imperfect world, but we too are imperfect. Acceptance of our own mortality enhances the meaning of life and, as Kushner reflected, gives each of us the opportunity to be productive and to impact others, so we'll be remembered as having contributed to this world. Knowing that our time is limited gives value to the things we do.

Can those of us who are afflicted with bipolar disorder, a mental illness characterized by alternating periods of manic and depressive behavior, accept our own frailty and imperfections? Are we prepared to meet rejection from others who don't understand our issues? Can we assume responsibility for our disorder without using it as an excuse for our actions? Regardless of the pain dealt us in life, can we focus on the positive and minimize the negative?

Many individuals who have suffered harshly have learned to survive great losses and find new ways of living full and productive lives despite their misfortunes. How does one cope with shame and humiliation, a grave illness, a disabling accident, disfiguring surgery that involves the loss of body parts, or the death of a loved one?

You will discover that it is possible to transform a serious loss or human affliction, such as receiving a diagnosis of bipolar disorder, into a positive and meaningful life experience by understanding and mastering the principles of a positive mental attitude. The human mind is resilient and capable of reversing a negative situation even in the midst of pain and cruelty. By learning how to live again and overcoming seemingly insurmountable obstacles people can emerge stronger and more self-reliant, with new goals and a renewed purpose in life.

Paraplegics, who have lost the use of limbs, often discover the ability to lead fulfilling, productive lives. Others, who have lost their sight or hearing, gain a deeper sense of perception in the aftermath of their loss. Likewise, many who are afflicted with bipolar disorder rise above their illness by adjusting to new lifestyles.

> *It's possible to transform a serious loss or human tragedy, such as receiving a diagnosis of bipolar disorder, into a positive and meaningful life experience by understanding and mastering the principles of a positive mental attitude.*

A diagnosis of bipolar disorder, which is also known as manic depression, can leave permanent scars. People with the disorder feel branded or stigmatized. The illness carries a bad connotation; it sounds awful and can be frightening. The mere mention of bipolar, or any mental illness, can adversely affect relationships, summoning as it does visions of the most severe forms of emotional disturbance. At the same time, each individual has a unique personality that influences his or her attitudes and conclusions regarding a given diagnosis, so everyone reacts differently.

A survey conducted by the Depression and Bipolar Support Alliance (DBSA), the organization which Jan Fawcett helped found in 1986, concluded that over 1.5 percent of the adult population in the United States (more than 2.5 million people) suffer from manic depression.

> *Nobody is immune—young or old, rich or poor. People from all walks of life are vulnerable, and bipolar disorder has confronted high-profile individuals in all fields of endeavor.*

Nobody is immune—young or old, rich or poor. People from all walks of life are vulnerable, and bipolar disorder has confronted high-profile individuals in all fields of endeavor. The revelations of these people clearly indicate that financial resources, status, gender, intellect, and even the devotion of friends and family cannot prevent the illness. In their candor they reflect exceptional courage and boldness, and their disclosures are gifts to those who feel they are suffering alone.

Many celebrated individuals have educated us, helping to reduce the stigma surrounding bipolar disorder, and supported those of us who believe we are outcasts feel less so. In addition, they have offered us hope that through openness and compassion we can more easily make sense of a mental illness such as manic depression. In this book, we will meet these people and discover how they have learned to cope with their illnesses—from unipolar depression to bipolar disorder. Here they candidly reveal their stories, specific symptoms, personal concerns, and reactions to being diagnosed with a mental illness.

JUDGE SOL WACHTLER: ON THE OTHER SIDE OF THE BENCH

One example of a powerful personality who suffered from bipolar disorder is Judge Sol Wachtler. Judge Wachtler began his government career in 1963 when he was first elected to the city council of North Hempstead, New York. Wachtler advanced to the New York State Supreme Court in 1968 and in 1972 was elected to the Court of Appeals, New York's highest court. In 1985 Governor Mario Cuomo appointed Wachtler chief judge of the State of

New York and the Court of Appeals. In an editorial for the *New York Times,* Alan Dershowitz wrote, "Sol Wachtler was not a good judge . . . he was a great judge."

Just as Judge Wachtler was on the threshold of becoming governor of New York, a cherished dream, he became instead Sol Wachtler, federal prisoner, assigned to solitary confinement. How did this happen?

The story of Sol Wachtler is one of illicit love and clandestine meetings, compulsive behavior and drug abuse, rejection and deceit, shame and self-reproach, depression with an attempt to self-medicate, and the fear of stigma—of being branded mentally incompetent.

Although it was a reckless act of compulsive behavior that abruptly led to Wachtler's self-destruction and ultimate fall, the root of Sol Wachtler's problem was his bipolar illness. It wasn't until 1992 that Judge Wachtler finally received the correct diagnosis, but by then his unchecked illness had destroyed his professional career and his life.

Though he made a courageous comeback from the abyss into which he had plunged, he dismisses any sentiments regarding the achievement. "I don't feel as if I've reclaimed my life," Wachtler says. "I've got a long way to go, and it will never be the same as before. I will always have deep scars. Take, for example, the times I hear myself talking to my students about 'my' court. But suddenly I realize that it no longer is my court. It was my court for twenty-five years, but that's all gone now."

Five years after his diagnosis, Judge Wachtler went public in a book about his experiences, *After the Madness: A Judge's Own Prison Memoir.* In

> *Just as Judge Wachtler was on the threshold of becoming governor of New York, a cherished dream, he became instead Sol Wachtler, federal prisoner.*

it, he maintains his dignity and sense of humor without excusing the actions that resulted in his arrest and conviction. Judge Wachtler's personal story can serve as a deterrent to others, as well as an inspiration.

There is no debating the pathological nature of manic-depressive illness. The disorder can unquestionably destroy lives, not to mention relationships. At the same time, the energy and the creativity that spills forth from this otherwise devastating condition can yield dividends for the afflicted and those who witness their lives.

In 2000, Judge Wachtler flew to Chicago for a personal interview with Nancy, Bernie Golden, and Deborah Bullwinkel.[1] At that time, Wachtler was teaching law again, twice a week, at a small college in New York, while also working at a mediation firm, writing his next book, and traveling extensively to lecture about bipolar disorder and his experience. Here is Sol Wachtler's personal account of his fall from grace.

Judge Wachtler was incarcerated in September 1993 for harassing his former mistress. At that time, he was a walking time bomb and was placed in solitary confinement for two weeks under close observation. The second and only other time that Wachtler was confined to solitary was for his own protection, after he was stabbed by another prison inmate. Although Wachtler never condoned his deviant behavior, it is clear that his bipolar disorder and abuse of prescription drugs contributed to his wrongdoing.

"Don't misunderstand," said Wachtler. "Bipolar is not, and should not be, an excuse for criminal conduct. If someone afflicted with the disorder commits a criminal act, that person should be stopped or arrested before more harm is done."

Wachtler's eminent position in the outer world did not earn him special treatment in jail. He was subjected to all the forms of inhumanity prisoners endure, including strip searches. During imprisonment, what he longed for most was privacy and freedom. "This loss was far greater than power or prestige," he said. "Prison was tough. Everything and every day was a constant reminder that I was a prisoner behind bars—the guards, the keys, mail call. At one time I considered suicide but quickly ruled it out as a viable alternative. Suicide takes courage, but I had none."

"It took more courage to live," observed Nancy.

"Perhaps. But I was stuck in the here and now, and with no future image. I saw nothing beyond life in prison. Days were endless, and each seemed like eternity. All thoughts were negative. I worried about what I'd do when I got out and how I'd make a living. I was also a patient in the mental health unit, and the treatment there was deplorable." Wachtler credits Prozac with keeping him going during his thirteen-month incarceration.

After his release, Wachtler had to contend with the public opinion of his actions. "Subtle things happened which were hurtful," he said. "For example, as former chief judge of New York I was invited to attend the presentation of an award to Ruth Ginsburg, a justice of the United States Supreme Court. Before the actual ceremony, recognition was extended to all distinguished former recipients of that award who were in attendance. I listened and waited, but my name was never called. I checked the program, then discovered that it had been omitted from the list."

"As if you never existed," said Deborah.

"Yes. Like a blot in history that was simply erased," he replied. "Around the same time, Mike Wallace invited me to do a segment of *60 Minutes,* but I declined."

"Why?" asked Nancy.

"He can be very rough," said Wachtler.

"What about your relationship today with Governor Cuomo?" said Nancy. "I know the two of you had been friends for years, but the friendship disintegrated and you sued him."

In 1991, Judge Sol Wachtler had filed a summons and complaint against Governor Cuomo in *Wachtler v. Cuomo.* The governor had threatened to cut the newly proposed budget of the state court system, which Wachtler had submitted to the legislature. At that time, Wachtler felt he "could not permit" Cuomo's budget cuts because of the damaging effect he believed they would have on the court system.

> *At that time I didn't consider my behavior strange. I thought they [others] were bizarre, not me. "I'm not talking too fast," I'd say. "You're listening too slowly."*
>
> —JUDGE SOL WACHTLER

"There's been a warming since then," said Wachtler, with a smile. "Just two weeks ago we lunched together, and Mario confided, 'Once you sued me, I knew you were crazy.'"

"How did you view your illness?" inquired Bernie.

"Bizarre," said Wachtler. "But at that time I didn't consider my behavior strange. I thought they [others] were bizarre, not me. 'I'm not talking too fast,' I'd say. 'You're listening too slowly.' Looking back, I don't see how I could have entertained that thought pattern. It's incomprehensible."

In his memoir, Wachtler sums up manic behavior and the unrealistic overconfidence and grandiosity that accompany full-blown mania: "Have a speech to deliver? I don't have to prepare—my head is full of the world's greatest speeches—just give me a platform."[2]

On the other end of the spectrum, he describes his state of mind at the height of depression as like the inner surface of an abyss. The physical manifestations of his depression included loss of appetite, constant weeping, sleeplessness, and fluttering in his stomach.

Before his diagnosis, he had convinced himself that he was suffering from a brain tumor. An MRI (magnetic resonance imaging) scan in 1992, however, revealed not a tumor but a mass of unidentified bright objects (UBOs) in the right parietal region of his brain. The discovery of UBOs, as Kay Jamison reveals in her book, *An Unquiet Mind,* heralded the scientific conclusion that bipolar disorder is a biological condition involving changes in brain chemistry (see chapter 3).

"It's important for anyone with mental illness to recognize the need for professional guidance before behavior turns antisocial," cautioned Wachtler. "Not to seek help is foolish, stupid, and terribly destructive. My wife, a trained certified social worker, pleaded with me to get counseling." Wachtler eventually did, and Prozac freed him. "Had I accepted my wife's advice earlier, today I'd be governor of New York."

> *It's important for anyone with mental illness to recognize the need for professional guidance before behavior turns antisocial. Not to seek help is foolish.*
>
> —JUDGE SOL WACHTLER

Wachtler resisted psychiatric help because of the stigma society imposes on those who "seek to remedy a defect of the mind." He recalled the lesson of Thomas Eagleton, the former U.S. senator and 1972 vice presidential candidate who was dropped from the ballot after it was leaked that he once received psychiatric treatment.

Psychotherapy helped Wachtler, and he still sees his psychiatrist regularly. "I'm on a maintenance program, but I also self-assess. I measure what I've done and how I've done it. For example, am I speaking too rapidly? I keep a reality checklist." Wachtler takes long walks for physical exercise, which also helps regulate his mood. Only now, looking back on the behavior that resulted in his public disgrace, can Wachtler see how out of control he was.

"I didn't realize the absurdity of my actions toward her [his mistress] until after I started on Prozac. I had low-level depression and mania prior to the relationship, but I was unaware of how ridiculous it was until later. Then I was helped to make sense of why I had sought out the relationship in the first place. I remember my wife's comment once that if ever I had an affair she didn't want to know about it. But then she read about my affair on page 1 of the *New York Times.*"

"Do you worry about depression returning?" asked Bernie.

"Constantly. As soon as I see it happening, I return to the doctor so he can adjust my medication."

At the end of the interview, Nancy commented that everything happens for a reason. "No!" Wachtler exclaimed, then added, "You have no idea how many people have told me that. But I can't accept it."

With no further word on the subject, Bernie and Nancy were left to speculate on the vehemence of Wachtler's last remark. The judge was approaching his seventieth birthday, and his very identity had been based on his judicial career and becoming the governor of New York. Now all that was gone; his dream had turned to ash. Not for several months would Wachtler reveal the reasons behind his vehement reaction that day in Chicago.

Since Wachtler's release from prison thirteen years ago, he has waged a crusade to help other people who, like himself, are afflicted with mental disorders. He travels extensively across the country lecturing about his bipolar condition. "Get help," he advocates. "Don't be stupid like I was." Yet, by reaching out to others in the hope of removing the stigma of mental illness, he has again positioned himself for public attack.

During an address in Albany, New York, for instance, Wachtler informed his audience that more people with mental illnesses are in prison today than are in hospitals receiving treatment. "Nobody is cured in prison," he said. "They become more dysfunctional." The very next day his words made headline news in New York: EX-CON TALKS ABOUT PRISON EXPERIENCE.

"Why talk," said Wachtler, "if every time it's like putting a pencil in my own eye. I'm not proud of having been in prison. But to refer to me as an 'ex-con' rather than by name or as the former chief judge is a constant bad reminder, like waking up a sleeping dog."

Despite obstacles, to this day Wachtler maintains a busy schedule as a mental health advocate, and educating others is at the forefront of his concern. He may not believe that things happen for a reason, yet the day Sol Wachtler permanently lost "his court" he began a new life as a source of inspiration and education to others.

MIKE WALLACE: LIVING WITH THE BLACK DOG

Mike Wallace, veteran news correspondent of *60 Minutes* since the show first aired in 1968 until his retirement in 2006, is another well-known personality who suffered from a mental disorder. In his case, it was depression, which

Winston Churchill, a fellow sufferer, referred to as "the black dog." Churchill's black dog image profoundly illustrates the all-consuming desolation experienced by people in this mental state.

Journalism's legendary tough guy, Wallace was shadowed with his first bout of depression after General William Westmoreland named him in a $120 million libel suit against CBS. "The Uncounted Enemy: A Vietnam Deception," a 1982 *CBS News Reports* documentary anchored by Wallace, charged Westmoreland with "cooking the books" in Vietnam in 1967. According to his charges, Westmoreland had failed to inform the American people of the truth regarding the number of enemy troops still fighting and how many more were coming down from North Vietnam to help drive Americans out of the country.[3]

In 1984, two years after Wallace accused Westmoreland of falsifying reports to the American public, he began an eighteen-week trial. It was a tough time for him as he was forced to sit helplessly by while being branded a "cheat" and a "liar." He was also trying to do his job, working nights and going off for a couple days at a time on a shoot. Because of his inability to concentrate on anything else, he

> *Fear of the stigma surrounding depression made Mike Wallace afraid of losing his job as a CBS news correspondent and anchorman. He felt it necessary, at all costs, to maintain his macho image.*

endured sleepless nights, weight loss, and depression so severe that he described himself as "feeling lower than a snake's belly."[4] Throughout this period, Wallace felt so ashamed at the prospect of being branded with the stigma of mental illness that he attempted to mask his feelings from everyone. Fear of the stigma surrounding depression also made him afraid of losing his job as a CBS news correspondent and anchorman. He felt it necessary, at all costs, to maintain his macho image.

While shame and guilt are typical components of depression, Mike Wallace's bout with depression was compounded by his tough-guy image. It was the meaning he gave to the illness (that depression is like a black hole), combined with his severe and unrealistically high self-expectations, that further exacerbated his shame and depression.

When Wallace was first diagnosed, he did not consider the public's reaction. He was too sick to care, and yet he didn't want to lose his job. He believed people knew something strange was going on, but they didn't know what it

> *By the time Mike Wallace was hospitalized and diagnosed with clinical depression, he was grateful to have some kind of diagnosis. He had worried that he had a brain tumor or that he was losing his mind.*

was. At that time, neither did Wallace. Not until later did he become aware of public opinion. When out in public places, he imagined that everyone was pointing at him, saying, "There's the cheat, the fraud, the fake."[5]

Wallace couldn't sleep, and because of his insomnia he started taking half a sleeping pill. From half it went up to one sleeping pill, and then if he still wasn't sleeping, he'd take another. He felt miserable all day long.

Wallace recalls his anguished calls to his personal physician. "I was really talking suicide and he would say, 'C'mon, Mike, you're not going to do that. You're strong and capable. This, too, shall pass.'"[6]

By the time Wallace was hospitalized and diagnosed with clinical depression, he was grateful to have some kind of diagnosis. Like Sol Wachtler, he had worried that he had a brain tumor or, alternatively, that he was losing his mind. But the pain associated with Wallace's clinical depression was more painful than Sol Wachtler's untreated manic episodes. People rarely seek help during manic episodes because they feel good. It's those who live around them, both family and friends, who suffer the most, as their lives are directly affected by the manic attacks of loved ones.

Wallace was released from the hospital after one week and sent home with a prescription for antidepressants and plenty to read on depression. He remained quiet about his own illness until a friend, novelist William Styron, the Pulitzer Prize–winning author of *Sophie's Choice,* came out of the closet about his mental health problems. Only then could Mike speak candidly about his affliction.

> *I think it's useful to talk about depression because it remains a mystery to so many people, and also verboten to so many people to talk about. If somebody has suffered it, survived it, and gone on about his business, and people know that, then it's got to be useful.*
>
> —MIKE WALLACE

"I think it's useful to talk about depression because it remains a mystery to so many people, and also verboten to so many people to talk about. If somebody has suffered it, survived it, and gone on about his business, and people know that, then it's got to be useful."[7]

In 1998, HBO broadcasted a special one-hour documentary, "Dead Blue: Surviving Depression." The program featured Mike Wallace along with William Styron and clinical psychologist Martha Manning, author of the book *Undercurrents*. The three featured guests spoke candidly about their illness with no reportage, script, narration, or "experts." Wallace noted how depression, despite epidemic proportions, was "shrouded in secrecy—something to hide, a skeleton in the closet associated with guilt, fear, and shame." Their message: "There is a way out of the darkness."

Wallace recovered from this bout of depression but suffered two relapses, in 1985 and 1993, before his health was fully restored. Depression-free ever since, Mike follows a strict maintenance program and returns to his doctor for semiannual checkups, which he's dubbed "lube jobs." Of his experience, he said, "I think I'm a wiser and kinder man for having been through it. That doesn't mean that I've lost the edge; I'm more empathic, more careful about making snap judgments, and I think I like myself better."[8]

COPING WITH DEPRESSION

As the daughter of famed news broadcaster Walter Cronkite, anchorman of the *CBS Evening News* (1962–1981), Kathy Cronkite has lived in the public eye all her life. Today she is a popular writer, journalist, public speaker, and one of the millions who suffer from clinical depression.

In the spring of 1990, Kathy Cronkite read an interview with Mike Wallace in *U.S. News & World Report,* in which Wallace openly talked about his battle with depression. His admission gave Cronkite the courage to face her own struggle.

"I've known Mike Wallace and his family all my life. Even when I was young, he was one of those rare grown-ups who seemed to take me seriously. Still, I never dreamed that as an adult I would interview him, as one professional to another."[9]

Cronkite had shared the same fear as Mike Wallace of publicly disclosing her personal battle with depression. She, too, had been worried that disclosure of her illness might have negative repercussions on her professional life. But it was the black dog that Cronkite most dreaded. "[Churchill's] black dog has really got me," she wrote in her book, *On the Edge of Darkness*. "[His] image of despair suits me better than 'the black hole.' A black hole just swallows you up. But, this dog, . . . I can't cope while he's there."

Kathy Cronkite eventually admitted to being in grave danger from her depression, but not until after she had contemplated swallowing a can of liquid Drano.

Academy Award–winning actor Rod Steiger also had suicidal tendencies. "You have moments when you're locked in an ever-increasing terror," he told Cronkite when she interviewed him for her book. "You begin to doubt your sanity. When you're depressed, there's no calendar. There are no dates, there's no day, there's no night, there's no seconds, there's no minutes, there's nothing. You're just existing in this cold, murky, ever-heavy atmosphere, like they put you inside a vial of mercury." Steiger insisted that you can't understand these feelings unless you've experienced them. Yet, no matter how sick he was, Steiger felt that acting was something he could always do. "Now I realize I didn't have as much control as I thought I had." When depressed, he was "acting in a fog."[10]

> *When you're depressed, there's no calendar. There are no dates, there's no day, there's no night, there's no seconds, there's no minutes, there's nothing.*
>
> —ROD STEIGER

Unlike the others, however, Rod Steiger was not ashamed to go public with his illness. "It might have damaged me to some degree in the profession, but across the country one in five has a mental disease. It's about time we begin to talk about this thing."[11]

Steiger believed that narcissism makes a person more vulnerable to depression. "If you've got a huge powerful ego and then all of a sudden it's proven that you're nobody but another human being, you can slide down a long way because you're way up there. I felt that I was gonna live forever. Why? Because my name's Rod Steiger."[12]

Writer Kay Redfield Jamison, who has bipolar disorder and knows the horror of deep depression intimately, describes the black dog in *An Unquiet Mind*:

Depression is awful beyond words or sounds or images. . . . It bleeds relationships through suspicion, lack of confidence and self-respect, the inability to enjoy life, to walk or talk or think normally, the exhaustion, the night terrors, the day terrors. . . . [Depression] gives you the experience of how it must be to be old, to be old and sick, to be dying; to be slow of mind; to be lacking in grace, polish, and coordination; to be ugly; to have no belief in the possibilities of life, the pleasures of sex, the exquisiteness of music, or the ability to make yourself and others laugh.

Depression is flat, hollow, and unendurable . . . tiresome. People cannot abide being around you. . . . You are tedious . . . irritable and paranoid and humorless and lifeless and critical and demanding and no reassurance is ever enough. You're frightened, and you're frightening.[13]

Like Kay Jamison, Nancy can identify with devastating episodes of deep and disabling depression. There is no minimizing its shattering, destabilizing effects, not only on the patient but also on family and friends. Depression is dark days and endless nights. Trivial, mundane tasks become insurmountable. Listening to music, taking a walk, or partaking in some otherwise pleasant outing with family and friends—none of these former pastimes bring joy to the afflicted, only sadness. All are sharp reminders of the past, a time when life felt good. Depression has a domino effect—one defeat leads to another and another and another . . .

"One of the mysteries of depression," said Kathy Cronkite, "is why people succumb when they do, why a blow that cripples one person is taken in stride by another, and why a person who has survived great adversity is laid low by one of life's predictable stumbling blocks." For example, Cronkite was deeply traumatized when her beloved dog was killed by a car. She had never experienced the death of a close relative or friend, and this loss plunged her into one of the deepest and longest depressive episodes that she had ever encountered.

While it may not be apparent in everyone with manic depression, frequently there are psychosocial stressors, as in Cronkite's situation, that trigger the illness in those who have a genetic predisposition for it. A casual observer may underestimate the severity of emotional distress caused by such events. Fortunately, Cronkite had the support and understanding of family and friends who were deeply attached to their own pets and could empathize with her loss.

> *When the black dog of depression rides along, you're in for a roller-coaster ride of exhilaration and despair. Those of us whose marriages survive seem to agree that it is largely because we are married to extraordinary people—"angels" or "saints."*
>
> —KATHY CRONKITE

Cronkite is candid about her personal relationships and the destructive nature of depression. After suffering a major crisis, she feared that her marriage was in jeopardy even though her husband had stood by her throughout her ups and downs. "No marriage runs on a smooth road all the time," she said, "but when the black dog of depression rides along, you're in for a roller-coaster ride of exhilaration and despair. Those of us whose marriages survive seem to agree that it is largely because we are married to extraordinary people—'angels' or 'saints.'"[14]

NANCY'S STORY: A DESPERATE CRY FOR HELP

"I felt like an oddball growing up," said Nancy. "I didn't fit. I was Jewish in a Gentile community, tall for my age, and older than most other students in my class. Being both older and taller created a sharp contrast between 'me' and 'them,' which made me feel isolated. My basic shyness and feeling of insecurity led to hero worshiping—the popular high school cheerleader, an older cousin, a beautiful aunt. I found safety in the shadow of others."

Nancy's moods continued to haunt her from childhood on. An emotional child who had been heavily doted on as her parents' firstborn, she continued to struggle with chronic low self-esteem and depression throughout her childhood. Although her moods became less severe and less frequent as she matured, they persisted well into adulthood.

Nancy's adult life was typical of the upper-middle-class suburban American housewife of the late 1960s to early 1980s. She sublimated her individuality to raise a family while living in the shadow of her husband's career. Although she had moments of uncertainty and sadness, not until her children entered adolescence and needed her less did she begin to experience a gripping, gnawing, and growing feeling of emptiness. She was nagged by the constant feeling that there must be more to life. At the same time, Nancy realized that she needed to develop her own identity. It was then, when Nancy was just entering her forties, that she found that identity working as a political activist. During this period she exhibited the first signs of bipolar disorder when she became obsessively involved in the rescue of a former Soviet scientist and political prisoner.

NANCY: HYPOMANIA

In the spring of 1996, at the age of fifty-four, Nancy was admitted to the hospital for a hysterectomy after being diagnosed with a uterine tumor. Her state of imbalance was immediately evident when she exhibited obvious signs of hypomanic behavior, or low-grade mania.

"The doctors and nurses kept shaking their heads, and one doctor suggested I be given lithium to control the mania," said Nancy. "But, since I realized that my manic state was only a temporary condition, I declined the doctor's 'offer.' I enjoyed the intensity of the moment, that feeling of being overly zealous." Although Nancy's laughter in the hospital was considered extreme, it probably prevented a bout with the blues. Furthermore, medicinal humor is psychologically beneficial and contributes to the healing process.

Nancy's normal daily antidepressant dosage, 50 mg of Zoloft, had apparently been insufficient in controlling the sudden hormonal shock to her system after the hysterectomy. Though aware of her manic state, Nancy had not been able to control it. In fact, she actually enjoyed the temporary mania.

Episode 1   Two friends, a husband and wife, stopped by to see Nancy in her hospital room, but the visit turned sour because Nancy was manicky and nearly out of control. When the husband asked Nancy what had happened during surgery to cause some "complication," she told them of the doctor's surprising discovery of an advanced case of endometriosis. The couple's reaction was anger. Apparently they had been very worried that something had gone seriously wrong because Nancy had exaggerated her condition during an earlier telephone conversation with them. Nevertheless, their emphatic response triggered an explosive reaction from Nancy.

"My alter ego began to speak," recalled Nancy. "Why on earth had this couple come to visit me if they were unable to be supportive? Were they disappointed I wasn't dying? Weren't visitors supposed to help buoy a patient's spirits? Should it be the patient's responsibility to guard her every word—and entertain? Isn't this nonsense?

"At the time I was furious," admitted Nancy. "I had just had surgery that morning, and although it had gone well, I was lying there uncomfortably while my two friends seemed to be arguing over semantics. Now I realize that the problem stemmed from me, not them.

(continued)

Episode 2   A second event occurred moments after the first. Still in pain from the first hospital encounter and her overreaction, Nancy was quickly transformed by a surge of mania. When another group of friends appeared in the doorway with cheerful faces, that was enough to cause a sudden change of mood from anger to giddiness.

"I was so happy to see my friends," said Nancy. "It was especially meaningful because they needed to travel some distance to see me in the hospital. I asked when they had made the decision to visit that evening. Dorothy replied that she had actually tried three times that day to ask me about visiting hours, but that it was hard to keep me on a single topic. I remember laughing apologetically and responding that visiting hours were all day and all night. As to the 'uplifting' experience of visiting me in the hospital after such a long trek, their response: 'It's more than we bargained for, even better than *Saturday Night Live!*' "

What Nancy's friends had witnessed was a hypomanic episode. People who become hypomanic can be very entertaining and fun to be with. They laugh a lot and are very talkative and animated. They are also prone to angry outbursts and downright meanness, however, and their energy levels can climb so high that sleep and concentration become a problem.

BIPOLAR DISORDER AND CREATIVITY

Since perfection does not exist among humans, all of us live with some kind of impairment or disability. It's how we adjust to our imperfections that determines our potential for happiness in life. When faced with challenge, what are the options?

"Is there life after manic depression?" questioned Patty Duke, who suffers from the illness.

In looking for an answer, Duke learned that people who share her disorder are frequently highly creative and successful individuals. The very nature of bipolar disorder is conducive to high energy and imaginative thinking.

Kay Jamison, Ph.D., and Frederick K. Goodwin, M.D., have presented a reasonable theory that supports the concept of bipolar "advantages," more commonly referred to as "fluency of thinking." They have shown a high correlation between creative personalities and bipolar illness. Jamison determined that highly creative people are usually most productive and prolific during periods of hypomania. In fact, it is the very intensity of such moods that propels and inspires creative thinkers. Jamison herself is an example of a highly creative and successful career person who lives with manic depression. She did not receive a diagnosis of bipolar disorder until after she had begun her career as a psychologist. Elements of creative thinking, many of which are associated with cognitive changes that take place during mild manias, include:

- Word fluency
- Associational fluency
- Expressional fluency
- Ideational fluency[15]

An artistic temperament and imagination, the by-product of such creative assets, have given rise to many celebrated and distinguished individuals. Among these talented people who have bipolar disorder we find poets, writers, artists, business tycoons, political leaders, and scientists.

Kay Jamison writes about her own experience with the illness. "I honestly believe that as a result of it I have felt more things, more deeply; had more experiences, more intensely; loved more, and been more loved; laughed more often for having cried more often; appreciated more . . . seen the finest and the most terrible in people, and slowly learned the values of caring, loyalty, and seeing things through. . . . But, normal or manic, I have run faster, thought faster, and loved faster than most I know. . . . It has made me test the limits of my mind.

"Extremes of emotions are a gift—the capacity to be passionately involved in life, to care deeply about things, to feel hurt; a lot of people don't have that. It's the transition in and out of the highs and lows, the constant contrast, that fosters creativity."[16] Impairment, the inability to function normally, does not occur until after the hypomanic stage has progressed into full-blown mania.

> *Highly creative people are usually most productive and prolific during periods of hypomania. In fact, it is the very intensity of such moods that propels and inspires creative thinkers.*

Without trying to romanticize or falsely exaggerate the positives, history has proven that people afflicted with bipolar disorder are in good company.

> *Extremes of emotions are a gift—the capacity to be passionately involved in life, to care deeply about things, to feel hurt; a lot of people don't have that. It's the transition in and out of the highs and lows, the constant contrast, that fosters creativity.*
>
> —KAY JAMISON

The ability to inspire is as important to public officials and world leaders as creativity is to people in the arts. Many of our most powerful men and women are among the afflicted. But not everyone who is creative or productive is manic depressive, nor is everyone with manic-depressive illness creative.

Goodwin and Jamison list certain bipolar characteristics common to many political dignitaries, including "high energy, enthusiasm, intensity of emotion, persuasion by mood, charisma, contagion of spirit, gregarious and extrovertish, increased belief in one's self and one's ideas, heightened alertness and observational abilities, and risk-takers."[17] Among the political leaders with bipolar disorder are Napoleon, Mussolini, Alexander the Great, Lord Nelson, and Oliver Cromwell, to name just a few.

Alexander Hamilton (1755–1804), first U.S. secretary of the treasury, suffered from extreme paranoia, hypersexuality, financial speculation and consequent indebtedness, rapid and fiery temper, extreme mood swings, and inordinate energy. Abraham Lincoln (1809–1865) struggled with suicidal depressions; Robert E. Lee (1807–1870), intermittent depressions; Winston Churchill (1874–1965), severe periods of depression alternating with periods of high energy; and, Martin Luther (1483–1546), periods of deep psychosis and, occasionally, suicidal melancholy.[18]

According to *Time* magazine, even current success heroes of our culture such as Ted Turner (*Time*'s "Man of the Year" in 1991) reputedly use mood-stabilizing drugs.

WORDS FROM THE WISE

The following are quotations from some famous, highly creative individuals who suffered from bipolar disorder.

Why is it that all men who are outstanding in philosophy, poetry, or the arts are melancholic?

—ARISTOTLE

By our own spirits we are defied;
We poets in our youth begin in gladness,
But thereof come in the end despondency
  and madness.

—WILLIAM WORDSWORTH

One must harbor chaos within oneself to give birth to a dancing star.

—FRIEDRICH WILHELM NIETZSCHE

Life is a train of moods.

—RALPH WALDO EMERSON

TIPPER GORE: DISPELLING MYTHS

"Coming out" about her illness was not easy for Tipper Gore. Yet she felt the only way of reducing the stigma of mental disorders was to educate the American public. Gore has remained mostly silent about the details of her own illness, citing just a few examples. Her struggle with clinical depression manifested itself soon after a car accident that had nearly killed her son.[19]

It is normal for people to experience grief when something terrible happens to a loved one or to themselves. Normal grief over a death, serious injury, or diagnosis of some catastrophic illness crosses the line and becomes "abnormal" only after it becomes apparent that one's grief has turned into prolonged sorrow, with no end in sight.

As the daughter of a woman who was twice hospitalized for depression, Tipper Gore was warned against revealing this "delicate" information to a reporter from the *New York Times.* "I think you want to dispute the fact that you had a difficult childhood," she was cautioned. "Right," said Mrs. Gore. "I had a great childhood."[20]

How does Gore maintain an even keel? What works for her is regular exercise and living with humor. "I think it's important to have a strategy for dealing with stress," she said. "I run, I Rollerblade, and I bike ride. It's important for me to be outdoors as much as possible." She

FOR ART'S SAKE

John Berryman, the Pulitzer Prize–winning poet, described the possible benefits to his art of being a manic depressive:

I do feel strongly that among the greatest pieces of luck for high achievement is ordeal . . . Beethoven's deafness, Goya's deafness, Milton's blindness. . . . And, I think that what happens in my poetic work will probably largely depend not on my sitting calmly on my ass. . . . But being knocked in the face, and thrown flat, and given cancer, and all kinds of other things short of senile dementia. At that point, I'm out, but short of that, I don't know. I hope to be nearly crucified.

As the daughter of a woman who was twice hospitalized for depression, Tipper Gore was warned against revealing this "delicate" information to a reporter from the New York Times. "I think you want to dispute the fact that you had a difficult childhood," she was cautioned. "Right," said Mrs. Gore, "I had a great childhood."

also cites the role of humor: "I think humor is a stress reliever, as is doing things we enjoy."[21]

Gore hoped her own story would help to dispel old myths by eliminating the need to whisper about mental illness. Her aim: to convince the nation that mental illness is not the result of bad parenting or lax churchgoing, but that its root is a chemical imbalance. Her problem was with her brain's "gas gauge."[22]

ROBERT BOORSTIN: HOPE FOR FUTURE ADVANCES

A colorful political figure, Robert Boorstin has struggled with bipolar disorder since his student days in college. Bernie Golden and Nancy interviewed Bob at the 1999 National DMDA Conference in Houston, Texas.

Bob was born into a well-to-do family from Beverly Hills, California. His privileged lifestyle—inherited wealth and an emphasis on high academic achievement (both father and grandfather were Yale graduates, and his mother was a Wellesley graduate who also studied at the Sorbonne)—did not replace what Bob missed most: love, peace, and family stability.

One month shy of Bob's tenth birthday, his forty-year-old father died suddenly from a massive heart attack. At the time of his father's death, Bob's parents were vacationing overseas. As he and his father had never developed a close relationship Bob was virtually unmoved by his father's death.

"My father was a driven, ambitious, and miserably unhappy man," he said. Later, Bob tried unsuccessfully to find some "emotional link" when, as an adult, he traveled to Greece to retrace his father's boyhood footsteps.

Boorstin's political career began in 1993 as a foreign policy speechwriter for President Clinton. Afterward, Bob was appointed senior adviser to the secretary of the treasury before resigning for private life. He still operates out of Washington and is politically active there, representing a firm that does international poll surveys. He admitted that driving up to work each morning at the White House had been very exciting, as was accompanying the president on Air Force One for his worldwide travels. Nevertheless, Bob was glad to leave the federal government behind after six and a half years. It meant that he could finally speak openly about his illness.

"There was no hint of emotional illness before I was seventeen or eighteen," he said. "Unlike my twin brother who followed the family patriarchs to Yale, I spent four enjoyable years at Harvard University studying international relations and acting as chief editor of the *Crimson* [Harvard's school newspaper]. But I had no idea what that constant feverish pace was doing to me [emotionally]. I was very manicky at Harvard.

"Then, I went to England and did my postgraduate work at James College in Cambridge. During my first year at Cambridge, everything seemed fine. I was also dating a woman whom I liked very much. The next year I broke off my relationship with her, and afterwards I was very lonely. Besides, I hated the English atmosphere—it was cold, bleak, and it rained all the time. I cried and couldn't get out of bed. At that time, I was teaching, studying Chinese and Russian, and trying to write my dissertation. I was overloaded.

"A combustible series of events that occurred within four months' time led to the ultimate upheaval in my life. First, my stepfather's death, then the broken relationship with a woman, and finally my decision to change professions.

"My stepfather and I were very close and I loved him desperately," said Bob. "He was a very supportive and caring person." After struggling with emotional problems for several years, Bob's condition was finally diagnosed as bipolar disorder at age twenty-four. His stepfather arrived in Cambridge to pay him a visit. "I talked, and he listened. Listening is very powerful, you know.

"I had suicidal flashes. I pictured myself dead, and that everyone would be happier without me. I also dreamed of being 'accidentally killed.' Finally, at the urging of my parents, I underwent psychoanalysis. I visited the shrink four to five days each week for two years and was never diagnosed. I'm still pissed about it. That doctor put me through needless torture. It was extremely stupid. Not until four years later, and after two hospitalizations, was I finally diagnosed with manic-depressive illness by another doctor."

> *I visited the shrink four to five days each week for two years and was never diagnosed. I'm still pissed off about it. That doctor put me through needless torture. Not until four years later, and after two hospitalizations, was I finally diagnosed with manic-depressive illness by another doctor.*
>
> —BOB BOORSTIN

Bob Boorstin could have easily been just another tragic statistic had he not been diagnosed. An untreated brain illness leaves an individual vulnerable to grossly distorted impressions as we saw with Judge Sol Wachtler. But bipolar disorder is also a biopsychosocial illness.

"Chemistry isn't everything," insisted Bob. "Focusing only on chemistry is mindless, but focusing solely on psychosocial influences is brainless."

Regrettably, Bob's stepfather's life was also cut short when he was killed in a freak highway accident. His death left Bob bereft. After years of pain and turmoil largely stemming from the incident, and many years of therapy, Bob has finally married and settled down.

"Ten years ago," said Bob, "had somebody predicted that today I'd be a happily married family man I would have vehemently disputed it. 'Hell no,' I would have insisted. 'It [marriage] is not for someone like me.'"

Both Nancy and Bernie experienced sorrow that anyone as gifted as Bob Boorstin could have such self-deprecating thoughts. It was not outside stigma that affected Bob but internal shame that directed his thinking in this area.

"When my wife and I were first married," he continued, "we had planned not to have children. 'Why,' we belabored, 'bring kids into this world knowing that any offspring of ours would have a 25 percent chance of being afflicted with bipolar disorder?' That seemed irresponsible." Bob credited ego with changing his mind. "Besides, my own condition is under control and I know what to look for. We also have hope of future advances in treatment and research," he added.

When Nancy and her husband were first married in 1966, neither was aware of her bipolar condition. As she now looks back, she can see early indications of the disorder, but it would be some years before her symptoms became obvious. In fact, at that time she had no idea that manic depression existed in her family, nor did she know what the illness was all about. Nevertheless, had Nancy been properly informed of her genetic predisposition to bipolar disorder, she still says her decision regarding children would have been the same. Like Bob Boorstin, Nancy's condition is now under control and she, too, knows what to look for in her kids.

> *Bipolar disorder is tremendously destructive to relationships. The divorce rate among marriages in which a spouse is manic depressive is very high.*

BIPOLAR DISORDER AND RELATIONSHIPS

Bipolar disorder is tremendously destructive to relationships. The divorce rate among marriages in which a spouse is manic depressive is very high. It is demoralizing for a husband or wife to endure a day-to-day relationship with someone from whom they can't get a positive response. Manic episodes can be as daunting for a partner to endure as can depressive ones. People like to believe they can contribute to their partner's getting better and are often disappointed to learn otherwise. "Count your blessings," a spouse will tell his mate. While the intention is to cheer and show support, such reassurances simply don't work for a person with bipolar disorder. A partner cannot alter the course of the illness, and the well-meaning spouse ends up feeling rejected and frustrated. People blame themselves for not being able to turn their partner's illness around.

When a person with bipolar disorder becomes intense, the very elevation of his or her mood can frequently create problems with interpersonal relationships. Intensity can fuel powerful manifestations of ebullience, overconfidence, and volatility. These episodes may fluctuate dramatically and be interspersed with periods of irritability and rage. "We, the afflicted, become transported into a world of unlimited ideas and possibilities. The sky's the limit!" said Nancy.

"While we're soaring, other people frequently are put off by such apparent grandiosity. We may seem too talkative, uninhibited, pompous, manipulative, or intrusive; our ideas may sound outlandish; or we may exhibit other irresponsible or inappropriate behavior. Such characteristics are manifested during periods of

> *When someone whose spouse is in a manic episode and refuses treatment asks me what he or she can do, I tell them to "close the bank account and wait it out."*
>
> —JAN FAWCETT

mania, or hypomania (less extreme), and our seemingly inexhaustible supply of energy and self-confidence can erode, and even torpedo, relationships.

"'You're not hearing me,' I've been told on numerous occasions," said Nancy. "Although I might have heard every word, at that moment I may not have been in a position to control my garrulousness. When my bipolar condition kicks in, oftentimes it's accompanied by irrational behavior. I feel distraught."

In a troubled marriage, the ill person is often the one blamed and receives little or no support from his or her partner. These relationships can quickly deteriorate. Statistically, women, more often than men, will stay around to nurture and support the relationship when illness strikes a loved one. That said, even the strongest relationships are susceptible to the ravages of stress over time.

The Effects of Stress, Intensity, and Trauma

Any traumatic episode can trigger symptoms in people with bipolar disorder, which likely appear overreactive to the uninitiated. While some individuals are better equipped to handle shock than others, the average person is not thrown completely off balance by a simple twist of fate. But in a person who has bipolar disorder, trauma produces an uncontrollable emotional upheaval, unwittingly leading to poor judgment and intrusiveness.

"I once was completely blown away by the apparent disloyalty of a former colleague," said Nancy. "Following the previous dissolution of our association due to irreconcilable differences, I had thought my troubles were over. But the nightmare of one unhappy episode returned to haunt me like a bad movie which flashed before my eyes. When betrayed, I felt instantly threatened and morally violated, trapped, once again, inside a vicious web. A temporary loss of faith in all humanity returned momentarily because of the injustice which I felt had been committed. The resulting trauma brought out the worst in me, and for twenty-four hours I was unable to function normally. I did not sleep or eat and was uncommunicative with everyone except my husband and Bernie." Someone not prone to bipolar disorder might have handled this situation in a more balanced fashion without "going off the deep end" as Nancy had.

Trauma can create the most insurmountable form of stress—pressure so intense that it not only inflames but also permanently damages an existing relationship. "As approval turns to contempt and friend to foe, we the afflicted find ourselves in a state of overwhelming despair," said Nancy. "Impenetrable walls seem to spring up before our eyes, separating 'us' from 'them.'"

Some relationships never recover from these painful, regrettable, and inopportune shock waves. But life is filled with endings and new beginnings. Relationships

> *As approval turns to contempt and friend to foe, we the afflicted find ourselves in a state of overwhelming despair. Impenetrable walls seem to spring up before our eyes, separating "us" from "them."*
>
> —NANCY ROSENFELD

may come and go, but no matter how fleeting, it is from these experiences that people gain strength and wisdom.

Living and thriving with bipolar disorder may not be easy, but it's possible—even probable—if you are willing to accept the challenge. As with any other obstacle, even some grave misfortune, there is a bright side. Moreover, everyone has choices when confronted with challenging situations. It is the responsibility of each one of us to determine how to overcome our individual problems and be able to turn negatives into positives. Survivors of this disorder need to understand that they are not their illness: The afflicted have bipolar illness, but they are not bipolar disorder.

CHAPTER 2

Diagnosis of Bipolar Disorder

A correct diagnosis conveys the cluster of symptoms that characterize a disorder and points the way to treatments that have proven helpful. If the medical field is sufficiently advanced in the area of a particular illness, understanding of its various causes and mechanisms ultimately leads to the development of better treatment. With this information, the physician can design a course of treatment based on the newest and most effective therapies available.

Psychiatric disorders are manifested by emotions, thoughts, and behavior. Yet our culture, and even the medical field, has erroneously separated concepts of the mind from the body as if they are totally unrelated. Too often mood and behavior are viewed as only the by-products of self-discipline, strength of character, and moral choice for which we bear responsibility, while physical illness is considered an unfortunate event outside of one's control. This narrow—and false!—definition ignores the fact that the mind is controlled by and dependent on normal brain function. The result of this misappropriation is an inability to understand the manifestations of psychiatric disorders in the same way that medical disorders are judged. If a person develops severe depression after a serious head injury, it is understood that a brain injury is related to the depressive behavior. If a person develops severe depression in conjunction with bipolar disorder, the behavior may be seen as a voluntary choice on the part of the patient.

WHY IS BIPOLAR DISORDER CALLED AN ILLNESS?

Although everyone experiences ups and downs among happiness, sadness, and anger, people with manic depression have mood swings out of proportion in intensity or totally unrelated to what is going on in their lives. While the occurrence of mania or depression may follow a life stress, the pathological mood state tends to persist long after the stressful situation is resolved.

A lack of good animal models for psychiatric illnesses, as well as the technical and ethical difficulties in studying human brain function, explain why research studies have only recently begun to collect data analyzing mood disorders. Historically, people believed that demonic possession was the cause of psychiatric disorders. While this belief has fallen out of favor, a different stigma has taken its place; today, the assumed cause is often a moral or character weakness. The reality is that chemical changes in the brain and genetic factors are to blame— not the whims and moral weakness of the patient.

> *Historically, people believed that demonic possession was the cause of psychiatric disorders. While this belief has fallen out of favor, a different stigma has taken its place; today, the assumed cause is often a moral or character weakness.*

As you may know, the original name for bipolar disorder was manic-depressive psychosis. One of the reasons for this change of terminology may well have been the stigma attached to the earlier name. At the time people frequently mischaracterized the diagnosis as "maniac" (rather than "manic") depressive illness. This is one way that some psychiatric diagnoses, such as bipolar disorder, become associated with "labels" (or tags). The social meaning for these illnesses is different from the medical diagnoses. These are labels that we understandably consider harmful and want to avoid, but arriving at a correct diagnosis is crucial to a patient's well-being even if they're at risk of such social consequences.

THE DIFFICULTY OF DIAGNOSING BIPOLAR DISORDER

Bipolar disorder can be a difficult illness to diagnose. The diagnosis may result in a patient's hearing social disapproval and shame because of its stigma. Fear and ignorance can even affect the attitude of people who might otherwise seem educated or sophisticated. Like clinical depression, bipolar disorder is frequently attributed to a weakness of character. As a result of this stigma, the details of a family history of mental illness, which aid in the diagnosis of bipolar disorder, may be hidden or "forgotten" by patients or relatives.

Manic or hypomanic episodes can increase other people's anxiety about the disorder because of the unpredictability of behavior and lack of control that often accompany such episodes. In general, families and friends are much more comfortable in dealing with depressive episodes rather than the manic or hypomanic stages of the illness.

> *In general, families and friends are much more comfortable in dealing with depressive episodes rather than the manic or hypomanic stages of the illness.*

On the other hand, some people in hypomanic states—characterized by euphoria, optimism, and increased confidence and energy—may be very charismatic, interesting, and uplifting to be around. They often exercise leadership qualities and make excellent salespeople of both things and ideas. These individuals rarely perceive such states as pathological but instead value the increased levels of energy, confidence, and creativity that they provide. Consequently, people in a hypomanic state may view hypomania as a normal pattern of behavior and refuse any treatment that compromises their energy and creativity.

The diagnosis of bipolar disorder is largely based on the history of prior behaviors, thought patterns, and moods, as well as family history of mood disorders. Therefore, it is important for a clinician to actively seek this information from the patient. Even though mood swings may not be initially apparent to the patient, this pattern provides the physician with critical data for diagnosis.

ONSET OF BIPOLAR DISORDER

Bipolar disorder can start in early childhood or as late as the forties and fifties (see figure 2.1). Over age fifty, the cause of an initial episode is more likely to be a problem that imitates bipolar disorder, such as neurological illness or the effects of drugs, alcohol, or a prescription medicine. Frequently, bipolar disor-

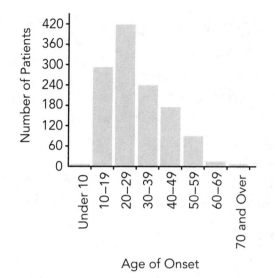

Figure 2.1. Age of Onset of Bipolar Disorder

(*Source: Manic-Depressive Illness* by Frederick K. Goodwin and Kay R. Jamison, copyright 1990 by Oxford University Press, Inc. Used by permission of Oxford University Press, Inc.)

der is manifested for the first time during adolescence, which is a time of "normal" turmoil. Some people may hold the view that normal adolescence is a kind of "psychosis" in itself. Since moodiness and various crises around school and relationships often occur during the teen years, it is easy to understand how the early symptoms of bipolar disorder might first be incorrectly attributed to "normal" adolescent problems.[1] Best-selling author Danielle Steel's son Nick, to whom we refer again, is an example of a troubled youth whose bipolar illness was neither fully understood nor properly managed.

Clinical scientists have found that the initial episodes of depression or hyperactivity, frequently attributed later to bipolar illness (when a doctor finally makes the diagnosis), occur in response to some life stress. The patient's history will clearly show subsequent episodes, which may have occurred without any identifiable trauma. Gradually the illness becomes autonomous and mood swings recur cyclically in a pattern that can be discerned in retrospect.

Some people in hypomanic states are very charismatic, interesting, and uplifting to be around. These individuals rarely perceive such states as pathological but instead value the increased levels of energy, confidence, and creativity that they provide.

EARLY DIAGNOSIS AS PREVENTION

Early diagnosis, proper treatment, and finding the right medication at a young age is crucial in helping people to avoid the following:

- Suicide
- Alcohol/substance abuse
- Marital and work problems
- Treatment difficulties
- Incorrect, inappropriate, or partial treatment

All too often doctors fail to arrive at an early diagnosis. People with bipolar disorder see, on an average, three to four doctors and spend more than eight years seeking treatment before receiving a correct diagnosis.

IMPORTANCE OF EARLY DIAGNOSIS

In young people, bipolar disorder can be severe enough to interfere with school. It may also cause its victim to miss the usual social and identity development associated with adolescence. Adolescent development can also be distorted by episodes of depression, nonfunction, crises resulting from impulsive behaviors, bad judgments made during manic mood swings, and repeated hospitalizations. The adolescent self-identifies as a patient rather than as a student who is building a future adult identity and career.

The additional problems of alcohol and substance abuse, which are hazards for all young people, are common with bipolar disorder. This is called a comorbid condition. Rates of alcohol and substance abuse comorbidity of 50 to 70 percent have been reported among those with bipolar disorder. The two illnesses augment each other in their power to damage or even destroy a young life. This happened to Nick Traina when he began to abuse over-the-counter medications at the age of eleven to "still the demons." Comorbidity finally killed him.

Family education leads to early diagnosis and treatment, resulting in harm reduction. An early response may help reduce or prevent the negative

> *In young people, bipolar disorder can cause its victim to miss the usual social and identity development associated with adolescence.*

consequences of bipolar disorder—social impairment, school failure, legal problems, hospitalizations, and many others. If a family history of bipolar disorder is present, this can provide a strong clue to the family and clinician. As mentioned above, however, shame and denial may spur family members to hide this history, making early recognition more difficult. In addition, as will be discussed later, adult victims may function at high levels despite the disorder, thus further obscuring the diagnosis and the establishment of a family history.

Some of these patients have a mild form of the illness known as cyclothymia (see page 37). This is characterized by depressive periods lasting weeks or months and then mild hypomanic periods during which the person experiences increased energy, mental alertness, confidence, and a decreased need for sleep that make considerable success attainable. Many people with a history of depression and hypomania do not seek treatment for several years.

SYMPTOMS OF BIPOLAR DISORDER

We have alluded to various types of bipolar disorder above. The variation in symptoms and in the severity of the illness in different individuals is one reason for the difficulty in obtaining a proper diagnosis. Even trained specialists in psychiatry might miss the diagnosis when it presents in certain atypical forms.

Mania, hypomania, and depression are the general categories of symptoms involved in bipolar disorder. Bipolar disorder differs significantly from clinical depression. In bipolar disorder, a person's mood alternates between mania and depression. One swing of the mood pendulum can last for days, weeks, or even months, or in other instances rapidly changing moods alternate with normal periods. It is important to inform your physician of all mood swings, past or present, so a correct diagnosis can be made.

> *The variation in symptoms and in the severity of bipolar disorder in different individuals is one reason for the difficulty in obtaining a proper diagnosis.*

Mania

Mania often begins with a pleasurable sense of heightened energy, creativity, and social ease. People with mania lack insight, deny anything is wrong, and angrily blame others for pointing out a problem. In a manic state, some or all of the following symptoms are present for at least one week, and the person has trouble functioning in a normal way:

- Heightened mood and exaggerated optimism and self-confidence
- Decreased need for sleep, without fatigue
- Grandiose delusions, inflated sense of self-importance
- Excessive irritability, aggressive behavior
- Increased physical and mental activity
- Rapid, pressured speech, flight of ideas from one topic to another, distractability
- Poor judgment, impulsiveness
- Reckless behavior such as spending sprees, rash business decisions, erratic driving, sexual indiscretions

Anyone experiencing these symptoms, which often alternate with symptoms of depression (see below), should seek help from a medical professional if the symptoms persist for several days and cannot be attributed to drug or alcohol abuse.

Hypomania

A milder form of mania, hypomania has similar but less severe symptoms and impairment. It is characterized by increased energy, increased activity, decreased need for sleep, increased confidence, sexual drive, poor judgment, impulsive behavior, euphoria or irritability, and sometimes grandiosity but without psychosis. Friends and relatives notice that the behavior is not usual for the individual. Psychoses (e.g., delusions of having special powers) is not present in hypomania but is present in mania in about 50 percent of cases.

Depression

Major depression is characterized by five or more of the following symptoms, lasting for at least two weeks and making it difficult to function normally:

- Depressed mood or markedly diminished interest or pleasure in almost all activities for most of the day
- Significant changes in appetite or sleep patterns
- Loss of enjoyment or pleasure in usual activities

- Loss of motivation
- Loss of energy, persistent lethargy
- Feelings of guilt and worthlessness
- Inability to concentrate, indecisiveness
- Slowing of speech, thought, and body movement
- Physical agitation and restlessness
- Recurring thoughts of death or suicide

In addition, although not criterion symptoms for the diagnosis, patients with major depression frequently show irritability, anger, worry, agitation, anxiety, and physical symptoms such as various types of pain and nausea. If you have thoughts of death or suicide, tell a medical professional, friend, or a member of the clergy immediately.

DIFFERENT PATTERNS OF BIPOLAR DISORDER

There is a spectrum of symptom severity in bipolar disorder that can obscure the diagnosis, as discussed above. There are also subtypes of the disorder that can confuse the picture. These subtypes may also require different treatment, which makes it even more important to arrive at a correct diagnosis. Reflecting the range of bipolar disorder, the official classification guide for diagnoses, the *DSM-IV* (*Diagnostic and Statistical Manual of Mental Disorders,* 4th edition), recognizes bipolar I disorder; schizoaffective disorder, bipolar type; bipolar II disorder; bipolar disorder NOS (not otherwise specified); and cyclothymia. Mood disorders owing to an organic condition (brain tumor, subclinical stroke, traumatic brain injury, or metabolic disease) or a

BIPOLAR DIAGNOSES

- Bipolar I disorder
- Schizoaffective disorder, bipolar type
- Bipolar II disorder
- Bipolar disorder NOS (not otherwise specified)
- Cyclothymia

SUBTYPES OF BIPOLAR DISORDER

- Rapid-cycling bipolar disorder
- Mixed or dysphoric mania
- Bipolar spectrum disorders
- Covert cycling
- Depressive disorders

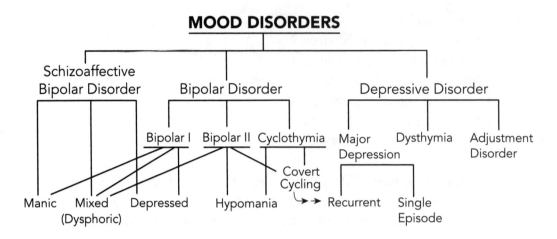

Figure 2.2. Bipolar Mood Disorders

substance-induced mood disorder (street drugs, alcohol, and certain prescribed medications) can create symptoms that resemble bipolar disorder.

Some people have equal numbers of manic and depressive episodes. Others have mostly one type or another. The average person with bipolar disorder experiences four episodes during the first ten years of the illness. Men are more likely to start with a manic episode, women with a depressive one. Cycles vary in duration, intensity, and frequency. Some people recover completely between episodes, but others continue to experience low-grade but troubling depression or mild mood swings.

Bipolar I Disorder

Bipolar I disorder is the most severe form of bipolar disorder, a condition that includes symptoms of hyperactivity progressing in some patients to agitation, irritability, paranoia, grandiosity, and even progressing to a delusional psychosis (characterized by an inability to appreciate reality). Additionally, patients may exhibit a progressive degree of grandiose delusions, pressured speech, distractibility, and flight of thoughts (the patient goes from one topic to another cued by words that trigger some other thought).

A high percentage of patients have symptoms

> *The average person with bipolar disorder experiences four episodes during the first ten years of the illness. Men are more likely to start with a manic episode, women with a depressive one.*

severe enough to warrant additional treatment (usually hospitalization) on top of a medication regime. Approximately 50 percent of patients with bipolar I disorder manifest a psychosis (the inability to distinguish reality from fantasy or belief). These patients' frequently exhibit poor judgment, impulsive behavior, and total lack of insight into their illness. Consequently, they may refuse treatment.

In chapter 1 you met Judge Sol Wachtler, who is a prime example of someone who lives with bipolar I disorder. Wachtler's illness was responsible for the bizarre behavior that led him to prison.

Schizoaffective Bipolar Disorder

This is another severe form of illness, considered by many to be an alternate form of bipolar I disorder that has characteristics of schizophrenia. These patients may manifest depression, mania, and persistent psychotic symptoms (hallucinations or delusions) that overlap with episodes of depression and mania and that persist beyond mood episodes. Differentiating bipolar disorder and schizophrenia can be a diagnostic challenge. (See figure 2.2.)

The differentiation between these two disorders is a controversial subject, and one that is met with considerable confusion. Are patients who have psychotic symptoms schizophrenic? Or manic? Or do they suffer from severe depression with psychotic symptoms? The term *schizoaffective disorder* was created as a separate diagnostic category, a hybrid type of mood disorder that overlaps the criteria for schizophrenia and bipolar I disorder. But there is some evidence to indicate that schizomanic conditions are more prevalent than schizodepressive ones.[2]

What is important to note is that mood-stabilizing drugs will help patients with schizoaffective bipolar disorder whereas mood stabilizers are generally not helpful to patients suffering solely from schizophrenia.

There are three stages of mania, essentially differentiated by the severity of the illness and manifested by an increasing amount of agitation and psychosis. Acute symptoms of irritability, anger, paranoia, and catatonic-like excitement could support a diagnosis of mania *or* schizophrenia.

> *There are three stages of mania, essentially differentiated by the severity of the illness and manifested by an increasing amount of agitation and psychosis.*

In a severe episode, it may be difficult to differentiate between the two without any prior personal history or family history. It is therefore understandable why some research clinicians suggest that schizoaffective bipolar disorder is really a severe form of bipolar I disorder and that families of patients with this diagnosis actually have histories of bipolar disorder, not schizophrenia.

Bipolar II Disorder

The subtleties of bipolar II disorder make it more difficult to diagnose than other forms of the illness. It is characterized by episodes of hypomania often alternating with extended periods of major depression that can be very severe and threatening. Although these people exhibit symptoms that are commonly recognized as "abnormal" by either the patients or their families, their symptoms are generally not severe enough to mandate hospitalization, even though there may be some interference in their normal level of functioning. However, these patients do not manifest psychosis and may not even recognize, much less report, their symptoms of hypomania, choosing to remember only their depressive episodes.

Individuals with bipolar II disorder are usually the ones to seek treatment for depression and give histories of recurrent depressive episodes. They may resist treatment for their disorder by electing not to take mood stabilizers, such as lithium, which tend to suppress the hypomanic periods that patients commonly associate with happiness or increased function and creativity.

Many of these patients go undiagnosed because they are treated for depression with antidepressant medications alone. This can actually increase their mood cycles and lead to recurrences of depression, rapid cycling, or the occurrence of mixed states. Doctors may also misdiagnose bipolar II disorder as a severe personality disorder.

Nancy's bipolar condition seems to be in the category of bipolar II disorder. Though she once contemplated suicide and has sought therapeutic counseling, Nancy was never hospitalized for her condition. She reports that her highs and lows have been extreme. With proper management of her illness (which includes a daily maintenance program of antidepressant medication), however, Nancy functions at a high level, with minimum occurrence of mild depression.

Bipolar Disorder NOS

Bipolar disorder NOS (not otherwise specified) includes disorders with bipolar features that do not meet specific criteria for other diagnoses of bipolar disorder. Examples might be rapid alternations of mood over a period of time that do not meet the duration criteria for other diagnoses or recurrent hypomanic episodes in the absence of depression.

Cyclothymia

Cyclothymia is the mildest form of bipolar disorder. Many patients with cyclothymia never seek diagnosis or treatment. They may function well, with some interruption during periods of mild or moderate depression alternating with mild hypomania and increased activity. These individuals can become severely ill to the point of impairment in response to certain substances or medications (including marijuana, alcohol, antidepressants, steroids, and, possibly, high doses of decongestants), which may increase the severity of their depression or precipitate full-blown mania.

Rapid-Cycling Bipolar Disorder

Patients are arbitrarily defined as having a rapid-cycling form of bipolar I disorder or bipolar II disorder if they have four or more episodes of mania or depression in one year (in any combination). Rapid cycling also implies an increased frequency of depressive or manic episodes with shorter times of normalcy between episodes. Between 5 and 15 percent of patients with bipolar disorder fall into this category at some time in the course of their illness. Patients can manifest mood cycling to the point of showing mood changes in the same day or even within an hour. This is termed ultrarapid cycling (ultradian cycling).

The significance of these variations in rapid cycling is that they can lead to a misdiagnosis of personality disorder or schizophrenia, which makes the condition even more difficult to treat effectively. Rapid cycling is a temporary phase of bipolar disorder that some patients, particularly women, are prone to, whereas bipolar disorder usually affects both sexes equally. Some bipolar patients go through rapid cycling for months, during which their symptoms are more difficult to control. At this time, the exact causes of rapid cycling remain unknown and there is no preventable treatment. Rapid cycling may occur at some point in a bipolar disorder and then revert to a previous pattern of an episode or two each year, depending on treatment response. Although the issue is debated, there is evidence suggesting that antidepressant agents can precipitate rapid cycling or mania in bipolar patients.

Goodwin and Jamison reported that the phenomenon of rapid cycling is of considerable importance both theoretically and practically. From a theoretical standpoint, rapid-cycling patients make up a disproportionate percentage of the total number of cases studied. Practically speaking, the treatment of patients with rapid cycling may be different from the treatment prescribed for patients with normal cycling patterns.[3] We discuss this further in chapter 4.

Mixed or Dysphoric Mania

This is the most disabling subform of bipolar disorder because symptoms of both mania and depression occur simultaneously or alternate frequently during the same day. The person becomes excitable and agitated but also irritable and depressed—feeling anxiety instead of the euphoria classically associated with mania.

This form of the illness can be found in either bipolar I disorder or bipolar II disorder. Mixed mania occurs in about 40 to 45 percent of bipolar cases. The patient manifests the restlessness, hyperactivity, irritability, and sometimes paranoia or mania, combined with symptoms of depression and distress.

Doctors may mistakenly diagnose the patient as having a schizophrenic psychosis with agitation, or a paranoid state. Doctors can miss the bipolar disorder diagnosis with milder forms as well, and erroneously diagnose the condition as a severe personality disorder or substance-abuse disorder.

Mixed mania is the most disabling subform of bipolar disorder because symptoms of both mania and depression occur simultaneously or alternate frequently during the day.

These patients are often more impulsive and suicidal than those who experience the other forms of bipolar disorder. Often they are not capable of being cooperative in a relationship, have a very low tolerance for stress, and frequently express anger or rage. These symptoms can also be the manifestation of rapid cycling, which also occur in patients with bipolar I or bipolar II disorder.

Bipolar Spectrum Disorder

The term *bipolar spectrum disorder* is often used to describe a class of disorders that have bipolar features, such as recurrent mood changes associated with increased activity, impulsive behavior, and irritability alternating with depressed or dysphoric mood. This term overlaps with the bipolar NOS diagnosis in many instances.

Covert Cycling

Covert cycling may not technically meet the formal criteria for bipolar disorder I or II but may meet NOS criteria. It is found in some proportion of patients who have a series of recurrences of depression following several months of antidepressant response to treatment. Frequently, the patient improves with the use of another antidepressant medication only to relapse once again.

In some cases, careful observation and talks with loved ones who know the patient well may reveal a pattern of hyperthymia (periods of mildly elevated mood and increased energy that seem within a normal range). This pattern is often associated with increased productive activity. Patients and those around them might consider the slight mood elevation as a positive "admirable quality" rather than viewing it as a pathological mania. The hyperthymia in these individuals is then followed by a depressive recurrence despite any maintenance program of antidepressant medication.

In covert cycling, antidepressant medication alone will not prevent depression once a hypomanic or hyperthymic mood shift has occurred, however the addition of a mood-stabilization drug may prevent these recurrences. In fact, in almost all cases of bipolar disorder, a depression follows a manic mood swing, so it is difficult, or impossible, to avoid the depressions while permitting the manic or hypomanic symptoms. Once patients with

In almost all cases of bipolar disorder, a depression follows a manic mood swing, so it is difficult, or impossible, to avoid the depressions while permitting the manic or hypomanic symptoms.

cyclothymia or bipolar II disorder understand this, they are more likely to accept mood-stabilization treatment.

Depressive Disorders

In sharp contrast to mania, depressive disorders are usually defined by a slowing down of almost all aspects of emotion and behavior, that is, rate of thought and speech, energy, sexuality, and the ability to experience pleasure. As with mania, the severity of depressive disorders varies widely.[4] The majority of bipolar patients usually spend more time in depressive states than in mania or hypomania.

At the most severe end of the spectrum is major depression; this state can be recurrent or occur as a single episode. Chronic depression, or dysthymia, is a lingering form of mild depression (limited to two to three symptoms) that persists at least two years. Patients may not fully recover from a chronic depressive episode without treatment, and remain generally lacking in energy with a negative outlook on life. Adjustment disorder, the mildest form of depression, is manifested by depressive symptoms emerging under situational stress and may impair social or occupational functioning. Any impairment is generally short-lived, however, and less pervasive than a major form of depression.

Doctors can fail to diagnose bipolar disorder owing to the frequent difficulty of obtaining an accurate history along with the multiple levels of severity and various forms in which the illness presents itself. The establishment of an accurate diagnosis is important because the untreated illness can be severely disabling, and even dangerous, to the patient. Given that fact and the effective treatments available to us today, early diagnosis can restore and even save lives. People who had lost a sense of meaning and joy in life can rediscover it and return to leading a productive existence. Early diagnosis and treatment can also save careers, not to mention marriages, and greatly reduce family strife.

Depressed Brain

Recovered Brain

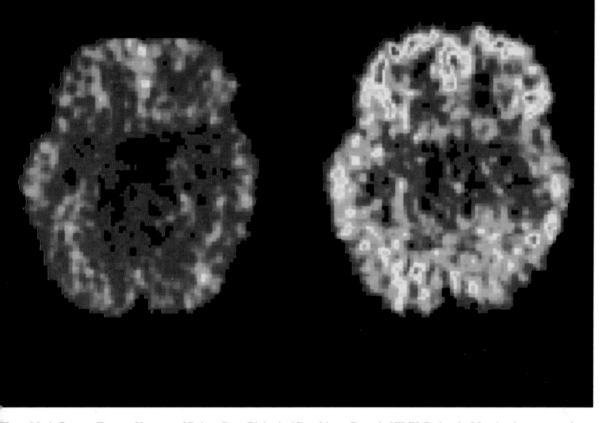

From Mark George, Terence Ketter, and Robert Post, Biological Psychiatry Branch, NIMH, Bethesda, Maryland, courtesy of Frederick K. Goodwin, M.D.)

PET (positron emission tomography) scans of the brain of a patient during depression and after recovery from depression. The colors in the scans correspond to glucose metabolic rates (which indicate activity of the neurons), with the lowest rates associated with the coolest end of the color spectrum (blue) and the highest rates with the warmest (red). If an area that normally reflects higher rates (red, yellow, or green) shows up blue on the scan, it implies that the neurons in that region are impaired in their function. The image made during a depressive episode (left) is dark, mostly blue, whereas the image created after treatment with medication (right) has more green, yellow, and red, showing that the activity of the neurons has normalized. See "Imaging Studies," page 56.

Rapid-Cycling Manic-Depressive Brain

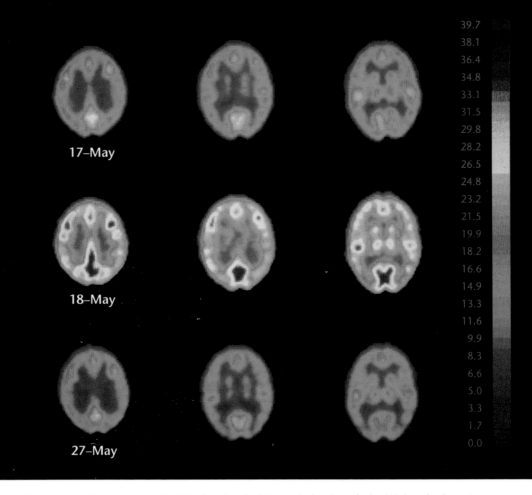

(Image and text adapted from Baxter et al., 1985. Reprinted with permission from Oxford University Press.)

PET scans of the brain of a drug-free rapid-cycling manic-depressive patient. The images in the top row were made when the patient was depressed. The second row shows the identical planes scanned the next day, when the patient had become manic. The third row shows scans taken ten days later when the same patient was again depressed. Impairment of metabolic function is expressed in the symptoms of clinical depression, such as slowed thought, lack of energy, loss of spontaneity, poor concentration, problems making decisions. In a manic state the metabolism of certain areas is increased at a supra-normal rate, correlating with increased energy, rapid thinking, rapid speech, decreased sleep, and hyperactivity. The scans show that this brain is in an abnormal metabolic state (either decreased or increased metabolic function) when the patient is in a depressed or manic state. See "Imaging Studies," page 56.

CHAPTER 3

The Biology of Bipolar Disorder

F or centuries, humans have sought to explain and understand disorders that manifest as emotional pain, adverse behaviors, and, in some cases, irrational thought. The causes we have attributed bipolar disorder to in the past and present are strongly correlated to the predominant thought of the time as well as the degree to which scientific knowledge has developed.

WHAT CAUSES BIPOLAR DISORDER?

Bipolar disorder often stems from a genetic vulnerability that runs in the family. Thus far, we have evidence that the interaction of this genetic vulnerability with everyday life stresses triggers the onset of symptoms, although over time symptoms can recur autonomously without discernible causes.

Researchers have identified a number of genes that may be linked to the disorder. If you have bipolar and your spouse does not, there is a 7.8 percent risk of an offspring developing bipolar disorder and an additional 11.2 percent chance for the development of unipolar major depression (for a total risk of a mood disorder of 19 percent). The chances may be greater if a number of your relatives are afflicted with the disorder or if the onset of the disorder occurred in childhood or adolescence. If both parents have a history of bipolar disorder, there is a 50 to 75 percent chance of their child developing a mood disorder. Note that the chances of an offspring developing unipolar major depression are greater than the chances of developing a bipolar disorder. Recent epidemiological studies have determined that just over 1 percent of the population has symptoms of various forms of bipolar disorder.

Epidemiological evidence can chart the scope of an illness, its predicted course, likely associated or comorbid conditions (such as anxiety or alcohol abuse disorders), and possible risk factors. In addition, these studies are used to link the occurrence of the illness with genetic, psychological, social, and environmental factors. These data can also be effective in planning research into the causes of the illness as well as designing treatment or even preventive programs.

> *Bipolar disorder often stems from a genetic vulnerability that runs in the family. Thus far, we have evidence that the interaction of this genetic vulnerability with everyday life stresses triggers the onset of symptoms, although over time symptoms can recur autonomously without discernible causes.*

In this chapter, we will review some of the large and rapidly growing bodies of evidence from family studies, as well as imaging neurochemical and pharmacological studies that convey what we know and are rapidly learning about the psychobiology of bipolar disorder. This area of study is progressing rapidly and newly developed methods of treatment are being used and tested every day. Therefore, some findings may not be in agreement with one another until more research has been done. One has to view the emerging findings in the perspective of the past. While groundbreaking studies establishing new methods of treatment for mood disorders such as bipolar disorder and major depression (e.g., the 1970 introduction in this country of lithium as a treatment for bipolar disorder) occasionally emerge, the majority of these scientific findings only advance our knowledge in small increments. Sometimes new discoveries can reverse, or even redirect, former ways of thinking. Scientific progress originates from this sea of findings, and yet the process can be tedious. It is the product of a mass of research efforts, one adding to another. With this caveat, we will attempt to summarize some areas of research into the psychobiology of bipolar disorder, as well as examine the newest directions and emerging findings in this field of study.

PSYCHOBIOLOGICAL FINDINGS

As knowledge has grown concerning the possible causes of bipolar disorder and related affective disorders, it has become clear that biological factors are at least necessary, if not sufficient, conditions for their occurrence.

Goodwin and Jamison's *Manic-Depressive Illness* presents evidence of contributing biological factors to the development of bipolar disorder, from the earliest recorded studies to 1990. Summary statements from this book challenge that any set of findings purportedly to be relevant to the causes of manic-depressive illness (bipolar disorder) must account for both genetic vulnerability and the cyclical (recurrent) nature of the illness.

Gene research is one cornerstone of the effort to explain the causes of bipolar disorder. Attempting to account for the cyclical nature of this illness has been difficult to study at the biological level because few, if any, suitable animal models of bipolar disorder exist. Animal studies permit the use of certain invasive scientific methods that cannot be used in humans. These

> *As knowledge has grown concerning the possible causes of bipolar disorder and related affective disorders, it has become clear that biological factors are at least necessary, if not sufficient, conditions for their occurrence.*

studies have been a major source of progress in our understanding of cancer, infectious diseases, heart disease, and other illnesses, but bipolar disorder only manifests itself in behaviors specific to humans.

Initial research focused on genetic vulnerability as the cause of bipolar disorder. Later, as a result of observing the effect of medications such as lithium and antidepressants on the course of the illness, scientists began to consider the contribution of alterations in brain chemicals called neurotransmitters. Dr. Lewis Opler explains in layperson's terms how these chemicals work: "We have nerve cells in our brain that are separated by tiny little spaces called 'synapses.' Chemicals called 'neurotransmitters' send messages across these spaces, and these messages signal our brain to do its job. Neurotransmitters come in all different forms, and these chemicals fit neatly into 'receptors' that are located on the surfaces of other cells."[1] Recent research is focusing on the chemical reactions initiated by these receptors within the nerve cell and their effect on complex chemical second messengers released within the cells, as well as the activation of certain genes.

GENETIC PREDISPOSITION TO BIPOLAR DISORDER

Scientifically based evidence supports the theory of genetic predisposition to bipolar disorder. Let's examine recent findings that support this correlation.

Dr. Elliot S. Gershon, distinguished investigator (2006) of the University of Chicago, and colleagues point out that the strongest evidence comes from studies of identical (monozygotic, or MZ) twins compared with fraternal (dizygotic, or DZ) twins. MZ twins share identical genes and environment, while DZ twins share a similar environment but have a slightly different genetic makeup.[2]

In these studies, the concordance rate, or rate of similarity between twins (meaning both twins had affective illness), for MZ twins was from 62 to 72 percent (with an additional 18 to 25 percent with unipolar depression), but only 0 to 8 percent (with an additional 0 to 11 percent with unipolar depression) for DZ twins.

In a more recent psychiatric review of twin studies, Norwegian psychiatrist E. Kringlen reported that genetics make a relatively strong contribution to Alzheimer's disease, bipolar disorder, schizophrenia, and childhood autism. Since the concordance rates are far from 100 percent in most of these illnesses, environmental factors must also be important.[3] This observation is important in light of increasing neurobiological research showing that experience can modify biochemical processes in the brain to a degree not previously appreciated. The implications of such "brain plasticity" will be discussed later.

Additional genetic evidence is found in adoption studies, a research method most frequently used in Scandinavian countries. Two studies of children whose biological parents also had bipolar disorder, but who were adopted at less than six months of age and raised by nonbipolar adoptive parents, have provided support for the theory of genetic familial transmission.[4] Data from over forty studies has revealed that the risk for the disorder is consistently higher for relatives of bipolar sufferers than it is for relatives of normal controls. Accordingly, the risk for both bipolar and unipolar disorders is

GENETIC VULNERABILITIES

Summarizing the studies of genetic factors in the transmission of vulnerability suggests the following conclusions:

1. Affective disorders run in families and this is due to a genetic vulnerability.
2. Unipolar depression is the most frequent affective disorder in relatives of bipolar patients; bipolar disorder ranks second.
3. Bipolar disorder tends to strike more frequently among relatives of unipolar patients than in control groups.
4. The likelihood of familial manifestations of affective disorders is more commonly associated with both early onset and the severity of the illness.

higher in the relatives of bipolar subjects, whereas first-degree relatives of unipolar depression subjects have a higher rate of unipolar depression alone.[5] We can therefore conclude that affective disorders are indeed the result of genetic transmission and that the most frequent affective disorder among relatives of bipolar patients is unipolar depression, not bipolar disorder.

In families where there is evidence of early-onset (childhood or adolescent) bipolar disorder, the likelihood that another family member will be affected by the disorder is above the average for affected families overall. Moreover, the more severe the form of bipolar or schizoaffective bipolar disorder (such as psychosis or rapid recurrences), the greater the risk of the illness appearing in another family member.

This review of the scientific literature also demonstrates that in bipolar disorder the mode of inheritance is complex and likely involves multiple interacting genes.[6]

Cohort Effect

Some epidemiological studies have shown what is called the cohort effect—increased occurrences—in both bipolar and unipolar depression, beginning in the 1930s and appearing to spiral upward thereafter. The cohort effect cannot be attributed to genetic alteration because it occurs over too short a period of time. Instead, it must reflect a cultural influence on the expression of vulnerability to the disorders. This suggests that while genetic vulnerability may be necessary, without certain stress factors it is insufficient for the full expression of the illness, similar to Kringlin's observation concerning incomplete concordance in identical twins.

We might ask ourselves just what in our culture is producing the increased incidence of these mental disorders and agitating the genetic vulnerability. Is it our ever higher, often unmet, materialistic expectations? Or is it the greater informational load from early age as a result of television and other media? Could the problem stem from dietary changes, such as a decrease in the overall intake of omega-3 fatty acids? It has been asserted that changes in agribusiness have reduced our sources of these important dietary constituents, which make up a good part of our central nervous system and which our bodies cannot produce. Fish, fish oil, and flaxseed oil are a few of the only remaining sources left. It has been reported that while cattle once fed principally on

> *Some investigators have found that the incidence of both bipolar and unipolar depression has been increasing, beginning in the 1930s and spiraling upward thereafter. Such an increase cannot be attributed to genetic alteration because it occurs over too short a period of time. We might ask ourselves just what in our culture is producing the increased incidence of these mental disorders and agitating the genetic vulnerability.*

plants containing omega-3 fatty acids, farmers now prefer to use special feeds that exclude these important nutrients. Furthermore, while these nutrients are highly concentrated in human breast milk, they are not presently included in infant formula.

The Harvard School of Public Health Study, conducted by C. J. Murray and A. D. Lopez for the World Bank, found that clinical depression is presently the world's fourth most frequent cause of disability; bipolar disorder is the sixth. These data take all possible causes of disability into account, from war and malnutrition to every disease known to humankind. Moreover, the study predicted that by 2020 clinical depression will be the world's second most common cause of disability.[7]

It appears that depressive illness becomes a more frequent and severe problem as populations become more technologically advanced. This could be a direct result of the rate of change, as increased competition and level of expectations (both for increased material wealth and performance requirements) often characterize periods of great technological progress.

While medical scientists can make observations concerning genetic transmission, eventually it becomes necessary to study ways of reducing biological vulnerability to life stress and to develop coping techniques (see chapters 8 and 9) in order to make progress in our understanding of the disease.

Molecular Genetics

Rapid advancement from powerful methods in molecular genetics, a relatively new field, has led to the discovery of genetic "markers" associated with bipolar disorders in specific areas on various genes. Technological advances have increased the capacity to scan for these markers. In little more than fifteen years, progress in molecular genetics has leaped from looking for gene markers associated with bipolar illness to looking for candidate genes that produce various substances that regulate neurochemical reactions in the brain (resulting in the symptoms of bipolar disorder).

Chromosomal Linkage

Studies have identified regions of interest in linkage studies (these establish linkage between a certain location on a chromosome from affected individuals as compared with unaffected relatives) on chromosomes 4, 8, 10, 12, 16, 18, and 21 and the X chromosome of the human genome. Research is currently looking at genes that code for receptors, reuptake transporters (these control the metabolism of neurotransmitters in the brain by regulating the rate at which they are taken back into the nerve for breakdown or restorage), or critical neurotransmitters known to be affected by medications that improve the course of bipolar disorder (lithium and antidepressants). Improved techniques increase the likelihood that scientists will one day identify critical mechanisms in the expression of bipolar disorder.

Genetic research studies also continue to identify predisposing genes for bipolar disorder. This work is leading to a reconsideration of the diagnostic categories used in psychiatry research. In a recent review of genetic findings, research investigator Nick Craddock and associates pointed out in England emerging evidence suggesting specific relationships between genotype and psychopathology. Two genes have shown susceptibility to a form of illness with mixed features of mania and schizophrenia. These researchers note that association findings across six different genes show increasing evidence of genetic susceptibility across all traditional classification categories. They believe that as further association between genes and various forms or symptoms of psychopathology are discovered, our understanding of disease psychopathology will be increased and this will lead to changes in both diagnostic classification and the clinical practice of psychiatry.[8]

GENETICS, STRESS TOLERANCE, AND DEPRESSION

Studies of A. Caspi, and more recently Kenneth S. Kendler, have shown that individuals with a particular short form (polymorphism) of the gene for the serotonin transporter (the mechanism that causes reuptake) and metabolism of the transmitter serotonin at nerve cell endings, which are blocked by many newer antidepressants, including fluoxetine (Prozac), are eight times more likely to experience clinical depression in response to minor life stress while individuals with the long form of this gene are unaffected.[9] It is interesting to note that Kendler and his colleagues found that the short form of the gene is *only* related to the occurrence of depression, and not the occurrence of generalized anxiety.

INSIDE THE HUMAN BRAIN

The human brain is a highly complex structure and is located at the upper end of the *spinal cord* (see figure 3.1). In its overall appearance, the brain is a large agglomeration of delicate nerve cells and crisscrossing nerve pathways. An average adult brain weighs about three and one-half pounds (no larger than a grapefruit) and is molded into two symmetrical halves, or *hemispheres.* This bulbous structure of gray and white matter consists of approximately one hundred billion nerve cells, or neurons, and blood vessels. Neurons consisting of a cell body and fibers are held together and connected by the fibers. Gray matter is composed of nerve cells and their surrounding mesh of fibers.

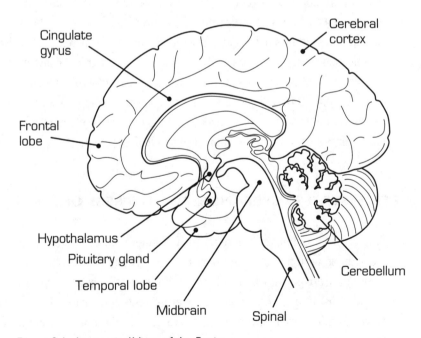

Figure 3.1. Anatomical View of the Brain

The *cerebral cortex* is the largest section of the human brain and accounts for about 85 percent of its weight. This section consists of the right and left hemispheres and is covered by a thin carpet of gray matter and is responsible for controlling our mental processes such as memory, speech, and thought.

The two hemispheres of the cerebral cortex are divided into lobes— *frontal* and *prefrontal, temporal, parietal,* and *occipital.* The frontal and prefrontal lobes are located behind the forehead and appear to be the center of human intelligence, refined emotions, and personality. Most important, the prefrontal lobe controls our ability to plan and to initiate thought and memory.

Deep in the temporal lobe is an almond-shaped center called the *amygdala* (see figure 3.2). The amygdala (and *hippocampus,* an underlying cortical structure) controls memory and determines emotional reactions such as elation, excitement, anxiety, agitation, rage, and aggression. It also regulates the capacity to start and stop behaviors associated with these emotions. The *cingulate gyrus* is a convoluted portion of the cortex that conducts many limbic system fibers.

Beneath the cortex is white matter containing nerve cells that connect the cortex with the brain stem, and one area of the cortex with another. Groups of nerve cells called the *basal ganglia* lie deep below the cortex.

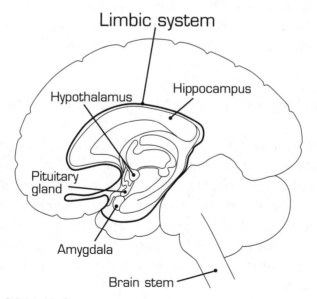

Figure 3.2. Limbic System

The *hypothalamus* is a walnut-sized cluster of cells that weighs about four grams. This governs the sex drive (or libido), regulates body temperature, controls appetite and sleep patterns, and is responsible for mood changes and emotions such as fear and rage. The hypothalamus also controls the pituitary gland. The *pituitary gland* is a major endocrine gland located at the base of the brain. Its hormones regulate growth and control the secretions of other endocrine glands, such as the thyroid and adrenals. The pituitary gland regulates the hormonal stress responses of the body, which have a direct effect on brain function as well.

> It is believed that depression is associated with a reduction of serotonin or norepinephrine transmitters. Conversely, a rapid increase of these chemicals may trigger mania.

The *midbrain* is the area on which most affective disorder researchers focus. The midbrain is an origin of neurons that produce the chemicals serotonin and norepinephrine. These chemicals are highly important in mood disorders. Nerve impulses are activated and carried from one brain cell to another by the sum total of neurotransmitters released. It is believed that there are numerous neurotransmitters, many of which are not yet known. It is further believed that depression is associated with a reduction of serotonin or norepinephrine transmitters. Conversely, a rapid increase of these chemicals may trigger mania. We will discuss this further in chapter 4.

The lower part of the brain is called the *cerebellum*. Situated beneath the cerebral cortex, the cerebellum controls muscle coordination, whereas the cerebral cortex controls our conscious thoughts and actions.

BEHAVIOR AND BIOLOGY AS TREATMENT TARGETS

We have stressed the importance of making an accurate diagnosis of bipolar disorder so that proper treatment can be initiated as early as possible to avoid the cumulative damage this illness can cause if left untreated. This section, which deals with some recent scientific advances, may at first seem to contradict this position. Early diagnosis and treatment will always remain a priority. However, as we review the findings of a wide variety of studies, new understandings relevant to the treatment of bipolar disorder and related depression may emerge.

For instance, we have discussed the fact that various subforms of bipolar disorder (e.g., rapid-cycling, mixed, or dysphoric states) may be more effectively treated by medications that better suppresses symptoms of that specific form of the illness. Studies have indicated that divalproex sodium (Depakote) may be particularly helpful in addressing mixed states of bipolar disorder, while lithium may be more useful to address depression and the long-term risk of suicide.

Both biological findings and the results of various treatment studies are beginning to point to the importance of the behavioral dimensions of psychological disorders. We will be considering this point as we review findings from this perspective and discussing some overlap between genetic studies of bipolar disorder and schizophrenia.

In particular, research has revealed overlap between schizophrenia and bipolar disorder in three regions on chromosomes 13, 18, and 22 of the genome. This raises the possibility that schizophrenia and bipolar disorder share some susceptibility factors. This is supported by the findings of family studies that first-degree relatives of bipolar and schizophrenic patients are at increased risk for both schizoaffective disorder (symptoms of both bipolar disorder and schizophrenia) and recurrent unipolar depression.

Oligogenic Inheritance

Dr. Elliot Gershon points out that the oligogenic inheritance (inheritance owing to several genes) of most diseases has frustrated efforts to establish linkages based on an assumption of single gene inheritance.[10] Figure 3.3 illustrates that it may require the occurrence of three or more susceptibility genes

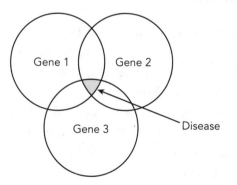

Figure 3.3. Oligogenic Inheritance

to produce a vulnerability. More advanced approaches taking oligogenic inheritance into account should lead to further progress in genetic research in bipolar and other disorders. As mentioned earlier, genetic research has gone beyond merely establishing a connection between markers for genes and bipolar disorder. The goal now is to isolate the genes, identify the proteins they code, and then determine the processes they activate that lead to the emergence of symptoms. Finding new ways to block the expression of identified "bipolar symptom component" genes could prevent the emergence of the symptoms of bipolar and other affective disorders.

It may take hundreds of studies or further breakthroughs in method to reach this point. Even then, researchers may find that the genetic vulnerabilities for these disorders are different in people from different ethnic or genetic backgrounds. The multiple-gene nature of illness vulnerability adds to the complexity of the search for answers.

It is possible that affective disorders are like fevers, with similar symptoms caused by different disease processes or vulnerabilities. Successful efforts to decode the human genome have already led to the identification of cancers with the same apparent cell type (but which can be differentiated on the basis of molecular-genetic studies) that have very different treatment responses. This same approach may identify types of bipolar disorder that respond to different medications despite identical clinical symptoms and clinical diagnosis. In short, genetic research holds great promise for the future, but the direct benefits and practical applications in diagnosis, treatment, and prevention are likely to take some time to emerge.

Studies of Neurotransmitters

Research into various neurotransmitters, the enzymes involved in their synthesis and breakdown, and the receptors they activate or inhibit is an outgrowth of the "psychopharmacological revolution" that started in the United States in the 1960s.

This revolution began with three developments in the area of medication: the success of chlorpromazine (Thorazine) in blocking symptoms of delusions and hallucinations, principally in schizophrenia but also in bipolar disorder; the discovery that imipramine (Tofranil) can reverse symptoms of severe depression; and the ability of a simple salt mined from the earth—

lithium—to reduce symptoms of mania and prevent recurrences of mania and depression.

These therapeutic advances literally caused a paradigm shift in the treatment of severe mental illness. In the early 1950s, prior to the introduction of chlorpromazine, the population in state hospitals was increasing at the rate of 10 percent a year. With no treatment other than restraints and crudely administered electroconvulsive therapy, these state hospitals resembled the "snake pit" mental institutions so vividly portrayed in the movies *The Snake Pit* and *One Flew over the Cuckoo's Nest.*

After the introduction of antipsychotic medications, these populations decreased by 10 percent a year, as more patients could be discharged and fewer required admission and long-term (sometimes lifetime) hospital stays. Unfortunately, this success prompted policy makers to close state hospitals without sufficient assurances of supportive services and continued treatment as outpatients in the community. The result has been the expansion of the ranks of mentally ill homeless individuals we see on the streets of our cities today. Sadly, county jails have also become a repository for acutely mentally ill persons without access to proper treatment.

Mechanisms of Drug Actions

The effects of chlorpromazine, imipramine, and lithium on mental disorders resulted in a torrent of basic laboratory studies and human clinical studies of the action mechanism of these medications. The resulting information led to the formulation of biochemical theories, which in turn led to more knowledge about the neurotransmitter and receptor changes underlying bipolar disorders, depressive disorders, and schizophrenia. Research focused on three major brain neurotransmitters: serotonin, related to depression, mood stability, and aggression/impulsivity; dopamine, related to schizophrenia, psychosis, and mania; and norepinephrine, related to depression. Further research led to the development of medications that affect like availability of these neurotransmitters in the brain. However, achieving a more complete understanding of how these neurotransmitters and their receptors—and second messenger systems within the nerve cell activated by receptors—are altered is made difficult by our limited ability to study their functions in the actual living human brain. The brain has a barrier that selects various biochemicals in the blood and controls their rate of passage in and out of the brain. This blood-brain barrier results in the brain maintaining a certain "metabolic independence," even though it depends on the body for nourishment and life. The significance of this in terms of research is that the blood-brain barrier limits simple generalizations about brain function based on samples of easily obtainable body fluids such as blood.

Diseases such as hypertension, diabetes, and cancer can be more readily studied in animals where organs can be probed after such conditions are created in the animal. Scientists have so far not found any animal models of bipolar disorder. The closest approximation has been the "kindling" model, which induces spontaneous seizures by repeated electrical stimulation of the brain. While it may present a good analogy for bipolar and recurrent mood disorder, it is hardly a "virtual" copy of bipolar disorder in humans.

> *Diseases such as hypertension, diabetes, and cancer can be more readily studied in animals where organs can be probed after such conditions are created in the animal. Scientists have so far not found any animal models of bipolar disorder.*

Despite our increasing understanding of how medications affect neurotransmitter systems and their receptors, these research limitations have restricted our understanding of how these systems are disordered and thereby lead to and maintain a state of mental illness. Research has revealed some information in this area, however. Studies have discovered increased densities of serotonin receptors in the brains of depressed suicide victims and correlated low serotonin turnover or function in the brain with violent suicide (e.g., violent methods such as guns, jumping from high places, or hanging as opposed to overdosing or self-poisoning) and impulsive, sometimes aggressive behavior.

Based on current studies, it is known that most antidepressant medications act to block a transporter site on a nerve ending that removes the neurotransmitters previously released by this nerve terminal from the synapse (the space between two neurons). This is hypothesized to result in a slower breakdown of the neurotransmitters and, therefore, an increased effect on receptors in the space between nerve endings or synapse, as well as on receptors on the adjacent nerve cell body. This results in a decrease in the number of receptors on the adjacent nerve cell (called a down regulation), which requires several weeks to occur—about the same length of time required for depression to improve significantly in response to antidepressant medication. In recent years, interest has focused on the "messenger systems" that are activated in the postsynaptic cell by receptors on the cell surface. There are studies suggesting that lithium has the ability to stabilize membranes and perhaps enhance serotonin function by an effect on certain second messenger systems in the cell. There is no clear understanding of the mechanism of divalproex sodium (Depakote) or carbamazepine (Tegretol) in bipolar disorder mood stabilization. It is thought that these medications affect mood stabilization by effects on the neurotransmitter glutamate, but evidence is limited.

While these studies have yielded few definite conclusions on how neurotransmitters mediate the symptoms of bipolar disorder, they do provide direction for the application of newer techniques to get at some of these questions. Researchers have had to devise other methods for getting inside the "black box," the relatively inaccessible human brain, to try to understand the workings of its complex chemical machinery (see Imaging Studies, page 56). As just one measure of its complexity, the brain is composed of at least forty million functional neurons, each with an average of five thousand connections with other neurons.

Neurotrophins and New Cell Production

Scientists have recently begun to explore an entire area of neurotropic factors now being measured in the brain. Additional studies illustrate clear evidence of neurogenesis (new cell production occurring in the brain), which may prove useful in the treatment of bipolar disorder and depression. Evidence has shown that chronic depressive illness and bipolar disorders, as well as certain anxiety disorders such as PTSD (posttraumatic stress disorder), actually cause a loss of nerve cells in both frontal areas of the brain and the hippocampus (see figure 3.2).

An article by Dr. Husseini Manji, chief of the Laboratory of Molecular Pathophysiology at the National Institute of Mental Health, and colleagues notes that "the expression of different genes, including transcription factors, is markedly altered by lithium administration. Chronic lithium treatment also robustly increases the expression of the neuroprotective protein Bcl2, raising the intriguing possibility that some of lithium's effects are mediated through neurotrophic (induction of new neuron growth) and neuroprotective effects."[11]

Work like that of Dr. Manji's illustrates the effect that certain medications have regarding new cell production. Recent research is also producing evidence that new cell formation (neurogenesis) can be induced in selected areas of laboratory animals' brains by way of exercise and new learning.

Recent work at Princeton has taken this research one step further. Molecular geneticists, under the direction of Dr. J. Z. Tsien, have developed in accomplishing a new technique to "knock out" or remove the gene required for the development of nonspatial intelligence on mice. This accomplishment required the team to create a genetic effect involving only "one" area and function of brain development. That in itself is an amazing feat, but these scientists went further. They placed a group of mice, bred for low intelligence, inside a barren cage and an equal number (also bred for low intelligence) into cages equipped with running wheels, tunnels, and mazes to provide environment. Astonishingly, the "mentally dull" mice inside the enriched environment illustrated the acquisition of abilities and intelligence for which there was no genetic basis.

Research is producing evidence that new cell formation (neurogenesis) can be induced in selected areas of laboratory animals' brains by way of exercise and new learning.

On close examination, the scientists discovered the growth of new nerve endings in the affected areas of the mice's brain tissue. The mice in the environmentally enriched group were able to transfer and develop new functions despite their innate lack of such genetic programming.[12]

The jump from mice to men may be a long one, but this revolutionary new evidence raises an important question: Can the biological functioning of the human nervous system also be shaped by new learning? If intensive "cognitive therapy" works for mice, it could possibly work for man to help reverse genetic vulnerabilities at the biological level.

Imaging Studies

It appears that our knowledge of the important neurotransmitters, combined with the emerging field of molecular genetics, is allowing us to "leapfrog" some of the barriers to learning about neurotransmitter function in the brain.

The development of brain imaging techniques has allowed researchers to get inside the "black box" of the human brain without invading the brain itself. This technology makes it possible to pinpoint anatomical differences and detect functional alterations in various areas of the brains of patients with bipolar disorder. Introduced ten years ago, initial brain imaging efforts focused on defining the differences between bipolar patients and people without the disease. Imaging has now evolved to studying the differences in aspects of brain structure and function between patients with schizophrenia, bipolar disorder, and recurrent depression. This methodology, together with molecular biology and genetic approaches, promises to further advance our knowledge of human brain function.

It appears that our knowledge of the important neurotransmitters, combined with the emerging field of molecular genetics, is allowing us to "leapfrog" some of the barriers to learning about neurotransmitter function in the brain.

Brain imaging techniques have the advantage of not employing X-rays to produce the image, thus avoiding the toxicity of radiation. Instead, imaging uses modified radio waves and strong magnetic fields to form images of the atoms and molecules that make up the brain.

Techniques such as magnetic resonance imaging (MRI) "image" brain structures and certain aspects of function, such as blood flow. A related technique, magnetic resonance imaging spectoscopy (MRI-S) allows measurement of certain chemical changes reflecting neuronal function in small areas of the brain. Through this type of imaging, we can measure various chemicals in targeted areas of the brain without interfering with their activity.

Another promising technique, positron emission tomography (PET), can measure metabolic processes in the brain and body. Much can be learned from measuring the rate of glucose metabolism, indicative of brain activity, in various areas of the brain in distinct disease states such as mania and depression. Specific neurotransmitters are "labeled" with radioisotopes and their behavior studied in various brain neural circuits.

The PET scans labeled "Depressed Brain" and "Recovered Brain" (facing page 40) show the brain of a patient during depression and after recovery from depression. The colors in the scans correspond to glucose metabolic rates (which indicate neural activity), with the lowest rates associated with the coolest end of the color spectrum (blue) and the highest rates with the warmest (red). If an area that normally reflects higher rates (red, yellow, or green) shows up blue on the scan, it implies that the neurons in that region are impaired. The image made during a depressive episode (*left*) is dark, mostly blue, whereas the image created after treatment with medication (*right*) has more green, yellow, and red, showing normalized neural activity.

The PET scans labeled "Rapid-Cycling Manic-Depressive Brain" (facing page 41) are those of a drug-free patient. The images in the top row were made when the patient was depressed. The second row shows the identical planes scanned the next day, when the patient had become manic. The third row shows scans taken ten days later when the patient was again depressed. The scans show that the brain is in an abnormal metabolic state (either decreased or increased metabolic function) when the patient is in a depressed or manic state compared with the rates of metabolism during periods of normal function.

These imaging techniques, guided by knowledge gained from studies elucidating the important neurotransmitter systems (despite all the limitations encountered), are leading to rapid advances in our understanding of bipolar disorder and other conditions. At this point, the techniques are purely investigational; they are not developed to a degree that they can be used in clinical treatment. While imaging points to functional and structural abnormalities, there is still some variation and inevitable lack of agreement from study to study because of the use of varying techniques and small numbers of patients. The findings are therefore unreliable for diagnosis and treatment decisions.

Still, valuable findings are emerging from these pioneer advances, and there is great promise for new understanding as these techniques become more powerful. One early finding was that certain left-sided frontal brain damage caused by stroke or trauma may lead to the development of major depression. Poststroke mania is associated with a right-sided brain injury and either an underlying subcortical loss of cells or a genetic vulnerability to bipolar disorder.

> *Recent studies highlight the brain's plasticity with evidence of cell atrophy and loss in response to severe prolonged stress and untreated depression. New evidence is emerging that treatment (antidepressants, divalproex sodium, and lithium) may reverse some of these processes.*

A recent report confirmed previous observations of neuroanatomic deep white matter changes (sometimes called unidentified bright objects, or UBOs), as well as subcortical gray matter changes, in primarily young bipolar patients. Both PET and functional MRI studies have shown decreased metabolism of various areas of the frontal lobes as well as in subcortical structures such as the basal ganglia.

A recent study of cell density in these same brain areas, using tissue taken from individuals dying while in an episode of depression (some with no prior treatment), has shown both reduced neuronal and glial cells (the metabolic support cells for neurons), which corresponds to both PET findings and MRI studies revealing signs of atrophy in some patients with these disorders.

Other MRI studies of bipolar patients have revealed atrophy of frontal, temporal, and subcortical areas. Though older patients showed a higher percentage of this trend, the finding appeared in 10 to15 percent of adolescent patients as well, suggesting an illness-related correlation. An MRI-S can measure changes in certain biochemicals in the living brain. Studies in bipolar patients have revealed decreases of the neurotransmitter glutamate in the anterior cingulate cortex (see figure 3.1). Recent studies highlight the brain's plasticity with evidence of cell atrophy and loss in response to severe prolonged stress and untreated depression. New evidence, reviewed above, is emerging that treatment (antidepressants, divalproex sodium, and lithium) may reverse some of these processes. Other studies have demonstrated signs of stimulation of neurotrophic and neuroprotective factors in the brains of bipolar patients who are taking lithium for their disorder.

Using both neuron-imaging and neuropsychological testing, Dr. Hilary Blumberg, associate professor in the Department of Psychiatry and director of Yale's Mood Disorders Research Program, has shown shrinkage of the ventral prefrontal cortex (VPFC) of adolescents with bipolar disorder as well as decreased control of functions of the amygdala in these patients. The amygdala is an almond-sized nucleus, occurring bilaterally in the brain, which informs judgments about negative or positive perceptions of situations. It is of great interest that patients with (more severe) rapid-cycling forms of the disorder had greater decreases in the VPFC and that those diagnosed, treated, and taking current medication had larger volumes of gray matter. This suggests that pharmacotherapy may protect effects of VPFC volume in patients with bipolar disorder.[13]

Review of the research on the biology of bipolar disorder reveals evident progress in molecular genetics and imaging studies. Additionally, investigations into the effects of medications on key neurotransmitters and messenger systems have significantly increased our knowledge of the brain and the systems affected by bipolar disorder. Relating findings from one set of methods to another (e.g., effects of medications related to findings on imaging studies) is leading us closer to knowledge that will result in the development of more effective treatments for bipolar disorder and possibly earlier diagnosis techniques and prevention strategies. Practical breakthroughs in early diagnosis and treatment will occur unpredictably as further research leads to new paradigms for understanding the biology of the illness. In the meantime, we must continue researching the effectiveness of new medications developed to treat it. In the next chapter, we will examine the latest medication strategies and treatment models.

CHAPTER 4

Medication Therapy

The past forty-five years have witnessed great progress in the treatment of bipolar disorder and clinical depression. It is important to note that bipolar disorder may appear in forms that are difficult to treat and, in some cases, may require multiple medications in several different combinations before an acceptable result is obtained. Progress has been made and there is reason for hope, but each patient requires the right combination of medications and often specific psychotherapies to get the desired result. It is important to persist with treatment. Here we will present the array of treatment possibilities open to patients and the importance of accessing them. Since the first edition of this book, there has been substantial development of effective medications for bipolar depression and mood stabilization. The development of safer, more effective, and easier-to-use medications has brightened the outlook for people who have depressive and manic-depressive conditions. With the increasing volume of research and the continued development of new medications, we see promise of even more effective treatments on the horizon.

Despite already considerable progress, many unanswered questions and doubts remain about the use of medications in the treatment of clinical depression. Some people find it hard to understand why a medication is necessary to treat what they mistakenly view as a purely psychological disturbance affecting only the mind. In actuality, mental illness results in a wide range of effects on all levels: physical, mental, emotional, and behavioral. Bipolar illness goes to the very center of a person's being, obstructing the ability to enjoy or appreciate life, see beyond oneself, and be productive or creative. Hopelessness and despair are common by-products. Other consequences include lack of energy and motivation, impaired insight and judgment, and a predisposition to physical illness. Lewis Judd and colleagues have shown that patients with bipolar depression average about half their time in depression versus about 2 percent of their time manic or hypomanic.[1] Bipolar disorder often extends way beyond the distortion of emotional responses, as it has a profound impact on the body's physiology and the brain's capacity to function.

Some people erroneously believe that those who experience depression would benefit from learning how to cope more effectively with life's disappointments. "Just deal with it," patients so often hear from others. "Count your blessings" or "confess your sins and turn to God." Others are under the misconception that suffering from depression or mood swings that require medication is a sign of weakness or a "cop-out." Still others believe the person is overlooking a simple panacea. "Try running every day. You'll feel better," some well-meaning friend or relative might say.

Some of these views undoubtedly originate from the stigma associated with a mental disorder, a belief in "true grit" or the concept of willpower. That depression might be the manifestation of dysfunctional brain mechanisms, and not purely a mind problem that can be overcome by "trying harder," is a difficult concept for skeptics to accept. Consequently, some people find a talking treatment (psychotherapy) philosophically easier to embrace than the idea of medication.

> *The idea that depression might be the manifestation of dysfunctional brain mechanisms, and not purely a mind problem that can be overcome by "trying harder," is a difficult concept for skeptics to accept.*

Unfortunately, the stigma surrounding bipolar disorder is not limited to the general population. It exists in the health-care industry as well, as evidenced by discrimination against paying for the treatment of "mental" disorders as if they are separate and distinct from "medical" disorders. Psychiatric patients have long suffered at the hands of health insurers whose drastic cuts in the funding of care have resulted in denial of coverage for mental illness. And yet health insurance covers expensive, highly technological procedures such as liver and heart transplants without question. Meanwhile, suicide is the eighth cause of death overall and the third cause of death among people fifteen to twenty-four years old. Many of these deaths could be prevented by access to effective treatment, which is now frequently lacking owing to insufficient medical coverage.

The failure of health-care providers to recognize mental illness as a legitimate health problem has reinforced the social stigma, contributed to a rise in mental disorders as they go untreated, and increased the cost to society.

A major problem in understanding clinical depression as an illness results from the fact that the word depression is an adjective used to describe mood states commonly resulting from disappointment or demoralization when things go wrong. Since we all experience this type of depression, and develop behaviors to cope with such feelings, many people conclude that clinical depression is the same thing—something that a person should be able to simply "get over." Unfortunately, clinical depression does not respond to such coping efforts.

THE UNDERTREATMENT OF BIPOLAR DISORDER AND DEPRESSION

In 1997, the Depression and Bipolar Support Alliance (DBSA), formerly the National Depressive and Manic Depressive Association (National DMDA) published *Expert Consensus Treatment Guidelines for Bipolar Disorder: A Guide for Patients and Families.* The report brought to light some damning facts, particularly regarding the long delay between the onset of symptoms and correct diagnosis and treatment. The report revealed that people with bipolar disorder see approximately three to four doctors and spend more than eight years seeking treatment before they receive a correct diagnosis. The report also pointed to the inability of some primary care providers to make a proper diagnosis because of their limited experience in dealing with psychiatric problems. The attending physician may lack sufficient information on the diagnosis and treatment of depression. In addition, many providers have limited training in managing emotional distress because general practitioners normally deal with physical ailments. This points to the importance of increased public as well as medical awareness of these disorders.

This report followed a 1996 National DMDA conference to investigate the reasons for the undertreatment of depression. A panel composed of

DEPRESSION AND BIPOLAR SUPPORT ALLIANCE

Headquartered in Chicago, the Depression and Bipolar Support Alliance (formerly National DMDA) is the nation's largest patient-run, "illness-specific" organization. It is a major source of support for people with unipolar and bipolar disorders. Since its inception in 1986, members have been working to combat the public stigma surrounding these illnesses. Rather than bow to stigma, members act to obliterate it through public education, which remains one of the primary purposes of the organization.

psychiatrists, psychologists, family practitioners, internists, managed care and public health specialists, and members of the community considered six key questions: (1) Is depression undertreated in both the community and the clinic? (2) What is the economic cost to society regarding depression? (3) What have been the efforts in the past to redress undertreatment and how successful have they been? (4) What are the reasons for the gap between our knowledge of the diagnosis and treatment of depression to the actual treatment received in the United States? (5) What can we do to narrow this gap? (6) What can we do immediately to narrow this gap?

The panel arrived at the following conclusions:

1. Depressive disorders affect 15 percent of the male population and 24 percent of females, an increase over the past several generations; the age of onset has also decreased. In a 1980 survey, approximately one-third of the people suffering depression sought treatment. Of those who sought treatment, only about one in ten received adequate help. Unfortunately, the vast majority of patients treated with antidepressants are prescribed an inadequate dose for an insufficient period of time. Although effective psychotherapies exist, few patients receive them or, when they do go for help, the allotted time frame is too short.

The Depression and Bipolar Support Alliance has a grassroots network of 275 chapters and support groups and is managed by an administrative board of directors, the majority of whom are patients themselves. It is also guided by a 65-member scientific advisory board comprising the leading researchers and clinicians in the field of depressive illnesses. Contact DBSA for free educational material, membership information, or to locate a patient-run chapter or support group in your community (see Resources, page 333).

2. Depression is one of the ten most costly illnesses in the United States and imposes an enormous burden on society. The many costs and consequences include decreased quality of life for patients and families, high morbidity and mortality, and substantial economic losses. A conservative estimate from a recent study calculated the annual national cost of depression at $43 billion. A new cost–benefit analysis estimated that the savings of appropriately treating depression outweighed the direct treatment costs by about $4 billion per year.

3. Depression, the world's fourth most common cause of disability in 2000, is projected to be the second most frequent cause of disability by 2020, with heart disease being number one. The gap between our knowledge of correct treatment of depression and what actually gets implemented can be attributed to patient, provider, and health-care system factors.

Patients: Patients don't recognize the existence of a problem, fail to identify the problem as depression, or underestimate the problem's severity. Some face limited access to treatment or are unwilling to stay with a recommended medical regimen. Many still experience a stigma attached to mental health issues, which, while it is on the decrease, remains a reality of our culture and is often reinforced in families.

> *Depression is one of the ten most costly illnesses in the United States and imposes an enormous burden on society. A conservative estimate from a recent study calculated the annual national cost of depression at $43 billion.*

Providers: Medical schools may fail to provide sufficient education about psychiatric diagnosis, psychopharmacology, or psychotherapy for depression. Other problems include physicians inadequately prepared to use the most modern methods, primary care providers who don't perceive psychiatric disorders as real illnesses, poor insurance coverage, inadequate dosage of antidepressants administered to patients, and some patients' reluctance to see a psychiatrist or other mental health care specialist.

Health-Care System: Some reasons for less than optimal treatment of depression include inadequate insurance reimbursement, lack of qualified specialists, cost-saving plans that discourage treatment and proper monitoring of patients, and insufficient follow-up care.

4. There is a need for additional research and analysis to narrow the gap between diagnosis/treatment determination and actual treatment of depression. The panel designed a slate of questions to help investigate this problem.

5. What can be done immediately to help narrow the gap? Increasing the knowledge of patients and families about treatment options and essential treatment requirements for depression diverts responsibility away from the providers and places it back in the hands of the afflicted. Developing performance standards for behavioral health care can make providers accountable for their standards of treatment. Other proposals included increasing provider knowledge and awareness about new effective treatment and screening for depression; increased collaboration among primary care providers, psychiatrists, and other mental health specialists; and giving more attention to further research, especially as it relates to children, adolescents, and senior citizens.[2]

EFFECTIVENESS OF PSYCHOTHERAPY

Psychotherapies are relatively untested in bipolar disorder. On the other hand, new evidence exists to support the effectiveness of interpersonal and cognitive psychotherapies in unipolar depression of mild to moderate severity. Evidence is mounting that a combination of medication and psychotherapy may ultimately provide the best results for most patients with depression.

> *Evidence is mounting that a combination of medication and psychotherapy may ultimately provide the best results for most patients with depression.*

Early studies have also shown that family education can improve the outcome of bipolar disorder. In chapter 5, we will discuss the benefits of psychotherapy in detail.

Clearly, psychotherapy ("talk therapy") can be helpful in dealing with issues that otherwise might aggravate bipolar disorder or depression even when the patient is on medication. It is simplistic and counterproductive to view psychotherapy and medication as competing treatments. These modalities are frequently complementary.

Poor outcomes follow attempts to replace one modality with the other rather than addressing aspects of the problem with the appropriate treatment. At this point, the evidence supports the need for mood stabilizers and, possibly, added antidepressants for bipolar disorder. Mood stabilizers, such as lithium or divalproex sodium (Depakote), and olanzapine (Zyprexa), address manic and/or hypomanic (mildly manic) cycles. Antidepressants address breakthrough depression, which is one of the most common problems in bipolar disorder. Additional psychotherapy (the appropriate type) depends largely on what other disorders or individual problems need addressing. These may include low self-esteem, excess perfectionism, problems in relationships, poor compliance (with taking prescribed medication), and family problems.

WHEN ARE MEDICATIONS A NECESSARY FORM OF TREATMENT?

During episodes of mania, symptoms of agitation and psychosis may occur. These can result in a state of high energy, with a rush of thoughts and a suspension of self-criticism (or concern about outside criticism, for that matter), which leads to positive feelings of creativity. Commonly, such lack of self-criticism simply leads to an overestimation of performance. In a minority of cases, however, the individual is more capable of a real sense of creativity, sometimes resulting in significant accomplishments.

Patients frequently are reluctant to have this state of mind "taken away" by the use of mood-stabilizing drugs. Without mood stabilizers, those who feel more creative and generative during a hypomanic episode but in fact are merely oblivious to realistic feedback, may end up suffering from an exercise of poor judgment. For them, it is clear that medication is in their best interest. For the small minority of individuals whose true creative achievements were the by-products of hypomania, reluctance to take mood stabilizers is understandable.

Both manic and hypomanic mood swings are frequently followed by episodes of depression, which are usually not prevented by antidepressant medications alone. The question becomes not only what are the consequences of

> *Both manic and hypomanic mood swings are frequently followed by episodes of depression, which are usually not prevented by antidepressant medications alone. The question becomes not only what are the consequences of mania, but what is the cost of the depression that is likely to follow?*

mania, but what is the cost of the depression that is likely to follow? In many cases, the creative period is not worth the intense suffering that results from depression. Nevertheless, this is a decision that must be addressed on an individual basis between the patient and his or her doctor.

There is no question that learning new adaptive skills can help patients better cope with life. Strategies to increase self-esteem, manage stress, and deal with interpersonal relationships through various types of psychotherapy are often helpful if an individual is in an appropriate state to respond to such interventions.

People with mood swings associated both with the milder and the more severe forms of bipolar disorder require appropriate medication to control their imbalance. There is also evidence that more severe depressions, characterized by more severe symptoms, prolonged duration, greater impairment of function, and increased suicidal risk respond more reliably and positively to medications.

A large and growing body of information confirms the theory (which the authors adhere to) that more severe forms of clinical depression and bipolar disorder are associated with biochemical brain changes. These changes in brain chemistry are more likely to develop in individuals with a family history of clinical depression and bipolar disorder, just as diabetes and high blood pressure tend to occur in families with a history of those disorders. Newer medical imaging techniques can demonstrate a change of metabolism in specific brain areas associated with depression (see color illustrations facing pages 40 and 41). Most of these brain changes return to normal after successful treatment.

WHEN THE USE OF MEDICATION IS INDICATED

Patients with mood swings of mania, hypomania, or mixed-dysphoric mania (an increasingly common form in which increased activity and agitation is combined with depression) require mood-stabilizing medications (e.g., lithium, divalproex sodium, and possibly other medications that will be discussed later). These untreated mood swings usually become more frequent and more severe rather than showing improvement over time.

For bipolar sufferers, periods of depression usually follow such periods of mania or hypomania. In milder instances, symptoms can improve with mood stabilizers alone. Sometimes results will only be seen after dosage increases or with the addition of lithium. Untreated, the depression can continually recur and become a major obstacle for patients with both bipolar I and bipolar II disorders. Such depression can result in disability, ruined careers, marital problems, life without happiness, or even suicide.

In the more severe forms of depression, antidepressant medications are added to the patient's regimen despite an increased risk of inducing manic or hypomanic cycles. This risk is much less pressing if the mood-stabilizing medications are taken in adequate doses prior to the use of antidepressant medications. In the case of severely worsening symptoms or prolonged depression, the risk of a mood cycle is far outweighed by the pain, damage, and suicidal risk of severe depression. However, recent studies showing that medications such as lamotrigine or quetiapine can relieve bipolar depression with a negligible risk of mood cycling present new treatment possibilities for bipolar depression. If a person in this situation mentions suicide, or wishes to die, it is imperative that lethal weapons or substances are removed and a physician, preferably a psychiatrist, is contacted. The patient should not be left alone until properly evaluated.

CHOOSING AND EVALUATING MEDICATIONS

For many years, doctors treating depression and manic depression had few options to choose from. In the 1980s and 1990s, however, the Food and Drug Administration (FDA) approved several new mood-stabilizing and antidepressant drugs including serotonin reuptake inhibitors, an anticonvulsant, and an atypical antipsychotic medication for depression and bipolar disorder. These newer drugs are safer, better tolerated, and at least as effective as the older medications.

The goal of mood-stabilizing medication (including lithium, the anticonvulsant divalproex sodium, and the atypical antipsychotic olanzapine) is the moderation or prevention of mood cycles, ideally for both mania (or hypomania) and depression. By controlling mania, these medications also limit the damage resulting from impaired judgment. While there have long been studies supporting the use of lithium, during the 1980s anticonvulsants such as carbamazepine (Tegretol), and later divalproex sodium (Depakote), were also proven helpful in mood stabilization. Depakote was later approved for use in acute bipolar disorder. More recently the first of a new series of medications called atypical antipsychotic medications, Zyprexa (olanzapine), has been approved for the acute and long-term treatment of bipolar disorder. It ushers in the availability of other medications in this new class including Risperdal (risperidone), Seroquel (quetiapine), Geodon (ziprasidone), and Abilify (aripiprozole), now studied and approved by the FDA for use in treating bipolar disorder. Some people feel stigmatized when they learn these medications are classified as "atypical antipsychotic medications." Originally designed as new treatments for schizophrenia, they have since been proven very effective in treating bipolar disorder patients without symptoms of psychosis. The introduction of these medications over the past five years is a major advance in our capacity to treat bipolar mania, hypomania, mixed mania, and depression. These medications will be discussed in greater detail later. In the past six years, studies have been published showing the effects of the antiepileptic drug Lamictal (lamotrigine), which demonstrate its capacity to reduce mood cycling and prevent or treat depression.

Antidepressant medications can decrease or eliminate "target symptoms" of clinical depression both in unipolar and bipolar disorder. However, antidepressants can also increase the frequency of mood cycles into mania and mixed states, usually resulting in another episode of depression for an indeterminate period of time. Once cycling begins, an antidepressant is no longer helpful in treating symptoms of depression.

> *New treatments for depression that do not depend on antidepressant medications have been demonstrated by studies in the past five to seven years. These include Lamictal, Seroquel, and the combination of Zyprexa and Prozac (fluoxetine). Some bipolar patients may still require antidepressant medications, and in these cases it is important that a mood-stabilizing medication is in place.*

Since the early 1970s, anticonvulsant drugs have been showing considerable therapeutic promise in the treatment of manic episodes even before FDA approval. Furthermore, the severity and debilitating effects of the depressive target symptoms vary from patient to patient. One patient may have no energy or motivation, sleep all day, and be prone to weight gain. Another patient may appear anxious and sleepless, with poor concentration and little or no appetite.

In each of these cases, a medication strategy would be designed to fit the patient's target symptoms and individual response. (For instance, while one person with bipolar disorder or depression may experience a vast improvement with medication X, another patient with similar symptoms may not benefit at all or suffer too many unwanted side effects. This patient might respond better to medication Y.)

Sometimes several medication trials, or a combination of medications, are necessary to achieve improvement. The patient's prior experience with medication is a good predictor of what drugs to try or to avoid. A personal record of treatment, including medication and dosages used, the length of time taken, and any positive or negative experiences, can be a valuable tool for the doctor in determining a medication strategy.

> *With a successful course of medication, the symptoms of depression should decrease, if not totally disappear. This should occur within two to eight weeks, but a full response sometimes takes twelve to sixteen weeks.*

With a successful course of medication, the symptoms of depression should decrease, if not totally disappear. This should occur within two to eight weeks, but a full response sometimes takes twelve to sixteen weeks. Some patients may require more than one course of treatment (or medication trial) to attain a good result. For others, improvement may occur even though personal troubles, such as a problematic relationship or unsuccessful lifestyle, remain. Medications benefit a patient by reducing or removing the symptoms of depression, not by changing negative life situations. In these cases, psychotherapy may well be warranted. As depressed patients improve, their ability to cope with life's adversities also improves.

It is important for patients to continue antidepressant medications long after their depressive symptoms have disappeared in order to avoid a relapse or recurrence. If medication is stopped prematurely, or without a gradual tapering of the dose, a relapse will occur. In the

> *It is important for patients to continue antidepressant medications long after their depressive symptoms have disappeared in order to avoid a relapse or recurrence. If medication is stopped prematurely, or without a gradual tapering of the dose, a relapse will occur.*

case of bipolar patients, antidepressants are often gradually discontinued after a stable response is obtained, while mood stabilizers are continued indefinitely.

Generally, the first one to three months of an antidepressant regimen is enough to establish acute response to treatment, with a subsequent six months of a stable effective dose in place to ensure stabilization and prevent a relapse. Depending on the duration of the depressive episode, and the number and severity of prior episodes, a doctor may recommend maintenance treatment for one to several years, sometimes indefinitely, since depression is often a recurring condition. We have evidence from a number of studies that symptom relapse rates are high if medications are not continued long enough. In the case of patients with bipolar disorder who take mood stabilizers, antidepressants may be tapered and discontinued somewhat earlier in some cases.

Just as patients with diabetes or high blood pressure must remain on their medication, those with bipolar disorder, who suffer recurrent depression and chronic depression, need long-term medication, which can prevent most, or all, of the recurrences that characterize the illness. Once symptomatic and diagnosed, bipolar disorder is likely to be recurrent for a lifetime if left untreated.

TYPES OF MEDICATION

It is not unusual for patients to require several sequential trials of mood-stabilizing and/or antidepressant medications before pinpointing an effective regimen with tolerable side effects. While large studies allow clinicians to assess the efficacy of various medications, individual physiological differences demand that most clinicians go through a sequence of trial and error before deciding on the best course of treatment for each individual patient with bipolar disorder. The nature and severity of the illness will determine the type of drug therapy. Options include antidepressants, mood stabilizers, anticonvulsants, and newer "antipsychotic" medications. Whenever a new drug or combination of drugs is tested, the patient must be carefully monitored for side effects.

Mood Stabilizers and Anticonvulsant Medication

The FDA initially approved three primary medications for the treatment of bipolar disorder: lithium, divalproex sodium (Depakote), and olanzepine (Zyprexa). Lithium is a mood stabilizer; Depakote is an anticonvulsant, as is carbamazepine. The latter is not FDA-approved for treatment of bipolar

HOW DO PSYCHIATRIC DRUGS WORK?

Most psychiatric medications act in the brain to either increase or decrease the effects of various neurotransmitters (which send chemical messages from nerve cell to nerve cell). This process attempts to normalize brain function. Recent studies indicate that both mood stabilizing and antidepressants may also act by stimulating neurogenesis or new cell growth in various brain areas.

disorder but is sometimes used "off label." Doctors can prescribe this because it has been approved for other illnesses. Zyprexa, the most recently approved medication, is classified as an atypical neuroleptic (antipsychotic). New medications that are currently being studied to establish their effectiveness are also in use. More recently, Lamictal, Risperdal, Seroquel, Abilify, and Geodon have been approved for at least acute treatment of bipolar disorder.

Lithium: Lithium, a naturally occurring element, was the first medication on the market for the treatment of manic-depression. Approved by the FDA in the 1970s for bipolar disorder, lithium is sold under numerous brand names: Lithobid, Lithonate, Lithotabs, Cibalith-S, Eska-lith, and Eskalith CR. A mood stabilizer, lithium is used to treat the manic phase of bipolar disorder and prevent a recurrence of manic and/or depressive episodes. Once the mania subsides, lithium is administered on a maintenance basis.

Scientists have not yet determined the specifics of how lithium works, but it is believed that lithium corrects chemical imbalances in certain brain cells. The drug can be effective when used alone, or in combination with other medications. For example, medicines that had been initially approved for the prevention of temporal lobe epilepsy (carbamazepine and divalproex sodium) are now administered in combination with lithium to treat bipolar disorder. Lithium is also being used to augment the effects of antidepressant medication when the response is less than optimal.

Divalproex Sodium (Depakote): Depakote was first developed for the treatment of epilepsy. Since the FDA approved its use for acute mania in 1995, doctors and patients have relied on it for both acute and long-term treatment. As an anticonvulsant, its mechanism of action is different from that of lithium, but it has similar effects and may benefit patients who don't respond or cannot tolerate lithium or carbamazepine. Depakote works effectively to stabilize patients during manic episodes and acts to reduce the severity of future mood swings.

Carbamazepine (Atretol and Tegretol): Anticonvulsants Atretol and Tegretol are used as alternatives to lithium and divalproex sodium. Originally marketed for seizure disorders such as epilepsy, doctors discovered that it helps to keep the manic phase of bipolar disorder under control and is effective (alone or in combination with lithium) in the treatment of patients with rapid-cycling bipolar disorder.

New Medications: Within the past ten years, bipolar drug development has advanced in three important ways: (1) ongoing trials have proven the effectiveness of what originally were considered antiepileptic drugs (AED), such as Lamictal; (2) atypical antipsychotic medications originally developed to treat schizophrenia were found effective in treating nonpsychotic bipolar disorder; and (3) doctors have developed new antidepressant medications, or combinations of them, that treat depressive symptoms without promoting mood cycling—a major drawback and danger of antidepressant regimens of days past.

Topirimate (Topomax): Topomax, one of the new AEDs approved by the FDA in the last ten years, has not been found efficacious as a single therapy but may be helpful as an add-on treatment. It also tends to decrease the appetite, an unusual and attractive feature for many patients. Atypical antipsychoic medications turn out to be important mood stabilizers with antidepressant and antiagitation effects in bipolar disorder. These medications have vastly increased our ability to help patients who suffer from various phases of bipolar disorder. We are not declaring victory on the war against bipolar disorder, but these medications are helpful in extending our therapeutic capacity.

Like all drug regimens, these new medications differ vastly from individual to individual in their therapeutic effects and side effects. Olanzapine (Zyprexa) was the first atypical antipsychotic used and the most studied. At the time of this writing, it also is the only one of its class to qualify for both acute and maintenance (long-term) treatment of bipolar disorder. Zyprexa is sedating, reduces anxiety and agitation, stabilizes mood, especially with mixed states, and contains antidepressant properties. It has proven useful for both psychotic and nonpsychotic patients. Side effects may include weight gain, possible development of insulin insensitivity, and secondary diabetes without close monitoring. Patients on this drug should be checking in at least every three to six months. Recently, the FDA issued a "black box" warning to patients who take atypical antipsychotic medications about the risk of increased serum lipids and secondary diabetes. Clinical observations and a recent study suggest that these risks may be greater with Zyprexa than other atypical antipsychotic medications.

Risperidone (Risperdal) and Quentiapine (Seroquel): Risperdal and Seroquel are two antipsychotics used as a mood stabilizer. Mildly sedating, they are also used to lessen patient agitation.

Seroquel reduces anxiety and agitation and has recently demonstrated a surprising degree of effectiveness in the treatment of bipolar depression. It is given in slowly increasing doses (usually at bedtime) to accommodate to sedating effects over time while building up a therapeutic dosage. Like Risperdal, it may result in moderate weight gain and should be closely monitored. Both have shown efficacy in acute treatment of bipolar disorder as well as long-term maintenance.

Aripiprozole (Abilify) and Ziprasidone (Geodon): Abilify and Geodon differ somewhat from other members of the antipsychotic class. They are effective in stabilizing mood and reducing anxiety/agitation, but they lack strong sedative effects and are therefore less powerful for some patients in reducing the acute agitation that leads to sleep deprivation. That said, they also do not sedate patients as heavily during daytime activities and don't cause nearly as much weight gain over time.

Managing the Side Effects of Mood Stabilizers

The following are steps you can take to reduce the side effects of lithium, mood stabilizers, and anticonvulsants.

Have blood tests. If you are taking lithium, your doctor should test your blood regularly to rule out rare effects on the kidney or thyroid, especially if you are in the initial stages of taking the medication. Once your doctor has determined the appropriate dosage and your blood levels of lithium have stabilized, a blood test every six months to one year should be enough.

Elderly individuals are typically more sensitive to lithium and may therefore require a lower dosage than younger adults. Lithium can be dangerous for people on low-sodium diets, for those who have lost sodium through severe vomiting or diarrhea, and for people who have kidney disease. This is because lithium tends to replace lost sodium in the body, leading to increasing blood levels that can be toxic and cause nausea, vomiting, impaired coordination of movements or gait, and mental confusion, as well as kidney damage. Lithium toxicity is a medical emergency.

If you are taking Zyprexa, Risperdal, Seroquel, Abilify, or Geodon, you should have blood tests for fasting blood glucose and blood lipids (LDL and HDL cholesterol and triglycerides) at least every six months.

Adjust medication dosage. Even when lithium blood levels are in the correct range, side effects can, and do, occur, although these vary widely from patient to patient. Some patients may notice a fine tremor in their hands. This symptom sometimes manifests itself when the body is under social performance stress. The tremor is not a sign of serious toxicity, but it is bothersome socially such as when you are holding and drinking from a cup when surrounded by a group of people. A small decrease in the lithium dose will often lessen this symptom; in other cases, such as when the tremor is overly pronounced or disruptive, switching to another medication may be the only answer.

Take medication at night. When you are on lithium, you may notice a tendency to urinate more frequently than usual. You also may experience increased thirst. This is a benign, if somewhat inconvenient, side effect. It may help to take your lithium in the evening but only if your doctor thinks it's safe.

Put things in perspective. Lithium can worsen acne and make your hair thin and brittle. Although rare, some people feel that they experience mental dulling or less creativity on lithium. However, it is wise to view the side effects of lithium in the context of its effectiveness in helping to prevent the social and career consequences of mania, ease the suffering of debilitating depression, and control mood swings so that they do not dominate your life.

If you must discontinue your medication, do so with care. Recent evidence has accumulated suggesting that lithium maintenance actually lowers the risk of suicide in bipolar and perhaps unipolar patients as well. But research also shows that a sudden discontinuation of lithium results in a higher likelihood of rapid mood swings into mania, and increased suicide risk.[3] Talk to your doctor if you plan on getting off the medication and work out a safe plan of action.

Watch for other side effects. Depakote is usually well tolerated, but even it can cause nausea, drowsiness, or tremors. Certain antacids (Pepcid) may quell the nausea, but a lowering of the dosage may be needed to regulate the other symptoms. Luckily, a slight readjustment is usually all that is needed. A small percentage of patients may experience thinning and breaking off of hair, leaving the impression that their hair is falling out. The hair will grow back although thinning may occur in the meantime. In menstruating women, a possible but uncommon side effect is polycystic ovary syndrome, characterized by menstrual irregularities, accompanied by weight gain. A gynecology consultation should be sought if this side effect is suspected.

Communicate all reactions to your doctor. It is very important to inform both the doctor who prescribed your medication and your family doctor of any symptoms you experience. You should do so even if you don't think there's a connection between the medication and the symptom. By way of illustration, a rare hypersensitivity to divalproex sodium can cause pancreatitis, a serious condition that usually manifests itself with abdominal pain and distress. Patients don't typically associate this abdominal pain with the medication and will often attribute the pain to flu symptoms or gastrointestinal issues. They also tend to consult their primary care physician, rather than their psychiatrist, who would be aware of rare side effects and could take effective action before the pancreatitis caused further damage.

To minimize pharmaceutical side effects, check with your doctor about periodic laboratory testing. Despite the above mentioned possible side effects, most patients tolerate divalproex sodium without difficulty.

Don't drink and medicate! Bipolar medications, especially Depakote and Tegretol, increase the sedating effects of alcohol and can lead to severely impaired judgment, motor skills, and alertness. Drinking should be avoided entirely or practiced with great care.

Get lab tests when taking Tegretol. Although it happens rarely, Tegretol can cause a drop in white blood cells. If you are on this medication, make sure you're getting periodic laboratory tests, especially if you find yourself afflicted with frequent infections, colds, or the flu. The body is very sensitive to too much Tegretol, and blood levels can result in high uncoordination or double vision. This is most likely to happen in the initial stages of taking the medication or after a dosage increase. *Safety alert*: If serious skin rashes, blotchiness, or itchiness occur, contact your doctor and stop taking Tegretol immediately. Be aware of possible adverse drug interactions (such as with the antibiotic erythromycin).

Don't take drugs during pregnancy. Women of childbearing age should be aware that lithium can cause a slightly increased risk of congenital heart defects, particularly in the first trimester of pregnancy. Depakote and Tegretol, as well as other anticonvulsants, can lead to serious defects of a baby's nervous system. Since 65 percent of all pregnancies are unplanned, this subject should be carefully discussed with your doctor ahead of time.

Antidepressant Medications

The occurrence and severity of side effects from antidepressant medications are difficult to predict in the individual patient. A study by Lewis Judd and colleagues illustrated that patients with bipolar disorder symptoms are in a depressed state 70 percent of the time, so it's easy to see why treatment of depression is a priority. However, when antidepressants are insufficiently counterbalanced with mood-stabilizing medications, they can actually worsen the course of the illness by increasing the frequency and severity of mood cycles and ultimately causing a continual recurrence of depression rather than eliminating it. Such complications highlight the importance of a correct diagnosis and regimen. When the physician knows the pharmacologic effects of the medication used, it is possible to estimate which side effects are more likely to occur.[4]

A physician has numerous options in treating a patient who is suffering from depression. More than twenty antidepressant medications are now on the market. Some of these, such as selective serotonin reuptake inhibitors (SSRIs) and the newer dual-action medications, are safer in terms of overdose toxicity and are safer for patients with heart diseases, especially as compared with the older tricyclic antidepressants (TCAs). In most patients, the newer medications produce fewer side effects than the older ones.

Before the advent of fluoxetine (Prozac), psychiatrists relied on two classes of antidepressants: TCAs and monoamine oxidase inhibitors (MAOIs). All of these medications are thought to work by increasing the effect of norepinephrine and serotonin. The older drugs produced more unpleasant side effects because they affected several different neurotransmitters and were more toxic when overdosed.

Most of the newer antidepressant medications act to increase neurotransmitter activity of the brain. One of the most studied neurotransmitters associated with mood disorders, serotonin is in a class of chemicals called monoamines. Other antidepressant medications have effects on other monoamine neurotransmitters, such as norepinephrine. Since patients with similar symptoms may respond differently with one medication or another, medications that have their therapeutic effect through different chemical mechanisms provide doctors with a wide range of treatment options.

Prozac, approved by the FDA in 1987, was widely accepted because it has fewer side effects than the TCAs and MAOIs. Prozac was the first of the SSRIs. The function of the SSRI is to block only the reabsorption of serotonin and no other neurotransmitters. This mechanism proved so effective that a second generation of SSRIs (Zoloft and Paxil) soon followed.

After serotonin stimulates the various receptors on neighboring neurons that tend to maintain normal mood, enzymes break down and inactivate the neurotransmitter. It then is reabsorbed by nerve cells and stored for future use. This process is called reuptake. If the brain is producing an insufficient number of circulating neurotransmitters, and consequently they're not available in sufficient concentration to stimulate their receptors, or if the receptors are in some way unresponsive, it is hypothesized that patients are then vulnerable to depression.[5]

SSRI medications block the reuptake of serotonin, resulting in an increase of serotonin in the gap between one nerve ending and receptors on the next ones. Different SSRI medications (e.g., Nefazodone and Remeron) have the capacity to block certain serotonin receptors; this has a tendency to reduce anxiety. Research in neuroscience is identifying other important neurotransmitters affected by newer medications.

Medications that affect two neurotransmitter systems at once are called SNRI medications (serotonin and norepinephrine reuptake inhibitors) and include the drugs Effexor XR (venlafaxine), Remeron (mirtazepine), and the relatively new drug, Cymbalta (duloxetine). Effexor XR must be gradually increased to doses greater than 150 to 200 mg to obtain this dual effect, whereas Cymbalta is an SNRI at starting doses of 60 mg, and the initial dose of Remeron is 15 mg with a maximum dosage of 60 mg. At 15 to 45 mg these medications may have this effect by helping some patients not benefited by SSRI antidepressants alone. Periodic liver function test should be checked in patients taking Cymbalta and Nefazedone. These medications are also useful for decreasing the body pains that often accompany depression.

> As more is known about the neurochemistry of the brain and its mechanisms in a depressed patient, the capacity to "design" more effective medications with fewer side effects improves.

Wellbutrin SR (buproprion SR) has a unique effect that sharply differentiates it from other antidepressant medications. Based on clinical experience it tends to be more activating, resulting in increased energy, but is perhaps less useful in treating the anxiety that often accompanies depression.

As more is known about the neurochemistry of the brain and its mechanisms in a depressed patient, the capacity to "design" more effective medications with fewer side effects improves. While each medication discussed has its own set of likely benefits and side effects, different people often respond dissimilarly to the same medication, making it hard to predict an individual's response to treatment. Trial and error is the key to pinpointing the right regimen. When it is difficult to attain a good response to treatment, switching medications, adding a medication (augmenting) or combining certain medications may be helpful.

Not all primary care physicians have the training and experience to diagnose depression and prescribe antidepressant medications. With less experience and training in psychiatry, they may miss the diagnosis of bipolar disorder and prescribe antidepressant medication without considering the worsening effects that may occur if given without mood stabilizers. Psychiatrists generally are better prepared to manage patients with bipolar disorder and are trained in the skillful use of mood stabilizers or antidepressant medications in the treatment of depression, which can reclaim, or even save, a life. If depressive symptoms persist or are either undiagnosed or unresponsive to two courses of medication, or if suicidal thoughts are present, ask for a referral or contact a psychiatrist.

Side Effects of Antidepressants

Nearly all effective medications have some side effects. These vary widely in severity from medication to medication and patient to patient and also depend on dosage and individual sensitivity. Although most side effects are merely inconvenient or interfere only slightly with quality of life, sometimes rare, medically significant, side effects can occur. Obviously, the benefits of the medication should exceed the difficulties.

Since 1988 it has been known, but not widely recognized, that patients can suddenly worsen to the point of increased suicidal thoughts and impulses soon after they begin their regimen before the medication begins to help. With the development of SRI antidepressants, which have fewer overall side effects, the use of antidepressants has increased markedly, and previously rare negative events are now reported more frequently. Recently the FDA analyzed studies on the effects of new antidepressants on depressed adolescents with various anxiety disorders. When the studies were reviewed together, researchers discovered that instances of increased suicidal thoughts, threats, and/or gestures occurred twice as frequently in patients on medication than they did for those patients taking a placebo, or inactive medication (2 percent on placebo vs. 4 percent on medication), although no actual suicides occurred. This finding resulted in a black box warning for the use of antidepressants in adolescents or children, stating that the risk of treatment should be weighed against the risk of not medicating. It further stated that patients and their parents should be warned of the possibility of paradoxical worsening with increased anxiety, agitation, or suicidal thoughts prior to the prescription of these medications. Patients and loved ones should immediately contact the prescribing physician for assistance if worsening or changes in behavior are observed. This means the physician prescribing these medications should be available and accessible.

The above warning should be given to all patients prescribed antidepressant medications. A small percentage of patients will be vulnerable to worsening symptoms within one to two weeks after beginning antidepressant medication. It should also be emphasized that the use of antidepressant medications is a major decision not to be taken lightly. If this level of practice is maintained and the prescribing physician is readily available to the patient, these medications can be safely and effectively administered with great benefit to patients.

Lists of possible side effects can be frightening or intimidating to anyone, but especially to a patient who is experiencing the distress, anxiety, or hopelessness associated with depression. However, side effects can usually be managed by changing dosage or switching from one medication to another. It is also important to note that most people only have slight side effects or no significant side effects at all.

Recent studies by G. E. Simon and colleagues of over eighty thousand exposures to antidepressants[6] and by M. S. Bauer and associates for the Step BD investigators[7] posed the question: Are antidepressants associated with new onset suicidality in bipolar disorder? A study of participants in the Systematic Treatment Enhancement Program for Bipolar Disorder followed 425 bipolar depressed patients and did not show any increased risk of suicide.[8] In fact, this study showed a reduction in the risk of attempts one month after the initiation of antidepressant medications. J. Angst has shown that patients with major affective disorders (including bipolar disorder) who continue maintenance medication including antidepressants have significantly less risk of suicide in a forty- to forty-four-year follow-up period. The absence of maintenance medication proved the greatest risk for suicide or attempts. A review of seven studies of suicide revealed the presence of antidepressants in only 12 to 23 percent of patients who committed suicide, suggesting that undertreatment is the greatest risk.[9]

It is sometimes difficult to separate side effects from the symptoms of the depression. Obviously side effects are the culprit if symptoms occur after the initiation or a dose increase of the medication. They almost always occur early in the treatment and rarely begin after weeks of symptom-free treatment. When medication therapy is actively reported to and managed by your doctor, the side effects should not interfere with the medical benefits of the drug.

Many of the newer antidepressants are likely to produce only one or two side effects, which decrease over a period of one to two weeks. Dosage adjustments may also minimize side effects. Antidepressant medications are not habit forming, and they sometimes are required to be taken for months or years to prevent a relapse. If you decide to stop taking them, do so gradually and only after consulting with your doctor.

Figure 4.1 summarizes patient-reported side effects in a recent survey of 1,370 people (of whom 46 percent were diagnosed with bipolar disorder) in treatment for depression. Results of the survey, which was conducted by the

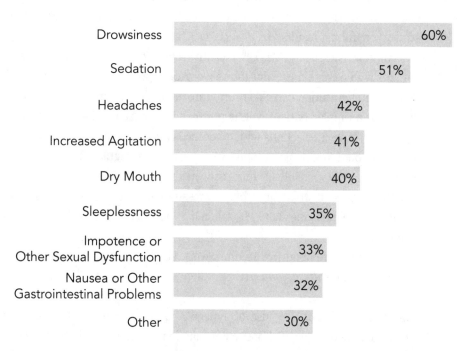

Drowsiness	60%
Sedation	51%
Headaches	42%
Increased Agitation	41%
Dry Mouth	40%
Sleeplessness	35%
Impotence or Other Sexual Dysfunction	33%
Nausea or Other Gastrointestinal Problems	32%
Other	30%

Figure 4.1. Side Effects Experienced by Depressed Patients While Taking Medication
(*Source:* 1999 National Depressive and Manic-Depressive Association online survey.)

National DMDA, show that drowsiness and sedation are the most commonly reported side effects. Many of these side effects can be managed, or decreased, by reporting them and working with your doctor. None represent a serious medical threat (although you should not drive a car or operate heavy machinery if you experience drowsiness or sedation).

This survey demonstrates that medications require careful management by a physician. It also indicates the need for the development of improved medications with fewer side effects and greater effectiveness.

Alternative Medicines

Saint-John's-wort: The herb Saint-John's-wort (*Hypericum perforatum*) is widely used in Europe to treat mild-to-moderate depression. It is available over the counter in the United States. The FDA does not regulate the purity and potency of Saint-John's-wort products because it is not considered a drug. Several large and small studies have been done to evaluate the antidepressant properties of Saint-John's-wort, with mixed results. Larger studies tend to show only modest effects in mild depression while smaller studies demonstrate more robust results.

Andrew Nierenberg, M.D.,[10] recently reported two cases of mania in patients who were taking Saint-John's-wort for depression. Conventional antidepressant medication can also precipitate mania in an unrecognized bipolar patient or a bipolar patient who is not mood stabilized. Saint-John's-wort is reported to have interactions with other medications, particularly antidepressants. Although use of Saint-John's-wort hasn't been regulated or institutionalized, it is true that all of our early medications (e.g., aspirin, digitalis, reserpine—used to treat high blood pressure) were discovered initially in plants, and no medicine should be taken lightly, whether it's medically recognized or not.

To learn more about Saint-John's-wort, see Dr. Steven Bratman's book, *Beat Depression with St. John's Wort.*[11]

The Omega Plan: The use of omega-3 fatty acids in the treatment of bipolar disorder has elicited positive results in medical research, but findings are mixed. As a breakthrough dietary plan, initially touted to replace harmful fats with beneficial ones, the plan derived from the theory that people who consume a lot of fish (which is high in omega-3 fatty acids), as evidenced in Japan, Taiwan, and Hong Kong, have a low rate of depression. Although we have seen some early results with this new approach that support its effectiveness, it needs further

> *The use of omega-3 fatty acids in the treatment of bipolar disorder has elicited positive results in medical research, but findings are mixed.*

confirmation. Studies on the use of omega-3 fatty acids alone did not confirm a significant individual benefit, but others show that it may be helpful when added to standard treatment for bipolar disorder.

OUT OF THE CUCKOO'S NEST: ELECTROCONVULSIVE THERAPY TODAY

Electroconvulsive therapy (ECT) was widely used in the 1940s and 1950s and remains the most effective and rapid treatment for severe depression. Although it is vastly safer and more humane today than it was in the past, it is still a controversial therapy and seldom employed.

It is not known exactly how ECT helps both severe and unresponsive bipolar disorder and depression, but it is proven to elicit results. There is evidence to suggest ECT works by causing a seizure, which stimulates most of the brain's systems and thereby increases neurotransmitter production in the brain. When successful (80 to 90 percent of the time), the effects of this treatment can last several months, although relapse is as high as 50 percent in one year without appropriate maintenance medication. There are side effects with ECT, notably short-term memory loss, which in most cases gradually disappears. ECT can be helpful in treating severe mania and mixed states.

The attending physician administers a short-acting barbiturate, such as sodium pentothal (an anesthesia), and a muscle relaxer to the patient. A brief electrical pulse is then given, which causes a brain seizure. Within seconds, the patient's body convulses, appearing to twitch, but without major spasms because of the muscle relaxant. An anesthesiologist usually administers oxygen, and the patient is carefully monitored throughout the procedure.

ECT is only used today for the most serious forms of psychotic depression, in which the depression is severe, often accompanied by suicide risk, and when the patient has not benefited from other courses of medication. For these patients, ECT may be a lifesaving treatment. ECT is frequently used in elderly patients who are frail and unable to tolerate or benefit from antidepressant medications. It is unquestionably safer than the treatments portrayed in Hollywood movies like *One Flew over the Cuckoo's Nest*. That film actually portrayed the most primitive use of ECT as it was administered in the 1940s, before the procedure was developed to its current state and before other medications were available.

HOW TO AVOID HOSPITALIZATION

When required, hospitalization does not usually continue for longer than one to two weeks. Hospitalization is used as a last resort to protect someone's life or to treat a patient who has not benefited from conventional treatment. Only if a life or future is at serious risk should admission be forced on a patient. Determining an individual's degree of suicide risk is a very difficult and touchy decision and should be left in the hands of a qualified medical health professional. Hospitalization is also required for individuals who have medical complications that make drug monitoring difficult or impossible or for patients with severe drug or alcohol dependency in addition to bipolar disorder or clinical depression.

> *Hospitalization is used as a last resort to protect someone's life or to treat a patient who has not benefited from conventional treatment. Only if a life or future is at serious risk should admission be forced on a patient.*

Early intervention and treatment of bipolar disorder can help reduce the likelihood of hospitalization. It is important to give serious consideration to slowing down the process so each patient has an opportunity to feel empowered. Hospitalization is appropriate to prevent an imminent suicide or violent act, as well as to treat patients who cannot be treated without protective custody. Hospitalization cannot be forced on a patient unless it is determined that the patient is suicidal, at risk to commit some violent act, or is rendered incapable of physically caring for him- or herself.

TALKING WITH YOUR DOCTOR

It is very important that you have a trusting relationship with your doctor and feel confident in his or her knowledge, skill, and interest in helping you. For your part, you must practice open communication and convey all the information your doctor needs to know, even if it makes you uncomfortable. Always tell your doctor about all medications, "natural" treatments, and other substances you are taking, as these substances could interact with medications that are prescribed. A complete medical history, including medication reactions, allergies, and prior experiences with medication, is important. A skilled and interested doctor will likely address many of the issues below. If he or she doesn't, you may want to ask about these issues yourself so that you are comfortable with and have confidence in your doctor and your course of treatment. If you prepare a written list of questions for your doctor prior to each visit, the doctor can provide better service in addressing your issues. Make sure to write down the answers and keep them handy. It is also very helpful to fill out a daily chart of your moods, as it is difficult to assess and remember every mood over time. This will help your doctor evaluate the effectiveness of your treatment, especially when adjusting medications. A mood chart designed by Dr. Robert Post and colleagues of the National Institute of Mental Health can be downloaded from the Depression and Bipolar Support Alliance (DBSA) Web site. Consider the following questions:

What is my medication dosage, and how should I implement an increase if you prescribe it?

What side effects might I expect, and what should I do if I experience one?

Will mood stabilizers or antidepressants reduce or change my mental performance or judgment?

How can I reach the doctor if I experience severe side effects or worsening of my condition? (Before you leave the appointment, be sure you have an emergency phone number for reaching your doctor.)

When should I expect some improvement?

What type of improvement should I expect?

Are there any hazards associated with this treatment and how will I recognize them?

How long will it be necessary to take the medicine?

If the medication needs to be stopped for any reason, how should this be done?

How often will I need to come for an appointment, and how long will my appointments be?

Is any type of psychotherapy recommended as part of treatment?

Are there activities or things I can do to improve my response to treatment?

Are there activities I should avoid in order to increase my likelihood of improvement?

If this medication isn't helpful, are there other alternatives for treatment? If so, what are they?

If someone asks me why I need medication or raises concerns about possible dangers of taking medication, how should I respond?

Voice any concerns you have about taking the recommended medication that you have not talked about.

INTERNET SURVEY RESULTS

The first Internet survey conducted by DBSA was made available in 2000.[12] A total of 1,370 people participated in the survey, all of whom had reported symptoms of depression.

Of the total participants surveyed, 46 percent were diagnosed with bipolar disorder. Out of this group, 87 percent reported that they had received treatment during the past five years.

As illustrated in table 4.1, 93 percent of those surveyed experienced depression nearly every day and for the better portion of the day. Also noted

TABLE 4.1. SYMPTOMS BEFORE AND AFTER TREATMENT

SYMPTOMS	BEFORE TREATMENT	AFTER TREATMENT
Depressed (sad or gloomy) mood most of the day, nearly every day	93%	28%
Loss of interest or pleasure in usual activities most of the day, nearly every day	93%	35%
Fatigue or loss of energy	96%	40%

(*Source:* Adapted from the 1999 National Depressive and Manic-Depressive online survey.)

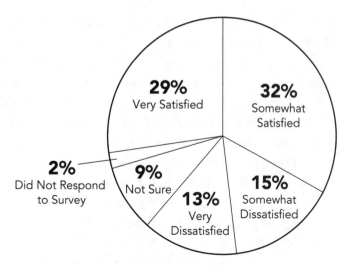

Figure 4.2. Satisfaction/Dissatisfaction with Treatment

(*Source*: Adapted from the 1999 National Depressive and Manic-Depressive online survey.)

in the survey are loss of interest or pleasure in usual activities, fatigue, and loss of energy.

Some 28 to 35 percent experienced no change of depressed mood or capacity for enjoyment after treatment, and 40 percent reported no change regarding fatigue or loss of energy. These results suggest the need for the development of even more effective medications to reduce depressive symptoms, especially fatigue and low energy. Participants who responded to being "very satisfied" or "somewhat satisfied" with their treatment constituted 61 percent of the sample, while 28 percent reported dissatisfaction (see figure 4.2).

Of those people who followed a course of antidepressant treatment, only 25 percent were still taking the original prescription while 75 percent admitted to having discontinued at least one of their prescribed medications. Simultaneously, 69 percent said they were continuing to medicate on a regular basis, and as ordered. This number of patients, along with the high percentage who had tried and stopped medication, suggests that many did not benefit from their initial course of treatment and needed to try something different.

Desire for some future medication that does not cause drowsiness, sedation, headaches, tension, or other similar side effects was conveyed by

80 percent of the participants. Of those patients who had considered not taking antidepressant medication, 23 percent feared that antidepressants would "change their personality." Some with chronic depression felt their personality improved with treatment. Another 18 percent of participants were concerned about the potential for the medication to become habit forming. To date, we have no substantiating evidence to support that concern. What has been ascertained is the importance of continuing medication to prevent recurring depression.

The survey also confirmed that 35 percent of sufferers considered not taking antidepressants, believing they could manage their symptoms on their own. Finally, 8 percent refused medication entirely.

It is clear from the National DMDA study that while more than 60 percent of those treated reported being helped and were satisfied with treatment, a significant number received no benefit, or only partial benefit, and had core symptoms of the illness remaining after treatment.

These new findings underscore the hope that help can be obtained from proper treatment, and also indicate the need for additional research and the development of more effective treatments for bipolar disorder.

A great deal of progress has been made in the treatment of bipolar disorder and depression, especially with the development of new medications. These treatments are not perfect. Often, either because a medication is not helpful to an individual patient or produces intolerable side effects, more than one trial of medication is necessary. In some cases, it may take a combination of several medications for symptoms to improve.

We do not know why one patient responds completely to one mood stabilizer or antidepressant and another patient with similar symptoms has difficulty getting a good response. This is true not only of psychiatric conditions but of all medical illnesses. Patients with ulcers, high blood pressure, arthritis, diabetes, and convulsions (epilepsy) show the same varied patterns of response. This is what makes medicine as much an art as a science.

The expert practitioner must keep up with the latest information on the use of medications and help each individual patient get the best possible response. Finding the right medication may take several trials, for there are limited data to predict response to a given drug in an individual patient. If a response is not forthcoming, it is worth getting a second opinion or an expert consultation. Never give up! Some rare individuals finally find the medication that works after failing to benefit from as many as ten to fifteen treatment trials. Even if you don't respond to your first treatment, keep hope in mind and understand that sometimes you need to stay with treatment for a longer period and try different methods in order to obtain a good result.

CHAPTER 5

Psychotherapy

A most comprehensive and advantageous treatment of bipolar illness will involve both medication and psychotherapy. Although bipolar illness is thought to be a chemical disorder, ultimately it is expressed through thoughts, mood, social interaction, physical well-being, behavior, and sense of self. Those living with bipolar illness need the skills and awareness to make sense of their illness and to develop proactive and reactive approaches that help minimize its impact.

Psychotherapy also offers those with bipolar illness the ability to distinguish between the effects of the illness and issues related to normal living. Treatment that is based on an open and trusting therapeutic relationship can help a patient distinguish between the debilitating aspect of severe depression and natural experiences of sadness as well as the differences between healthy optimism and the boundless unrealistic optimism associated with severe mania. In treatment, patients are encouraged to explore patterns in their thoughts, moods, and behavior until they can recognize how daily life events affect them and learn skills to cope better with life's challenges.

Another function of psychotherapy is to help patients uncover the meaning they assign to their illness and how that influences their response to it. For example, while one patient will steadfastly comply with medication and view her illness as a part of her life challenge, another might embrace his illness to such a degree that his self-identity becomes embedded in being bipolar. Psychotherapy can therefore play a tremendous role by influencing how a patient responds to living with bipolar illness. Psychotherapy can also be helpful in exploring issues that are unique to each individual's personality, such as those related to dependency, free will, optimism, and self-esteem.

Another major challenge that psychotherapy can address is medication compliance. Empathic therapeutic relationships help people who live with bipolar illness make sense of and manage the many emotions, motivations, and attitudes that influence whether or not they adhere to the recommended treatment.

> *Psychotherapy offers an understanding of the differences between healthy optimism and the boundless unrealistic optimism associated with severe mania.*

A psychotherapeutic session offers patients a haven. In this environment, a patient can safely explore the full range of emotions that accompany the experience of living with bipolar illness. Here, they are invited to acknowledge their anger and fear and to release any competing motivations that play against each other when balancing the pros and cons of medication. In this intimate setting, the patient recognizes and makes use of "self-talk": "I want to feel better, but I don't want to give up my energy; I want to feel better, but I don't want to feel dependent on medication; I want to feel better, but I will lose my creativity; I want to feel better, but I don't want to give up that wonderful feeling of being totally unself-conscious when I am manic." Patient and therapist can discuss these subjective experiences so the patient will fully understand and take responsibility for his or her choices in coping with bipolar illness.

For psychotherapy to be effective, it must foster increased self-awareness. It is most advantageous when it also helps a patient discover specific skills for problem solving and for coping with the complexity of life's everyday challenges. One powerful form of therapy that addresses these concerns is cognitive behavioral therapy (CBT). This form of psychotherapy is most effective in dealing with depression. Specifically, individuals who exhibit stable moods, mild, or moderate depression are helped the most. In contrast, those with severe depression or mania lack the capacity for the structured and objective self-reflection essential to the therapy. For them, stabilization by medication is a necessary prerequisite. Finally, those experiencing low levels of mania are minimally motivated to seek treatment. So it is during depression or periods of greater stability that those with bipolar illness may achieve the best results.

COGNITIVE BEHAVIORAL THERAPY

"I can't do anything right. My life is a complete waste. I am nothing. I am totally inadequate. Nothing is going to change. I might as well give up!"

These are some of the paralyzing thoughts that pervasively dominate one's awareness during severe depression. As viewed by cognitive behavioral therapists, it is the intense and compelling nature of such thoughts that deeply influences mood and, ultimately, one's behavior and physical well-being. The intensity of these thoughts and the emotions they arouse leave little room for objective reasoning. The thoughts and type of thinking that lead to them are the focus of "cognitive restructuring." In a collaborative effort, therapist and client work together to identify these thoughts and evaluate, challenge, and, ultimately, replace them with thoughts that are based on more objective reflection.

Two other forms of CBT are coping-skills therapy, which focuses on specific behaviors, and problem-solving therapy which helps individuals develop adaptive means for dealing with everyday life. Some of the cognitive behavioral approaches may fall into more than one category. Comprehensive CBT draws on each of these approaches.

COGNITIVE RESTRUCTURING

"You feel the way you think," says David Burns, a researcher and author who specializes in depression.[1] Hormone problems, chemical imbalance, or other physiological changes can trigger some forms of depression, while others are precipitated by negative events. As emphasized by cognitive behavioral therapists, your thoughts about such events are what lead you to become upset, so by altering such disabling thoughts you can alleviate depression.

For psychotherapy to be effective, it must foster increased self-awareness. It is most advantageous when it also helps a patient discover specific skills for problem solving and for coping with the complexity of life's everyday challenges.

Sadness and hurt are natural reactions to negative events in one's life. It is when negative feelings are out of proportion to the event that a depressed mood is triggered and maintained. Often, a loss of self-esteem also leads to depression, characterized by the feeling that you are no good, that your worth has decreased, or that you are inadequate. Patients with low self-esteem often convince themselves that things will never get better and lose interest in trying to improve their situation which merely fosters and keeps the depression alive. While negative feelings are always an appropriate reaction to upsetting events, it is the conclusions you draw regarding such feelings and events that lead to this debilitating state.

Aaron Beck, a pioneer in the development of cognitive therapy, assumes that depressed people are subject to the "cognitive triad": feelings of negativism, pessimism, and helplessness about themselves, their world, and their future. These feelings derive from core patterns of distorted belief systems. To the degree that individuals lack awareness of their belief systems, these systems influence their daily thinking and are especially powerful during times of emotional stress.[2]

Core Beliefs

In CBT, these core beliefs are called schema. In a sense, they inform the underlying philosophy one has about life, serving as a lens, or template, for information processing. We view, categorize, and interpret all of our experiences according to these core beliefs.

The following statements exemplify core beliefs: "I need to have everyone love me"; "I need to be perfect"; "I need to have, and should have, complete control over my life." These beliefs are deeply rooted and often unconscious, and they predispose us to entertain thoughts that may actually foster negative moods, including depression. For example, when you operate from a deeply held core belief that any experience, short of perfection, is equal to a failure, it is easy to understand how you might automatically think, "I am inadequate, I don't measure up, I am no good."

Cognitive therapy describes these kinds of thoughts as "automatic." In a sense, they form our "automatic pilot," guiding us through the day. Cognitive behavioral treatment for depression involves helping the patient become aware of these automatic thoughts as they occur. While at times unconscious, automatic

> *Core beliefs are deeply rooted and often unconscious, and they predispose us to entertain thoughts that may actually foster negative moods, including depression.*

thoughts are more accessible to one's awareness than those that form the core beliefs.

Self-Talk

Self-talk is conversation that we have with ourselves every day, as internally voiced dialogue about others, the world around us, and ourselves. Everyone practices self-talk, whether at home, at work, in a car or in a store, while interacting with loved ones or observing people on a bus, in the company of others or alone; however, some of us are more aware than others of these ongoing thoughts, and each of us varies in the amount of self-talk we engage in.

When we are busy and focused on an activity or very engaged with people, we are typically unaware of self-talk. In fact, we are living in an age in which we are increasingly bombarded by external stimulation, and so strongly encouraged to be active and productive, that we often lack awareness of such dialogue. In many ways, our culture reinforces us to be overly concerned with the thoughts and attitudes of other people rather than to more fully identify and value our own way of thinking.

Throughout the day we all make decisions, some of which are based on thoughtful consideration, while others are based on an internal automatic pilot. These decisions result from ideas that become our knee-jerk thoughts, rapid and immediate self-talk that is usually based on our core beliefs and influenced by distortions in thinking. Again, we *all* have emotional reactions, make decisions, and take actions based on self-talk whether we're aware of it or not.

> *Those living with bipolar illness are predisposed to operate on an automatic pilot that is constricted during depression and without limits during manic periods.*

Those living with bipolar illness have emotional reactions, make decisions, and take action based on self-talk that is strongly influenced by the schema associated with depression or mania. These individuals are predisposed to operate on an automatic pilot that is constricted during depression and without limits during manic periods.

To better understand the idea of unconscious self-talk, it is helpful to understand how we focus our attention, shift attention, and attend to one area while ignoring another.

Selective Attention

Imagine that you are in a restaurant and actively engaged in talking with your best friend. At some point in your conversation, you hear two individuals at a nearby table mention the name of your company's CEO. Your interest is piqued. Although you had not been tuned in to that conversation before, now you're continuing to speak with your friend while paying attention to that intriguing discussion going on behind your back. You may even find yourself listening to the dialogue behind you rather than to your friend. This is an example of selective attention. We have the ability to choose to shift our focused attention to one of two separate conversations.

This same process occurs with our internal conversations. While we may be consciously aware of certain thoughts, other ideas may be taking place at a deeper, quieter level. It is only by attending to the unconscious self-talk that we can become more acutely self-aware and know the wider range of our thoughts and emotions.

Core beliefs, as previously illustrated, are based on distortions of thinking that may predispose us to entertain automatic thoughts grounded in faulty thinking. Core beliefs influence our thinking to the extent of guiding us to pay too much attention to some details while ignoring others. A core belief that you need to be perfect may frequently lead you to the automatic assumption that you are a "failure" even if you make just one mistake at any given task. Core beliefs may similarly lead you to other distortions in information processing that reflect a negative focus.

The process of identifying automatic thoughts leads to identifying the core beliefs that underlie such thoughts. Cognitive behavioral therapists utilize a wide variety of techniques to foster this process. Some therapists focus on shared discussion exploring the details of an experience that may have preceded feelings of depression. Patients may be helped to identify specific situations and their reactions to them. They may be encouraged to explore their thoughts, emotional reactions, observations, or other experiences related to the event in an effort to gain insight regarding automatic thoughts and core beliefs. For example, a patient may recall being ignored by her husband during dinner. Through shared discussion and self-reflection, she may recognize automatic thoughts as conclusive regarding her experience. Automatic conclusions may include "He doesn't really love me," "I'm so boring," or "I'm

EXAMPLES OF DISTORTED THINKING

Overgeneralization   A pattern of drawing a general rule or conclusion based on one or more isolated incidents and applying that rule or conclusion to related and unrelated situations.[3] Examples:

"Since I wasn't accepted for that job, I'm convinced I shouldn't bother applying for those other positions."
"If I'm depressed, it must be because I have bipolar illness."

Selective abstraction   Focusing on a detail of a situation and then conceptualizing the whole experience on the basis of that one detail.[4] Examples:

"I'm sure I won't get that position. I made a mistake in that one answer."
"If I get dry mouth with this medication, I need to discontinue taking it."

Dichotomous thinking   Thinking in extremes and labeling experiences in one or two extreme categories (e.g., flawless or defective, saint or sinner).[5] Examples:

"If I'm not accepted for that position, I'm a failure."
"If I don't feel comfortable with that therapist, I should give up therapy."

Discounting the positives   Focusing only on the negative aspects and discounting the positive aspects of a scenario.[6] Examples:

"I performed weakly in every part of the interview."
"I had one brief manic period during this past year. That proves I'm not getting better."

Labeling   Applying a global label to oneself instead of viewing an incident as a mistake.[7] Examples:

"What I said at the party was really foolish. I'm such a jerk."
"How could I have taken that medication while taking lithium? I'm so stupid."

responsible for making this enjoyable." They may also suggest assignments between sessions that encourage the patient to increase her attention to events and specific thoughts, which are then presented during the next session.

Other therapists are highly structured in their approach. As part of the initial assessment, these therapists may ask patients to complete questionnaires in order to identify their attitudes. One such questionnaire is the Dysfunctional Attitude Scale, an inventory that assesses attitudes such as vulnerability ("Asking for help is a sign of weakness"), attraction/rejection ("I am nothing if a person does not love me"), and perfectionism ("My life is wasted unless I am a success").[8]

Therapists may ask their patients to keep a daily journal in an effort to identify thoughts that might help "turn up the volume" on quieter thoughts. Another approach is to have patients use forms to monitor their experiences; on the forms, they record the emotions, thoughts, and behaviors that accompany their experiences. These methods enable patients to develop more objective attitudes in assessing themselves.

"I encourage my clients to monitor their thoughts in a variety of ways," says Bernie Golden. "First, you might keep a journal that involves any ongoing narrative regarding specific experiences. Or you may be helped to identify your thoughts by keeping a structured log." Such a log may include the following:

- The date of some particular incident
- A description of the situation
- Any emotions surrounding the event (with a rating of their intensity)
- Automatic thoughts (rating the intensity)
- A rational response (rating the intensity)
- An outcome that includes a rating of the intensity of your belief in the automatic thought and the intensity of your emotion following the challenge of rational thinking

Therapists work with clients to develop skills that increase their capacity for self-reflection and thereby foster an increased awareness of their thoughts. Role-playing and discussion are useful tools. Through repeatedly asking themselves questions and identifying the content of their thoughts, clients increase their awareness of the distorted thinking that influences their thoughts and moods. Some therapists use cognitive therapy in combination with psychodynamic therapy. When these approaches are practiced together, they help the client identify the dynamics and patterns of past experiences that may have influenced the development of the client's core beliefs.

Case Study: Moderate Depression and Cognitive Therapy

In his first cognitive therapy session, Matt, a twenty-eight-year-old lawyer, described how he had become increasingly depressed. While he did well professionally for the first two years after joining a law firm, in the past four months he had suffered setbacks, losing two significant cases. He also shared that against his desires a five-year relationship ended six months prior to his seeking treatment. Matt described feeling inadequate, weak, anxious, and depressed. Similarly, he reported difficulties in sleeping, a reduced appetite, and lethargy at work and during activities that previously provided him pleasure. In addition, he reported increased social isolation over the past few weeks. Although Matt experienced no active suicidal ideation, he did have some fleeting ideas about welcoming "the end" if it were to occur.

Matt evidenced a moderate level of depression. If it had been more severe, medication therapy might have been in order. Depressive thoughts can be paralyzing, and the tunnel vision it engenders can hamper a severely depressed patient from receiving any measurable benefit from cognitive therapy. In a severely depressed state, the patient is sometimes unavailable to engage in the collaborative effort and process of standing back and observing his or her own thoughts. During this phase, medication therapy is usually an essential component of treatment.

Through repeatedly asking themselves questions and identifying the content of their thoughts, clients increase their awareness of the distorted thinking that influences their thoughts and moods.

In Matt's case, cognitive therapy helped alleviate his depression. In addition to therapy sessions, Matt kept a personal journal and adhered to a variety of structured exercises to identify his thoughts during those moments when he felt most depressed.

Through discussion of his journal entries and guided interventions in the sessions, Matt was able to identify and clarify the automatic thoughts that coincided with and followed his depressed moments. By increasing his skills in recognizing his thought processes, he was then able to identify the thoughts he had during meetings at his law firm. These automatic thoughts included "I need to be a senior partner in the firm by age thirty or I'm a failure," "I'm feeling that my successes were just luck," and "I'm feeling completely inadequate."

Therapy helped Matt identify thoughts he had outside of work as well. He reported moments when he wanted to relax but quickly reconsidered because of the guilt he would feel over not working more productively on his cases. When he would so much as entertain the thought of seeking companionship, he automatically thought, "I will never again love anyone as much as I loved Jane."

It took several sessions before Matt was able to recognize, and appreciate, his "quiet" thoughts. He began to turn up the volume on his self-talk, something he had not attended to previously. In addition, Matt recognized the frequency of these thoughts. He became increasingly aware of how his thoughts influenced his experience of fear, tension, irritability, and depression. Later, he was in a better place to recognize the distortions in his thought processing that had led to these debilitating automatic thoughts, namely labeling, discounting the positives, selective abstraction, and overgeneralization.

The next step in Matt's treatment involved helping him to challenge these distortions with more objective thoughts. A challenging thought is one that offers an alternative by which we can more objectively gauge our expectations and conclusions. Through repetition, the challenging self-talk replaces the unrealistic thought and becomes a part of our automatic pilot.

> *A challenging thought is one that offers an alternative by which we can more objectively gauge our expectations and conclusions. Through repetition, the challenging self-talk replaces the unrealistic thought and becomes a part of our automatic pilot.*

A challenging thought is one that draws attention to the real world and illustrates how people actually behave. Focusing on more mature logic, we call attention to the realistic probability of things happening a certain way. Whereas unrealistic expectations may really be "wishes," the challenging thought is strictly bound by reality.

In a way, this approach pits the objective reasoning part of us (the rational, mature, reasonable, parental, and nurturing part) against the unrealistic reasoning part of us (the part that creates distorted appraisals, has unrealistic expectations, and is impulsive and sabotaging). The objective reasoning part must be activated in treatment of any kind.

A challenging statement is often very simple, both in wording and message. The more concise and basic the language, the more easily it becomes a part of our internal dialogue and influences our expectations and conclusions. Cognitive therapy helped Matt develop challenges for each of his automatic thoughts, as outlined in table 5.1.

TABLE 5.1. AUTOMATIC THOUGHTS AND CHALLENGES

AUTOMATIC THOUGHTS	CHALLENGES
"I need to be a senior partner in the firm by age thirty or I am a failure."	"What if I don't make it, what then?"
	"I am not my feeling."
	"I will still survive."
	"While I *wish* to be a partner, I do not *need* to be a partner."
"I'm feeling that my successes were just luck."	"Just because I feel that way does not make it so."
	"I would have had to have an extreme percentage of luck to win all those cases."
	"I studied for years to gain that knowledge and put in many hours of work to win those cases."
"I'm feeling completely inadequate. I'm a failure."	"I am not my feeling."
	"I've won ten of twelve cases!"
	"Disappointment makes me think that way."

In the process of learning to challenge distorted thinking, we learn skills in self-soothing. This is a major part of effective change in the management of depression, as well as other uncomfortable emotions. Therapy helped Matt develop challenging thoughts related to his sadness concerning the ending of his relationship. With further work, he became aware of core beliefs that served as the foundation for some of his automatic thoughts. The core beliefs he uncovered included "I need to be perfect at everything I do" and "I am not worthy of love."

These core beliefs predisposed Matt to the intensity and pervasiveness of his depression, which was precipitated by losing the legal cases and his relationship. After helping Matt identify the core beliefs, his therapist then worked with him to develop numerous challenges to these core beliefs. As stated previously, through repetition, these challenges are integrated as part of our automatic thoughts, thereby permitting change to occur at a deeper level.

To the degree that depressed individuals do not recognize thoughts based on distorted thinking, they are, in fact, prisoners of their thoughts. If distorted thoughts are not recognized as such, they go unchallenged and options for changing our mood or behavior seem unavailable. In severe depression, any hope for change is absent. The sufferer experiences futility at having an impact on oneself or on others and a sense that the condition is permanent. The consistent and enduring attitudes are hopelessness, helplessness, and despair.

Tunnel Vision and Depression

Kay Jamison describes the overwhelming influence of tunnel vision during her depressive periods. "My thinking, far from being clearer than a crystal, was torturous. I was used to my mind having analytic thought. Now, all of a sudden, my mind had turned on me: it mocked me for my vapid enthusiasms; it laughed at all of my foolish plans; it no longer found anything interesting or enjoyable or worthwhile. It was incapable of concentrated thought and turned time and again to the subject of death: I was going to die, what difference did it make?"[9]

Clearly, Jamison's thoughts became compelling and left little, if any, room to consider alternative attitudes. During those moments, she was a prisoner held captive by the intensity of her despair.

Most individuals with severe depression need medication therapy to help reduce symptoms, including negative thinking. Judge Sol Wachtler, whose story appears in chapter 1, states that Prozac is what most helped him deal with his depression. While some research suggests gains without medication, most mental

> *To the degree that depressed individuals do not recognize thoughts based on distorted thinking, they are, in fact, prisoners of their thoughts.*

health professionals emphasize the use of medications as a major component of treatment for the severely depressed.

Though medication can decrease the intense hold of depressive thinking, cognitive therapies have their greatest impact in responding to mild and moderate levels of depression. It is during this phase of mood disorder that clients are more genuinely available to step back and observe their thoughts. In doing so, they gain increased freedom from their automatic pilots and, subsequently, gain more control of their moods and attitudes.

While not immediately apparent, those with mania can also be constrained by their thinking. Typically, we associate mania as boundless in energy and thought. In contrast to those with depression, people experiencing mania are often held hostage by their energy and impulses. In severe mania, individuals lack the capacity to accurately assess the reality, safety, and/or appropriateness of their behavior. These individuals are compelled by thoughts that race and propel them into action, thoughts that reflect little or no restraint, and, in the extreme, thoughts dominated by a "logic" that lacks reality-based cause-and-effect thinking.

It is this faulty thinking and the inability to control one's thoughts and activities that are most debilitating in severe mania. Core beliefs are often at the foundation of obsessiveness in mania. Here, the patient's unrealistic optimism and manic energy fuel the obsessive actions that the individual takes in response to underlying and predisposing core beliefs, such as "I must be perfect."

> *In contrast to those with depression, people experiencing mania are often held hostage by their energy and impulses. In severe mania, individuals lack the capacity to accurately assess the reality, safety, and/or appropriateness of their behavior.*

While individuals who exhibit mania may be helped to identify automatic thoughts and distortions in thinking, those who experience low-level mania clearly have little motivation for such treatment. Automatic thoughts associated with mania may be overly optimistic and grandiose. Subsequently, these thoughts do not promote discomfort, which is so often the motivating force to seek treatment. Patients encountering more severe mania are even less available to stop and reflect on their thoughts. Individuals with mild depression and mania, however, as well as those in a more stable mood, can greatly benefit from coping-skills therapy, another form of CBT.

COPING-SKILLS THERAPY

While cognitive restructuring involves attention to internal thoughts, coping-skills therapy focuses on helping individuals alter the way they respond to external negative events. In this context, individuals learn to identify and alter thoughts, images, and actions that may help reduce the negative impact of such events.

Take the example of a person with bipolar illness who loses her job. Coping-skills therapy can help her alter her thoughts, images, and actions by being responsive to her feelings regarding that loss—anxiety, frustration, hurt, and anger. In therapy, she can learn relaxation exercises to decrease her anxiety. Therapy can help her identify the actions she can take to move on. It can also assist her in developing assertiveness skills or communication skills that will enable her to respond better to external stressors. Certainly, through coping-skills therapy, she can identify how her illness may have contributed to her reactions to losing her job, however, the primary focus in this approach is on action.

In the case of someone with a predisposition for depression, coping skills provide alternative ways of responding to bad events. This helps prevent a spiraling sense of negativism from dominating how we feel, think, and act in response to loss. The goal of such therapy is not to eliminate the emotional reactions to loss but rather to decrease their intensity by reducing the pervasiveness, longevity, and global quality of thoughts prompted by loss. As would be expected, some aspects of cognitive restructuring may be useful in conjunction with coping-skills therapy.

> *In the case of someone with a predisposition for depression, coping skills provide alternative ways of responding to bad events. This helps prevent a spiraling sense of negativism from dominating how we feel, think, and act in response to loss.*

Clearly, coping-skills are useful for those with bipolar illness. As with other forms of therapy, the benefit is greatest when the patient is in a stable mood. While such skills are useful following upsetting events, it is most effective as part of an everyday proactive approach toward mood stabilization.

PROBLEM-SOLVING THERAPY

Problem-solving therapy focuses on helping individuals learn processes that help them identify, discover, or invent a variety of ways to cope with specific problems encountered in everyday life.[10] Problem-solving processes then help one select the most effective response from these self-prescribed choices. "A problem is defined as a life situation that demands a response for effective functioning, but for which no effective response is immediately available to the individual (or group) confronted with the situation."[11]

The solutions to these life situations involve strategies that help individuals either alter their environment or respond to it. Problem-solving therapy is most beneficial for individuals when it is approached as a proactive rather than reactive program. Again, the best window of opportunity to learn such skills is during low-level depression or mania or a period of mood stability.

Every day each of us encounters problems in our daily lives. You may be confronted with a friend who is habitually late for scheduled meetings. When you brainstorm to arrive at alternative ways to respond to this situation, you are using problem-solving skills. You decide on the advantages and disadvantages of the various ways of responding. As a result of engaging in this problem solving, you might decide to learn and practice a coping strategy, such as assertiveness skills, so you can feel comfortable communicating to your friend how you are affected by his lateness. Or you may choose not to spend time with him or her. Other possible solutions include scheduling your meeting ten minutes earlier than you actually want to meet or bringing a book to read to give you something to do while you're waiting.

In contrast, you could focus the problem solving on how to interpret his lateness. As a result of this work, you might decide to develop skills to monitor your predisposition to self-criticism (as reflected by self-doubt concerning the correct time of the meeting) or to wrongly interpret the lateness as a sign of rejection or lack of caring.

Problem-solving therapy helps the individual come up with a range of alternative responses to a situation. The client then judges each potential solution by considering four areas:

1. Problem resolution
2. Emotional well-being
3. Amount of time and effort required
4. Overall personal/social well-being[12]

The process of problem solving is dependent on a variety of skills that anyone can learn. Some cognitive behavioral therapists identify five key phases of problem solving:

1. General orientation
2. Problem definition
3. Generate alternatives
4. Decision making
5. Verification

General orientation refers to how we view problems in general. We can identify our general orientation by answering such questions as "Do I take it for granted that problems are a natural part of life?" or "Am I optimistic or pessimistic about problems and my ability to solve them?"[13]

Defining a problem involves stating it as a conflict between a goal and an obstacle. Generating alternatives involves giving oneself permission to brainstorm, with an emphasis on not being self-critical and on listing as many alternatives as possible. Decision making entails weighing the advantages and disadvantages of the alternatives and deciding which ones to use. Finally, verification involves taking action and assessing the outcome.

Learning these skills offers those with bipolar illness (and others) an organized approach to dealing with the problems that are an invariable part of daily life. The process of problem solving emphasizes resolution.

Cognitive therapy makes an important distinction between treatment that is problem focused and treatment that is emotion focused.[14] Problem-focused treatment emphasizes goals for changing the problem situation. In contrast, emotion-focused treatment emphasizes changing one's reactions to the situation in order to reduce the stress it arouses. In this case, treatment assists the individual in changing the "meaning" or appraisal of the situation, challenging automatic thoughts, reducing autonomic (physiological) arousal, and enhancing personal growth.

Self-management is another component of treatment that falls in the category of problem-solving skills. Self-management involves helping an individual identify strategies to maintain the practice of certain behaviors. A major premise of this approach is that the individual is available to observe, monitor, reflect on, or even initiate behavior. As part of a comprehensive program for manic depression, self-management is an especially important component for regulating sleep, eating habits, exercise, nutrition, and other habits that promote stability and overall well-being.

Once again, it is during the low level of depression or mania that an individual is most open to develop new habits, behavior, and thinking that foster stability. To a great extent,

> *It is during the low level of depression or mania that an individual is most open to develop new habits, behaviors, and thinking that foster stability. To a great extent, the goal of practicing self-management skills during these periods is to make them a natural part of one's repertoire.*

the goal of practicing these skills during these periods is to make them a natural part of one's repertoire. Through continued rehearsal, patients gain the capacity to observe signs of escalating mania or depression. Through repeated monitoring, they become more able to regulate relevant behaviors and/or seek support regarding them. Self-management involves self-monitoring, self-evaluation, and self-reinforcement.

TREATMENT COMPLIANCE

A major challenge in the treatment of bipolar illness is the lack of compliance with medication treatment and with psychotherapy. While some clients readily adhere to a medication regime that helps reduce the debilitating effects of bipolar illness, others refuse to take medication, take too little, determine their own dosage, or develop their own schedule for taking it. In a similar manner, some individuals with bipolar illness refuse psychotherapy or make minimal use of it.

Numerous factors contribute to a lack of compliance with both medication and psychotherapeutic treatment. Patients with severe depression may not be available to utilize such treatment. The intensity and pervasiveness of depressive thoughts and emotions compete with optimism and open-mindedness. A patient's negative attitude about treatment can also interfere with compliance. This is especially true when these attitudes are based on the same patterns of distorted thinking that fostered the depression in the first place. Examples of negative attitudes that obstruct compliance include:

"I feel controlled by the therapist if I do a journal, engage in self-reflection, monitor my thinking, or take medication."

This attitude may be related to core beliefs, such as "I need to solve my problems by myself," and automatic thoughts, such as "I am too emotionally weak . . . I'm just too dependent!"

"I need a guarantee that it [the medication or therapeutic suggestion] will work."

This attitude may derive from a core belief that "I should never be disappointed" and the overgeneralization that "if one medication does not work, others will not work either."

"I enjoy the emotional high when I am manic and don't want to give it up, even though it might have many negative consequences later."

This attitude may be based on selective attention.

"I am afraid of doing the exercises. Something bad will happen."

This may be an expression of a core belief that "change is not good."

"Nothing will change, and there are too many side effects."

This reaction may be derived from discounting the positives.

"I will lose my creativity, spontaneity, and my very personality if I take medication or engage in psychotherapy."

The core belief "I should not have to experience uncertainty in order to get better" may underlie this attitude.

"I need to make these changes immediately."

This attitude may derive from the core belief "When I want something to happen, it should, and it should come quickly and easily."

When individuals with bipolar illness focus only on the positive aspects of their manic episodes and minimize, deny, or ignore the overall impact of the illness, it presents another obstacle to compliance. Such clients struggle with the real loss they may experience as a part of treatment and with the perceived losses they may anticipate. They need help both in dealing with that loss and in recognizing that most of their fears are not realistic.

Psychotherapy is an invaluable component in the treatment of bipolar illness. Such treatment offers knowledge, self-understanding, and life-coping skills. Most significantly, psychotherapy fosters empowerment and addresses the difficult experience of facing life's challenges while living with bipolar illness.

Successful treatment depends on the ability to recognize and openly discuss all pertinent concerns as outlined above. This requires a trusting therapeutic relationship that allows a candid exploration of the underlying emotions, attitudes, and behaviors that compete with the attitudes and behaviors favorable to compliance.

CBT can help individuals with bipolar illness challenge distorted thoughts, learn self-monitoring techniques, develop coping strategies, and recognize and manage motivations that may compete or interfere with overall improvement. The success of therapy depends on a patient's commitment to the therapeutic process and the open sharing of his or her concerns. Simultaneously, successful therapy requires a therapist who is aware of the issues surrounding medication and psychotherapeutic treatment for bipolar illness.

CHAPTER 6

Evolving Forms of Psychotherapy

I n the first edition of this book we highlighted cognitive behavioral therapy (CBT) because it is the most widely researched and practiced form of treatment for depression. Since that time there has been accumulating research regarding more focused techniques based on a CBT model, as well as other emerging psychotherapies that have a significantly different emphasis than CBT. Research with these approaches has shown increasingly positive results in the treatment of various patients. The evolution of these therapies further provides increased hope and proven strategies for the effective treatment of bipolar disorder.

COGNITIVE BEHAVIORAL THERAPY

Although originally focused on treating depression, further studies in the application of CBT have led to models of treatment that are more comprehensive.[1] This research is essential because a long-term therapeutic commitment must address not just depression but all aspects of bipolar disorder. CBT involves helping clients manage the different phases of the disorder and the many issues and attitudes that are part of the diagnosis.

> Accordingly, "the clinician's task is to not only help a person overcome the symptoms of the illness and recover from its psychosocial consequences, but also to prepare for its inevitable return. This means that the course of therapy may follow an untraditional pattern."

Accordingly, "the clinician's task is to not only help a person overcome the symptoms of the illness and recover from its psychosocial consequences, but also to prepare for its inevitable return. This means that the course of therapy may follow an untraditional pattern."[2]

In one study, CBT was used with a group of patients with bipolar disorder who had strong histories of medication nonadherence.[3] After six months, those who had been engaged in CBT showed significantly fewer symptoms and greater improvement in social functioning than a group that was wait-listed and did not receive treatment. When those who were wait-listed received CBT they also showed significant improvement in symptoms and functioning and had significantly fewer hospitalizations when compared to the six-month wait-list period. Other studies have shown CBT's effectiveness in reducing the frequency of episodes.[4, 5]

Growing research with this approach has identified a range of interventions that address the full range of symptoms and attitudes associated with bipolar illness. According to one model, the first phase of treatment involves helping patients learn skills to reduce their symptoms.[6] With the alleviation of initial stress, treatment may occur biweekly and then monthly depending on the needs of the patient. Once stable, the patient may not return to treatment until she experiences a return of symptoms, a major stressful event, or a significant life transition. It is often recommended that the client return every six months as a way to monitor progress and to provide feedback.

One phase-specific treatment involves helping clients address specific thoughts related to grieving over the illness. These may include denial (reflected in thoughts such as "It will pass"), anger ("It's not fair that I have this illness"), bargaining ("I'll just make sure I get enough sleep"), depression ("I will never be able to achieve my goals"), and acceptance ("I have to give up some goals, but I will still be able to achieve many of the goals I most value").

One phase-specific treatment involves helping clients address specific thoughts related to grieving over the illness.[7] These may include denial (reflected in thoughts such as "It will pass"), anger ("It's not fair that I have this illness"), bargaining ("I'll just make sure I get enough sleep"), depression ("I will never be able to achieve my goals"), and acceptance ("I have to give up some goals, but I will still be able to achieve many of the goals I most value").

This approach teaches clients the cognitive model (as described in chapter 5) and shows them that their ongoing interpretations of themselves, events in their lives, and the future can tremendously impact the management of their bipolar illness. They are taught that cognitive skills can be used to manage strong emotions and behavioral impulses, reduce a sense of hopelessness, develop greater objectivity in decision making and in their relationships, and reduce the impact of stigma.

With this treatment, patients become more objective in recognizing that they have no control over certain events and that a lack of control does not imply a weakness in character. This further reduces their vulnerability to self-criticism.

This approach also helps clients address the constellation of thoughts associated with mania. As such, they are helped to challenge thinking that reflects, for example, an overestimation of their capabilities, an underestimation of luck, an obsessive urge to take action, and a driving compulsion to take on too much.

A secondary focus of CBT supports clients in recognizing those events that impact their reactions, including conflicts with family or work, deadline pressures, changes in sleep schedule, and so on. Through this approach clients are asked to take a proactive approach in their own treatment.

> *With this treatment, patients become more objective in recognizing that they have no control over certain events and that a lack of control does not imply a weakness in character. This further reduces their vulnerability to self-criticism.*

Lastly, the cognitive approach helps clients become more objective in their thinking regarding the usefulness of medications. Questions posed by the therapist which encourage self-reflection, including journaling and other forms of self-monitoring, are used to help clients recognize the increased control they experience through medication adherence.

EMERGING PSYCHOTHERAPIES

In addition to research regarding CBT, a number of emerging psychotherapies have been studied and proven effective in the management of depression and bipolar disorder, including:

- Behavioral activation therapy
- Acceptance and commitment therapy
- Dialectical behavioral therapy

- Cognitive behavioral analysis systems of psychotherapy
- Interpersonal and social rhythm therapy
- Mindfulness-based cognitive therapy

While several of these share some of the same strategies in their approach, each places a different emphasis on the cognitive, behavioral, emotional, and social components of functioning and their role in treatment. Several also look beyond identifying and challenging distorted thoughts, focusing on the context in which these arise. In this way they broaden the focus of change by employing experiential and indirect change strategies.

Several of these have been evaluated as they may specifically impact the course of bipolar disorder. Taken together, they reflect the continuing search to identify the most appropriate treatment and effectively manage the range of reactions that accompany bipolar disorder.

Behavioral Activation Therapy

Although originally described as self-activation therapy, this approach focuses not on negative inhibiting and constriction of thoughts that lead to depression, but on behavior. Behavioral activation therapy (BAT) views depression as a mental conflict in which the client is no longer experiencing sufficient reward to engage in behaviors that previously were rewarding and reinforcing.[8]

When practicing this approach, the therapist helps patients identify those specific moments during which they may think of taking some action but fail to do so. According to BAT, these moments are marked by a constellation of thoughts, emotions, and images that reduce the experienced cost–benefit for engaging in any action. While the patient may have experienced a reward in the past for taking an action, now the reward for acting does not seem to warrant the effort to do so. Additionally, to some degree, past experiences may have provided insufficient reward or negative consequences for taking actions. The inertia resulting from a perceived decrease in the cost–benefit of taking action begins the onset of a depressed state.

BAT places an emphasis on the importance of behavior as contributing to mood rather than on the influence of cognition. It recognizes that a depressed mood creates inertia that feeds into further depression, while traditional cognitive therapy focuses on the internal experience of the client. More specifically, it helps clients identify how external factors—the relations between the individual's behavior and the environment—affect his or her mental state, and not the other way around.[9] The goal of BAT is to help patients identify behaviors that will help elicit a positive cost–benefit assessment that supports and promotes action.

This approach does not completely negate the influence of genetic factors, but it does suggest that depression may in fact be triggered by a disruption of life routines. The comparison has been made that just as our circadian rhythms are triggered by light, our physical–emotional stability may be disrupted by key changes in our life routines. Subsequently, the loss of a loved one, interpersonal conflict, the loss of a job, or a major physical injury may all serve to disrupt this internal balance. As such, BAT emphasizes the reestablishment of routine and the maintenance of routine. This includes maintaining a routine for daily activities such as eating, working, socializing, and sleeping.

> *BAT places an emphasis on the importance of behavior as contributing to mood rather than on the influence of cognition. It recognizes that a depressed mood creates inertia that feeds into further depression, while traditional cognitive therapy focuses on the internal experience of the client.*

In one major study comparing BAT, traditional CBT, and medication therapy with 241 depressed adults, it was found that behavioral activation was comparable to antidepressant medication, and both significantly outperformed cognitive therapy alone.[10] Patients received treatment over a sixteen-week period. The findings also note that the most significant results were among those patients who were most severely depressed. This research strongly supports the contention that changes in behavior can dramatically reduce symptoms, whether or not change occurs in what or how one thinks.

BAT first helps clients monitor the behaviors that have negatively impacted their moods.[11] Specifically, they must log their activities and the moods associated with those activities over a span of one week. It then asks the client to record the activities engaged in while experiencing a negative mood. Through this process clients become increasingly aware that their withdrawal, whether by inactivity, sleep, or avoidance of potentially uncomfortable experiences, actually further increases a sense of depression and the fatigue that may accompany it. Such withdrawal may be rewarded in the short term, but in the long term, it further exacerbates depression.

Following this assessment, clients are asked to identify alternative actions that they perceive as fulfilling. These should be short-term activities that they believe will yield a more positive emotional reaction, and are viewed by the client as sufficiently rewarding and doable in order to move them beyond the inertia of the moment. Although the specific activity may require little time, it is often part of a larger or more long-term goal that the client has defined.

> *Following this assessment, clients are asked to identify alternative actions that they perceive as fulfilling. These should be short-term activities that they believe will yield a more positive emotional reaction, and are viewed by the client as sufficiently rewarding and doable in order to move them beyond the inertia of the moment.*

For example, if a client indicates that he used to enjoy taking long walks, he may identify a ten-minute walk as the first step toward conquering his inertia. If a client genuinely believes that socializing with a particular friend is usually rewarding, he may be encouraged to make a brief phone call or a short visit with that friend when he would otherwise feel unable to take action.

Patients are supported in gradually developing an expanded repertoire of behaviors that, through their engagement, help to "pull" them through the depressive state.

Bernard Golden offers an example of this approach in his work with Sharon, a thirty-two-year-old bipolar woman who started treatment shortly after hospitalization for depression. She was on a leave of absence from her job, and while she hoped to be able to return, at that time she barely had sufficient energy to manage the upkeep of her apartment.

As part of the treatment plan, Sharon was asked to identify how she felt upon waking in the morning. She described a terrible fatigue attributed in part to the effects of a new medication regime. Even thinking about organizing her apartment seemed overwhelming in terms of the energy it would require. Sharon was asked to start small (an essential strategy in BAT) and identify several activities that she could engage in during the first few minutes after awakening that would be rewarding for her. She was encouraged to imagine these activities rather than the initial moment of engagement. In this way, she could come more fully in touch with a mood of increased satisfaction and reward even before beginning the activity. The emphasis was on helping her overcome inertia rather than focus on the more long-term goal of returning to work.

Sharon identified several activities that included clearing the top of the bathroom vanity, organizing one area of her kitchen counter, hanging up some of her clothes, and spending ten minutes cleaning the refrigerator of food that was no longer edible. She was taught to view these activities as a series of individual tasks, serving a distinct reward and contributing to a larger goal.

In addition, Sharon reported that video games, walks, sketching, and talking to some of her friends were rewarding prior to her depression. The goal of this aspect of her treatment was to help her continually identify and engage in activities as a way of overcoming her inertia.

According to this model, even self-devaluing thoughts associated with depression are viewed as distractions from facing the discomfort of a particular action. As such, the behavioral activation therapists help clients recognize such thoughts as distractions rather than addressing and challenging them for the content they convey. They're taught to increase their awareness of how time spent engaging in such thoughts further fuels depression and encouraged to observe these thoughts without judging them. Simply recognizing such thoughts without judgment helps avoid getting stuck trying to eliminate them. An underlying premise of BAT is that self-critical or hopeless thoughts are so ingrained in our psyche that they cannot be challenged, but by learning to acknowledge them and remain nonjudgmental toward them, their frequency and intensity will decrease.

This approach has been receiving much attention and offers increased hope as a powerful treatment in managing the depression associated with bipolar disorder.

> *According to this model, even self-devaluing thoughts associated with depression are viewed as distractions from facing the discomfort of a particular action. As such, the behavioral activation therapists help clients recognize such thoughts as distractions rather than addressing and challenging them for the content they convey.*

Acceptance and Commitment Therapy

While much of acceptance and commitment therapy (ACT) has evolved from a behavioral emphasis, it has expanded to integrate a broad variety of theories regarding psychopathology and change. This approach has a broad focus that asks clients to

*A*ccept their reactions and be present with them
*C*hoose and commit to a valued direction
*T*ake actions that are increasingly consistent in working toward that goal

More specifically, it focuses on six processes by which clients are helped to move forward. These include acceptance, contact with the now, a transcendent sense of self, defining values, committed actions, and cognitive diffusion.[12]

ACT teaches that "it is not possible to influence psychological variables (emotions, thoughts, tendencies toward action), without changing their context."[13] To some degree, ACT may at first seem counterintuitive in its goals. Rather than reacting to uncomfortable emotions, thoughts, or bodily responses by challenging them and trying to diminish them, it prioritizes the acceptance of such experiences as the first step to move beyond them. From negative thoughts to the rumination associated with the worry of anxiety, ACT emphasizes that we have little control over when these experiences "visit" us. However, by acknowledging and accepting them we can gradually grow to just observe rather than respond to them with judgment.

> *Rather than reacting to uncomfortable emotions, thoughts, or bodily responses by challenging them and trying to diminish them, it prioritizes the acceptance of such experiences as the first step to move beyond them.*

Another major component of this approach, and one that distinguishes it from many other approaches, is that depressed clients are supported in identifying what is meaningful in their lives and the values to which they aspire. Patients are then supported to engage in behaviors associated with these values and goals.

When distractions arise, they are asked to take note of them and gradually move on. As such, they attain a life guided by these values, rather than governed by the avoidance of pain and suffering.[14] Commitment means actively choosing to be fully present with one's experiences while remaining committed to these identified values. In practice, clients are encouraged to accept rather than run from, stifle, ignore, or challenge their thoughts and emotions. Accepting and acknowledging depressive thoughts does not imply passively giving into them. In fact, it does not require giving them any meaning. It emphasizes the development of an objective curiosity regarding one's experience, not unlike watching a parade marching by. It involves perceiving the mind as the receiver of signals, thoughts, moods, emotions, and even sensations that do not necessarily reflect who we really are as a person.

ACT is derived from many roots, including Eastern ideas, the human potential movement, and behavior therapy. Clients develop an increased openness and acceptance of psychological events regardless of how irrational or negative they may seem.

What determines whether an event will be targeted in treatment depends on what function it serves. However, none of these approaches involves challenging the experience in an attempt to dispute it. In treatment, the ACT therapist does not help the client reduce, eliminate, or avoid uncomfortable internal experiences. Rather, treatment involves helping clients identify and accept what they are feeling and thinking.

> *Accepting and acknowledging depressive thoughts does not imply passively giving into them. In fact, it does not require giving them any meaning. It emphasizes the development of an objective curiosity regarding one's experience, not unlike watching a parade marching by.*

These strategies look at the function these experiences serve and help clients to explore the context of their situation and those internal events and behaviors that can bring them closer to their desired goal. For example, a client may learn that feelings of hopelessness are a natural reaction in the context of her history. She may be helped to understand how depression was a useful reaction in certain contexts to avoid the discomfort of actions toward achieving her goals. As such, patients are helped to understand how depression serves to undermine a life built on their most meaningful values and impede their advancement toward personal goals.

The foundation for ACT rests on relational frame theory.[15] This theory focuses on language and cognition, how language informs the patterns of our cognitions, how these patterns interact with each other, the context in which they are formed, and how these relationships impact our behavior. According to this perspective, bipolar illness is viewed as rigidity in thought based on distorted relational "frames" that narrow the range of our ability to seek out or choose alternative explanations or actions. These frames, or patterns of expectation, account for our thoughts and reactions to others, the world around us, and to ourselves. We are not accustomed to looking outside the frame, thereby neglecting to notice the details and uniqueness of the situation we are encountering. As such, these patterns make "an individual less in contact with the here-and-now experience and direct contingencies, and more dominated by verbal rules and evaluations." This is described as cognitive fusion.[16]

Based on such relationships, as described by Steven Hayes, a child who has previously been scratched by a cat may cry and run away when she hears her father indicate he sees a cat. According to relational frame theory, her reaction is not simply overlearning and generalization but instead a product of many relationships in language that she has made that keep her from considering being close to the cat, even though this particular cat may not be harmful.[17]

Her flight reflects what ACT therapists describe as experiential avoidance. This process takes place when a person avoids uncomfortable bodily sensations, emotions, thoughts, memories, images, or behaviors by avoiding the events and contexts that may arouse them.

As such, it is through the labeling of experiences with language that the girl becomes closed to experiencing the uniqueness of the cat that her father has just encountered. Her flight reflects what ACT therapists describe as experiential avoidance. This process takes place when a person avoids uncomfortable bodily sensations, emotions, thoughts, memories, images, or behaviors by avoiding the events and contexts that may arouse them. Ultimately, the emotional or cognitive states associated with these experiences also acquire a negative connotation. For example, experiencing anxiety associated with specific events can lead one to associate and experience all anxiety as bad. Although it ties directly to the specific events, this reaction is actually due to the intricate webs of relationships in language and the conceptualization of our experience, rather than the event itself.

The goal of ACT then becomes assisting patients in gaining greater psychological flexibility, an increased ability to engage in certain contexts when doing so remains in the interest of one's identified values. This is achieved by teaching individuals to be more present with their experiences; helping them to learn cognitive diffusion skills to impact behavior in new ways rather than relying on established cognitive patterns; teaching choice from mindfulness; and emphasizing skills to foster commitment, persistence, and change associated with chosen values.

Interventions based on ACT involve paradox, metaphor, stories, behavioral tasks, and experiential processes. The goal is not to remove a belief system but rather to expand on it to provide a more flexible repertoire in experience and action. The specific techniques fall into three broad categories: mindfulness, acceptance, and values-based living.[18]

Mindfulness involves shifting our perspective of internal experiences to that of an observer rather than a puppet. It involves identifying without judging and a decreased, often useless compulsion to engage with, act on, or change experience. Through techniques that encourage mindfulness, individuals are taught to identify emotions, thoughts, images, sensations, and urges but not to avoid, attempt to change, or react to them all. This promotes a perspective of oneself as an observer who is free to choose to respond or not respond to such experiences. Most significantly, these techniques help eradicate the association between experiences and identity, and expose them as merely events as transient, time-limited experiences. Mindfulness helps one to recognize that our reactions to our experiences, and not the experiences themselves, are what lead to our suffering. Our thoughts about our thoughts,

Interventions based on ACT involve paradox, metaphor, stories, behavioral tasks, and experiential processes. The goal is not to remove a belief system but rather to expand on it to provide a more flexible repertoire in experience and action. The specific techniques fall into three broad categories: mindfulness, acceptance, and values-based living.

feelings about our feelings, and opinions about both combine to create suffering. In this process, suffering intensifies precisely to the degree that we react to our internal experiences. For example, we may feel slightly depressed but then become guilty and depressed about our depression. We may feel inadequate about managing a task and consequently may experience and foster shame-inducing thoughts about feeling inadequate.

Through a variety of exercises, clients are helped to move from experience avoidance to experience acceptance. According to ACT, when we focus on trying to eliminate our pain, we become distracted from living who we are and who we can become. The focus on commitment involves taking an active stance in exerting one's will toward living according to identified values. The identification of such values is an essential component of ACT and distinguishes it from many forms of the emerging therapies.

Dialectical Behavioral Therapy

Dialectical behavioral therapy is a derivative of cognitive behavioral therapy that integrates more traditional aspects of CBT, mindfulness, social skills, and a contextual emphasis. Although originally developed for work with suicidality and then with borderline personality disorder, this approach has increasingly been applied to other disorders involving depression and anxiety.[19]

DBT is a compassionate type of behavioral therapy intended to help clients effectively manage problems stemming from emotional dysregulation. As such, it is geared to helping individuals tolerate distress, silence, negative self-talk, and resolve inner dialectical conflict—self-talk that promotes seemingly contrasting and conflicting perspectives: "My life is completely changed now that I have bipolar disorder!" or "I am really the same person I have always been!" DBT paints experience in a greater context to get the truth: "My life is somewhat changed now that I have bipolar disorder and, in most ways, I am really the same person I have always been!" As such, DBT emphasizes evaluating and conceptualizing issues as gray rather than as black and white. This is fostered and achieved by considering the specific context in which we make such explanations and mindfulness of details that may lead to a more integrated view.

> *A major focus of DBT is the underlying premise that we are all doing the best we can at any given moment, even though we can learn strategies to become more constructive and effective in attaining our goals. Fostering self-acceptance while emphasizing the capacity for change is a core underpinning of DBT.*

A major focus of DBT is the underlying premise that we are all doing the best we can at any given moment, even though we can learn strategies to become more constructive and effective in attaining our goals.[20] Fostering self-acceptance while emphasizing the capacity for change is a core underpinning of DBT.

DBT offers the patient empathic and sympathetic acknowledgment of the pain they are experiencing, validating the patient's sense of truth about that pain, while at the same time helping the patient to gently build on and expand their perspectives and behaviors.

Like ACT, it emphasizes that much of our difficulty managing our emotions is related to the secondary emotions we develop in reaction to experiencing the primary emotions. These may include feeling angry about feeling angry, becoming anxious about feeling fear, or feeling shame for feeling anxious. These reactions are the result of internal judgments about how we "should" be feeling.

In actual treatment, DBT techniques help the client recognize that pain is a natural part of life, but if they can reduce the rigidity of their expectations and dichotomous thinking, they can reduce unwarranted and excessive suffering as well.

This emphasis on acceptance reflects an integration of Eastern and Western psychological perspectives and practice. But acceptance does not mean having to attend to, react to, or in any way become engaged with our reactions. The exercises and practices of DBT help the client become more flexible in thinking rather than overly attached to how he or she "should" feel or behave or how others, or the world, "should" be. For example, an individual who experiences disgust with a diagnosis of bipolar disorder may intently focus on the disparity between how she functions and how she "should" function. However, it is only by accepting where she is at in the present that she can more compassionately work toward how she would like to be or develop new strengths and behaviors to deal with the changes in her functioning. Her erroneous, internal judgment of the type that inhibits medication adherence or seeking appropriate treatment will ultimately lead to more years of unnecessary suffering.

> *In actual treatment, DBT techniques help the client recognize that pain is a natural part of life, but if they can reduce the rigidity of their expectations and dichotomous thinking, they can reduce unwarranted and excessive suffering as well.*

> *The exercises and practices of DBT help the client become more flexible in thinking rather than overly attached to how he or she "should" feel or behave or how others, or the world, "should" be.*

A major strategy in this form of treatment involves increased mindfulness to internal experiences, including emotions and the judgments about emotion. The goal of such mindfulness is to develop a perspective of the one as the "receiver" of emotions and thoughts, and not respond with judgment. We must become "observers" to our experiences. At the same time, the goal is to help the client recognize an increased choice not to respond to these internal experiences.

Recognizing emotional triggers, or patterns of reactions that trigger negative emotions and judgment, is an important aspect of this form of treatment. Detailed journaling, in the form of maintaining a mindfulness diary, is encouraged to help fine-tune such mindfulness so as to recognize patterns and to develop more constructive choices and actions in response to internal reactions. The focus is also on validating the experienced emotions while taking actions to promote and experience a more positive outlook.

Challenging self-talk, a major component of CBT, is also employed in this approach. Here self-talk is defined in the broadest terms to mean any judgment of thoughts or emotions, or how others or the world "should" be.

DBT also strongly emphasizes interpersonal skills such as the ability to ask for what we want and saying "no" as a way to deal with interpersonal conflict. In doing so, it highlights assertiveness.

The holistic approach of DBT is reflected in its emphasis on evaluating how factors inherent in our lifestyle can cause us to be vulnerable to become too emotional. This is especially relevant in dealing with relapse in bipolar disorder. As such, treatment also considers nutrition, sleep, physical fitness, socialization, use of leisure time, and the overall balance in life as important components of wellness.

> *The holistic approach of DBT is reflected in its emphasis on evaluating how factors inherent in our lifestyle can cause us to be vulnerable to become too emotional. This is especially relevant in dealing with relapse in bipolar disorder. As such, treatment also considers nutrition, sleep, physical fitness, socialization, use of leisure time, and the overall balance in life as important components of wellness.*

DBT involves the use of "exposure" techniques, helping clients face their fears directly. Through a combination of mindfulness, relaxation techniques, maintaining a nonjudgmental stance, and other skills, resilience is fostered to confront fear or anxiety-provoking behavior. This can be used when dealing with depression as well as general anxiety.

Cognitive Behavioral Analysis Systems of Psychotherapy

James McCullough Jr. is the therapist most responsible for the development of the cognitive behavioral analysis systems of psychotherapy (CBASP).[21] This approach reflects an integration of theory and application from several different areas of research. Specifically, CBASP

- Hypothesizes as a contributor to depression, arrested maturational development (based on a Piagetian perspective)
- Highlights the role of attachment in the course of therapy
- Addresses the patient's habitual patterns of social interaction in the context of the therapeutic alliance
- Includes attention to cognitive and behavioral analyses of patient interactions with the environment as reflected by learning theory

The basic theoretical position of this approach is that individuals with depression fail to predominantly think in a way that reflects mature causal relationships. Specifically, they are seen as failing to plan ahead, and recognizing that their actions have impact, factors which negatively affect their social skills.[22] As such, thought and conclusions are based on immature logic that is self-focused and lacks attention to other causal factors.

> *The basic theoretical position of this approach is that individuals with depression fail to predominantly think in a way that reflects mature causal relationships. Specifically, they are seen as failing to plan ahead, and recognizing that their actions have impact, factors which negatively affect their social skills.*

The paralysis of depression may be addressed as distinct moments in time that the client is helped to explore more fully. They are asked to describe a distressing event, how they evaluated it, and their reactions. They are then asked to articulate their desired outcome. Through these analyses, patients can identify how their judgments and conclusions or the meaning they attach to the situation, actually influences it. They are then helped to identify and consider alternative meanings and actions that determine a more desirable outcome.

"When patients are positively affected by the environment and can produce what they want by enacting adaptive cognitive and behavioral strategies, several intrapersonal changes will have occurred: Primitive preoperational functioning has been replaced by formal operations thought."[23]

CBASP therapists help patients recognize patterns of emotions, thoughts, and behaviors that may stem from childhood experiences and are reenacted within the therapeutic relationship. To foster this awareness, they are asked to identify significant others in their past and how their relationships with them influenced their capacity to express and satisfy their needs, interpersonal skills, and management of emotions. In this context, a therapist may help a patient identify how her striving for perfection, instilled by a parent, may lead her to feel inadequate in interaction with the therapist. This need to be "perfect," to gain approval, and acceptance in general, may be enacted in the therapy session. Collaboratively, the therapist and patient can then explore the difficulty in accepting acceptance and even positive comments regarding her progress.

Focusing on and altering the therapy relationship is another dimension of this form of therapy. Patients are helped to identify how they have difficulty accepting positive emotions within the therapeutic relationship. These interactions are explored in terms of how they reflect the patient's ongoing history. By helping clients become more open and realistic in their appraisal and experience in this specific relationship, their learning can generalize to their relationships with others. This focus on the therapeutic relationship distinguishes CBASP from many of the emerging cognitive therapies.

Difficulty empathizing with others and interpersonal skills deficits are also addressed as major contributions to the depressive experience. This issue is further explored within the therapeutic relationship, as well as in the context of other patient relationships.

A major technique used in CBASP is situational analysis. Through careful exploration of a specific event, patients identify their contribution to the outcome. A focused evaluation of the details of their experiences helps them recognize the control and impact they may have on the world in general and realize that acting on alternative solution strategies can actually reduce their suffering. They may learn to be more flexible and compassionate with themselves, more open to consider a range of alternative reactions to a situation, and more realistic in general.

> *A focused evaluation of the details of their experiences helps them recognize the control and impact they may have on the world in general and realize that acting on alternative solution strategies can actually reduce their suffering. They may learn to be more flexible and compassionate with themselves, more open to consider a range of alternative reactions to a situation, and more realistic in general.*

Mindfulness training is a major component of this form of therapy as it is in several other emerging therapies. Specifically, it highlights the use of Zen meditation, described by J. Kabat-Zinn, in an effort to help patients become more aware of thoughts, emotions, and bodily sensations occurring in the moment.[24] If all goes well, they develop the capacity to observe experiences as just experiences, and not as reflections of their core and fixed identity. As described in ACT and DBT, these experiences do not need to be judged or responded to in any way. The thought that occurs during depression—"I have bipolar illness and I will never change!"—is viewed as a transitory event, and the patient is encouraged to develop an attitude of nonresponse. Through this process the patient is helped to disengage from his predisposition to maintain such thought patterns.

Numerous studies of CBASP have been made, focusing on the use of CBASP alone, CBASP with medication, or medication alone. These emphasize the combination of treatments as the most effective for chronically depressed patients.[25] CBASP is now being studied to determine which types of patients are most responsive to this approach.

Interpersonal and Social Rhythm Therapy (IPSRT)

This approach, developed by Ellen Frank, focuses on the maintenance of interpersonal and social rhythms as they impact bipolar disorder.[26] She has introduced the term *zeitgebers,* physical and social cues that can influence an individual's social and biological rhythms. These may include the rising and setting of the sun, the timing of sleep, work, meals, leisure time, and interpersonal interaction. Underlying this approach is the premise that life events have the potential to disrupt social zeitgebers, which in turn disrupt social rhythms, which then disrupt biological rhythms, which lead to somatic symptoms and ultimately to mania or depression for individuals with bipolar disorder. This approach is based on theory and research from physiology and psychology.

Those who advocate this approach emphasize that biological/genetic vulnerability factors influence one's predisposition to biological rhythm instabilities that may ultimately lead to mood instability. They suggest that "the state of increased somatic symptoms that precedes to depression or mania is a normal social and psychobiological response to a disruption in social rhythms and is usually self-limiting and reversible in nonvulnerable individuals."[27]

IPSRT emphasizes the maintenance of stability in these rhythms in an effort to reduce the potential for relapse. According to this theory, relapse is related to nonadherence to medications, stressful life events, and a disruption in social rhythms. As such, treatment focuses on the management of symptoms through medications and the stabilization of social rhythms, and effectively managing interpersonal problems.

The Social Rhythm Metric, a self-report inventory, is used to monitor and develop routines. This inventory helps patients detail the variety of activities in which they participate throughout the day.[28] These include identifying the time of getting out of bed and indicating whether it is earlier or later than usual; the time of the first contact with another person; the start and finish time of various activities throughout the day; the time when the patient had lunch and dinner; the time engaged in leisure activities; and the time the patient went to bed. Additionally, patients are asked to rate their experienced mood of the day. Through close monitoring discussion patients are taught the skills necessary to adapt to new routines.

> *Like CBT, this approach also emphasizes psychoeducation, self-monitoring moods and symptoms, activity-scheduling, and a focus on present problems and relationships. However, the focus is on exploring these as they are related to routines and the promotion of overall stability, rather than on emphasizing the internal cognitive processes that may foster depression or mania.*

Like CBT, this approach also emphasizes psychoeducation, self-monitoring moods and symptoms, activity-scheduling, and a focus on present problems and relationships. However, the focus is on exploring these as they are related to routines and the promotion of overall stability, rather than on emphasizing the internal cognitive processes that may foster depression or mania.

IPSRT is based in part on various theories and research regarding disruption of the sleep cycle, social stressors, social demands, and social-role stress, as well as their impact on other physiological functions. Theoretically, these trigger changes in mood for individuals whose biological predisposition leaves them especially sensitive to even slight social/physical alterations.

One two-year study compared IPSRT to an intensive clinical management approach (a form of psychotherapy that addresses causes, symptoms, and treatment of bipolar disorder) for 175 individuals diagnosed with bipolar disorder I, the more serious form of the illness.[29] The main factors assessed were time to stabilization in the acute phase and time to recurrence during the maintenance phase. All groups received standard medication throughout the study. Researchers found that there was no significant difference in the time it took for stabilization; however, those who received IPSRT during the acute phase were more likely to remain well during the two-year maintenance phase. Most significantly, the degree to which this was true was directly related to the extent to which patients increased the regularity of their social routines. It should be emphasized that the effects were not as significant for individuals who also had medical problems such as diabetes or heart disease.

As part of a much larger study, IPSRT is being compared with both CBT and family focused treatment. The results of this study are not yet available, but this study will help determine the strength of IPSRT for patients with bipolar disorder.

Mindfulness-Based Cognitive Therapy

Mindfulness-based cognitive therapy (MBCT) is intended to reduce relapse in recurrent major depression and for implementation as part of maintenance psychotherapy rather than during an acute phase of depression.[30] It rests on the premise that depression is marked by the negative contents of thoughts as well as the ongoing rumination of such thoughts. According to several major researchers, "Such ruminations revolve around a globally negative view of self and are reinforced by feedback loops involving the effects of depression on the cognitive systems (e.g., attentional and memory processes) and on the body (e.g., sensations of sluggishness and fatigue)."[31]

While CBT emphasizes challenging and replacing the content of such thoughts, MBCT focuses on helping patients alter the ways in which they respond to or process them. This approach helps individuals increase their capacity to choose what to attend to, rather than falling victim to the automatic, ingrained content of negative thoughts. Mindfulness training helps patients alter their awareness of and response to their thoughts, emotions, sensations, and images. Specifically, they are helped to view these experiences that do not necessarily define who they are. They learn that these experiences may not be accurate assessments of themselves or the situation they are confronting.

Through mindfulness training, patients learn to alter their way of processing or attending to thoughts rather than trying to alter their internal experiences. Thus, they reduce the rumination that can potentially foster relapse. In the process of mindfulness training and mindfulness meditation, patients can learn to

> *Through mindfulness training, patients learn to alter their way of processing or attending to thoughts rather than trying to alter their internal experiences. Thus, they reduce the rumination that can potentially foster relapse. In the process of mindfulness training and mindfulness meditation, patients can learn to attend to experiences correctly and recognize the early warning signs of a potential relapse.*

attend to experiences correctly and recognize the early warning signs of a potential relapse.

MBCT is presented over eight weekly two-hour group sessions with up to twelve recovered, recurrently depressed patients. Homework includes exercises and recordings that help increase nonjudgmental awareness of thoughts, feelings, sensations, and images, with an emphasis on applying such skills to everyday life. With increased awareness, patients learn to be more present in each moment without falling into habitual ways of thinking. Follow-up sessions may be scheduled.[32]

This approach was first studied with 145 patients who were in remission from major depression.[33] They were divided and considered according to recency of recovery (0–12 months vs. 13–24 months) and number of episodes (two vs. more than two). They were randomly selected to receive either conventional treatment as usual or MBCT. A one-year follow-up found that those with three or more episodes of depression had a relapse rate of 37 percent, compared with 66 percent for those who did not receive MBCT.

A second study of seventy-five patients in 2003 yielded the same results with a relapse rate of 36 percent for those trained with MBCT versus 78 percent for those receiving conventional treatment.[34]

FAMILY-FOCUSED TREATMENT

In the first edition of this book we briefly discussed new research supporting the application of a family-focused treatment (FFT) for individuals with bipolar disorder. A variety of studies have continued to support this approach as yet another treatment perspective that can help both patients and their families.

FFT can help the family develop new skills in communication, problem solving, and stress management. Most significantly, further research continues to support the conclusion that family treatment helps reduce the degree of negative expressed emotion (EE).[35] This has been found to help medication adherence, foster healthy sleep patterns, and support overall commitment to treatment.

Another study compared FFT with individual treatment.[36] Of fifty-three individuals hospitalized for bipolar illness and in a manic state, twenty-eight were assigned to individual treatment and twenty-five to FFT for a nine-month treatment period. Follow-up assessments occurred at three-month intervals for a one-year period of active treatment and for a one-year period following treatment. The FFT followed a manual prepared by researchers D. J. Miklowitz and M. J. Goldstein.[37] This model emphasized the teaching of information related to a vulnerability-stress model of bipolar disorder and such communication skills as active listening—giving one another positive and negative feedback and framing requests in a positive manner. It also taught problem-solving techniques, including the identification of problems, brainstorming for solutions, assessing the advantages and disadvantages of alternative solutions, and implementing and assessing chosen solutions. Crisis intervention was made available when needed.

> *This model emphasized the teaching of information related to a vulnerability-stress model of bipolar disorder and such communication skills as active listening—giving one another positive and negative feedback and framing requests in a positive manner.*

Individual treatment focused on education, increasing and monitoring the patient's awareness of symptoms, conducting crisis intervention, and reducing ongoing life stress. In the year following treatment, 28 percent of those who had received FFT relapsed, in contrast with 60 percent of those receiving individual treatment. Additionally, only 12 percent of those receiving FFT were rehospitalized compared with 60 percent of those in individual treatment.

This research has encouraged the National Institute of Mental Health to support further study of the family-focused approach. One such study randomly assigned 101 patients with bipolar illness to FFT and pharmacotherapy or to a less intensive crisis management intervention and pharmacotherapy.[38] Outcome assessments were performed every three to six months for a period of two years. FFT consisted of 21 sessions of the model previously described. Those receiving FFT had fewer relapses (35 percent compared with 54 percent) than those receiving crisis management. Patients undergoing FFT similarly had greater reductions in mood disorder symptoms and better medication adherence during the two years than patients in crisis management treatment.

Clearly, FFT provides another effective strategy for individuals confronted with bipolar disorder.

Since these approaches are still evolving, you may need to do research to find out which therapists in your community are available to provide a specific approach. Some of these approaches are more available than others. We encourage you to use the Internet as well as the Resources (page 333) to help you find the treatment you are seeking. It is our shared view that this research encourages hope and provides increased assurance in new and proven strategies to help manage this disease.

In recent years there has been a vast expansion of theory and interventions for the psychological treatment of bipolar disorder. Some of these reflect an evolution of core aspects of cognitive behavioral therapy. Other approaches are based on an integration of theory and practice that emphasizes social context, family systems and communication, the importance of routines, and the application of mindfulness meditation. In sum, these provide an expanded range of treatment choices to address the broad diversity of symptoms and the many challenges associated with bipolar disorder. Taken together, they instill hope for the effective treatment and management of bipolar disorder.

CHAPTER 7

The Prevention of Suicide in Bipolar Disorder

S uicide is the eleventh leading cause of death in the United States and third in youth ages fifteen to nineteen, resulting in more than thirty thousand deaths each year. The rate of suicide has increased in the past five years, and several studies have suggested this is correlated with an increase in the use of the lower antidepressants.

Suicide is a major risk in people with bipolar disorder. To state it plainly, we are losing too many. As we have pointed out in previous chapters, early diagnosis and treatment, which results in a stabilization of the illness, is the basic approach to reducing suicidal risk. But in some instances, even treated patients may break through with symptoms of depression or mixed states of bipolar disorder. The accurate assessment and rapid treatment of these patients can be lifesaving. In this chapter, we will discuss the assessment of acute and chronic suicide risk in patients with bipolar disorder.

WHO IS AT GREATEST RISK AND WHEN?

Completed suicide is four times more frequent in men (5:1 in adolescents) than in women, but two times more women than men attempt suicide. Of people who complete a suicide, 60 to 70 percent had talked to friends about it in the preceding six months. Statistics indicate that eight to twenty-five suicide attempts are made for every suicide that is completed.

Suicide is four times more frequent in men than women (5:1 in adolescents), but two times more women than men attempt suicide. Of people who complete a suicide, an estimated 60 to 70 percent had talked to friends about it in the preceding six months.

A recent study by Benjamin G. Druss, M.D., and Harold Alan Pincus, M.D., in the *Archives of Internal Medicine* presented data on suicidal ideation and behavior. The study involved a standardized psychiatric interview from a sample of 7,589 adults (ages seventeen to thirty-nine). The survey found 16.3 percent of the sample reported suicidal ideation, and 5.5 percent reported suicide attempts, in an otherwise healthy group. The incidences of suicidal ideation reported by those with one or more than one medical diagnosis were 25 to 35 percent for suicidal ideation and 8.9 to 16.2 percent for reported suicide attempts. The risk for suicidal ideation increased 1.3-fold for patients with a diagnosis of major depression or alcoholism. Suicide attempts showed a fourfold increased risk if the patient suffered from asthma or cancer. Suicides occur most commonly in the month of May, with April and June being the next most common times. Although most patients suffer depression more severely between Thanksgiving and New Year's Day, it is in the burst of spring that suicide exerts its greatest threat.

We find the highest risk for suicide attempts among those single, white, or Native American males over the age of fifty, especially if suffering from a chronic medical illness and anticipating a future of continued poor health. Completed suicides occur more frequently among men over sixty-five years old.[1] That said, the recent tripling of suicide rates in males ages fifteen to twenty-four, and doubling of the rate in young females, has now established suicide as the third most common cause of death in adolescents in this country. Among college students, it is the second leading cause of death.

The mental health profession has been and is still reluctant to label children and adolescents with diagnoses traditionally applied to adults. Similarly, physicians are more reluctant to prescribe medications to children and adolescents since the "black box warning" from the FDA. It is also difficult to distinguish bipolar illness from a variety of other conditions that may occur during what is viewed as normal adolescent turmoil. The behavior and emotions of children and adolescents can reflect a broad range of influences from disabilities, attention deficit disorder, delayed emotional development, or antisocial behavior.

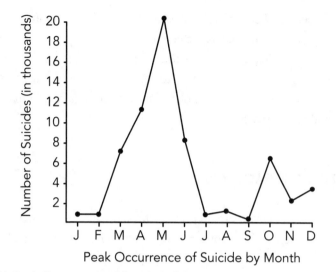

Figure 7.1. Peak Occurrence of Suicide by Month

(Source: *Manic-Depressive Illness* by Frederick K. Goodwin and Kay R. Jamison, copyright 1990 by Oxford University Press, Inc. Used by permission of Oxford University Press, Inc.)

In the bipolar population, statistics are high for suicide. Many studies show that approximately 15 percent of all people who suffer from manic depression commit suicide. A recent English study, however, found the rate to be lower, at about 6 percent. This later study found the risk was greatest early in the course of the illness. The difficulty in preventing suicide is compounded in this group by the difficulty in identifying which factors lead one individual with the illness to cope and another to take his or her own life.

> *In the bipolar population, statistics are high for suicide. Approximately 6 to 15 percent of all people who suffer from manic-depression commit suicide, often early in illness.*

Psychosocial stressors are often responsible for triggering irrational and antisocial behavior in children or adolescents with bipolar disorder. A child may not acquire a sufficient mastery of the challenges of adolescence and will thus be ill prepared to move on to adulthood. Even low-level stress (let alone mental illness) can be painful and overwhelming for teenagers as they face the increasingly complex tasks of maturation. While such stresses are common to many, the presence of clinical depression, substance abuse, significant anxiety, and/or a history of conduct disorder or impulsiveness can create a vulnerability to suicidal behavior.

Early diagnosis and treatment can help prevent a disaster. Effective treatments are currently available to help stabilize mood disorders, so that the millions who suffer from bipolar disorder can regain, and maintain, a fulfilling and productive life.

SUICIDE RISK FACTORS

Table 7.1 shows common risk factors for suicide in patients with bipolar disorder, depressive disorders, alcoholism, schizophrenia, and borderline personality disorder.

If suicidal thoughts or behaviors become apparent, or if relatives even suspect that a patient is thinking about suicide, the treating psychiatrist should be called immediately. It is possible that hospitalization may be required. As with the development of chest pains in a heart patient, the development of suicidal feelings or several other risk factors in a person with bipolar illness indicate the need for immediate expert evaluation.

Although this study identifies the only risk factors for patients with the psychiatric disorders, it should be recognized that even seasoned experts cannot accurately predict suicide in any given individual. If the presence of risk factors suggests the individual may be in a high-risk group at the time observed, an evaluation, followed by appropriate treatment, should be obtained.

> *The risk of suicide in bipolar disorder is highest during the depressive phase or during episodes of dysphoric mania.*

The most common methods of suicide appear to be the most violent: death by shooting (58 percent) or hanging. Moreover, violent suicides are typically carried out in settings where there is little chance of being rescued.[2]

The lifetime risk of suicide in bipolar disorder is about 15 percent, approximately 1 percent of all patients per year. As noted above, a recent English study reported a lower long-term rate of 6 percent but stressed the fact that suicide tended to occur early in the course of illness. Although some clinicians believe that the risk is higher with bipolar disorder than with unipolar depression, most studies show that the risk is the same. There is some evidence that the

TABLE 7.1. ACUTE AND CHRONIC RISK ASSESSMENT FACTORS FOR SUICIDE AND SUICIDE ATTEMPT

RISK FACTORS	ACUTE RISK (hours to days)	CHRONIC RISK (months to years)	TREATMENT RESPONSE (hours to days)	TREATMENT RESPONSE (weeks to months)
High Risk Diagnoses				
Bipolar		+		+
Major Depression		+		+
Schizophrenia		+		+
Alcoholism-depression		+		+
Borderline disorder with depression		+		+
Other Risk Factors				
Suicide ideation (past)		+		
Suicide impulse and plan	+			
Past attempt		+		
Recent attempt	+/–	+		
Severe psychic anxiety	++		+	
Panic attacks	++		+	
Severe agitation	++		+	
Impulsivity	++	++	+	+
Recent alcohol abuse	++		+	
Past drug or alcohol abuse		+		
Global insomnia	++	+/–	+	
Severe anhedonia	+			+
Psychosis		+		+
Recent loss (relationship support, job)		+		
Discharge from psychiatric hospital within 6 to 12 months	+	+/–		
Male >65		++		
Male		+		
Living alone		++		
No child < 18 at home		++		

+some risk ++high risk +/– possible risk

state of dysphoric mixed mania (which can occur in either bipolar type) and bipolar II disorder may carry a higher suicide risk than other forms of the illness. The risk of suicide in bipolar disorder is highest during the depressive phase or during episodes of dysphoric mania (see page 38).

CAN SUICIDE RISK BE DETECTED IN TIME TO PREVENT A SUICIDE?

Unfortunately, it is not generally possible for even mental health professionals to accurately predict an individual suicide. That said, it is important to learn to recognize the features that place a person in a high-risk category and to get an evaluation by a trained expert. People who take their own lives may have had depression or bipolar disorder with suicidal ideas for some time. Suicidal thoughts result from hopelessness and recurrent severe anxiety that can eventually produce an intolerable "psychic pain" that cries for relief. In ruminating about suicide, some patients even develop a specific suicide plan. The development or rehearsal of a plan greatly increases the risk of a suicide attempt. Criteria for high risk must be further examined, and, where indicated, an individual must receive treatment, which may include hospitalization. The following questions are most useful in determining a patient's suicide risk:

Do you feel hopeless about life or sometimes feel like life is too painful to continue living?

Are you suffering from constant worry, anxiety attacks, and/or the inability to sit still?

Are you unable to sleep at night?

Do you have frequent severe panic attacks?

Have you started using alcohol to sleep or reduce your anxiety?

Are you fearful of the future, and do you have episodes of pacing?

What are your reasons for living at this point?

Do you have any thoughts of dying or of ending your life?

Have you attempted suicide in the past, or have you acted self-destructively on impulse?

Do you have a suicidal plan?

Do you have the means to carry it out (e.g., a gun, a high balcony)?

Communicated suicidal ideation—vocalized thoughts such as "I wish I was dead" or "I won't take this any longer"—and prior suicide attempts are standard high-risk indicators. Suicidal communications prior to an attempt are much more commonly imparted to family and friends than to doctors or mental health professionals. Anyone who receives such a communication should report it immediately to someone who can help.

> *Of those who expressed suicidal thoughts in the year prior to their actual death, 60 percent communicated suicidal ideation to spouses, 50 percent to friends, and only 18 percent communicated to helping individuals such as doctors and counselors.*

The classic studies of Eli Robins concluded that approximately 70 percent of patients who committed suicide had mentioned the thought during the year prior to their actual death. Robins found that 60 percent of patients communicated suicidal ideation to spouses, 50 percent to friends, and only 18 percent communicated to helping individuals such as doctors and counselors.[3]

That means that although a loved one, relative, or friend talks to you about suicidal thoughts, that person may not be leveling with their doctor or therapist about them. If there is evidence of preoccupation, a suicide plan, or talk of lethal means (such as a gun, hanging, jumping, or carbon monoxide from a car), take it seriously and consider it an emergency situation.

Recent studies have shown that before taking their lives people frequently deny any suicidal ideation or intent to commit suicide when asked by their doctor or other professional. Therefore, it can be naive to dismiss suicide as a potential risk simply because a patient denies it, especially if other risk factors are present. A careful clinical evaluation can result in lifesaving treatment; many patients have been lost because this was not available to them.

A history of suicide attempts, especially over time, increases the risk of suicide. This is supported by follow-up studies of patients who attempted suicide; studies found that 7 to 12 percent completed suicide over a ten-year period.[4] Any history of attempted suicide is important when evaluating a depressed individual. A positive family history of suicide also increases suicide risk.[5]

The presence of impulsiveness, a trait frequently apparent in individuals with a history of alcohol or substance abuse and certain personality disorders (antisocial personality, borderline personality, and rapid-cycling or mixed states of bipolar disorder), adds another high-risk factor for suicidal behavior when depression is also present.

The Role of Anxiety in Suicide Risk

In recent studies we have found that severe psychic anxiety, often of a ruminative type, and the occurrence of panic attacks and agitation are also associated with acute high risk in the presence of depression.[6] Ruminative anxiety is a severe, pervasive, and recurrent anxiety that dominates a person's thoughts over everyday problems, such as financial concerns, possible legal problems, or problems with relationships.

When panic attacks occur together with the hopelessness that accompanies depression, some patients feel that suicide is their only way out. In a study of 954 hospital inpatients, followed for over ten years, 62 percent of those who killed themselves within one year of evaluation had panic attacks together with major depression. We know that panic attacks occur in approximately 25 to 30 percent of all patients with major depressive disorders. The presence of total or global insomnia, the inability to concentrate, severe anhedonia (the inability to experience usual interest and pleasure), and recent moderate alcohol abuse are also high-risk indicators.

> *When panic attacks occur together with the hopelessness that accompanies depression, some patients feel that suicide is their only way out.*

Anxiety may be present in several different forms, such as the ruminative anxiety mentioned above. The anxiety becomes pathological when the particular problem consumes almost all of the individual's attention and is out of proportion to the actual danger of harm. All other issues become secondary when a patient's mind is otherwise focused on a central negative theme. For instance, a person may become persistently worried over a minor legal violation or become concerned that he is suffering from a life-threatening disease such as cancer, even before there is clear evidence. There is no escaping this fear, and the patient is unable to focus on anything else.

Some unfortunate individuals seem plagued by common worry over a lifetime. However, when someone develops a new pervasive, severe anxiety, especially when there is evidence of depression—such as social withdrawal, poor sleep, or loss of appetite—it is then not the topic of concern that is most important to blame, but the inescapable, fearful preoccupation combined with the hopelessness that accompanies depression. As President Roosevelt said at the onset of World War II, "The only thing we have to fear is fear itself."

Anxiety also occurs when panic attacks are superimposed on depression and greatly increases the risk of suicide attempts. Depression associated with panic attacks, in contrast to depression alone, increases the risk of suicide within a few weeks to a few months. A high level of anxiety was found to be the most important short-term predictor of suicide, and perhaps the most treatable one, in a recent study.[7]

Some people have repeated panic attacks without depression. This condition is often diagnosed as panic disorder. The attacks are of a sudden onset and may occur in a stressful situation, in a crowd, while flying, or "out of the blue," as when someone is woken from sleep by a panic attack. Panic attacks are characterized by heart palpitations, a rapid (>100 beats/minute) pulse and, often, acute difficulty breathing or a feeling of not being able to get enough air. Chest pain, leading to fear of a heart attack and feelings of being on the verge of fainting, losing control, or going "crazy" frequently also occur. Panic attacks may manifest themselves in angry outbursts or even sudden diarrhea.

A third form of severe anxiety state is agitation. Although often associated with severe psychic anxiety, agitation is also demonstrated by physical restlessness (pacing, the inability to sit still) and sometimes by moaning, shouting, or angry outbursts. Patients might express the feeling of being about to "jump out of their skin." Someone suffering this kind of anxiety may seem inconsolable. These agitated states can come and go quite abruptly but may be persistent, or recurrent, in a person with ongoing symptoms of depression.

Immediate treatment for anxiety attacks is crucial to the depressed patient's health. The reduction of severe anxiety symptoms and agitation can reduce suicide risk, even if the depression takes longer to respond to treatment. Several medications can quickly reduce anxiety, but the patient must be observed and the treatment continued. If the depression has not been successfully treated, anxiety symptoms may recur rapidly once

> *Frequently, people assume an anxious, agitated person is better, only to have the same state recur with tragic results after the "improved" person is left to manage alone.*

medication has worn off or the reassuring presence of a supportive person is no longer there. Frequently, people assume an anxious, agitated person is better, only to have the same state recur with tragic results after the "improved" person is left to manage alone.

WHAT CAN BE DONE TO PREVENT SUICIDE?

Suicide invariably induces a mixture of guilt and anger in friends and loved ones. In some cases, the suicide occurs even after every possible effort was made to help. When people become depressed, they often become less communicative and more socially withdrawn. It is common for a person, just prior to attempting suicide, to act as if no special problems are present, misleading loved ones and even expert clinicians.

Some people with severe depression often appear markedly improved just before committing suicide. Some, though clearly distressed, refuse treatment after deciding that their situation is hopeless or because they want to avoid the stigma of admitting a need for treatment. Other high-risk individuals reject help even more overtly, pushing away everyone's efforts to comfort, reason with, or understand them.

Case Study: From Suicidal to Successful

Daniel, in his early forties, was undergoing treatment consisting of lithium and psychotherapy. He was recovering from episodes of mania that had resulted in the loss of his job and previous career. While recovering and trying to begin a new career, he encountered major financial pressures and uncertainties. Despite his prior improvement, Daniel experienced a breakthrough depression related to this stress. In tangent with the depression and financial worry, he also developed intolerable anxiety attacks that increased in frequency and severity. All of this progressed to the point where he could no longer see the way out of his dilemma or tolerate the pain of his persistent anxiety. He purchased a gun and went off to a secluded place to take his life. After test-firing the gun, however, he decided to make one final attempt at treatment before ending his life.

Daniel called his psychiatrist who saw that this was an emergency and hospitalized him at once. Daniel received antianxiety medication to control his overwhelming anxiousness, and he started on antidepressant medication as well. Although antidepressants commonly take from one to four weeks to lift a severe depression, the antianxiety medication relieved his severe anxiety almost immediately even though he was still plagued by financial problems.

Of the experience, Daniel said, "I felt overwhelmed. With the constant feeling of impending doom, I could see no way out. I couldn't stand the pain. Death seemed like the only relief from intolerable pain and failure. Then, when my anxiety decreased I began to see some long-term solutions to my very real problem. I realized it wasn't a life-and-death issue, and that I could work my way out of it."

Within two days, Daniel was discharged from the hospital, his condition markedly improved. With continued supportive treatment and medication, he gradually turned his life around and has since found a new and meaningful career helping others.

The Importance of a Strong Support System

Abraham Lincoln's story (see page 144) is historical proof of the effectiveness and importance of concerned, supportive, and giving friends to a severely depressed and suicidal person. It appears that Lincoln's friends played a major role in his recovery, thereby permitting the man once described by a friend as "the most ambitious man in the world" to express his talents on the nation's behalf.

In Lincoln's case, however, he had made his distress known to his friends and accepted their help. In some ways, the severity of his state, which rendered him helpless, may have made it easier for his friends to come to his rescue. They could be empathic, and he was in no position to resist the help offered. This is not always the case.

In many instances, people hide hopelessness, inner turmoil, and anxiety from friends and loved ones and even deny the existence of these emotions. The hopelessness that is intrinsic to suicidal depression often leads the person to reject help, especially treatment. It is as if the suicidal patient cannot

SUICIDAL TENDENCIES: THE CASE OF ABRAHAM LINCOLN

In *The Inner World of Abraham Lincoln,* biographer Michael Burlingame depicts the period in the young Lincoln's life when he was rejected by a woman he had hoped to marry and was consumed by serious financial problems. Moreover, he had a childhood history of maternal loss and physical abuse. These factors added to his vulnerability at a difficult period in his life and caused him to suffer severe depression and become preoccupied with suicide.

Lincoln's friends were so concerned that they literally moved in and stayed up with him day and night, after removing knives and guns from his presence. He remained agitated, spoke as if delirious, and was sleepless, with recurrent suicidal impulses. His friends maintained a constant vigil for a week or more until the crisis abated. Later, a friend invited Lincoln to live in his lodgings and paid his daily expenses as well as his law school tuition.

Gradually, Lincoln recovered and, despite other disappointments and depressive recurrences, was able to serve as the sixteenth president of the United States. Lincoln held the nation together during the grave crisis of the Civil War— not bad for someone "weak" enough to suffer suicidal depression!

Throughout his life, Lincoln exhibited many signs of continued high risk for suicide, including frequent recurrences of severe melancholic depression and suicidal ideation.

How did Lincoln survive well enough to be able to manifest such strength in the service of our nation? What enabled him to get through the periods of high suicide risk when medical and psychological treatment was unavailable? What seemed to be a major factor, as depicted in this biographical sketch of Lincoln, was his capacity to attract empathic and helpful friends and, most important, to accept their help in times of crisis.[8]

tolerate one more disappointment, such as the possible failure of efforts to improve what he or she experiences as a hopeless situation.

Depression narrows a person's vision of any positive alternatives. Any new direction, such as treatment, is viewed as just another source of uncertainty, pain, and failure. The obliteration of consciousness along with feelings of responsibility, torturous anxiety, failure, and guilt seems suddenly desirable.

Often, the person experiences a fleeting vestige of hope regarding therapeutic treatment and its positive direction, but the sirens singing of relief from all of life's psychic pain and self-hate are very seductive. Uncanny as it may seem, patients often appear suddenly and dramatically improved just before their suicide.

> *The hopelessness that is intrinsic to suicidal depression often leads the person to reject help, especially treatment. It is as if the suicidal patient cannot tolerate one more disappointment or failure.*

Talking with patients after a medically serious suicide attempt, one is struck by the sense of peace and calm derived from the apparent freedom from all anxieties and criticism that the decision to commit suicide can create. Sadly, those people die not realizing that it is possible to attain a similar state without having to exchange their conscious life for it. Unfortunately, they often cannot see beyond the distortions imposed by their state of depression.

Maintaining Effective Medications Can Prevent Suicide

Recently the question has been raised whether antidepressant medications can worsen depression, especially in the first one or two weeks of use, and increase the risk of suicide attempts or suicide (see chapter 4). At the same time, data have been published to show that the majority of patients who commit suicide have no evidence of the presence of antidepressants in their blood at their time of death. An average of seven toxicology studies show that 12 to 23 percent of patients who committed suicide had evidence of having taken antidepressant medications, suggesting that patients who die by suicide are generally undertreated with medication.

Even more important is the recent study by Bauer and colleagues that shows no increase of suicide or suicidal thoughts/attempts in 425 bipolar patients studied one month after the initiation of antidepressant treatment.[9] Simon and associates have shown in a sample of 82,285 episodes of antidepressant treatment, studied for six months after first use, no increased risk of death from suicide in the month after treatment initiation; the risk of suicide attempts was found to be greatest before treatment was begun and decreased progressively as the treatment continues.[10]

While there is some evidence that antidepressant medications do not reduce suicide risk over eight to twelve weeks of treatment, a 2005 study by

Jules Angst and colleagues has shown that continued treatment (minimum six months) reduces mortality and suicide.[11, 12] One of the most important deterrents to suicide is the continuation of antidepressant treatment, which reduces the likelihood of relapse or recurrence. Stigmatizing a person who is taking antidepressant medications is the same as urging a diabetic patient to stop using his insulin. Promoting continued use of effective medications can save lives.

In recent years it has been shown by many studies that lithium carbonate has a protective effect against suicide, such that patients who continue lithium maintenance have eight times less risk.[13]

Demoralization Versus Clinical Depression

We frequently confuse a state of demoralization with clinical depression. People can try hard, do all the "right" things, be a "good" person, persevere, and still fail in their efforts or be struck down by some unexpected occurrence, such as an illness, tragic accident, or natural disaster. People often feel demoralized in such situations—beaten down, sad, and wanting to give up. They may even develop a clinical depression in response to these adverse events. But if they persist and fate finally rewards them, as God finally stopped testing Job, things begin to turn positive and life, once again, becomes happy.

> *The deeply depressed state of mind, pervasive no matter how it seems to the sufferer, can be completely lifted and held at bay by successful treatment. Doctors see this happen many times, and it is an amazing miracle to behold.*

In the case of a clinical depression, no possibility of redemption seems to exist. Clinically depressed people no longer experience success as positive. They view every occurrence, positive or negative, as having some fearful implication without any positive outcome even imaginable. The clinically depressed person on the verge of suicide can anticipate only further suffering and failure.

Even more problematic is that this mind state is not always continuous but may alternate with some moments of distraction, during which the anxiety and suffering cease temporarily, only to return again. Intermittent self-destructive impulses are the most frightening of these distractions because of their unpredictability. A chronic negative state with its terrible predictability is sometimes easier to tolerate than attaining a glimmer of hope, only to be again plunged into fearful despair. Depression that views suicide as a solution is fueled by suffering—psychic pain colored by the fear and anticipation of increasing, uncontrollable, interminable pain. Is it any wonder that death becomes attractive to a mind in this state?

We are all either prisoners or beneficiaries of our outlooks and attitudes, which determine how we experience life. We can all learn to endure pain with the anticipation of a better future. Depression can negatively distort a person's entire outlook, yet this state of mind, no matter how it seems to the sufferer, can be completely lifted and held at bay by successful treatment. Doctors see this happen many times, and it is an amazing miracle to behold.

SUICIDE: A PERMANENT SOLUTION TO A TEMPORARY PROBLEM

Depression distorts the problems of the afflicted into a never-ending state of suffering from which death seems the only relief. If patients survive suicidal impulses, however, they may regain their will to live.

One such case involved a man who hiked into the woods with full intent of ending his life. In an attempt to portray his suicide as an accident, he placed his rifle on a log, pointing the firearm at his chest. As he leaned over to pull the trigger, the rifle moved and accidentally discharged. Although the man was seriously wounded in the thigh, he crawled on his hands and knees for two miles, through deep snow, to get help.

This example clearly illustrates the tremendous will of people able to get beyond the point of suicidal crisis. After the crisis, the human instinct for self-preservation often reasserts itself.

Of course, in an untreated bipolar disorder or major depression, the hopelessness, pain, and suicidal wishes are likely to recur.

When depression is lifted by appropriate treatment, another problem has been solved. In the presence of depression, there is no way out, and it seems certain that more suffering and failure can only become more intolerable. It is difficult to imagine through empathy if you haven't been there. Many people are reluctant to entertain the possibility that, despite free will (the ability to control one's own thoughts), people's views can, and do, become so negatively distorted. To most of us who have never experienced clinical depression and utter hopelessness, it is difficult to conceive of not being able to overcome this state with our own efforts as we do with "normal" sadness and disappointment.

A doctor told a patient who did not respond to a series of treatment efforts that if he could just hang on and stay alive, the doctor was sure he would get better. A new treatment approach was finally successful and the patient returned to a normal state. The patient subsequently confided to the doctor, "I didn't believe you for one minute when you told me I could get better, but you were so persistent in trying to help me that I decided you either believed what you were saying or you were delusional. Your refusal to quit made me decide not to kill myself and to stick around to see what would happen."

IMPLICATIONS FOR MANAGED CARE

Managed care criteria for predicting suicide, such as expressed suicidal threats or a recent attempt, are often inadequate for the assessment of suicide risk and the need for hospital care. Even severe agitation and anxiety, panic attacks, and global insomnia may be considered insufficient indicators of the need for hospitalization if the patient denies suicidal ideation.

The physician must be able to evaluate a patient without restriction by a managed care "protocol," which often overrides the clinical judgment of the doctor. When managed care plans disqualify patients from receiving coverage for psychiatric services on an inpatient basis, doctors frequently are at a loss to find alternative solutions. Not only does this exacerbate a patient's already high level of anxiety, but insufficient medical coverage also leads to lower levels of care.[14]

An important caveat for supportive friends and relatives is that even a severely depressed patient may experience some transient hope after first seeing a skilled physician or counselor. When improvement is not immediate, the patient may feel disappointed that no miracle turnaround occurred. Profound hopelessness, cynicism, and recurrent anxiety can rapidly supplant transient hope following this disappointment. The risk of suicide can be very high at this time.

It is important to stress that improvement may take time. Any first attempt at treatment, or the first medication tried, may need to be changed or modified before the best treatment is found. Hope is a fragile state in the mind of a clinically depressed person, and hope can turn into hopelessness in the absence of immediate success, especially if the patient is not given realistic expectations.

> *When managed care plans disqualify patients from receiving coverage for psychiatric services on an inpatient basis, doctors frequently are at a loss to find alternative solutions.*

Preventing suicide is not easy. First, you have to sense when a person with depression is in a state of immediate risk. Once that has been determined, the person should never be left alone until they have been examined by a professional and possibly hospitalized. If they can be induced to get help, it is wise to communicate with the professional about available options.

Offering a patient support until improvement has gradually occurred is very important. Be suspicious of dramatic recovery: When a patient seems to rebound too quickly, it may indicate that he has given up, decided to commit suicide, and is pretending to be improved. Gradual recovery over days is much more reliable. Even then, sudden setbacks can occur. Remember the case of Abraham Lincoln and how the sustained support of friends got him past his suicidal crisis.

Even professionals can't always accurately predict or prevent a suicide, but if you think you recognize a high-risk period, stay with the patient or get someone else to stay until he or she is safe. Do not leave a person alone in a high-risk state. Also remove all firearms and other dangerous weapons and substances. Don't just think about it. Act! If you do your best—and that is all anyone can be expected to do—you may save somebody's life.

Those who have previously attempted suicide and/or have a family history of suicide should take the following preventive measures:

- Be informed. Educate yourself through books, lectures, and support groups, and consult with your local advocacy chapters (see Resources, page 333).
- Contact your psychiatrist, therapist, crisis intervention team, or others who are trained to help.
- Ask for written information on all drugs you take, and be on the alert for any side effects.

PREVENTIVE MEASURES FOR SUICIDE

The Depression and Bipolar Support Alliance lists the following recommendations for preventing the suicide of a family member, friend, or other person:

Take seriously the person's condition.

Stay calm, but don't underreact.

Involve other people. Don't try to handle the crisis alone or jeopardize your own health or safety. Call 911, if necessary.

Contact the person's psychiatrist, therapist, crisis intervention team, or others who are trained to help.

Express concern. Let the patient talk about suicidal thoughts without loved ones appearing to convey shock and condemnation. Give concrete examples of what leads you to believe the person is close to suicide. If this understanding is conveyed to the patient, then he or she may feel less guilty about possessing such suicidal thoughts.

Listen attentively. Maintain eye contact. Use body language, such as moving close to the person or holding his or her hand, if it is appropriate.

Ask direct questions. Inquire whether the person has a specific plan for suicide. Determine, if possible, what method of suicide the person is thinking about.

Acknowledge the person's feelings. Be empathetic, not judgmental. Do not relieve the person of responsibility for his or her actions, however.

Reassure. Stress that suicide is a permanent solution to temporary problems. Insist that the problem can be helped, even if past attempts have failed. Provide realistic hope. Remind the person that things can get better if the right help is made available. Stress that you will help them find effective treatment.

Don't worry about confidentiality! Confidentiality is secondary to a life-and-death situation. Don't hesitate to speak with the person's doctor in order to protect that person.

Do not leave the person alone, if possible, until you are sure that he or she is in the hands of competent professionals.

CHAPTER 8

The Stigma of Mental Illness

S tigma refers to being characterized as deviant, flawed, limited, undesirable, or not measuring up in some way. When associated with mental illness, stigma is based on the view that such disorders reflect a weakened genetic strain, flawed heredity chain, weakness in character, purposeful malingering, lack of self-control, and/or immoral behavior.

HISTORY OF THE STIGMA OF MENTAL ILLNESS

Historically, stigma has always been associated with mental illness although the details have varied as our collective understanding and attitudes toward individual will, responsibility, human behavior, and personality have changed over the years. Fear, ignorance, and shame have largely informed this history.

For centuries, mental illness was associated with mysticism and theology. Those who evidenced bizarre behavior were often thought to be influenced by the spirit world or by the forces of evil. Centuries later, when individual responsibility was emphasized, the mentally ill were viewed as having been sinful or as having lost faith in God. While sometimes sought out for having useful knowledge, these most often became victims of stigma and were both marginalized and ostracized.[1]

In ancient Greece, people who evidenced bizarre behavior were often shunned or locked up. At that time, explanations of mental illness were based mostly on beliefs regarding religion or magic, but the Greeks were the first to consider that this sickness might be physically rooted in disease. Hippocrates identified epilepsy, melancholia, postpartum psychosis, and hysteria as medical illnesses rather than effects of divine influence.[2] While this explanation served to reduce some of the stigma, those with mental illness were still associated with shame and humiliation.[3]

Historically, frightening developments in the human condition were attributed to punishment by the gods. People found it comforting to blame the victim when facing tragedy. In biblical times, when friends of the long-suffering Job could find no other plausible explanation for the inexplicable tragedies that struck him, they all blamed him, despite the fact that Job had lived a moral life.

During the Middle Ages, people regarded symptoms of mental illness as evidence of communication between the afflicted individual and good or evil spirits, often citing demonic possession. Witch-hunts reflect the extreme consequence of such attitudes.

The extermination of those with mental illness during the Holocaust is another heinous response to stigma coupled with scapegoating. Even today, stigma is perpetrated in countries that label dissidents as being emotionally disturbed, when in fact they may simply disagree with state politics.

Public reaction to mental illness is greatly influenced by a general lack of knowledge. This ignorance leads to public fear, which has served to exacerbate the shame of the afflicted and their loved ones. Despite seeming advances in fairness and disability legislation, stigma associated with mental disorders has, unfortunately, not abated.

Luckily, efforts to teach public awareness while finding new ways of treating mood disorders continue to advance despite this ongoing stigma. These efforts have helped reduce fear and ignorance while paving the way for a more compassionate, humane, and realistic response to one of life's most complex challenges.

It should come as no surprise that the stigma of mental illness has been very strong in Western culture. Our society

> *It should come as no surprise that the stigma of mental illness has been very strong in Western culture. Our society places a high value on self-control, free will, and individual responsibility and expects us to exert self-control over our feelings and behavior. These values, coupled with ignorance, have led to the public view of mental illness as a sign of character weakness.*

places a high value on self-control, free will, and individual responsibility and expects us to exert self-control over our feelings and behavior. These values, coupled with ignorance, have led to the public view of mental illness as a sign of character weakness.

This attitude may be especially prevalent toward individuals with bipolar illness. Those living with the disorder demonstrate wide variability in functioning, from healthy and "normal" to depressive or psychotic. This capacity to function in a normal manner, at least some of the time, may lead observers to conclude that episodes are merely evidence of weakness in willpower and self-control. The fact that many symptoms of low-level mania are positive and fall within the parameters of a "normal" personality may similarly lead observers to point to a lack of self-control when more severe symptoms develop. All too frequently we hear people insinuate that the mere exercise of willpower would repel psychotic, depressive, or manic behavior.

CONTRIBUTORS TO STIGMA

The major factors creating and perpetuating the stigma attached to mental illness are fear, ignorance, and shame.

Fear

Fear is a powerful determinant of stigma. It is often a reflexive reaction when observing behaviors that don't make sense and appear unpredictable. People may be especially fearful of the impulsive or confusing behaviors evidenced during psychosis or severe forms of mania. Despite all the research demonstrating that people with mental illness are actually less prone to violence than others, many people erroneously associate aggressive behavior with mental disorders. Although only 3 percent of mentally ill patients can be categorized as dangerous, television programming, including the news, plays up the role of the mental illness in a vast number of crimes, including murder.[4]

Fear and anxiety must be anticipated in some degree among those unacquainted with a mood disorder. In the presence of severe depression, hopelessness, helplessness, and despair are evident. People can feel how all zest for life is gone from the depressed individual, and this can raise fear and anxiety, especially in those who have the slightest propensity for depression. They are reminders of the uncomfortable attitudes and emotions that we all struggle to avoid. Even those who usually approach life with optimism and passion may experience anxiety when a loved one is severely depressed, as well as confusion, a lack of understanding, and a sense of helplessness to make things better.

Extreme mania raises similar concerns. The behaviors associated with mania might be especially threatening to people who are concerned about losing control of their own passions and impulses. In a culture that values self-control, the bold, daring, and colorful actions of those with mania may seem outlandish, "over the edge," and overly self-focused.

Ignorance

Ignorance is a major contributing factor to the responses of fear and anxiety. Between lack of knowledge and basic confusion over manic-depressive behavior, people are likely to become anxious and concoct subjective and irrational explanations for the behavior as a means of easing their own anxiety. This is as true for the observer of such behaviors as it is for the person suffering through them.

A lack of knowledge about the causes and treatment of mental illness keeps stigma, and the practices based on stigma, firmly in place. Insufficient training or experience may lead a family physician, relative, or friend to minimize the need for further assessment and treatment of an individual suffering bipolar symptoms. Quickness to minimize or deny depression and a tendency to evaluate symptoms of mania as within the norm both reflect and promote the stigma that interferes with an accurate diagnosis.

Lack of knowledge also fosters the social isolation of those with mental illness. A lack of knowledge regarding the course of bipolar disorder or its treatment, naive assumptions about willpower, intensify the stigma that dissuades the afflicted from seeking treatment.

> *A lack of knowledge about the causes and treatment of mental illness keeps stigma, and the practices based on stigma, firmly in place.*

In the late 1960s, the mental health field made an effort to provide more humane treatment for patients with mental illness by transferring many of them back to their communities from state psychiatric hospitals.

Community mental health centers (outpatient services, inpatient units, day-care programs, and group homes) were established to provide the necessary continuum of care for patients. With the advent of improved medications and the structure provided by these community mental health centers, it was hoped that patients would experience less isolation, be helped to stabilize, and return to a higher level of functioning.

During these years, it was the philosophy of mental health treatment teams to make every effort not to hospitalize patients experiencing emotional crises. Staff would spend hours, even days, with as many family members as possible to provide structure and stabilize the patient. Avoidance of using the community inpatient unit was not based on cost efficiency (HMOs were not yet a dominant force in health care) but on the clinical view that hospitalization would have an extremely negative impact on the patient's overall self-esteem. Although well intended, this approach unwittingly communicated a stigma associated with hospitalization. Embedded in the philosophy of the approach was the message that hospitalization equaled failure. When hospital admission was deemed necessary, the patient felt defeated, experiencing admission as lost self-control, failure to measure up to self-expectations and the expectations of others, and letting down one's family and treatment team.

Shame

The experience of shame is at the core of stigma. Shame affects not only the mentally ill but also those living with the afflicted. Recent studies reflect the notion that the foundation of shame involves the awareness of not living up to one's own code of standards, rules, or norms or those of others.

Shame derives from and further fosters the negative self-judgment or evaluation that follows this awareness. The degree to which the standards of the normative "code" are perceived as important and widely held by others dictates how frequently they are internalized. Violation of these internalized standards leads to a negative self-assessment. Much of the fear, anxiety, and guilt surrounding mental illness are based on ongoing and pervasive efforts to avoid this painful experience of shame.[5]

> *The experience of shame is at the core of stigma. Shame affects not only the mentally ill but also those living with the afflicted.*

> *While guilt is painful, it is not all-encompassing. Shame is much more profound; it is experienced as a sense of wanting to disappear, hide, or even die—a total escape.*

Michael Lewis clearly articulates the experience of shame and differentiates it from guilt. Shame is a self-reflective observation that involves an appraisal of one's whole self. In contrast, guilt is a self-reflective emotion by which one identifies a specific action as not measuring up to self-expectations or the standards set by others. While guilt is painful, it is not all-encompassing. Guilt often points to defining an action that can be taken to rectify a situation, whereas shame does not. Shame is much more profound; it is experienced as a sense of wanting to disappear, hide, or even die—a total escape.[6]

Reflections on Shame

Kathy Cronkite, who had her own experience with depression, interviewed celebrities and politicians who experienced severe depression or bipolar illness. The following is Cronkite's compilation of how those with mood disorders view shame.

Mike Wallace said he did not experience shame over the prospect of losing his job. Nevertheless, he worried about being fired for depression.[7]

William Styron told Cronkite that he did not experience shame. "You feel shame only when you've done something that you're derelict about," said Styron. "I had enough awareness to know that this was not my fault."[8]

"Jane Doe," a Washington, D.C., professional who did not wish to be identified, reported that shame and related stigma are prevalent in our nation's capital. "People don't have feelings here, and they don't have problems, nor disease, nor depression, nor sadness."[9]

In her conversation with Cronkite, Kitty Dukakis suggested that we often think of people who can't function in society when we look at mental illness. "That's probably one of the reasons that more people don't come forward and get the help they need. I hid it, but other people who are mentally ill can't put up a veil and hide it. The tragedy is that so many people, particularly people in highly visible positions, don't get the help they need because of their concern about what the public will perceive."[10]

Whether in the public eye or not, shame can lead to isolation by those living with bipolar disorder. When they or those living with them ignore,

EXPERIENCE OF SHAME

The four key features that form the experience of shame are:

1. **The desire to hide.**   "Hiding" occurs on many levels. Feeling shame may lead a person to isolate physically from others. People may practice social isolation or withdrawal in an attempt to decrease their vulnerability to shame and to new shame-provoking experiences. Increased inhibition in all forms of self-expression may be another attempt to avoid potentially shame-provoking experiences. Others may subconsciously distract themselves from shame by emotional substitution, focusing on other emotions instead of the shame. Through denial and minimization, the person becomes consciously aware only of the anger and/or depression that are consequences of experiencing shame.[11]

2. **Feeling intense pain, discomfort, and anger.**   The pain experienced in shame is very intense. Negative self-evaluation leads to hurt, sadness, and overall shame. Anger can develop as an outgrowth of these negative emotions and may be directed at oneself or toward others, serving as a distraction from the painful root issues.

3. **Feeling no good, inadequate, and unworthy.**   The interplay of self-devaluation and pain escalates and intensifies to produce a feeling of complete worthlessness. Scholars who have studied attribution theory (the area of inquiry that tries to identify the factors that people attribute to their successes and failures, self-esteem, and optimism–pessimism) emphasize that depression is related to internalizing blame for negative events.[12] Shame is based on a negative assessment of the whole self and experienced as permanent.[13]

4. **Self-involvement.**   When we reflect on ourselves, assessing our shortcomings from an intensely negative and "all-encompassing" point of view, all objectivity is lost; self-doubt, confusion, and anxiety prevail; and any action is viewed as futile. This paralyzing consequence of shame inhibits one's capacity to think, talk, or act normally.

When the shame of mental illness is so culturally ingrained and pervasive, leading to a generalized reaction involving the whole person, it is understandable why people with bipolar disorder view themselves as a "depressive" or "bipolar" rather than victims of a mood disorder. For these individuals, the illness has become their identity, and shame further exacerbates their depression.

minimize, or deny the seriousness of this illness, they only serve to foster such shame. Even statements intended to provide support may further shame and promote isolation. Seemingly encouraging advice to force oneself to be happy a little at a time or to "Say some positive affirmations when you wake up and before you go to sleep," may provide some measure of support for those with low-level depression. However, severely depressed individuals experience these gestures as isolating exhortations, as they're unlike the "rest of the world," powerless to implement such practices. These gestures of help only increase shame and remind the afflicted of their failure to measure up to expected standards. That said, the mere avoidance of any discussion about the illness, however well intended, may also contribute further to the stigma of bipolar disorder.

In several of her books, author Susan Sontag explores the meanings that we have come to associate with various illnesses. For example, according to Sontag, we developed a romantic view that those with tuberculosis (TB) experienced tremendous, unexpressed passion. In contrast, she says, "The romanticizing of madness reflects in the most vehement way the contemporary prestige of irrational or rude (spontaneous) behavior (acting-out), of that very passionateness whose repression was once imagined to cause TB, and is now thought to cause cancer."[14]

> *The tragedy is that so many people, particularly people in highly visible positions, don't get the help they need because of their concern about what the public will perceive.*
>
> —KITTY DUKAKIS

The meaning given to illness has certainly changed through the ages. While the former view was that a certain illness corresponds to a specific character, in recent years, illness has been seen more as an expression of the character. As Sontag notes, "It is a product of will. Recovery from a disease depends on the healthy will assuming dictatorial power in order to subsume the rebellious forces of the sick will."[15]

This view has serious implications for the promotion of shame. Walk into any bookstore and you'll see many books in the medical, psychology, and self-help sections focused on improving physical or emotional well-being. While many of these offer powerfully constructive ideas, others reflect Sontag's concern: "The romantic idea that the disease expresses the character is invariably extended to assert that the character causes the disease because it has not expressed itself."[16]

This notion promotes shame and perpetuates stigma as it puts the onus of disease on the patient. Sontag states that our culture views illness as a psychological event and encourages people to believe that they unconsciously will it. It is this view of illness that even in our "enlightened" society still places stigma on both those who experience mood disorders and on their families. When language implies that the individual is responsible for his or her illness, it reinforces blame, guilt, and shame, and reduces the desire to seek treatment.

RESPONSIBILITY AND STIGMA

Frequently, those who blame victims of mental disorder for their illness suggest that the afflicted are just giving in, being self-indulgent, avoiding responsibility, or being manipulative. Exploring these charges in more detail illuminates their circular reasoning. What might be the motivation of "giving in" to depression or psychosis? If one is self-indulgent, what is the incentive to indulge oneself in feelings of shame, guilt, and even paralysis of thought as experienced in severe depression? What intensely uncomfortable subjective experience makes one feel unable to be responsible or work toward meeting his or her own needs? What intensely negative internal experience leads one to avoid responsibility or to try to manipulate others?

When we focus on the idea of pretense, that the illness is a ruse or a strategy for attention, we fail to acknowledge the real pain associated with mental illness. In fact, maintaining this belief is a way to avoid recognizing pain in others. However, if we acknowledge that someone's pain is real, we also accept the needs and desires of that person. This capacity to understand serves as the foundation for compassion.

Let us consider the evolution of how our attitude toward responsibility influences our view of mental illness. As suggested in the writings of Sontag, we are more likely to blame people for their condition to the degree that we can attribute responsibility to them. Sontag cited one study that found that more stigma is attached to overweight people and to those with AIDS than to people with cancer. The assumption is that individuals can do something about their weight and sexual behavior but have no control over developing cancer.

Research that demonstrates the biological and neurochemical etiology of severe depression and bipolar illness encourages the afflicted to feel less responsible for the illness. Both the medical community and advocacy groups emphasize these findings to provide education about appropriate attitudes and treatment and, thereby, reduce stigma. This educational thrust should be supported and applauded.

At the same time, this view may have tremendous implications for establishing guidelines for compassion. Does it indirectly suggest that we develop a hierarchy for compassion? Should we feel more compassion for nonsmokers with cancer than for smokers with the disease? What about people with severe depression whose condition is chemical in origin—should we have more compassion for them than for those who experience less severe depression? If our focus is on the concept of free will as fundamental to guiding behavior, we are more prone to blaming a victim of depression, especially if we don't believe in the biological or neurobiological basis. When that is the case, we are in fact limited in compassion.

Part of the blame, as reflected by the culture of self-help, lies in the way we view the underlying motivations of individual thought, feelings, and action. If we do not identify a biological component, we more readily look for the role individuals play in developing and maintaining their state of depression. To the degree that mental health practitioners have made us aware of competing or unconscious motivations, we can use these motivations as ammunition against those who experience emotional disturbance. But is it really in our control?

> *If our focus is on the concept of free will as fundamental to guiding behavior, we are more prone to blaming a victim of depression, especially if we don't believe in the biological or neurobiological basis.*

A more discerning and mature adult might say, "If only I had the wisdom then that I have now, I would have made better decisions." That small word—*if*—makes all the difference. Once depression sets in, the condition takes over and the afflicted individual exhibits symptoms of the disorder: lack of awareness, narrowed vision, and constriction of thought, behavior, and emotions. During periods of extreme depression or mania, the person only minimally experiences choice, if at all. In addition to chemical imbalance, depression can be related to a lack of resilience as a result of genetic factors, cumulative stress, and experienced trauma. Should people with these conditions be the target of anger, either self-directed or derived from others?

"HOW GOOD DO WE HAVE TO BE?"

In his book *How Good Do We Have to Be?*, Harold Kushner discusses how we have raised our standards from "striving to do well" to concentrating on the need for perfection. This is the standard we apply when we stigmatize mental illness. We invariably sow the seeds for depression through unrealistically high self-expectations. These expectations are activated by a society bent on perfection; we seek perfection in our weight, in our appearance, and in all the expectations we have of ourselves and others.[17]

How do Kushner's views apply to the stigma of mental illness? It is our idealization of perfection that keeps us from exercising compassion, not only toward others but toward ourselves as well. If we accept our common humanity and that we are all imperfect beings, compassion will follow. Whether mood disorders are biologically related, stress related, or a result of trauma, we can be accepting.

Lack of compassion, which is both a cause and a result of stigma, has a significant impact on the experience of individuals with mood disorders. Regardless of the etiology of the illness, part of the experience of being depressed is helplessness, hopelessness, and reactions that extend beyond sadness and hurt to despair. Stigma affects the management of depression before, during, and after all stages of the illness. The very thought of saying out loud that you are depressed often leads to fear of what people will think, fear of rejection and/or abandonment, and fears about job security. Those who are depressed may be surrounded by family and friends who support these same fears, either consciously or unconsciously.

The lack of knowledge about mental illness that is associated with stigma can also foster the isolation of the afflicted person. If you are unaware of appropriate treatments for depression, you might engage in self-talk, such as "I'll let it pass and see what happens," "It'll go away," and "I need to keep my image up." Consequently, untreated depression leads to increased isolation, exacerbating one's experience of decreased productivity, unanswered needs, and lack of connection with others. It also fosters and reflects a loss of compassion for oneself.

To draw a parallel with physical illness, imagine ignoring severe and lingering chest pains, fever, a suspicious and expanding growth, or the onset of blurred vision. Delaying medical treatment can have serious consequences and make the condition more difficult to reverse.

Depression can produce an inability to concentrate that may interfere with work performance. Frequent mistakes lead to interpersonal conflicts and tension, which exacerbate the fears of the afflicted person and diminish performance quality. Stigma and shame, already associated with the disorder, are worsened as the afflicted individual feels less and less effective in his work.

A severe manic episode may also interfere with effective work and overall performance. However, a sense of shame and related stigma may not arrive until a later period of emotional stability, when the victim is more able to reflect on bizarre or inappropriate behaviors.

> *Stigma affects the management of depression before, during, and after all stages of the illness. The very thought of saying out loud that you are depressed often leads to fear of what people will think, fear of rejection and/or abandonment, and fears about job security.*

It is equally important to identify the impact of stigma on the friends or family of the afflicted person. Their reactions often influence the seeking or avoidance of treatment. Even when those around us are trying to be compassionate, they may be affected by fear, ignorance, or shame. Sometimes these can stem from a friend or relative not feeling helpful, being fearful of saying or doing the wrong thing, becoming frustrated, feeling anxious about the future, or even experiencing shame or guilt by association.

Fear, ignorance, and shame related to stigma can combine to induce anger and resentment. As mentioned previously, people may even believe that their depressed or manic friend is malingering, overly self-indulgent, or manipulative. But a severely depressed person is self-focused, not necessarily procrastinating or being overly self-indulgent or controlling. Nobody wants to remain in the depths of depression.

If manipulation occurs, it is because depressed people are also fearful and feel ashamed. They might be unprepared to exercise self-help owing to lack of knowledge. Although some individuals develop an identity around an illness, severe depression is not an experience one chooses to maintain. Using illness as a crutch rather than attempting to improve the situation is a sign of fear, anxiety, deficient knowledge, lack of trust, or another block that keeps the person feeling unable to move forward. Regardless of the origin of depression and manic depression, mental illness deserves compassion, not anger; acceptance, not stigma; understanding, not ignorance and bias; and respect, not devaluation.

> *Regardless of the origin of depression and manic depression, mental illness deserves compassion, not anger; acceptance, not stigma; understanding, not ignorance and bias; and respect, not devaluation.*

RESPONDING TO INTERNALIZED STIGMA

While everyone with bipolar disorder is subjected to the pervasive influence of stigma, not everyone with this illness experiences it in the same manner. To a great extent, the impact of stigma is most destructive when it leads to internalized stigma, a constellation of self-critical attitudes associated with shame and a feeling of isolation. Response to this stigma significantly affects a person's openness to accept a diagnosis and subsequently seek, obtain, and adhere to effective treatment.

The capacity for resilience to such stigma rests on several key factors. These include the degree to which the illness has come to define identity, the degree to which individuals admired and respected are perceived as genuinely accepting of the illness, and the intensity of anger regarding the stigma.[18]

In chapter 5, we discussed a form of distorted thinking described as dichotomous thinking. The individual who practices this distortion in thinking experiences her diagnosis as all-encompassing, as an integral and dominant aspect of her personality, and is more likely to feel overwhelmed by the disorder. Such rigid thinking interferes with the capacity to recognize her own complexity and many areas of daily living that when effectively managed may not be affected by a mood disorder.

Those who evidence such thought patterns are more prone to exert tremendous energy denying, ignoring, and minimizing any evidence that is indicative of a diagnosis. This is the case for many who never seek treatment.

Bernard Golden describes a young man who was referred to him by faculty from a graduate psychology program. He reluctantly came to the first session reflecting fear and anger in his words and demeanor. He indicated that he had been diagnosed with bipolar disorder about two years prior to entering the program. He had not disclosed his diagnosis with anyone at the school because he was so intensely fearful of being rejected, even in a program that valued understanding and compassion regarding mental illness. He was referred only after several faculty observed symptoms reflective of his illness. He was extremely angry, both with being referred and about the diagnosis. He stated he had no intention to seek treatment for the disorder and that he would be able to manage it on his own. While his anger was understandable to some degree, his rage reflected underlying resentment that he should have to face such a challenge. This anger only got in the way of seeking and receiving the support and treatment he desperately needed and reflected the internalized stigma he had associated with the diagnosis. In spite of attempts to help him be more flexible in his perception, he refused to return for treatment.

In contrast, others diagnosed with bipolar disorder may have the capacity to recognize and acknowledge their interests, skills, competencies, and strengths evidenced in their unique personalities. They can maintain a multi-faceted self-identity. They may also become angry but often channel their anger constructively, by directing their energies toward effective management as well as toward advocacy. For this reason, effective therapeutic treatment focuses not just on the impact of the illness but also on helping clients identify and recognize their unique passions, interests, strengths, and qualities that are reflective of an evolving and complex personality.

The work of Patrick Corrigan, a major contributor in the study of stigma, emphasizes that when those who are meaningful to us can accept diagnosis, it becomes easier for us to accept it.[19] Their response helps buffer the impact of society's stigma. In effect, their empathy offers an antidote to internalizing stigma and supports self-compassion. When those who are meaningful to us communicate in word and deed their disgust, disappointment, and anxiety regarding a diagnosis, these reactions undermine the acceptance that is essential for the effective treatment and management of bipolar disorder. Unrealistic expectations, blaming, devaluing, demeaning, and negative communications create a conflictual interpersonal environment as well as foster internal tension and turmoil, as discussed previously (see chapter 5). It is for these reasons that the positive communications of family and loved ones is so effective in reducing the potential for relapse.

To Disclose or Not to Disclose

For those living with bipolar disorder, stigma demands attention in the context of relationships, engaged throughout the day. Deciding whether or not to disclose the illness at work, to family members, or to close friends is a major challenge that everyone with bipolar illness must somehow resolve. It is too easy for observers such as a caring, courageous partner, a well-meaning therapist, or a supportive and empathic friend to encourage such candor and support an individual's "outing." However, the reality is that people still maintain fear, ignorance, and shame with regard to this illness. Unfortunately, a study of case law regarding the Americans with Disabilities Act (ADA) and such disclosure, suggests that "the law offers little protection against anything but the most overt and blatant discrimination, and courts rarely grant employees with psychiatric disabilities the accommodations they seek through litigation."[20] Unfortunately, while there are laws in the workplace that protect individuals with disabilities, both physical and emotional, these are often misinterpreted or carefully evaded when it comes to really honoring them.

In the workplace itself, those who disclose may experience others' overt or subtle withdrawal. While many people view themselves as compassionate in theory, their own anxieties often interfere with their capacity to maintain connection to someone with emotional difficulties.

"In general, this is one area of concern where I find it difficult to be more directive in providing guidance," says Bernard Golden. "I help clients explore their reasons and attitudes regarding disclosing or not disclosing. I then help them explore the past history of their relationship, or the nature of their work setting, in an effort to help them make the best estimated guess of the possible consequences for revealing their difficulties."

The challenge of revealing emotional disorders has been compared to the issues one encounters when revealing sexual orientation.[21] Within both, there is a fear of rejection or ridicule if not outright abuse. Disclosure may proceed through phases, beginning with those with whom the individual feels the most secure bond and the greatest potential for acceptance. It may or may not progress to being fully open about the stigmatized sexuality or illness.

However, as Golden indicates, "This comparison falls short when we view emotional difficulties as a debilitating challenge that is often fully revealed by overt behavior in the public arena. The difficulties inherent in bipolar management may involve periods of inability to work or a need for some alteration in work schedule, a temporary decrease in work demands, and a required outside understanding of mood instability.

The issue of self-disclosure arises especially when reentering the workforce. This is especially true when emotional difficulties have led to an erratic work history. In part, this decision may be influenced by the need for special accommodation at work, as authorized by the ADA. Such accommodations can only be made when the employee has disclosed some aspect of his or her mental health condition.

In one study involving disclosure, thirty-two individuals recovering from significant symptoms of psychiatric disabilities were followed over a two-year period.[22] Some relied on vocational rehabilitation benefits. Key factors contributing to their decision to disclose had to do with their knowledge of the ADA, their experience with stigma and prejudice, and their beliefs about their job abilities. It is significant to note that although they occasionally experienced symptoms, most felt better at the time of the two-year follow-up interview.

Some reported favorable experiences regarding their disclosure. Others indicated a sense of being more closely watched and having their supervisor maintain greater expectations for them than for their coworkers. Those who did not disclose preferred to see themselves and have others also perceive them as "normal."[23]

Some chose to selectively disclose their conditions. One individual, for example, indicated she suffered with anxiety and that she was taking medications for it. She did not disclose a diagnosis. This allowed her to seek ADA protections but also helped to maintain her privacy. However, further inquiry is permitted by the ADA to determine the nature of the disability.

One individual disclosed only after he had been working in his position sufficiently to develop trust in others. The ADA allows disclosure to be made at the last possible minute prior to requesting accommodations.

The most frequently made requests for accommodations were for part-time work or a flexible schedule. Golden reports, "This is in keeping with my experience that many individuals with bipolar disorder may have difficulty in the morning, especially as they adjust to medications or when their symptoms are exacerbated." I have also found that being able to contact a significant individual or the therapist during the day for a brief supportive phone call is often sufficient to help address a particularly stressful moment in the day. An employee may similarly need to take time off to see a doctor both for medication monitoring as well as when responding to a flare-up of a condition.

Many people with bipolar disorder "self-accommodate," carefully identifying strategies to help them accommodate to the demands of the work environment so that coworkers and supervisors are not aware of their efforts. Grace, a patient counseled by Golden, reflects this experience. "I channel all of my energy to function on my job," she said. "During evenings and weekends I feel so emotionally drained that I withdraw and hibernate, having little energy or motivation for friends or for leisure activities."

The Family Medical Leave of Absence Act, in permitting less intrusive inquiry regarding the health issue, offers another option in responding to these types of demands.[24]

Clearly, advocacy and education need to be emphasized for employers, those dealing with emotional disorders, therapists, patient families, and others who play any role in helping someone with bipolar disorder deal with the very challenging task of negotiating employment and the decision regarding self-disclosure. And yet, with all of these challenges to disclosure, the capacity to be oneself without the need to carefully protect one's identity can foster a greater sense of internal harmony. As such it allows for energy to be more constructively channeled in directions that support the effective management of the disorder.

REDUCING STIGMA: PRACTICING CARE

The practices that work most significantly to dispel stigma fall into four specific categories: compassion, advocacy, recognition, and education, or CARE.

Compassion

Compassion is an essential ingredient in reducing stigma, whether practiced by a person who suffers from bipolar disorder, a friend or relative of someone who is afflicted, or merely an interested bystander. Compassion is not a goal but a way of being that is part of an ongoing process. When someone is sympathetic to the pain of another, it reduces stigma. When someone expresses sensitivity and respect toward self and others, it challenges fear. When a person is forgiving rather than holding out for perfection, it eliminates stigma.

Compassion demonstrates and fosters connection with oneself and others, challenges isolation, and promotes healing. It involves a fully conscious choice and commitment to this way of being. As an ongoing process, we need to choose compassion on the many occasions that require it. Those who live with people afflicted with bipolar disorder can choose compassion. In contrast, only minimal choice exists for those who are severely depressed or manic because during an acute episode too much is happening for an ill person to handle.

Much has been stated about the need for compassion by those who live with others who have bipolar disorder. However, the capacity to practice such compassion toward themselves is a major source of resilience for those who have bipolar disorder as well as any other major obstacle that one may face in dealing with life's challenges. The capacity to practice such compassion needs to be modeled by how others react. At the same time, a major goal of any psychotherapy treatment should also include skills to help foster such compassion. Since the development of "self-compassion" is so significant in living with bipolar disorder, it will be expanded upon in chapter 13.

Advocacy

Advocacy is a major activity in reducing stigma. Advocacy may involve the promotion of increased education, the funding of research, the support of legislation, or any of a variety of activities that both directly and indirectly reduce stigma. Through individual efforts or group involvement, advocacy both empowers and is an expression of empowerment. Advocacy helps alleviate stigma by influencing political, social, economic, and medical policies. Advocacy is most strongly epitomized by the work of organizations such as the Depressive and Bipolar Support Alliance (DBSA), formerly the National Depressive and Manic-Depressive Association (National DMDA). Through their active community involvement with politicians, doctors, lawyers, religious leaders, and educators, these groups help reduce stigma. Professional mental health organizations, such as the American Psychiatric Association and the American Psychological Association, also play an effective role in advocating for patients' rights and for the practices and policies that eliminate stigma. Each group provides and generates funding for education and continued research to improve the quality of treatment for bipolar disorder.

Since the first edition of this book there have been several major initiatives that reflect the ever-growing strength of such organizations to advocate against stigma.

StigmaBusters: StigmaBusters is a program established by the National Alliance on Mental Illness (NAMI) to encourage reporting of incidents that are hurtful representations of mental illness presented in the mass media, whether through television, radio, theater, movies, or print. StigmaBusters advocates strive to educate society about the realities of mental illness and actively contact and challenge these depictions in the media. They follow up by contacts with the source of the material and a dialogue is encouraged to address the stigma as well as to reduce the possibilities of such incidents occurring. This program relies on the participation of advocates who become active members of the program. Each month they receive the NAMI StigmaBusters Alert, which informs them about various incidents. They are also provided the name and e-mail or mailing address to educate those responsible for the offending depiction. For more information visit www .NAMI.org. Those who become aware of such incidents are encouraged to contact the newspaper editors, radio/TV station managers, and advertisers.

In Our Own Voice: Living with Mental Illness: Another program initiated by NAMI is In Our Own Voice (IOOV): Living with Mental Illness. This is a consumer recovery education program, named in 2002 (formerly Living with Schizophrenia), for family members, friends, professionals, students of all academic levels, and lay audiences. It involves a comprehensive presentation about mental illness that includes personal narratives, a video, and education. As of 2005 the program has been active in thirty-seven states.

Stigma Watch: The National Mental Health Association similarly tracks news and entertainment coverage of mental health issues for fairness and accuracy. Its line for reporting incidents is 1-800-969-NMHA. NMHA also works with the New York City–based National Stigma Clearinghouse to identify and respond to media depictions of mental illness that are stigmatizing.

Based on a review of studies assessing the effectiveness of various stigma prevention and reduction programs, the most effective approach in stigma prevention occurs when "each program targets a specific group and corresponding attitudes and behaviors for change."[25] In doing so, they address specific groups that make important decisions about the resources and opportunities available for individuals with mental illness. According to this perspective, once the groups are identified, they would then identify the best approach, whether it is education, contact with individuals with psychiatric illness, or some form of protest. While there is more effort than ever before regarding dealing with the impact of stigma, more concerted research appears necessary to determine the most effective programs.

Recognition

Recognition of mood disorders is needed before we can put a "face" on mental illness. It is no surprise that movements to combat stigma associated with illnesses such as bipolar disorder were initiated by those who live with the conditions. Celebrities and noncelebrities alike who publicly address their trauma or illness give bipolar disorder a face. Their courage in going public helps reduce fear and ignorance by reminding everyone of our shared humanity; we feel more connected. Whether we're informed about breast cancer by a well-known actress, bipolar disorder by a noted television news journalist, AIDS by an Olympic gold-medal swimmer, substance abuse by the wife of a U.S. president, or domestic violence by a relatively unknown man or woman in rural America, sharing helps everyone deal more effectively with life's many challenges. The courage of others enables those who are afflicted with bipolar disorder to feel less isolated in their own struggles.

Education

Education combats stigma and promotes compassion by presenting facts that help to eliminate fear and ignorance. Education is the primary goal of advocacy groups like NAMI and DBSA—as well as the American Psychiatric Association and the American Psychological Association, both of which provide books, pamphlets, and videotapes on all forms of mood disorders. Each year, the American Psychological Association schedules a day for screening depression at hundreds of sites nationwide. While adults have traditionally been the targeted audience, other programs are being developed to reach out to young people. In a pilot project conducted in a rural area of northern Mississippi, a high school presented a program through discussion, lecture, and contact with those afflicted to help reduce the stigma of mental illness and prevent adolescents from being ridiculed about the disorder. Several months later, when students who had participated in the program were reassessed about their attitudes toward mental illness, they consistently responded with more positive attitudes than those who had not taken part in the program.[26]

Recently, the American Psychological Association initiated the most comprehensive campaign ever to fight the stigma of mental illness among young people.[27] Launched in June 2000, and supported by Tipper Gore as an outgrowth of the White House Conference on Mental Health (1999), this five-year program seeks to transform the public's basic perceptions and attitudes about mental health. Joining with the American Psychological Association's executive director for practice, Dr. Russ Newman, Gore emphasized, "We cannot discriminate just because the illness happens to emanate from the brain, which is a part of the human body, a part of the human condition . . . but apparently we have to educate people about that."

> *Celebrities and noncelebrities alike who publicly address their trauma or illness give bipolar disorder a face. Their courage in going public helps reduce fear and ignorance by reminding everyone of our shared humanity.*

Partners in this effort include the offices of the U.S. Department of Health and Human Services, the U.S. Surgeon General's Office, the National Institute of Mental Health, the Office of the Assistant Secretary for Planning and Evaluation, and the Substance Abuse and Mental Health Services Administration. Specific goals include greater access to health care for people with mental disorders and decreased discrimination for them regarding employment and housing.

Based on a highly successful campaign against youth violence called

"Warning Signs," the American Psychological Association, in conjunction with MTV, has developed and begun airing sixty-second announcements that urge the audience, "Change your mind about mental health." Viewers are encouraged to call a toll-free number (800-964-0009) or log on to www.NoStigma.org in order to obtain the pamphlet "Change Your Mind About Mental Health: A Get-Help Guide for Teens and Young Adults." The brochure discusses depression, panic disorders, and eating disorders and presents guidelines for getting help.

Schools should be the starting point to help combat stigma. Even in the lower grades, teachers can inform children about mental illness at a level commensurate with their intellectual and emotional understanding. These issues need to be addressed, not treated as if they don't exist. Only by openly confronting the subject can we hope to broaden public awareness, understanding, and sensitivity so that society can embrace a higher level of compassion. Since fear of the unknown is the most frightening fear of all, education is our best tool for eliminating stigma.

The combined efforts of the four practices of CARE—compassion, advocacy, recognition, and education—offer powerful avenues for expression and empowerment while helping to dissipate stigma by transforming shame to compassion.

CHAPTER 9

Optimism, Hope, and Transcendence

What role does optimism play in the life of someone with bipolar illness? If optimism can influence the course of illness, what impact does it have leading up to, during, and following a severe depressive or manic episode? Are hope and optimism related? Can a person be inoculated with optimism, just as one receives a preventative vaccine? Is it possible to transcend bipolar illness or develop better coping skills to manage the disorder?

OPTIMISTS VERSUS PESSIMISTS

In recent years, optimism has become a topic of concern for those who study attribution theory, the area of inquiry that identifies factors people attribute to successes and failure. According to Martin Seligman, one of the more widely recognized writers on this topic, pessimists tend to believe bad events will last a long time, undermine everything they do, and are entirely their own fault. Optimists, on the other hand, view even defeat as a temporary setback and grant it a cause specific to the situation. Optimists tend to believe circumstances, bad luck, or other people caused the event to happen. Confronted by a bad situation, they perceive it as a challenge and try harder.[1]

The Art of Hope

Hope may be best described as a close cousin of optimism. Seligman views "the art of hope" as the ability to find temporary and specific causes for misfortune. He suggests that "temporary causes limit helplessness in time, and specific causes limit helplessness to the original situation."[2] Another definition of hope is "uncertain pleasure" in the anticipation that one's wishes will come to pass. Depression and mania both cause marked shifts in the ability to experience optimism and hope.

Transcendence

Transcendence refers to the ability to move beyond one's current situation. It reflects the concept that people are evolving, dynamic, and shifting beings rather than static creatures. We are not stagnant in our thinking, emotions, or behavior. This concept places a high value on self-awareness and the realistic observation of our own life as a moment in transition. Transcendence gives us the power to step outside ourselves and imagine a wide range of potentially different situations.

Transcendence is sometimes reflected by behaviors that span years, months, or mere moments in time. We can learn from an example related by Bernie Golden of an event that took place during a vacation in Hawaii. His group of six friends discovered an isolated beach. Within ten minutes after two of them had gone off swimming, the other four heard someone scream for help. At first they thought it was a joke, until they spotted one friend thrashing about in the water. Both swimmers had been caught in a riptide, but only one was in serious trouble. Bernie, a former lifeguard, dashed immediately into the water to rescue his panic-stricken friend. As he helped him to shore, his friend stared dazedly, and Bernie noticed the man's face turning blue. The friends on the beach assisted him as Bernie waded out again to help the second swimmer to shore. This swimmer was calmer, alternating between swimming parallel to the shore and lying on his back. He met Bernie halfway out and they returned to shore together.

> *Transcendence refers to the ability to move beyond one's current situation. It reflects the concept that people are evolving, dynamic, and shifting beings rather than static creatures.*

That evening, the others questioned the more relaxed swimmer about what he'd been thinking during the riptide mishap. He answered that he had instinctively instructed himself to remain calm. "Don't panic," he told himself. When in a riptide, one needs to swim with the tide instead of fighting it. He knew to stay parallel to the beach until he was able to move closer to shore.

Even when caught in a riptide, Bernie's friend had been able to focus visually and emotionally by imagining a passage back to shore. A major aspect of transcendence is abstract thinking: being able to project an image of oneself over time toward a positive shift from the current predicament rather than fixating on the plight and the fear and anxiety it provokes. Transcendence is the ability to orient oneself beyond the immediate limits of given time and space, to think in terms of "the possible." According to Rollo May, the author of *Existence,* it is this capacity to imagine and look beyond the current situation that we refer to as the basis of human freedom.[3]

A unique characteristic of the human brain is the ability to see a vast range of possibilities in any situation, on a level consistent with our self-awareness and imaginative capacity.[4]

OPPOSITE POLES: DEPRESSION AND MANIA

Anyone who has experienced or observed someone experiencing severe depression or mania knows that during this intense phase objective self-awareness is radically diminished. During more severe episodes of depression, a person is unable to see possibilities, while during severe mania they are consumed by them. Clearly, the *capacity* for self-awareness and self-reflection is present before, after, or during certain periods of bipolar illness. It follows that optimism, hope, and transcendence are possible, too. They become more relevant when we accept this view of mood disorders and can identify their presence or absence during the various stages of mood transition. This exploration leads to increased understanding and management of both the depressive and manic experiences.

We might characterize the alternate states of bipolar illness as representing two opposite ends of a continuum. While the manic state, in its most severe form, encompasses feelings of inflated self-esteem with heightened grandiosity and delusion, an extreme depressive experience is burdened by

> *During the more severe episodes of depression, a person is unable to see possibilities, while during severe mania they are consumed by them.*

an overriding sense of inadequacy. Extreme mania is characterized by the experience of unlimited possibilities and potential with absolute disregard for danger or social structure. Depression, in its most severe form, is characterized by negative tunnel vision. Mania focuses on movement toward a future that is optimistic and without bounds; severe depression reflects emotional entombment of the past with no perceived potential for change.

During severe depression, we experience only pessimism—the absence of hope and constriction by negative thoughts that don't allow for self-awareness or objective reflection on experience. In sharp contrast, during severe mania, we experience unrealistic optimism and undaunted hope but at the same time are so distracted that the capacity for self-awareness and objective reflection barely exists.

> *While bipolar disorder is often conceptualized as on a linear continuum, that image does not fully reflect the illness. Although manic and depressive symptom patterns clearly have a polar quality, the overlapping, transitional, and fluctuating aspects are enormously important in describing and understanding the illness as a whole.*

While bipolar disorder is often conceptualized on a linear continuum, that image does not fully reflect the illness. As Kay Jamison has observed, although manic and depressive symptom patterns clearly have a polar quality, the overlapping, transitional, and fluctuating aspects are enormously important in describing and understanding the illness as a whole.[5]

Depression

In *Touched with Fire*, Kay Jamison recounted her personal experience with bipolar illness, which began in high school with a manic period that spanned several months, followed by severe depression. Here she describes that depression: "The bottom began to fall out of my life and mind. My thinking . . . was torturous. Nothing made sense . . . all of a sudden my mind had turned against me. . . . It was incapable of concentrated thought and turned time and again to the subject of death; I was going to die, what difference did it make?"[6]

During this period of despair, Jamison lacked optimism or any sense of hope. She focused on death, decay, and the hopelessness she perceived all around her. She emphasized key aspects of depression, including helplessness and hopelessness, and the perceived inability to change her condition. Perhaps most debilitating, she despaired that her future held no promise of change whatsoever. While not directly articulated, her thoughts suggested an overall feeling of inadequacy. Though unvoiced, many people in Jamison's severely depressed state also experience intense shame.

In the midst of this despair, what was the quality of her self-awareness, her capacity for self-reflection, and her potential for transcendence? Her detailed description of her subjective experience itself is evidence of her capacity for self-awareness during and after the experience. Significantly absent during the episode was the capacity to envision herself as having a different subjective experience, one with greater openness, optimism, and hope. Vividly, she described the paralysis of not being able to imagine an alternative experience that is the hallmark of intense depression.

In its most severe forms, depression not only involves constricted thinking and emotions but may also be reflected in the person's physical demeanor through muscular rigidity, slowness in movement, and diminished fluidity in facial expression.

While still characterized by pessimism and lack of hope, these qualities are less intense at a less severe level of depression, and there is often a greater range of potential for realistic observations. Jamison explored this issue in her comprehensive study of manic-depressive illness and temperament. As mentioned previously, Jamison found considerable data suggesting a profound correlation between bipolar disorder and creativity, with the highest creativity occurring during the early, or less severe, episodes of mania. Many of her subjects described the ability to respond creatively and be actively productive during periods of less intense depression.

According to studies presented by Seligman, mildly pessimistic individuals also appear more realistic than those on the optimistic end of the spectrum. They are able to realistically assess the potential for negative events to occur. This view is further supported by Shelly Taylor, the author of *Positive Illusions*. While Taylor is controversial in her view that positive mental health is in fact fostered by positive self-illusions, she also suggests that those who fall into the category of "mild depressive" can be more realistic in overall perceptions.[7]

While experiencing mild depression, people are better equipped for self-awareness and transcendence. Not bound by positive illusions, they are able to attend to the full range of positive and negative realities of life. At the same time, low-level depression still leaves them with energy that may be channeled through creative expression Artistry—writing, painting, or composing music—reflects a capacity to translate subjective experience into something different. This clearly involves a forward momentum and active engagement, even if the creative work focuses on pessimism and lack of hope. Artists are able to disengage from the moment long enough to reflect on their experience and translate it into a new form of expression. Their art may be motivated by personal catharsis or the wish to connect with others.

Mild Mania

Further exploration of optimism, hope, and transcendence, and their relationship to bipolar disorder, is inescapable when we delve more deeply into the mild level of mania. Most of us can readily identify with the experiences of this level of mania. However, most people have these experiences only occasionally, whereas for those prone to low-level mania, these episodes represent a more constant, pervasive state.

Mild mania (hypomania) is marked by a constellation of positive thinking and emotions, and can occur at any time, whether the person is engaged in work or leisure. Nancy describes her experience of this state as follows: "At times I've encountered this experience when actively involved in writing, or thinking about writing. Then I am immersed in my thinking, my thoughts flowing one into another, choosing one path to follow, ignoring another, but with a momentum that feels almost self-propelled. The ideas flow with minimal hesitation and inhibition, while I print my thoughts with a sense of visceral, emotional, and intellectual excitement. It is with a sense of abandon and sheer joy that I select words to articulate my beliefs, attitudes, and feelings. Momentum increases and words flow easily. During these moments of heightened creativity, I experience little self-doubt and, as the momentum escalates, little self-consciousness. I might literally lose awareness of my surroundings because I'm so totally immersed in work; all sense of time is lost. This experience of complete freedom to be myself enables me to feel 'in control.' Both during and after this time, I may experience an elevated sense of self-esteem because my writing clearly matches and reflects externally my internal experience. Being fully engaged in the here and now with no sense of past or future, the intense joy of the moment is greatly amplified. While engaged, several hours may slip away without my even realizing that I have forgotten to eat!

"Intense involvement may interfere with patterns of sleep. When I'm engrossed in self-expression, I find it difficult to disengage long enough to get to bed at a 'respectable' hour. In fact, I don't mind continuing the process in my head for hours on end because this heightened sense of clarity furthers my emotional high, excitement with life, sense of engagement, and overall feeling of self-worth. I feel driven and experience the strongest sense of optimism and hope at these times."

> *Most of us can readily identify with the experiences of this level of mania. However, most people have these experiences only occasionally, whereas for those prone to low-level mania, these episodes represent a more constant, pervasive state.*

Intensely pleasurable experiences like Nancy's may fill entire days for those with low-level mania. Kay Jamison also described the positive aspect of her early manic episodes: "My manias, at least in their early and mild forms, were absolutely intoxicating states that gave rise to great personal pleasure, an incomparable flow of thoughts, and a ceaseless energy that allowed the translation of new ideas into papers and projects."[8]

During this phase, hope and optimism abound and are influenced by thinking that is for the most part realistic, but may occasionally reflect faulty, unsound reasoning. A decrease in self-consciousness and self-awareness occurs as the person becomes totally engaged in thinking about and enjoying the intense pleasure of the activity. Thus transcendence is part of this experience, reflected in the immersion of self into creative pursuits.

Optimal Experience: In the Flow

What has been described, up to this point, is part of the constellation of experiences of someone who lives with low-level manic intensity. Given the list of "symptoms," many people might express eagerness for similar experiences in their own lives.

In recent years, researchers, while not necessarily focusing on manic depression, have tried to examine what factors contribute to enhancing the general quality of life. Mihaly Csikszentmihalyi, a leader in this field and the author of *Flow: The Psychology of Optimal Experience,* studied the psychology of optimal experience and identified its components. His specific findings and conclusions are based on a study of hundreds of individual responses. The participants, who came from different economic levels, different cultures, and had different career paths and interests, were asked to describe optimal experience—those moments of deepest joy.

> *The conditions defined as necessary components for optimal experience seem to parallel certain qualitative aspects of the core experience of low-level mania.*

Csikszentmihalyi refers to the optimal experience as "flow": "The state in which people are so involved in an activity that nothing else seems to matter; the experience itself is so enjoyable that people will do it even at great cost, for the sheer sake of doing it; it is something that we make happen, a moment when a person's body or mind is stretched to its limits in a voluntary effort to accomplish something difficult and worthwhile."[9]

The conditions Csikszentmihalyi defined as necessary components for optimal experience seem to parallel certain qualitative aspects of the core experiences with low-level mania:

- A task that can be completed
- Full concentration on the task at hand
- A clear set of goals
- Immediate feedback
- Acting with a deep, effortless involvement that removes from awareness the worries and frustrations of everyday life
- An enjoyable experience that allows one to exercise a sense of control over one's actions
- A concern for self disappears, yet paradoxically the sense of self emerges stronger after the flow experience is over
- An altered sense of duration of time; hours pass by in minutes, and minutes can seem to stretch into hours

As Csikszentmihalyi suggested, "The combination of all these elements cause a sense of deep enjoyment that is so rewarding people feel that expending a great deal of energy is worthwhile simply to be able to feel it."[10]

Such moments of optimal experience encountered while working, strolling through a park, enjoying a good book, engaged in an interesting discussion, or participating in an enjoyable pastime like scuba diving, swimming, or dancing involve deeply felt positive experiences in which one feels completely immersed in the activity of the moment. Much of the experience of low-level mania appears to encompass such optimal experience. Whether we're talking about emotional reactions, thoughts, actions, or visceral reactions, people with low-level mania report experiences that involve aspects of flow.

Kay Jamison's research into the lives of artists and writers diagnosed as manic is relevant to flow and low-level mania. In a review of changes experienced by these artists and writers, she discovered patterns of behavior during periods of intense creativity that were strikingly similar to the major components of flow.

The Downside of Low-Level Mania

If low-level mania were characterized only by positive experiences, there would be no need for a diagnosis. Hope and optimism flourish and provide the impetus for envisioning a wide spectrum of possibilities in daily life. Hypomania includes more than the positive qualities that foster optimal experience, however. It can also involve irritability, distractibility, inflated self-esteem, and a decreased need for sleep (perhaps a maximum of three hours or less). These qualities can interfere with concentration during flow, reduce one's capacity to disengage from the flow experience, and may involve unrealistically positive judgment of the experiences. Similarly, a person may become excessively involved in pleasurable pursuit; even during periods of low-level mania this has a high potential for painful consequences, such as neglecting one's responsibilities or the need for sleep.

> *If low-level mania were characterized only by positive experiences, there would be no need for a diagnosis. It includes more than the positive qualities that foster optimal experience, however.*

Ellen, twenty-two years old, was diagnosed as hypomanic. When Bernard Golden first met her, she appeared extremely light and energized in both her tone of voice and in her movements. Ellen wore her hair in a free-flowing style, which she rapidly and repeatedly brushed away from the side of her face. Her makeup was noticeably bright; though not garish, it overly accentuated her cheekbones and intense eyes. Ellen's animated speech was somewhat pressured as she spoke about her career as an executive secretary and her delight in finally deciding to return to school to pursue a graduate degree in English. She chatted nonstop about her love for poetry, plays, and fiction and recited passages from her favorite works. Ellen appeared affable and personable, was passionate about life, and showed vitality, hope, and optimism.

As the symptoms of mania increase in intensity, the overall experience can move in a more negative direction. Optimism and hope continue strong but are increasingly influenced by less rational thinking.

Kay Jamison wrote of a similar positive state, "Mood in hypomania is usually ebullient, self-confident and often transcendent, but it almost always exists with an irritable underpinning, fluctuating and volatile. I raced about like a crazed weasel, bubbling with plans and enthusiasms, immersed in sports, staying up all night, night after night, out with friends, reading everything that was not nailed down, filling manuscript books with poems and fragments of plays, making expansive, completely unrealistic plans for my future. The world was filled with pleasure and promise; I felt great. Not just great. I felt really great. I felt I could do anything, that no task was too difficult. My mind seemed clear, fabulously focused, and able to make intuitive mathematical leaps that had up to that point entirely eluded me."[11]

In Ellen's case, it was only after several meetings with Golden that she discussed the difficulties she was experiencing. Her troubles were quickness to become irritated, especially when experiencing blocks to her self-expression; escalating impulsiveness; and increasingly unrealistic self-expectations regarding time commitment and the balance of her involvement with her work life, leisure activities, and friends.

As the symptoms of mania increase in intensity, the overall experience can move in a more negative direction. Optimism and hope continue strong but are increasingly influenced by less rational thinking. The person can envision various possibilities and opportunities throughout the day, and are less based in rationality. Self-awareness and the ability to observe patterns in one's thinking, emotions, or actions diminishes as mania increases.

Extreme Mania

In describing her own experience, Jamison sums up the more intense period of a manic episode: "Almost everything was done to excess; instead of buying one Beethoven symphony, I would buy nine; instead of enrolling in five classes, I would enroll for seven; instead of buying two tickets for a concert I would buy eight or ten. I was working 20 to 30 hours a week in order to pay my way through college, and there was not a margin at all for the expenses I ran up during these times of high enthusiasm. Unfortunately, the pink overdraft notices from my bank always seemed to arrive when I was in the throes of the depressions that inevitably followed my weeks of exaltation."[12]

As mentioned previously, extreme mania encompasses inflated self-esteem with extreme grandiosity and delusion, and the experience of unlimited possibilities and potential with disregard for any real danger or social structure. It focuses on movement toward a future that is unrealistically optimistic and without bounds.

It was this extreme optimism and distorted thinking that propelled Ellen, during one of her most severe attacks of mania, to saunter boldly into the director of admissions office for a graduate program. There, she demanded immediate acceptance into the master's program. She was determined to be admitted despite being three courses short of completing her undergraduate degree. Ellen had never engaged in any formal application process and in fact had never spoken to, nor made an appointment with, the director of the program. She was finally admitted to the hospital following this bizarre episode and related altercations with campus security.

It is a major challenge in manic illness to monitor and modulate the positive attributes and experiences before they escalate and shift toward a destructive outcome. It is the lure of flowlike experiences that takes hold at the onset of a manic episode and maintains a stranglehold against seeking medication, much less continued compliance.

THE ROLE OF OPTIMISM, HOPE, AND TRANSCENDENCE IN TREATMENT

In Martin Seligman's view, a healthy and rewarding life is greatly influenced by the individual level of optimism versus pessimism. Similarly, he focuses on how a person's "explanatory style" may influence his or her placement on the optimism–pessimism scale. According to Seligman, the explanatory style is the manner in which you habitually explain to yourself why events happen.[13] It is that inner voice that offers meaning, makes appraisals, and explains events. As mentioned in an earlier chapter, this internal voice can be so inner and so habitual that we are unaware of being engaged in self-dialogue.

To illustrate the explanatory styles of pessimism and optimism, let's consider the example of a screenwriter who fails at his first attempt to sell a script to a movie company. Intense pessimism is reflected in an explanatory style that concludes that he will never sell the script, that he is most likely to fail at other endeavors, and that his failure is based on poor writing skills or, even worse, on overall inadequacy. An optimistic explanatory style, on the other hand, views the rejection as a single event, without assuming that his other projects are heading for a similar fate. The writer looks for other explanations of rejection, such as lack of budget, timing, and insufficient interest in the subject. He weighs all factors equally, and his focus is outward rather than thinking the fault lies with him.

Optimists are more realistic about externalizing the cause of negative events. The word *realistic* needs emphasizing, as Seligman indicates, because during depressive episodes people frequently exaggerate their personal responsibility for a negative event. Likewise, falsely externalizing the causes is an escape from responsibility. Seligman suggests that some degree of pessimism is healthy, especially when based on a good "reality check." This implies assessing the realities of a situation before taking an action, or during it.

Our behavior is largely the result of modeling and internalizing the styles of people with whom we shared significant relationships during our formative years. For example, a parent may instruct a six-year-old to think optimistically by helping the child understand that a writing mistake is a specific error rather than a sign of the child's general inclination to make mistakes continuously.

Seligman's views have many implications for bipolar illness as he has developed programs based on his theories to help instill optimism and treat various forms of depression. His methods help people recognize and monitor the underlying thoughts that foster an optimistic or pessimistic explanatory style. Once

> *People can reduce catastrophizing by identifying specific and temporary causes in contrast to their global and pervasive explanations for negative events.*

they recognize these underlying thoughts, the program helps them acknowledge the realistic optimistic thoughts and challenge the pessimistic one with more accurate and realistic explanations. For example, people can reduce catastrophizing by identifying specific and temporary causes in contrast to their global and pervasive explanations for negative events. Similarly, they can challenge their quickness to overvalue their contribution to negative events by identifying a variety of realistic external explanations for what caused the event.

Cognitive behavioral psychotherapy (see chapter 5) incorporates Seligman's ideas about explanatory style. As with other therapies, more severe forms of depression, especially when connected to manic-depressive illness, require drug therapy before an individual can benefit from his approach to optimism.

Hope, as discussed earlier, involves identifying temporary and specific causes for misfortune. This capacity is one of the major ingredients in an optimistic explanatory style.

Understanding explanatory style can provide new insight into the experience of transcendence as it applies to bipolar illness. People who are severely depressed or manic are unable to experience basic transcendence because they have lost the ability to envision realistic possibilities for themselves. But how do people with bipolar disorder explain or make sense of the illness when they are only slightly depressed or manic (before and after an episode)? How does the explanatory style surrounding the condition impact the illness?

If we maintain a pessimistic explanatory style about our bipolar illness, this "explanation" can foster depression about the depression. We will feel more depressed, less hopeful, and less optimistic if we envision a permanent state of mania or depression, overgeneralize all negative aspects of life as related to the illness or core being, or personalize the cause of the illness (as something we have control over or contribute to). We are then constricted in our sense of potential and more likely to label ourselves manic depressive (as distinguished from a person with the illness). This difference, though subtle, has tremendous implications for the way we view our illness and the manner in which we seek and follow an appropriate course of treatment.

When the larger society communicates negative messages about illness, afflicted individuals are bound to internalize and adopt this thinking as their own. They learn to accept a pessimistic explanation for mental illness, which, in turn, diminishes their capacity to transcend the effect of the illness.

Seligman's concepts regarding depression also help to provide insight into the social impact on bipolar illness. The afflicted, and those with whom they have significant relationships, are all part of a larger culture that influences explanatory style. Our society sends very clear messages regarding mental illness, particularly bipolar disorder. It's been a relatively short time since people have begun to view mental disorders more realistically and compassionately. It's been an even shorter period since the public first began to recognize bipolar disorder as a condition of intense mood cycles that can be regulated with medication and are time limited, not permanent.

When the larger society communicates negative messages about illness, afflicted individuals are bound to internalize and adopt this thinking as their own. They learn to accept a pessimistic explanation for mental illness, which, in turn, diminishes their capacity to transcend the effect of the illness.

It is a lifelong challenge for those who live with bipolar illness—an ongoing process of developing and maintaining optimism and hope in the face of all the internal and external factors that could convince them otherwise.

ENHANCING OUR CAPACITY FOR TRANSCENDENCE

Bipolar disorder involves a constant struggle to remain alert to the signs that this illness, by its very nature, is constantly working to undermine accurate self-judgment. Vigilance in developing an explanatory style that favors realistic optimism and hope is essential. Patients must rethink how they explain events and especially the illness itself. In recent years, new strategies have been identified to help develop this vigilance and to increase the capacity for meaningful transcendence.

Researchers have devoted much attention to finding new ways of managing emotions, since our emotions impact our behavior and attitudes. Psychologist and author Daniel Goleman has written extensively about the concept of "emotional intelligence." This form of intelligence refers to our abilities to motivate ourselves by persisting in the face of frustrations, to control our impulses and delay gratification, to regulate our moods, to empathize and to hope. Goleman notes, "When emotions are too muted, they create dullness and distance; when out of control, too extreme and persistent, they become pathological, as in immobilizing depression, overwhelming anxiety, raging anger, manic agitation."[14]

According to Goleman, emotional intelligence is a "meta-ability," a constellation of abilities that allows us to oversee, monitor, make use of, create balance with, marshal, and integrate our emotions. A weakened capacity to think realistically and implement emotional intelligence during depression leaves us unable to move forward.

While Goleman has identified thirteen groups of abilities that compose emotional intelligence, four are most relevant for coping with bipolar illness. These are described below.

Self-Awareness: Self-awareness involves the ability to reflect on ourselves and recognize our own feelings, vocabulary for labeling those feelings, and a full grasp of the relationships between thoughts, feelings, and reactions. Self-awareness is a key issue for anyone with mood disorders. The ability to recognize and differentiate emotions, as well as the intensity of each emotion, allows us to identify markers on the path of escalating mania or spiraling depression. Similarly, self-awareness focuses

> *A weakened capacity to think realistically and implement emotional intelligence during depression leaves us unable to move forward.*

differentiating thoughts from feelings and recognizing the interaction between and among them. This type of awareness does not require obsessive, paralyzing, self-conscious self-absorption. It can be fostered by the use of daily journaling, as often suggested in treatment and in self-help books. External feedback, in the context of psychotherapy or support groups, is essential to identify patterns of thinking and associated emotions more clearly.

Personal Decision Making: Personal decision making includes the abilities to explore your actions, recognize and anticipate their consequences, and be aware when emotions or thoughts serve as their basis. Personal decision making pushes the pause button on the forward movement action, allowing for self-reflection, clarification of actions and potential outcomes, determining whether thoughts or emotions are ruling the action, and recognizing what is in your best interest.

Insight: Insight includes the ability to identify patterns in your thoughts, emotions, and actions and to recognize patterns in others. Insight into your own emotions, thoughts, and actions makes you more sensitive to the complexity of their interplay in the actions of others.

Managing Feelings: Identification of self-critical automatic thoughts and complex interaction of emotions (e.g., anger is so often a secondary emotion to feeling hurt, devalued, or rejected) enables us to manage negative emotions such as fear, anxiety, anger, and sadness. This control increases your tolerance for frustration. Recognizing, identifying, and challenging negative self-dialogue greatly contributes to the ability to manage feelings.

We live in a world that is highly complex and continually changing, a society in which we experience constant challenge to learn new skills. It is important in this environment to regard emotional growth and development as an ongoing process—it takes time, patience, and commitment. Likewise, it is an ongoing process to develop one's emotional intelligence.

Recognizing, identifying, and challenging negative self-dialogue greatly contributes to the ability to manage feelings.

By describing the experience of bipolar illness, we have more clearly identified the challenges that must be addressed in managing and coping with this illness. In addition to identifying the challenges faced by people with bipolar disorder, this analysis offers insight into the form and timing of treatment. These concerns can best be addressed by viewing a summary of our exploration of the ebb and flow of optimism, hope, and transcendence associated with bipolar illness.

As reflected in table 9.1, severe depression brings with it intense pessimism, hopelessness, and diminished ability to step outside of experience and objectively observe the situation. This reduced capacity to observe our

TABLE 9.1. THE EBB AND FLOW OF OPTIMISM, HOPE, AND TRANSCENDENCE IN BIPOLAR ILLNESS

	SEVERE DEPRESSION	MILD DEPRESSION	STABLE PHASE	MILD MANIA	SEVERE MANIA
Optimism–Pessimism	Extremely pessimistic	Pessimistic	Typical for person	Highly optimistic	Unrealistically optimistic
Hope	Hopeless	Some	Typical for person	Hopeful	Unrealistically hopeful
Openness to transcendence	Closed	Somewhat	Typical for person	Extreme	Unrealistic in extreme
Realistic thinking	Impaired	Increased	Typical for person	Mixed	Impaired
Objective self-reflection	Impaired	Increased	Typical for person	Mixed	Impaired

own thinking and emotions interferes with the ability to be optimistic, experience hope, and envision transcendence beyond the current situation. During this phase, those with bipolar illness are very much in need of external support and involvement.

With severe depression, treatment focuses predominantly on strengthening and restorative approaches rather than proactive approaches. Most severe, paralyzing forms of depression require medical attention. Medication therapy and maximized contact with others, especially those who can be hopeful, empathic, and realistic, provide needed support during this phase. Those with severe depression can benefit from psychotherapy that focuses on providing support and education rather than learning completely new skills for managing emotions and thinking.

The primary focus of treatment during this phase is to prevent symptoms from worsening and promote a slight increase in the patient's capacity for optimism, hope, and transcendence. Another major focus should be on helping the person establish and maintain emotional connections, with loved ones as well as with others who have had similar experiences with depression. The severely depressed patient is faced with concerns about trust, issues about illness, and accepting help in general. So while he or

> *This reduced capacity to observe our own thinking and emotions interferes with the ability to be optimistic, experience hope, and envision transcendence beyond the current situation.*

she may be least open to socialize, even with others who have had similar experiences and can provide support, it is at this time that such support is most necessary.

Similarly helpful are strategies that help reduce constriction in thinking. This is facilitated by helping the afflicted to revisit memories of times when they experienced more optimism, hope, and transcendence. While severely depressed, they may not be receptive to new perceptive strategies, but should be encouraged to rely on realistic self-talk that has previously been employed to challenge pessimistic, devaluing, and negative thoughts. Reviewing journals written at a time when they experienced feeling optimism, hope, and transcendence can help challenge the severe depressive thinking of this phase. It is important to remember, however, that depression drains energy and concentration, so even these strategies may not be consistently well received.

During mild depression, people have an increased capacity for self-awareness and some ability to reflect on thoughts and emotions and the patterns they form in influencing the current life experience. In this phase, they can engage in more strengthening and restorative approaches and constructively channel their energy to manage the depression.

Mildly depressed individuals may be more open to participation in individual or group psychotherapy or in self-help groups. They are often willing to learn strategies for fostering constructive optimistic thinking, skills for challenging mental distortions as practiced in cognitive therapy, and emotional skills in the context of therapy. Although the depression is less severe, the afflicted still very much need the support of others, especially as such assistance offers sound reality checks to their negative views of themselves and life in general. In fact, they may be most open to treatment during this phase because they are motivated to alleviate the discomfort of the depression.

During the stable phase, people experience optimism, hope, and transcendence in ways that are typical for their particular personality and least influenced by the deteriorating impact of extreme depression or mania. During this period, they can learn strategies of coping with their illness that are proactive rather than reactive and restorative in focus. It is during mild depression, the stable phase, and mild mania that people are most available to channel their energies and concentration for developing skills of coping. As depression is alleviated, as a greater sense of well-being emerges, or as mild mania intensifies, motivation for treatment may begin to diminish.

The stable phase offers the inflicted an ideal opportunity to step back and observe their illness. They are encouraged to develop new ways of thinking that become a natural part of their repertoire, so they can respond more favorably to future life challenges that might otherwise foster depression or mania. Whether keeping journals, maintaining logs of their experience, making use of bibliotherapy (incorporating the use of self-help books in treatment), or therapy techniques focused on pausing to self-reflect, this is a time for increasing the skills of self-monitoring thoughts, emotions, and behavior.

As people become more strongly influenced by mania, the increase of energy, optimism, and experiences that approach the flow experience can decrease the motivation to take time to reflect and learn new skills.

During severe mania, people are least motivated to make use of treatment and least able to recognize the need for it. Unfortunately, conflicts with others, including the law, during this period often lead to a treatment referral.

It should be emphasized that major change can still occur during the extreme phases of both mania and depression. Specifically, the individual may acknowledge the need for medication and other treatment. It is during the other phases, however, that the most significant changes take place in terms of learning how to understand and manage bipolar illness.

> *As depression is alleviated, as a greater sense of well-being emerges, or as mild mania intensifies, motivation for treatment may begin to diminish.*

We have explored how optimism, hope, and transcendence impact and are impacted by bipolar disorder. Complete management of bipolar disorder requires transcendence—the collaboration of emotion and intellect—in order to move forward. We need to be able to shift our thinking beyond a knee-jerk response and regulate our emotions. This requires close monitoring. To the degree that we can learn to anticipate and recognize the subtle and not-so-subtle signs of shifting moods, and to the degree that we can learn new skills to modulate these moods, it is possible to constructively channel our energies toward a life that yields greater joy, fulfillment, and productivity.

Certainly drug therapy is essential to help manage severe depression and mania. However, the works of Csikszentmihalyi, Seligman, and Goleman provide specific ways of observing our emotions that can also help. This is not passive observation of uncontrollable prevailing moods and thoughts but rather an active engagement in feeling and living. With these abilities, we can directly observe and alter our emotional life in a positive way. These are the essential ingredients for optimism, hope, and transcendence; for coping with emotional trauma; and for the management of manic depression.

The advent of new medications and the increased awareness of the psychological and emotional needs of the afflicted with bipolar disorder (and those who live with them) make it possible for them to learn to value themselves, maintain rich lives, and develop new strategies to reduce the negative and devastating effects of their illness.

CHAPTER 10

The Spirit of Self-Help

I have suffered, but I know that without the suffering, the growth I have achieved would have been impossible.

—VIKTOR E. FRANKL

If Viktor Frankl could survive a Nazi concentration camp and rise above the horror of it all, those of us with bipolar disorder ought to be able to find ways of managing our situation. But where do we find a safe haven? Frankl found peace at Auschwitz when he looked up and saw the clear blue sky. Something in him allowed him to open to beauty despite surroundings of war and hate. At that moment, Frankl was no longer a prisoner; his body was held captive, but his soul remained free.

Our biological needs must be met to maintain good physical and mental health, but a true and lasting happiness also rests on our ability to reach beyond the basics. Frankl was stripped of everything except life itself, but he credited his survival to persistent and undying hope. "Only those who were oriented toward the future, toward a goal in the future, toward a meaning to fulfill in the future, were likely to survive," said Frankl.[1]

Rather than search for the meaning in life, those of us with bipolar disorder must first acknowledge that our primary goal should be to improve our quality of life. Since our very survival depends on our well-being, to compromise health jeopardizes life. The basic ingredients of life are sleep, food, love, sex, and work. All of them must be addressed. First, we must force ourselves to get adequate rest. During periods of low mania it is easy to go for long periods of time with minimum sleep and function on adrenaline alone. But lack of sleep affects our body's immune system, making us more vulnerable to disease. Exercise can help, too, and furthermore it builds healthy bodies and helps keep us "balanced" by diffusing excess energy and warding off bouts of the blues. Diminished appetite and compulsive eating habits are also traits of manic depression, and a concerted effort must be made to concentrate on a healthy diet. Maintaining relationships with friends and family is also essential and meets our most basic need of all: to love and be loved. Romantically, paying close attention to the needs of a partner brings people closer together and cultivates harmony and generosity in relationships. Money, perhaps the least important spiritually, still greatly affects mood and anxiety. Here, if possible, sustainability should be the goal. Happiness cannot be purchased, and nothing compares with peace of mind.

When taking a proactive approach to bipolar illness by monitoring health, in these areas, we can focus on pursuing meaningful goals.

SETTING A GOAL

We can start by setting a realistic goal, a unifying purpose for the things we do in our everyday lives. A realistic goal means one you can reach. If your goal is unrealistically high, you might feel threatened, insecure, or unqualified to achieve it. If you underchallenge yourself, the goal won't serve its purpose of providing meaning and orienting you to the future.

Mini-goals are the stepping-stones that lead you to your final target. Setting mini-goals allows you to experience success and to manage frustration while in pursuit of your main objective. If you succeed in meeting all necessary requirements to accomplish the final goal, then you will have gained the necessary tools and confidence to reach even further.

With every passing decade our society becomes more advanced technologically. To survive, and thrive, in such a fast-moving culture we must continue to grow as individuals. Rather than cling to old patterns of behavior, we can find untold fulfillment and joy by adapting and learning fresh skills. However, those of us who live with bipolar disorder also have the additional burden of maintaining emotional balance while pursuing our goals. The following list will provide guidance:

1. Establish your basic needs. As individuals, we vary greatly in our basic needs and in our ability to achieve them. For some, mere survival is paramount and overrides everything else, which by comparison represents unaffordable luxury. Basic survival is dependent on having a roof over our heads, food, clothing, and companionship. To succeed in life, we must monitor our health. When our bodies are sleep deprived or lack proper nutrition, the result can be eyestrain, headaches, and general malaise and fatigue.

2. Expand your horizon. After the basics of food and shelter have been met, you can begin to expand your horizon by turning your attention and energy to other aspects of life. An individual who has achieved personal security has the ability to be more open and available to family, friends, and the community. For some, life becomes focused around job concerns, educating children, and doing their best to provide for their family's happiness and well-being. Each of us is challenged in different ways, but our best moments often occur when our mind or body is stretched to the limits. Enjoyment and fulfillment can be attained by forward movement, a sense of novelty and accomplishment that may have seemed unimaginable before. Some experiences may not be pleasurable at the moment, but appreciation comes later when we look back. The result of such encounters lead to personal growth.

3. Achieve a healthy and safe interdependence. Some people develop strength and self-confidence by clinging first to family for security, then branching out independently. Some women, for example, become more independent after marriage because of the security they derive from the relationship with their spouse. A healthy and safe interdependence allows both spouses to become more independent.

Since we are social creatures by our very nature, bonding and accepting intimacy plays an integral role in our sense of satisfaction with life. Intimacy involves feeling close, open, honest, and trusting with another human being. The ideal relationship becomes a mutually bonding one, connecting our life with others—parent, teacher, sibling, spouse, lover, or friend—in mutually beneficial ways. In a healthy relationship, no one dominates over the wishes of another, yielding mutual respect, trust, and love in the partnership.

4. Set limits. People who have achieved a high level of independence have learned to prioritize goals and set limits. People who fail to set limits and are controlled by success are vulnerable to obsession.

5. Watch out for obsession. In working to meet the goals we have set, those of us with bipolar disorder need to be wary of falling prey to obsession, a symptom of bipolar illness. Obsessiveness can have both positive and negative outcomes. Spending too much time being extremely organized and focused certainly speeds the mastery of skills in any new area of growth; however, when practiced in excess, success may come at the cost of intimacy or full participation in family life. Too frequently, the end result is a wrecked marriage and estranged children. People in this situation may be left wondering if their success was worth it.

If your goal is so exciting that you become fixated on it, the price you pay to attain that goal may be too high. People in a state of fixation can focus nearly all of their attention and energy on themselves. Others become absorbed in a compelling project or cause to the exclusion of relationships with family and friends (self-indulgence and inattentiveness to others are traits of mania/hypomania). Anyone can fall victim to this trap when limits have not been set. This is what happened to Nancy.

"When I first dove in as a Soviet Jewry activist, I had no special skills or training for this job, other than the desire to be involved and to help," said Nancy. "I enjoyed the camaraderie of belonging to a group, I found a mentor, and little by little I learned. Our organization had a goal and collectively we were determined to accomplish our mission. Not until later did my preoccupation with Yuri become so intense that I became an unsuspecting victim. Had I first established limits, I would not have been entrapped.

"Yet it was the mania in me that supplied me with fuel—the energy and strength I needed to accomplish things that might otherwise have seemed impossible, or off-limits! The mania gave me the courage to telephone important political figures.

"Since every manic episode is followed by depression, when you are high there is no place to go but down. The more manicky the episode, the greater the plunge."

During the cold war era of the former Soviet Union, Nancy was offered an opportunity to become politically involved with a national movement to help rescue Soviet Jews from their persecuted state. What first began as curiosity and concern led to a deep commitment and, ultimately, a serious destructive obsession. Nancy began to lose her way after traveling to the Soviet Union and meeting Yuri, a former Russian scientist and political prisoner. Back at home she was catapulted into spearheading his rescue on a worldwide basis. Nancy's life's purpose became Yuri's emancipation. Involved in international affairs and interacting with prominent public figures, Nancy's glamorous and exciting activities were far beyond anything she had ever imagined herself doing.

"I found it exciting and terrifying, and I could not concentrate on other things."

Nancy's commitment to Yuri's rescue turned into an obsession. Tension soon mounted. Nancy started taking risks that imperiled not only her personal security but her family's. What had started as a noble cause to save another human being turned into a larger-than-life crusade that nearly cost her her sanity.

"I gambled with my marriage and jeopardized the welfare of my children," said Nancy. "I was not always home for them or was home but unavailable. Other 'needs' took precedence. Nevertheless, I could not stop nor alter my path. I was obsessed with my mission. I wouldn't permit anyone or anything to stand in my way before I had reached my objective."

When Yuri was liberated and at last permitted to emigrate, Nancy found herself without the cause that she had focused her entire being on for five years. Nancy's personal life was in an upheaval, as she and her family were growing desperately apart. She had risen from dilettante to savior but failed to prepare herself for the "real" world following Yuri's emancipation.

After losing all sense of perspective and control, Nancy eventually found herself on a one-way path going nowhere but down. As a chronic obsessive compulsive, she was looking for trouble and found it. Nancy's fixation ended in 1994 with a major depressive episode and a failed attempt at suicide.

"I remember feeling paralyzed by hopelessness, inadequacy, and failure," said Nancy. "A great black abyss held me captive and no exit seemed to exist. When I no longer could tolerate the pain, I reached for a bottle of aspirin and swallowed a handful of pills. At that moment, it felt as if I had lost my balance and had plummeted to the bottom of the earth from the peak of Mount Everest. Everything around me appeared to be going up in smoke, and life was being snuffed out." Yet Nancy's attempt at self-annihilation didn't work. Instead of snuffing out her tortured life, she became violently ill. This irrational episode was a desperate cry for help.

Obsessions may also involve rumination about depressive thoughts, those regarding perceptions of inadequacy, hopelessness, or helplessness. Obsessions related to a manic phase may focus on tasks that one feels compelled to complete. Those induced by depression inhibit taking any action while manic induced periods leave little room for attending to other concerns.

For example, many people with bipolar disorder report tremendous difficulty completing several tasks within a day. Rather they become obsessed with one task and become paralyzed, unable to shift their focus of attention until it is completed. Cleaning a room, which may require an hour, instead leads to reorganizing it, repairing a knickknack or a torn pillow, or even painting a wall. Such difficulty disengaging may subsequently interfere with buying groceries, eating, bathing, or even sleeping.

The appropriate medication for depression and mania help to address these symptoms of bipolar disorder. A number of psychotherapies described in chapter 6 may also be helpful in specifically addressing such obsessions, regardless of their content. When stable, learning and practicing mindfulness meditation as described in chapter 13 may also help one "gain distance" from and feel less compelled to act on such obsessions. Well-integrated people don't fall into the trap of obsession but are able to achieve their goals while observing healthy limits and move forward toward the goal of a truly meaningful life.

INGREDIENTS FOR A FULL, HAPPY, AND BALANCED LIFE

Let us return to the basic ingredients of life, our primary needs: sleep, food, love, sex, and work. If we accept these needs as something greater than mere human sustenance, and the philosophy that the body is capable of many forms of enjoyment, life is suddenly granted that much more promise and meaning. However, those of us who live with bipolar disorder find ourselves in trouble when we go overboard with these basic enjoyments and become obsessive. We can all learn to find and appreciate beauty in every aspect of life if we follow the guidelines below.

The Importance of Sleep

"Just five more minutes," pleads the child who is glued to the television set and doesn't want to go to bed. Five minutes is never enough, nor is any amount of time satisfactory for a bipolar patient who is determined to finish a project.

Just as we need food and water, adequate rest is also necessary for a properly functioning body. This is especially true of people with bipolar disorder.

Nancy may intellectually understand her need for sleep, but she still struggles with the issue. "It is difficult for me to put down a good book that I am reading, let alone put aside a consuming writing project. This is the mania in me! My head refuses to listen to the cries of my body when it screams out for sleep." When Nancy stays up to work and doesn't sleep, she invariably suffers the next day. She feels sluggish, irritable, and suffers from eyestrain after staring at the computer screen all night.

The Importance of Routine

Increasingly, it has been found that maintaining routines in other areas of daily living can foster emotional stability and reduce the vulnerability for relapse (see Interpersonal and Social Rhythm Therapy, page 127). Toward this end, carefully monitor and try to maintain a consistent routine in scheduling activities such as the time of your meals, social contacts, the use of leisure time, exercise, or relaxation. Even maintaining a specific time during which you call friends or relatives can further a sense of stability.

At the same time, be alert to changes of routine. You may find your moods suddenly shifting when the pressure of deadlines, social demands, physical demands, or expectations regarding your role at work change. Such changes in routine or the availability of social support may influence your mood variability and should serve as warning signals to seek greater stability before symptoms escalate.

The Importance of Exercise

While exercise is important for everyone, it is critical for people with bipolar disorder. Not only does exercise help to create balance by diffusing the excess energy that is symptomatic of mania, but it is equally effective in helping ward off bouts of the blues.

Low-impact exercises such as swimming and walking are less stressful on the body than some of the more rigorous forms of exercise. Eastern body training methods, such as yoga, help cultivate deep relaxation techniques that improve flexibility, soothe the body, and clear the mind. Other Eastern disciplines include judo, jujitsu, kung fu, karate, tae kwon do, aikido, and t'ai chi.

The Importance of a Healthy Diet

Since diminished appetite and compulsive eating habits are traits of manic depression, those afflicted with bipolar disorder need to make a concerted effort to follow a healthy diet regime.

Allocating sufficient time to eat may not always be possible or practical. While nutritionists point to breakfast as the most important meal of the day, it is frequently rushed because everyone is in a hurry. Men and women rush off to work, and children hurry out to catch their school bus; a continental breakfast (coffee/tea/milk, juice, and toast) too often becomes standard fare. Unfortunately, lunch is frequently eaten on the run, too (if at all). That leaves dinner supplying the bulk of daily nutritional needs. If you are bipolar, your chemical balance is exacerbated by faulty eating habits. By skipping meals, indulging in fast foods, and frequently pigging out on junk, people with bipolar are more at risk than others in terms of compromising health and diminishing the overall quality of life.

Dr. Artemis P. Simopoulos, a renowned expert on nutrition, believes that a moderate amount of fat in our daily diet is essential for both mental and physical well-being. In her book *The Omega Plan,* coauthored with Jo Robinson, we learn how the right fats increase our chances of living a long, lean, and healthy life. "Fat," state the authors, "is the raw material for hormone-like substances that virtually influence every function in your body, from your blood pressure to your sensitivity to pain. Your brain is composed primarily of fat, including the neurons that transmit electrical messages; if you don't eat enough of the right types of fats, you are depriving your brain of a critical nutrient and risk falling prey to depression and other mental disorders."[2]

What is the right type of fat? What is the wrong type? Studies have shown that the most harmful fat is saturated fat. Found in meat, dairy products, and some tropical oils, saturated fat increases the risk of coronary artery disease, diabetes, and obesity. Another harmful fat is trans fatty acid. These acids are man-made molecules produced during hydrogenation (e.g., the production of vegetable oil). Many nutritionists have demonstrated that an earlier theory, which prompted the switch from butter to margarine, was a bad idea.

Beneficial fats include olive oil and canola oil, which reduce the risk of certain metabolic disorders while protecting the body's cardiovascular system. Essential fatty acids (EFAs) are necessary for normal growth and development and help guard against depression. Two researchers from the National Institutes of Health, Joseph Hibbeln and Norman Salem, found that people who consume a large amount of fish have a low rate of depression. For example, in Japan, Taiwan, and Hong Kong, fish consumption is high and the depression rate is low. If our diet does not contain EFAs, we become deficient in these important fats. Omega-6 fatty acids are most abundant in vegetable oils such as corn, safflower, cottonseed, and sunflower. Omega-3 fatty acids are primarily found in seafood, green leafy vegetables, canola oil, and walnuts. An imbalance of EFAs is linked with a long list of serious conditions, including depression.[3]

The Need for Relationships

We tend to seek out partners who complement us and help us create balance. "In our family," said Nancy, "my husband is the more pragmatic of the two of us. His mathematical mind is quick to focus and he thinks in terms of the bottom line. I, on the other hand, am a detail person and prefer to elaborate. Were it not for my husband's curtailment, I might ramble forever. As an accountant, he is also more practical in financial matters; I'm less conservative.

"As a person who lives with bipolar disorder, I also add spark to our marriage. Being compulsive, I am driven to complete projects, whether they are personally oriented or ones benefiting both of us. My husband's complaint: If he wakes up in the middle of the night to go to the bathroom, the bed is made by the time he returns. A slight exaggeration, but you get the point!"

Attentiveness to the signals of one's mate tend to bring people closer together; so do shared experiences, raising children, the melding of families, mutual friends, and common goals. But, when people with bipolar disorder are focused inward, they often miss these important signals. A general malaise may develop, and partners may drift apart and form new relationships.

Sex is a powerful yearning, yet it pales in intensity when compared with our most basic of all emotional needs—to love and be loved. Love brings peace, harmony, and fulfillment. Since self-indulgence and inattentiveness to others are traits of bipolar illness, those of us who suffer from the disorder must be particularly mindful of the welfare of our loved ones. During periods of heightened mania, we are also more prone to episodes of flirtatiousness and promiscuity. Sex outside of marriage can be addictive and depleting. The dangers are obvious and everybody ultimately gets hurt—spouses, children, parents, and friends alike.

The Joy of Sex

The depth we feel from a sustained relationship can more than compensate for transitory romance. No honeymoon lasts forever; a healthy marriage depends on substance for its long-term survival. Don't bow to temptation when heightened sexuality becomes a problem. Force yourself to think ahead instead of focusing on an immediate sense of gratification. Remember: The cost of your transgression may be too high.

Can Money Buy Happiness?

Success in our society is often equated with how much money a person earns. But money does not equal happiness. We cannot purchase happiness, although spending sprees are symptomatic of bipolar illness. Money may improve our standard of living, but it cannot replace what is missing in our life if we are struggling with internal discontent. Our most profound need is peace of mind.

SELF-MONITORING

Self-monitoring is an essential strategy for taking a proactive approach to bipolar illness. Ongoing attention to one's stress level and change of moods is a major component of self-monitoring. With bipolar disorder, stress more profoundly impacts the onset of the initial depressive episode than subsequent ones. The body chemistry is thrown off-balance, thereby blocking one's natural ability to respond appropriately to environmental conditions. Stressful events such as loss or separation can create fear, anxiety, and depression.

> *Self-monitoring is an essential strategy for taking a proactive approach to bipolar illness. Ongoing attention to one's stress level and change of moods is a major component of self-monitoring.*

How vulnerable are you to stress? Have you ever taken a stress test? Are you vigilant about watching for early symptoms of depression or mania? What are your warning signals? Dr. Susan Musikanth, a psychologist from Cape Town, South Africa, and author of *Stress Matters* and *Depression Matters,* developed the questionnaires that follow to measure stress level and depression. The manic/hypomanic inventory was adapted from Mary Ellen Copeland's *Living Without Depression and Manic Depression.* You can use these questionnaires as tools to monitor your levels of stress, depression, and mania.

Stress Questionnaire

Answer the following questions to establish your level of stress. Choose one statement that best describes your response to each question.[4]

1. Your partner's or colleague's behavior upsets you. Do you:
   (a) explode?
   (b) feel angry, but suppress it?
   (c) feel upset, but do not get angry?
   (d) cry?
   (e) none of the above

2. You have a huge pile of work to get through in one morning. Do you:
   (a) work very hard and complete the lot?
   (b) leave the work and look for other ways to pass the time?
   (c) complete what is within your capability?
   (d) prioritize the load and complete only the important tasks?
   (e) ask someone to help you?

3. A friend makes some unkind remarks about you in conversation with someone else that you happen to overhear. Do you:
   (a) interrupt the conversation and tell the person exactly what you think of them?
   (b) walk straight past and forget about the incident?
   (c) walk straight past but start thinking about revenge?
   (d) walk straight past and think about the person?

4. You are stuck in heavy traffic. Do you:
   (a) honk?
   (b) try to take another route to avoid the congestion?
   (c) switch on the radio or CD player?
   (d) sit back and try to relax?
   (e) sit back and feel angry?
   (f) do some work?
   (g) you do not have a car so you would not be in a position to make these choices

5. When you play a sport, do you play to win?
   (a) always
   (b) most of the time
   (c) sometimes
   (d) never; I play for enjoyment

6. When you play a game with children, do you deliberately let them win?
   (a) never
   (b) sometimes
   (c) most of the time
   (d) always

7. A deadline is looming, but you are not satisfied with the work you have done. Do you:
   (a) work on it all hours to ensure perfection?
   (b) panic because you think you will miss the deadline?
   (c) do your best in the time available without worrying about it?

8. Someone tidies up your house or office and never puts things where you left them. Do you:

    (a) mark the position of everything and ask the person to put your things in the places you have indicated?

    (b) move everything back into place once the person has left?

    (c) leave most things as they are because the occasional change does not bother you?

9. A close friend asks you for your opinion about a room that has just been decorated. You think it's terrible. Do you:

    (a) admit it?

    (b) say otherwise?

    (c) only discuss the aspects that you like?

    (d) offer suggestions on how to make it better?

10. When you do something, do you:

    (a) always try to produce something perfect?

    (b) do your best and not worry about achieving perfection?

    (c) think that everything you do is perfect?

11. Your family complains that you spend too little time with them because of work. Do you:

    (a) worry, but feel that you have no control over the situation?

    (b) take work home so that you can be with them?

    (c) take on more work?

    (d) find that your family has never complained?

    (e) reorganize your work so that you can be with them more?

12. How would you describe an ideal evening?

    (a) a large and swinging party

    (b) doing something with your partner that you both enjoy

    (c) escaping the rat race by yourself

    (d) dinner with a small group of friends

    (e) a family evening doing things that you all enjoy

    (f) working

13. Which of the following do you do?

    (a) bite your nails

    (b) feel constantly tired

    (c) feel breathless without having been physically active

(d) drum your fingers

(e) sweat for no apparent reason

(f) fidget

(g) gesticulate

(h) none of the above

14. Which of the following do you suffer from?

(a) headaches

(b) muscle tension

(c) constipation

(d) diarrhea

(e) loss of appetite

(f) increase in appetite

(g) none of the above

15. Have you experienced one or more of the following in the last four weeks?

(a) crying or wanting to cry

(b) difficulty in concentration

(c) forgetting what you were going to say next

(d) irritation over trivialities

(e) difficulty in making decisions

(f) wanting to scream

(g) feeling that you have no one with whom you can really discuss things

(h) feeling that you are jumping from task to task without really completing anything

(i) none of the above

16. Have you experienced any of the following during the last year?

(a) a serious illness (your own or someone close to you)

(b) family problems

(c) financial problems

(d) none of the above

17. How many cigarettes do you smoke a day?

(a) 0

(b) 1–10

(c) 11–20

(d) 21 or more

18. How much alcohol do you consume in a day?

    (a) none

    (b) 1–2 drinks

    (c) 3–5 drinks

    (d) 6 or more drinks

19. How many cups of coffee (not including decaffeinated) do you drink a day?

    (a) none

    (b) 1–2 cups

    (c) 3–5 cups

    (d) 6 or more cups

20. How old are you?

    (a) 18 or under

    (b) 19–25

    (c) 26–39

    (d) 40–65

    (e) over 65

21. You have a very important appointment at 9:30 a.m. Do you:

    (a) have a sleepless night worrying about it?

    (b) sleep very well and wake up reasonably relaxed but thinking about the appointment?

    (c) sleep well and wake up looking forward to the appointment?

22. Someone close to you has died. Naturally, you are very upset. Do you:

    (a) grieve because no one can fill that terrible gap?

    (b) grieve because life is so unfair?

    (c) accept what has happened and try to get on with your life?

23. You have gotten into trouble over a problem. Do you:

    (a) assess the situation on your own and try to find another solution?

    (b) discuss the problem with your partner or close friend and try to work something out together?

    (c) deny that there is a problem in the hope that it will go away?

    (d) worry about it but make no attempt to try and solve it?

24. When did you last smile?
    (a) today
    (b) yesterday
    (c) last week
    (d) can't remember

25. When did you last compliment or praise someone in your family or at
    work?
    (a) today
    (b) yesterday
    (c) last week
    (d) can't remember

SCORING

Add up your score for each question.

1. a = 0   b = 0   c = 3   d = 0   e = 1
2. a = 1   b = 0   c = 1   d = 3   e = 2
3. a = 0   b = 3   c = 0   d = 1
4. a = 0   b = 0   c = 2   d = 3   e = 0   f = 2   g = 1
5. a = 0   b = 1   c = 2   d = 3
6. a = 0   b = 1   c = 2   d = 3
7. a = 0   b = 0   c = 3
8. a = 0   b = 0   c = 3
9. a = 0   b = 0   c = 3   d = 1
10. a = 0   b = 3   c = 0
11. a = 0   b = 0   c = 0   d = 0   e = 3
12. a = 1   b = 3   c = 0   d = 1   e = 2   f = 0
13. a = 0   b = 0   c = 0   d = 0   e = 0   f = 0   g = 0   h = 1
14. a = 0   b = 0   c = 0   d = 0   e = 0   f = 0   g = 1
15. a = 0   b = 0   c = 0   d = 0   e = 0   f = 0   g = 0   h = 0   i = 1
16. a = 0   b = 0   c = 0   d = 2
17. a = 3   b = 1   c = 0   d = 0
18. a = 3   b = 2   c = 1   d = 0
19. a = 3   b = 2   c = 1   d = 0
20. a = 3   b = 0   c = 1   d = 2   e = 3
21. a = 0   b = 1   c = 3

22. a = 0   b = 0   c = 3
23. a = 2   b = 3   c = 0   d = 0
24. a = 3   b = 2   c = 1   d = 0
25. a = 3   b = 2   c = 1   d = 0

SCORE

51–68: Your stress level is low. You show very few signs of stress. You are not a workaholic. You thus show type B behavior and generally cope very well with stress.

33–50: Your stress level is moderate. You show some stress. You are not a workaholic, but there is some tendency toward it. You therefore show mild type A behavior and generally do not cope well with stress.

16–32: Your stress level is high. You show many signs of stress. It is likely that you are a workaholic. You thus display type A behavior and do not handle stress very well.

0–15: Your stress level is very high. You show a great deal of stress. You are a workaholic. You display extreme type A behavior and your ability to deal with stress is very poor.

Depression Inventory

This assessment tool can help you measure the level of your depression or determine that you are depression-free.[5]

MOOD

0	I do not feel sad.
1	I feel blue or sad.
2a	I feel blue or sad all the time and I can't snap out of it.
2b	I am so sad or unhappy that it is very painful.
3	I am so sad or unhappy that I can't stand it.

PESSIMISM

0	I am not particularly pessimistic or discouraged about the future.
1	I feel discouraged about the future.

2a   I feel that I have nothing to look forward to.

2b   I feel that I won't ever get over my troubles.

3   I feel that the future is hopeless and that things cannot improve.

SENSE OF FAILURE

0   I do not feel like a failure.

1   I feel I have failed more than the average person has.

2a   I feel that I have accomplished very little that is worthwhile or that means anything.

2b   As I look back on my life, all I can see is a lot of failure.

3   I feel I am a complete failure as a person (parent, husband, wife, etc.).

LACK OF SATISFACTION

0   I am not particularly dissatisfied.

1   I feel bored most of the time.

2a   I don't enjoy things the way I used to.

2b   I don't get satisfaction out of anything anymore.

3   I am dissatisfied with everything.

GUILTY FEELINGS

0   I don't feel particularly guilty.

1   I feel bad or unworthy a good part of the time.

2a   I feel quite guilty.

2b   I feel bad or unworthy practically all the time now.

3   I feel as though I am very bad or worthless.

SENSE OF PUNISHMENT

0   I don't feel I am being punished.

1   I have a feeling that something bad may happen to me.

2a   I feel I am being punished or will be punished.

2b   I feel I deserve to be punished.

3   I want to be punished.

SELF-HATE

0   I don't feel disappointed in myself.

1   I am disappointed in myself.

2a   I don't like myself.

2b   I am disgusted with myself.

3   I hate myself.

SELF-ACCUSATIONS

0   I don't feel that I am worse than anybody else.

1   I am very critical of myself for my weaknesses or mistakes.

2a   I blame myself for everything that goes wrong.

2b   I feel that I have many bad faults.

SELF-PUNITIVE WISHES

0   I don't have any thoughts of harming myself.

1   I have thoughts of harming myself, but I would not carry
         them out.

2a   I feel that I would be better off dead.

2b   I have definite plans about committing suicide.

2c   I feel that my family would be better off if I were dead.

3   I would kill myself if I could.

CRYING SPELLS

0   I don't cry any more than usual.

1   I cry now more than I used to.

2   I cry all the time now; I can't stop.

3   I used to be able to cry, but now I can't cry at all even though
         I want to.

IRRITABILITY

0   I am no more irritated now than I ever am.

1   I get annoyed or irritated more easily than I used to.

2   I feel irritated all the time.

3   I don't get irritated at all at the things that used to irritate me.

SOCIAL WITHDRAWAL

0   I have not lost interest in other people.

1   I am less interested in other people now than I used to be.

2   I have lost most of my interest in other people and have little feeling for them.

3   I have lost all my interest in other people and don't care about them at all.

INDECISIVENESS

0   I make decisions about as well as ever.

1   I am less sure of myself now and try to put off making decisions.

2   I can't make decisions anymore without help.

3   I can't make any decisions at all anymore.

BODY IMAGE

0   I don't feel I look any worse than I used to.

1   I am worried that I am looking old or unattractive.

2   I feel that there are permanent changes in my appearance and they make me look unattractive.

3   I feel that I am ugly or repulsive looking.

WORK INHIBITION

0   I can work as well as before.

1a   It takes extra effort to get started at doing something.

1b   I don't work as well as I used to.

2   I have to push myself very hard to do anything.

3   I can't do any more work at all.

SLEEP DISTURBANCE

0   I sleep as well as usual.

1   I wake up more tired in the morning than I used to.

2   I wake up 1–2 hours earlier than usual and find it hard to get back to sleep.

3   I wake up early every day and can't get more than 5 hours of sleep.

FATIGUE

0   I don't get any more tired than usual.

1   I get tired more easily than I used to.

2   I get tired doing anything.

3   I get too tired to do anything.

LOSS OF APPETITE

0   My appetite is no worse than usual.

1   My appetite is not as good as it used to be.

2   My appetite is much worse now.

3   I have no appetite at all anymore.

WEIGHT LOSS

0   I haven't lost much weight, if any, recently.

1   I have lost more than 4 pounds recently.

2   I have lost more than 10 pounds recently.

3   I have lost more than 15 pounds recently.

SOMATIC PREOCCUPATION

0   I am no more concerned about my health than usual.

1   I am concerned about aches and pains, an upset stomach, constipation, or other unpleasant feelings in my body.

2   I am so concerned with how I feel or what I feel that it's hard to think of much else.

3   I am completely absorbed in what I feel.

LOSS OF LIBIDO

0   I have not noticed any recent change in my interest in sex.

1   I am less interested in sex than I used to be.

2   I am much less interested in sex now.

3   I have lost interest in sex completely.

SCORING

Add together the numbers you circled. Your total score indicates your depth of depression.

0–9:   none

10–18:   mild

19–25:   moderate

26–35:   moderate to severe

36 and above: severe

Manic/Hypomanic Inventory

This tool can help you assess your susceptibility to manic or hypomanic episodes by monitoring your symptoms. You need to learn what your own early warning signals are and be vigilant about watching for them. Put a checkmark next to each symptom that applies to you.[6]

- ❏ insomnia or diminished need for sleep
- ❏ surges of energy and restlessness
- ❏ euphoria
- ❏ flight of ideas
- ❏ excessive planning
- ❏ disorganization
- ❏ inappropriate anger
- ❏ excessive spending
- ❏ diminished appetite or compulsive eating
- ❏ false superiority and grandiosity
- ❏ obsessiveness
- ❏ overambitiousness
- ❏ oversensitivity
- ❏ assuming too much responsibility
- ❏ nervousness and excitability
- ❏ inability to concentrate
- ❏ irritability and outbursts of temper
- ❏ out-of-body sensations
- ❏ others appear "slow"
- ❏ hyperactivity
- ❏ incessant chattering
- ❏ excessive telephoning
- ❏ self-indulgence and inattentiveness to others
- ❏ heightened sexuality, flirtatiousness, and promiscuity

Use this list as a reminder of your personal vulnerabilities so you can more effectively monitor the first signs of trouble.

TAKE CHARGE OF YOUR LIFE

> *It wasn't until I realized that it was up to me to get my moods under control, that there was no magic cure, that I began to turn the corner on the road to wellness.*
>
> —MARY ELLEN COPELAND

To begin taking charge of your life, it helps to keep a personal calendar (a template is available through the Depression and Bipolar Support Alliance; see Resources, page 333). In this way, you can participate in your own treatment by monitoring your mood elevations and depressions. This provides you an opportunity to work collaboratively with your doctor, enabling him or her to regulate your medication more closely. The sample page in figure 10.1 is from Nancy's personal calendar.

Support of Family and Friends

Take a proactive role by alerting family members and friends to possible warning signs of depression and mania. They can encourage you to stick with treatment. If you become ill, an informed relative or friend will not be offended by potential hostility on your part but will see it as a sign of your illness.

During periods of relative calm, it may be helpful to discuss strategy with a loved one to avoid any future problems should another attack occur.

Any threat of suicide must be taken very seriously. If the situation becomes desperate, friends and relatives should know that a suicide attempt is a cry for help and to phone the doctor, a hospital emergency room, or 911 immediately.

When you're in the recovery stage, advise friends and relatives not to push or be overprotective. They need to understand that you will get well at your own pace, and you need to be treated as normally as possible.

Where possible, be mindful of those relationships that are tension and conflict provoking versus those that are supportive, nurturing, and stabilizing. Communications that are devaluing, stigmatizing, and do not consider the realities of bipolar disorder can foster increased instability. Certainly, every relationship may involve some conflict. However, as part of effectively

DAY OF THE WEEK	MEDICINES I TOOK (List medications)	SIDE EFFECTS (How the medicine made me feel)	SYMPTOMS (How I feel on a scale of 1 to 10 0—most depressed, 5—normal, 10—most manic)	ACTIVITIES/ SLEEP/MAJOR LIFE EVENTS (Include "homework" for psychotherapy)	APPOINTMENT SCHEDULE
Monday, January 2	None	None	2—Depressed Low energy Irritable Inability to concentrate	Slept poorly.	
Tuesday, January 3	One pill at 8 a.m.	None	3—Improved mood	Slept better. Forced myself to concentrate on work. Took a walk.	
Wednesday, January 4	One pill at 8 a.m.	None	6—Feeling better	Good day at work. Made a list of good things about myself.	Dr. Miller 1 p.m.

Figure 10.1. Sample Personal Calendar

managing vulnerability to relapse, you need to be more alert to the overall quality of ongoing relationships and how they impact you.

This places the burden on you to articulate what you need, how you are impacted, and to set limits on how you wish to be treated. If, in spite of constructive discussion, you find a relationship unchanged, you may need to redefine or reduce your expectations of that relationship. This is not an easy task if you are dependent on the relationship. However, in some circumstances you may need to decide if you want to work on that relationship, if you need to limit the quality and frequency of interaction or conclude that it is in your best overall interest to sever the relationship. This can be a very challenging decision.

At the same time, a close relationship can be invaluable in helping you to effectively manage bipolar disorder. *Loving Someone with Bipolar Disorder*, written by Julie Fast and John Preston, offers a comprehensive approach by which you can solicit the help of a loved one in this difficult challenge. It offers specific and detailed strategies for working together to monitor and address shifting emotions, thoughts, and behaviors, especially when they reflect the beginning stages of a relapse. This excellent guide can be extremely helpful for anyone who is seriously committed toward helping you with this illness.[7]

Empowerment

In the spirit of self-help, empowerment is key to achieving the necessary strength and confidence to help yourself. Empowerment describes self-assurance, assertiveness, and the ability to say no. To feel empowered, you must be able to acknowledge your inner strengths and feel worthy, thereby appreciating your inner self. When you attain self-confidence, you will succeed in gaining the respect, and the attention, of others.

> *Empowerment describes self-assurance, assertiveness, and the ability to say no. To feel empowered, you must be able to acknowledge your inner strengths and feel worthy, thereby appreciating your inner self.*

Becoming empowered is a process and cannot be quickly achieved. Like anything else, it takes practice. A piano player does not become a concert pianist overnight. So while there is no magic pill to make us feel empowered, success can be attained in a step-by-step process. The following steps are suggested:

1. Develop an adequate support system. A nurturing and healthy interrelationship with another person will offer you a safe haven from which you can grow and develop.

2. Learn problem-solving skills, time management and stress management skills, and take assertiveness training. Self-help books, such as this one, can offer suggestions and guidance. You can further develop problem-solving skills by attending psychological education workshops (see Resources, page 333).

3. Take control of yourself. The actual process of taking control involves great strength, self-determination, and complete self-discipline. It's tough! But keep in mind that anything worthwhile is worth striving for, and this goal has the potential to transform your life.

Authors Ada Kahn and Sheila Kimmel offer suggestions of how to enhance your quality of life through self-empowerment and improved self-esteem. Their method is based on finding ways to eliminate "squashers" (elements that hold you back) while establishing "boosters" (factors that help raise your self-esteem and give you strength).[8]

Emotional baggage—unresolved past issues—is the root cause of many squashers as well as low self-esteem. By confronting negative issues head-on, it is possible to overcome many problems. These issues may have plagued us for years, undermining our self-esteem and making us feel small. Eliminating our "squashers" will reduce stress, pave the way to self-assertiveness, and help us recognize untapped talents and potential ability. Kahn and Kimmel's Booster Questionnaire (see page 219) will help you become more aware of your own strengths and overcome your squashers. You may want to refer to this list on a regular basis to remind yourself of your personal strengths, your accomplishments, and your personal pride.

Increase Your Self-Awareness

Swiss psychiatrist/psychologist Carl Jung (1875–1961) was a follower of Sigmund Freud before breaking away to establish his own school of thought: analytical psychology. Jung emphasized the dynamic forces within the individual. Rejecting Freud's focus on sexuality, he believed that the will to survive is more compelling than sexual drive. Jung focused on current problems, rather than childhood conflicts, and developed a theory based on the unconscious mind. "Man is an enigma to himself," said Jung. He concluded that the key to peace of mind is self-knowledge. "An individual, willing to fulfill the demands of rigorous self-examination and self-knowledge . . . will discover important truths about himself."[9]

For many people with bipolar disorder, the turning point in their life comes when they understand their situation, accept responsibility for their actions, and are willing to work hard to change their lives. Finally, they see the light. Although the task ahead may be painfully difficult, simply understanding the problem makes it easier to bear.

"My first confrontation with the need to make radical life changes hit me right after I had plunged into a deep depression following the break with Yuri," said Nancy. "At that critical moment, I felt loveless, friendless, and completely lost, without a career or even a job to fall back on. I turned to my therapist for help."

The challenge of altering one's course in life, after recovering from shock, may ultimately become the motivating force that rewards one with pleasure. In refocusing on something new and different, the change itself can be exciting and stimulating.

Guidelines to Help You Get Well and Stay Well

Mary Ellen Copeland suffered recurring episodes of deep depression, followed by occasional mania, from early childhood until finally seeking medical and psychiatric help as an adult. She went on to become a scholar, teacher, lecturer, and author. Copeland lives with manic depression, but after conquering her illness she wrote a book to help others get well and stay well. The following guidelines are excerpted from her book and summarize many of the topics we've discussed in this chapter.[10]

1. Believe in yourself! Recognize yourself as a unique and valuable individual, then work at improving your self-esteem.

Booster Questionnaire

My strengths are

_____

_____

_____

The aspects of my personality I like best are

_____

_____

_____

I am proud of

_____

_____

_____

What I appreciate about me is

_____

_____

_____

The physical features I like best about myself are

_____

_____

_____

My accomplishments are

_____

_____

_____

Ways in which I take care of myself are

_____

_____

_____

Risks I have taken with successful outcomes are

_____

_____

_____

The personality qualities that make me likable are

_____

_____

_____

What others have told me they admire about me are

_____

_____

_____

Difficult life situations I have lived through, handled, and survived are

_____

_____

_____

When I feel powerful I can

_____

_____

_____

2. Create a network of support, people you care about and can trust to be around when you need them most. These may include family, friends, neighbors, health-care professionals, or members of a support group.

3. Eliminate physical causes of mood disorders:

- Allergies
- Diabetes
- Reactions to prescription drugs or over-the-counter medications
- Drug or alcohol abuse
- Premenstrual syndrome or menopause
- Sexual dysfunction
- Thyroid imbalance
- Viral infections
- Vitamin and mineral deficiencies

4. Get a complete physical and neurological examination, starting with your medical history.

5. Discuss the cost factor with your health-care providers (they're in a position to help direct you to affordable programs). Check covered medical services as well as limitations on coverage and its requirements. You can also call the American Medical Association.

6. Set realistic goals.

7. Stick to a regular exercise program, eat a diet consisting of fresh and natural foods grown without chemicals, and get proper rest.

8. Look for a comfortable living space that is affordable, easy to maintain, and close to community services, family, friends, or other support members.

9. Make time for pleasurable pursuits.

10. Adopt a pet or spend time with someone else's. Pets are healing, reduce stress, and offer unconditional love.

11. Enjoy your career! If your job is not interesting or stimulating, is too far from home, or you don't like your coworkers, change it. Remember, we all have choices. A new job may be your next goal.

12. Get rid of negative influences in your life—people, places, or situations. Anything that causes you stress, anxiety, or depression should be eliminated.

13. Empower yourself! Learn to assume positive action on your own behalf, and take charge of every aspect of your recovery.

IDENTIFYING AND ASSESSING THE REWARDS OF A JOB

You are beginning to take charge of your life by developing a sense of inner awareness. When you begin to feel empowered, take time to evaluate your job. Are you satisfied with your working conditions? Since a large portion of our waking hours is spent at work, every effort should be made to ensure that this part of your daily life is rewarding. If you enjoy what you're doing, you won't feel dissatisfied and bored. For sufferers of bipolar illness, boredom can be a contributing factor to a depressive episode. It frequently leads to anxiety, restlessness, irritability, and anguish. If you remain anchored at a place where you are unhappy, you may feel trapped. Unhappiness and discouragement exacerbate mood disorders.

A positive mental attitude is energizing and helps to encourage you to make whatever adjustments are necessary to improve working conditions. This, in turn, will increase your job satisfaction while simultaneously boosting your self-image and helping you avoid any sense of failure.

When properly challenged, you will not feel bogged down by tedious, repetitive routines that are common to every industry. Although few careers match the responsibility and challenges bestowed on scientists and surgeons, even they can eventually grow tired of their work.

To feel satisfied and fulfilled in your chosen work, it is important to feel appreciated and recognized for your skills. Kahn and Kimmel refer to this as "jobpower." To test jobpower, they developed the Jobpower Scale[11] (see page 224).

If the Jobpower Scale reveals that you are not finding your job satisfying, you may want to consider looking for other employment.

The sad reality is that job motivation is low in the United States and many people find themselves daydreaming. They might wish they were somewhere else, anywhere else, as long as that "other" place was some distance from work. At the end of the day they return home fatigued and irritable. If you are bipolar and feel trapped in your job, you need to remedy your situation immediately.

How Can You Improve the Job You Have?

If your work environment is uncomfortable but you like what you do, you might be able to remedy the situation by improving your relations with coworkers and bosses. If you want to stay at your job but find it monotonous at times, look for ways to add variety to your basic job description. Break that routine!

Identify what needs your job satisfies. Not all needs can be met in any one position. You might experience a "lack of fit" when certain needs are satisfied while others are not. Think through whether you can alter your job description to meet more of your needs, or more fully meet some of your needs. Decide if some of your needs can best be satisfied elsewhere. For example, you may work in a position that meets your needs for a good income, social connection, and challenge, but that does not allow you the opportunity for enough creativity. You may decide to maintain the job and seek other outlets for your creativity. Or, you may pursue classes in your area of interest so, with perseverance, you can gain an income from your area of creativity.

If, in the end, nothing you have tried improves your working conditions to your satisfaction, it might be time to look for other employment. A fresh start may be just the thing you need to revitalize your life. Boredom on the job can create major depressions—don't let this happen to you. Perhaps a lateral change might be all that's necessary (same type of position, but in a new location), or you may be ready for a career change. Keep your options open.

The Jobpower Scale

	Yes	No
Are you satisfied with your job?	❏	❏
Do you feel professionally fulfilled?	❏	❏
Do you feel that you are using your talents and skills?	❏	❏
Are you appreciated at work and recognized for your accomplishments?	❏	❏
Are you in a field you like?	❏	❏
Do others respect you at your job?	❏	❏
Do you feel competent to do the work you do?	❏	❏
Are you paid according to your ability?	❏	❏
Are you getting promotions you deserve?	❏	❏
Are you happy going to work most of the time?	❏	❏
Are you willing to go the "extra mile" to help others in your workplace?	❏	❏
Can you appreciate others' successes at work?	❏	❏
Are you able to speak up to your boss and coworkers?	❏	❏
Are you really interested in the work you do?	❏	❏

The following four questions apply to women only:

	Yes	No
Do you feel you have equality with men at your workplace?	❏	❏
Is your salary comparable to men's for the same job?	❏	❏
Do you get the advancements that men get?	❏	❏
Do men respect you for your professionalism?	❏	❏

If you answered no to more than 5 or 6 of the above questions, your present job may be a poor match for your skills and you may feel trapped.

On the Job: To Disclose or Not to Disclose?

A major challenge faced by almost everyone with bipolar disorder is whether to inform an employer of your illness (see chapter 8 regarding stigma). Your friends, family, and even your therapist may offer you a variety of suggestions on how to address this concern. Some may suggest complete honesty. Part of the rationale for being candid is that you will not have to constantly be on guard to protect your secret. Additionally, your employer may become more sensitive to your needs, and your company may make special accommodations to address those needs if necessary.

However, the reality is that some work settings are more positively supportive than others. Disclosure may also lead to negative consequences owing to the prevalence of stigma in a particular workplace. Such stigma could lead to lowered expectations for an employee, reduced confidence, or even a quickness to "pathologize" the employer, seeing the impact of the illness where it does not exist. Even when legally challenged to make special considerations, courts have not been as favorable toward individuals with emotional illness as it has toward those with physical disabilities.

We recommend you do as much research as possible regarding your work setting to help you make your decision. Reflect on the pros and cons you may personally experience from disclosure. On one hand, well-supported disclosure can lead to an increased sense of empowerment and integrity. At the same time, you have to assess your capacity to manage the potential fallout of such a decision.

One approach, as previously described, is to admit to the symptoms of the illness when they are in fact interfering with your capacity to carry out your job functions. As such, you may choose to describe symptoms of depression or anxiety rather than a clinical diagnosis.

Self-Help Books

In recent years the self-help movement has inspired the publication of numerous workbooks regarding the management of depression and bipolar disorder. While these can be helpful, their benefit is greatest when used in conjunction with psychotherapy. This is especially true for several of these books that reflect a specific psychotherapeutic approach.

We recommend the following guidelines to consider when using such books.

1. Be patient. Self-help books are to be used as reference points to provide increased understanding and skills regarding the management of various aspects of bipolar illness. They therefore require that you take time to do the various exercises in order to establish new skills as part of your behavioral repertoire.

2. Learning new skills can feel frustrating at first. These books are intended to inspire and not to add to your stress. As such, they require patience and commitment in their use. You may feel unable to do some of them at first. This is a common reaction to trying any new skill for the first time.

3. You do not have to agree with every idea presented in a book. Although each has something positive to offer, you may want to first research or review them to help you decide which makes the most sense for you. If possible, contact others who have used them or read the reviews on Web sites that sell them.

4. You may need to be sufficiently stabilized before being able to fully practice many of the strategies provided in these books.

Below is a partial list of useful self-help books with a brief description of each.

Living Without Depression and Manic Depression, by Mary Ellen Copeland. Oakland, CA: New Harbinger, 1994. This is one of the first workbooks to specifically address the management of bipolar disorder. It offers comprehensive suggestions to effectively live with the illness. The fact that it is still widely read attests to its practicality and overall relevance.

The Depression Workbook: A Guide for Living with Depression and Manic Depression, 2nd ed., by Mary Ellen Copeland and Matthew McKay. Oakland, CA: New Harbinger, 2002. This edition offers newer research-based self-help strategies for managing depression and for a variety of other symptoms.

Loving Someone with Bipolar Disorder: Understanding and Helping Your Partner, by Julie Fast and John D. Preston. Oakland, CA: New Harbinger, 2004. This book provides detailed guidelines to help anyone committed to living or supporting someone with bipolar disorder. It is filled with practical ideas and truly addresses the complexities of effectively responding to this challenge.

Mind over Mood: Change How You Feel by Changing the Way You Think, by Dennis Greenberger and Christine Padesky. New York: Guilford Press, 1995. This is one of the most widely used workbooks presenting a cognitive behavioral approach to help manage moods. It helps the reader to understand and effectively manage the interaction of thoughts and emotions that can lead to depression, anxiety, panic attacks, and stress in general.

Overcoming Depression One Step at a Time: The New Behavioral Activation Approach to Getting Your Life Back, by Michael E. Addis and Christopher R. Martell. Oakland, CA: New Harbinger, 2004. Offers a wide variety of strategies and understanding based on behavioral activation therapy. These skills help the reader to reengage in action as a way to manage depression.

Get out of Your Mind and into Your Life: The New Acceptance and Commitment Therapy, by Steven C. Hayes with Spencer Smith. Oakland, CA: New Harbinger, 2005. This book is based on the research surrounding acceptance and commitment therapy. It emphasizes a range of skills and exercises to help reduce depression and suffering in general. Additionally, as emphasized by this psychotherapeutic approach, it helps the reader to identify core values that form guidelines for living life meaningfully.

Don't Let Your Emotions Run Your Life: How Dialectical Behavior Therapy Can Put You in Control, by Scott Spradlin. Oakland, CA: New Harbinger, 2003. This workbook, based on dialectical behavior therapy, offers a wide range of strategies to help the reader better tolerate sorrow, anger, and fear. As such, it can provide skills for dealing with depression and the range of negative emotions that may surface as a product of living with bipolar disorder.

The Bipolar Workbook: Tools for Controlling Your Mood Swings, by Monica Ramirez Basco. New York: Guilford Press, 2005. This book provides strategies for recognizing and managing the symptoms of bipolar disorder and for helping to forestall relapse.

The Cyclothymia Workbook: Learn How to Manage Your Mood Swings and Lead a Balanced Life, by Price Prentiss. Oakland, CA: New Harbinger, 2005. This workbook is specifically for those who have this milder version of bipolar disorder. It helps the reader to recognize and manage symptoms that may trigger an escalation toward depression or mania.

The Bipolar Disorder Survival Guide: What You and Your Family Need to Know, by David J. Miklowitz. New York: Guilford Press, 2002. This is both a guide and workbook that provides a comprehensive understanding of bipolar disorder and practical strategies for self-management.

The Interpersonal Solution to Depression: A Workbook for Changing How You Feel by Changing How You Relate, by Jeremy W. Pettit, Thomas E. Joiner, and Lynn P. Rehm. Oakland, CA: New Harbinger, 2005. Based on interpersonal psychotherapy, this book offers a range of strategies that focus on interpersonal skills, managing dependency, and decreasing inhibitions central to depression.

CHOOSING YOUR OWN DESTINY

The privilege to choose your own destiny and take control of your life offers unconditional freedom. But attaining this freedom requires a big investment, perseverance, and self-discipline. If you live with bipolar disorder it is of paramount importance not only to self-monitor but to strictly self-discipline. The prerequisite for this freedom is a positive mental attitude. If you are prepared to meet all the demands of a long and difficult journey, the rewards can be great. It is possible to achieve mastery over your life, and with that comes peace and personal fulfillment.

Your feelings act like a barometer, an internal warning system that is trying to tell you something. Pay attention to those feelings—don't push them away. Accept that a problem exists, think about it, analyze it, and learn from it. If your primary goal is happiness and inner peace, you need to eliminate the obstacles. What is really important? What are your priorities in life? Is it possible that some of your choices may actually have been in conflict with your initial goals?

> *Know thyself, and listen to your feelings. The little feeling person inside you is saying, "You matter. You deserve to be heard, and I care to listen."*
>
> —JOHN GRAY

Stop! Be aware of the warning signals, and do not be afraid of them. Find some quiet time and space to clear your mind of all extraneous, distracting, and self-defeating thoughts. Listen to what your feelings are telling you, or trying to tell you, and heed their warnings. Trust your own intuitions. If you schedule time each day for quiet thought, follow through by sticking to your schedule; it will help you remain "on track."

Krishnamurti described freedom as the ability to see, cast doubt, question everything, and then act on one's feelings and convictions. Those who learn to take action for themselves will find enjoyment and heightened self-esteem in having discarded former dependencies in exchange for freedom.[12]

Independent people are far better equipped for life than those who are dependent on others. That said, not all dependency is unhealthy. A healthy independence involves knowing when to allow for a healthy dependence; that is, interdependence.

In times of crisis, independent thinkers rely on their own strengths and instincts before going into action. They process, study in detail, and then evaluate every piece of information on possible options. If they choose not to act alone, thinking people can elect to solicit others as team players.

Teammates can learn to work together toward a mutually accepted goal. Independent people know how to ask for help, without being pressed to blindly follow someone else. We are bound to make mistakes as we learn to live in this new, healthier way, but this is a learning process that we all must go through, and success will come to those who refuse to give up.

EXPECT THE UNEXPECTED

What do you do when your best-laid plans are suddenly turned upside down by some unforeseen misfortune? You have prepared for everything—except, of course, the unexpected! A person may feel comfortable and content, both at home and at work, until something happens to upset that delicate balance— sudden illness, problems at work, the loss of one's job, or even a forced move out of town. A sudden twist of fate—one that seems to jeopardize our very security and well-being—can plunge even the strongest person into despair or a temporary state of imbalance. What then? When "certainty" turns to "uncertainty," how do we cope?

As creatures of habit, it is human nature to fall back into old patterns of behavior. Some of these old habits may be self-destructive; this does not mean to imply that your efforts to take control of and manage your life have failed. Just be prepared to face obstacles. Learn to "let go" when something is beyond reach. Unrealistic expectations are universal, but get past it!

> *The ability to shift gears and move forward in a new direction when confronted by such obstacles is something each of us must learn in order to lead a healthy, well-balanced life.*

Acknowledge and accept that not everything in life is controllable. Things don't always happen the way we want them to, nor will people always respond favorably to us. The ability to shift gears and move forward in a new direction when confronted by such obstacles is something each of us must learn in order to lead a healthy, well-balanced life.

The ability to make sense out of chaos and rebound quickly is a skill that takes time. Many individuals who have faced challenging problems have ended up not only surviving but also thriving. When you have succeeded in developing the necessary skills to help you manage and take control of your life, then you will be ready to appreciate the beauty that life has to offer. Try living in the moment.

The best, most comprehensive way to beat manic depression is by adhering to the following prescription: psychotherapy, drug therapy, and self-therapy (self-help). No quick cure is available, nor will a pill make the symptoms go away. Bipolar disorder has both biological and psychological roots, and it is a daily struggle to combat the attacks of mania and depression.

Life is an endless series of challenges, but those who take positive action are true champions. Be honest with yourself and in your relationships. Accept the fact that all people are human and possess human failings. As with any other human weakness, living with bipolar disorder is not easy.

Nevertheless, our case studies have illustrated that people with this disorder can, and do, lead very full lives.

You can restore balance to your life, and with balance comes peace. Those who have survived the pitfalls of bipolar illness have discovered health and happiness waiting at the other end. But the ability to get well and stay well is up to each individual. Remember this motto: *The difficult we do immediately, but the impossible takes a little longer.*

CHAPTER 11

A Special Concern: Childhood/Adolescent Bipolar Illness

What is it like to parent a child who has bipolar disorder? The challenge of this undertaking presents one of the most difficult relationships between parent and child. In preparation for this chapter, we contacted parents who are members of the Child and Adolescent Bipolar Foundation. We asked them about their experiences and what they most want others to know about living with children and adolescents with bipolar disorder. A common response was, "Our children can be normal and safe when stable." The following examples highlight other responses from the parents.

- **Bipolar illness can manifest at extremely young ages.** "We've been dealing with Steve's illness since he turned one year old. He was such a calm, easygoing infant that we can actually tell you the exact day everything changed with him. Just three days before his first birthday, Steve woke up agitated. When his moods intensified and then continued our family doctor explained our son's behavior by saying that Steve was going through the "terrible twos" even though he was just a year old.

  "Each day with him was worse than the day before. Constant irritability, extreme violence, rage, sensitivity to stimuli—touching, lights, sound, everything set him off. He was even affected by tightly fitting clothes, socks with bumps . . . bright lights, loud noises. He was always sensitive to taste and smell. When he was only three years old, the doctor began to suspect he might have bipolar disorder, and by age four we had tried various holistic and behavioral methods. Steve has been on virtually every medication and combination thereof!"

- **Health-care professionals: Please, listen to what we say.** "Kevin was such a happy baby his first year," said his mother, "but after fourteen months, he became very clingy and sad. He couldn't handle changes in routine. In preschool he couldn't focus, he couldn't stay in his seat, and he was very distractible. Kindergarten was more of the same, and by first grade he was on Ritalin. By fifth grade he seemed very unhappy and often cried, but the doctor assured us that our son was not depressed.

  "The following year Kevin began to ask questions about what would happen if he were to kill himself. That's when he finally was diagnosed with depression and was started on antidepressants. One year later, in the seventh grade, he experienced his first manic episode and was hospitalized. At that time, we were informed of his bipolar disorder condition and the doctor put him on a combination of Depakote [mood stabilizer] and Zyprexa [antipsychotic/anticonvulsant, originally approved for schizophrenia]."

- **Insurance companies: Please cover this illness like any other medical illness.** "Brian cried constantly as an infant. He was bothered by hair combing, washing, or touching his head, face washing, and even some unexpected touch. At age two, Brian was aggressive toward his brother and parents. He cursed as a child, showed his genitals, and destroyed property. In school he has been disruptive in the classroom—acting out, deliberately knocking over his desk, and doing anything and everything for attention. At home he is equally uncontrollable—he runs around on the roof, hits his brother with a bat, and has daily rages."

EARLY-ONSET BIPOLAR DISORDER

Imagine waking up and finding your child extremely unmanageable and vastly different from the day before. He may be rageful, have tantrums for hours on end, be impulsive, aggressive to himself and others, and express irritability in his interactions. You become increasingly perplexed as you observe your child's behavior.

> *As parents, you may find yourselves increasingly at odds as the two of you try to cope. A sense of helplessness and frustration often results when a child develops early-onset bipolar disorder.*

You blame yourself, you blame him, you may even blame your spouse. With each of these reactions, you feel guilt and shame. As parents, you may find yourselves increasingly at odds as the two of you try to cope. A sense of helplessness and frustration often results when a child develops early-onset bipolar disorder.

You may find your neighbor less friendly, perhaps telling her children not to associate with yours. Perhaps they have observed him, or they may even have been the target of his aggressive behavior. Your neighbor's children don't need to be told to withdraw from him. They instinctively do so.

Early diagnosis is essential for optimal treatment of bipolar disorder, and yet mood disorders in children and adolescents represent one of the most underdiagnosed categories of mental illness. This is especially problematic

MESSAGE FROM THE PARENTS

The following are what the parents we interviewed most want others to know about living with bipolar children and adolescents:

Our children can be normal and safe when stable.

Bipolar illness can manifest at extremely young ages.

When possible, health-care professionals should ask the child's history without the child present so he doesn't hear a list of negative behaviors. He already knows!

Don't tell your kids to stay away from mine. He's not contagious.

Health-care professionals: Please, listen to what we say. Do not blame us! Have compassion and understanding for us. We need more doctors who specialize in this disorder.

Insurance companies: Please cover this illness like any other medical illness. No more discrimination on mental health care. My son deserves treatment without our worrying about using more than our "twenty days a year" coverage!

It takes a multimodal approach to effect positive change and achieve some stability.

Parents are the child's number-one advocate. Listen to them. There is hope for stability.

Please continue to educate others about this illness.

since childhood bipolar disorder greatly interferes with a child's capacity to develop the skills necessary for the complex challenges of maturity.

Since 20 to 30 percent of adult bipolar patients report having had their first episode prior to age twenty, early diagnosis is particularly important.[1] Despite these realities, doctors rarely identified bipolar disorder in children (and slightly less rarely in adolescents) until the 1980s.

While some parents may first seek help for a toddler or young child, parents involved in the Child and Adolescent Bipolar Foundation report that symptoms were either present from birth or developed suddenly during adolescence.[2]

One of the largest studies to date on pediatric bipolar disorder has been a multisite Course and Outcome of Bipolar Illness in Youth funded by the National Institute of Mental Health. Findings from this study of 263 children and adolescents, ages seven to seventeen years, indicate that this disorder affects children and adolescents more severely than adults.[3] Follow-up indicated that approximately 70 percent of all participants recovered from their initial episode and 50 percent had at least one relapse, particularly depressive episodes. Earlier age of onset, low socioeconomic status, and the presence of psychotic symptoms were factors associated with worse outcomes.

Comparing the group to adults with bipolar disorder I, the study found that those with pediatric bipolar disorder evidenced relatively longer periods of time with symptoms and more frequent cycling or mixed episodes. Additionally, children and adolescents also converted from a less severe form of the disorder to a more severe form at a much higher rate than evidenced by adults.

SYMPTOMS OF BIPOLAR DISORDER IN CHILDREN AND ADOLESCENTS

The symptoms of mood disorders in children and adolescents are expressed somewhat differently than in adults. For example, while a child's depressed mood may at times mirror the negative emotions, withdrawal, helplessness, and hopelessness characteristic of adult depression, both the mania and depression of bipolar disorder in children are more frequently expressed by behavioral symptoms.

Extreme Irritability and Emotional Lability

Extreme irritability and emotional lability (changeability) are hallmark signs of depression and mania in childhood. Intense irritability may lead to severe tantrums, characterized by their intensity and prolonged duration. Many young children have tantrums that last twenty to thirty minutes and occur occasionally beyond early childhood. In contrast, some children with bipolar illness, as in the case of Brian, cry for several hours during infancy, require little sleep, and evidence a general level of physical excitement and activity well beyond that of the normal infant.

The child with bipolar illness can engage in tantrums for hours without showing signs of reduced intensity. Also symptomatic of bipolar illness are tantrums that seem to abate for several hours only to be resumed again, and for extended periods of time, either that same day or during a consecutive period of days.

Intense Rage

Children and adolescents with bipolar disorder can exhibit intense rage that is expressed both verbally and physically toward peers, parents, siblings, teachers, and even themselves. They may be precocious in the profanity they use to express their rage. Such anger may seem totally unexpected and with no identifiable precipitant. This quickness to act aggressively further reflects the extremely impulsive quality of their thoughts and actions.

Hyperactivity

A lack of impulse control is further demonstrated by the extreme hyperactivity of children and adolescents with bipolar illness. Whereas the average child may have periods of great physical energy, the child or adolescent with bipolar disorder has periods of energy that are out of control and lacking in structure and direction.

Children and adolescents with bipolar disorder can exhibit intense rage that is expressed both verbally and physically toward peers, parents, siblings, teachers, and even themselves.

The average child may jump from couch to floor while proudly proclaiming, "I'm Superman." He may do this a few times, but the hyperactive child may repeat it twenty times. The child with bipolar disorder may take it to an extreme and jump from the top of a staircase or even the roof. Such behavior may stem from his activity level, coupled with a sense of grandiosity that may impel risk taking or underlie genuine suicidal ideation.

Sleep Disturbances

Mania in childhood is demonstrated by a variety of behaviors. The manic child may be too preoccupied at bedtime to sleep. Instead of sleeping, the child may play with toys, rearrange furniture, work on several craft projects simultaneously, move about his bedroom, or rove around the house. At all hours of the night, the child may complete many projects and leave others undone. However, the manic adolescent, with greater freedom than his younger counterpart, manifests sleeping difficulties much more dangerously. They might experiment with drugs, party through the night, and drive recklessly or speed while intoxicated.[4]

Miscalculated Life-Threatening Risks

The manic child can endanger his life by miscalculating the potential risk that an average "risk-taking" child or adolescent would not consider. An example of this is physical challenge involving jumps, leaps, or balancing acts that stretch beyond what is considered reasonably calculated risk. The older manic adolescent or adult may be prone to fast driving or excessive purchasing.

Overestimation of Ability

Risk-taking behavior may in part be driven by the influence of grandiose thinking. Such thinking could lead to stealing without any sense of wrongdoing, dictating to adults (teachers, parents, and others) on how things really should be, or earning poor grades with little or no sense of possible consequences. Similarly, an adolescent may express strong convictions of his great achievements in sports or music, when in fact he lacks the skills for such achievement. Children may exhibit pressured speech and describe racing thoughts.

Precociousness

Some children and adolescents with bipolar disorder are very precocious in language skills and other talents. For example, Kevin, whom we met at the beginning of the chapter, knew his multiplication tables by age four and was drawing weather maps of all fifty states. He spoke in paragraphs at the age of thirteen months, became interested in electronics between fourth and fifth grade, and was able to read diagrams and charts in books on electricity.

Hypersexuality

Hypersexuality is another symptom that can occur in some children, but it is more prevalent in adolescents with bipolar disorder. A young child, even without a history of sexual abuse or unusual exposure to sexual activities, may use language or behave in ways that are sexually provocative. Sexual profanity and excessive or even public masturbation can be observed in early childhood. Adolescents demonstrate symptoms of bipolar disorder that are closely associated with those of adults; they may be extremely sexually active and with multiple partners.[5]

Extreme Elation

Euphoria, or extreme elation, may be demonstrated by children and adolescents. Such elation may appear despite depressing or stressful circumstances. The child or adolescent may be too giddy or positive in his behavior even to recognize that his peers are not joining him in laughter. The "jokes" he presents, either verbally or by actions, may seem bizarre or beyond what others consider funny.

Hallucination

Some adolescents and young children with bipolar illness may even hallucinate. Most commonly, such hallucinations are auditory; the child or adolescent hears voices or holds imaginary conversations with another person. These conversations can be friendly, menacing, or commanding in nature. Although less typical, children can also hallucinate visually. What they think they are seeing might not be there at all, or they may be viewing extreme distortions of what is present.

Suicidal Ideation

The harsh reality is that these children and adolescents do in fact attempt suicide, and some succeed. Actual examples of methods tried include tying ropes or belts around their necks, cutting or poking themselves with scissors or tableware, laying behind the wheels of a parked car, or running into traffic. One of the most challenging and disturbing experiences for a parent is to witness these acts or hear their four- or five-year-old discuss jumping from a car or from the window of a tall building. Suicidal ideation is a part of the symptom profile for both adolescents and young children who suffer from mood disorders. Take seriously any such discussion or any gestures toward self-injury.

> *Suicidal ideation is a part of the symptom profile for both adolescents and young children who suffer from mood disorders. Take seriously any such discussion or any gestures toward self-injury.*

Night Terrors

While it is natural for children to have the occasional nightmare, children with bipolar disorder often experience night terrors that are much more severe in their imagery. Children who are not bipolar might dream of being chased by animals or monsters, but they manage to awaken before actually being injured. Conversely, children who are bipolar dream through experiences of physical attack that involve blood and gore. These children frequently report bloody images associated with torn skin and broken bones.[6]

Extreme Anxiety

Children with bipolar disorder can experience extreme anxiety. Separation anxiety in both infants and toddlers may be so severe that these children refuse to go to school. They might be extremely clingy and in need of constant reassurance. Children and adolescents may be preoccupied with death, separation, and abandonment. This anxiety may clear up with treatment, but some children require antianxiety medication.

Extreme Sensitivity to Stimuli

Children and adolescents with bipolar disorder are often extremely sensitive to stimuli. They are "thin-skinned" children who, like Brian, may be highly sensitive to touch, light, sound, taste, and/or smell.

In general, many of the symptoms of bipolar disorder in childhood and early adolescence may be reflective of an extreme lack of the capacity to self-calm, coupled with a tolerance for frustration. This is evidenced by the child's extremely diminished ability to regulate his affect, his quickness to become irritable and angry, his discomfort in making the slightest change in his activities, and, at times, his inability to maintain logical thought processes. During rapid-cycling or manic episodes, it may appear as if all his regulatory capacities are being challenged.

THE IMPACT OF EARLY-ONSET BIPOLAR DISORDER

The impact of bipolar illness for children and adolescents is severe and pervasive. While some children may become targets for positive attention, most are shunned or ridiculed by peers as too overbearing, aggressive, or irritable.

> *The impact of bipolar illness for children and adolescents is severe and pervasive. While some children may become targets for positive attention, most are shunned or ridiculed by peers as too overbearing, aggressive, or irritable.*

At home, a bipolar child draws on all of the family's emotional resources. Such children are challenging for parents as well as siblings. They need attention, special nurturing, limit setting, and the most forgiving love. The challenge of coping with a child's bipolar illness can lead to marital conflict and divorce.

Bipolar disorder in children and adolescents competes with channeling cognitive and emotional energies essential for academic achievement. The older adolescent may have extreme difficulty continuing school.

Although a bipolar child may be extremely bright

and creative in certain areas, bipolar illness interferes with a child's capacity to master skills or meet the challenges associated with normal emotional and social development.

Most alarming, bipolar illness can lead to suicide; it is a contributing factor in the significantly increasing rate of suicide among children. Between 1980 and 1992, the rate of suicide for children ages ten to fourteen increased by 120 percent.[7] In one five-year study of bipolar adolescents, 20 percent made at least one significant suicide attempt.[8]

DIAGNOSING CHILDREN AND ADOLESCENTS WITH BIPOLAR DISORDER

Diagnosing bipolar disorder in children and adolescents presents a difficult challenge. As reflected in the examples of Steve, Kevin, and Brian, a diagnosis of bipolar disorder may take years and involve numerous consultations before a correct determination is made. A part of this challenge is that there is still considerable controversy regarding the clinical presentation of pediatric bipolar disorder. A ten-year review of studies regarding pediatric bipolar disorder highlights this difficulty.[9]

For example, in 2001 the National Institute of Mental Health Research Roundtable on prepubertal bipolar disorder concluded that pediatric bipolar disorder can present as "narrow" or "broad" phenotypes. Children and teens with the "narrow" phenotype were described as experiencing multiple episodes of mania and depression with rapid cycling. They fit the diagnosis of bipolar disorder type I or II. However, since they often do not exhibit these symptoms for the duration of four to seven days, which is required to fulfill the *DSM-IV* (*Diagnostic and Statistical Manual of Mental Disorders,* 4th ed.) criteria for hypomania or mania, they may instead be diagnosed as bipolar disorder NOS (not otherwise specified). This is the diagnosis given when there are bipolar features but they do not meet the criteria for an official diagnosis of bipolar I or II.

In contrast, those with the "broad" phenotype are most frequently referred to clinicians and exhibit severe irritability, mood lability, severe temper outbursts, depression, anxiety, hyperactivity, poor concentration, and impulsivity. Because of the variability of symptoms evidenced with pediatric bipolar disorder, more children than adults may at first be diagnosed with bipolar disorder NOS (*DSM-IV*).[10]

In 2005, a team of doctors, clinicians, and members of the Child and Adolescent Bipolar Foundation identified guidelines for the treatment of child and adolescent bipolar disorder.[11] Regarding diagnosis, they emphasized the need to distinguish normal childhood misbehavior from that specifically due to bipolar disorder. Key factors identified were the frequency, intensity, number, and duration of symptoms. That said, the context of a situation also needs to be taken into account. For example, many children become giddy, irritable, or moody in a variety of circumstances, but their behaviors may not reflect bipolar illness.

Specific symptoms and factors to be on the alert for include the following.

Frequency and Rapidity of Cycling from Depression to Mania: Young people may first present with either manic or depressive periods. Some researchers indicate that children and adolescents exhibit greater frequency and rapidity of cycling from depression to mania than do adults with bipolar disorder. Young people move from one mood to another within several days and/or several times in one day. This is described as a mixed state and can include a demonstration of each mood minutes apart or with overlap.[12]

Somber Appearance, Negative Self-Statements, Suicidal Threats, Withdrawal, and Expressions of Hopelessness and Helplessness: These symptoms are evidenced during depression by some children and adolescents with bipolar disorder. While children may experience euphoria, they rarely experience the extended periods of euphoria, characterized by inflated self-esteem or grandiosity, that are typical of adult bipolar illness. As stated earlier, their bipolar disorder is more often reflected by irritability, intense angry outbursts, physical hyperactivity, aggression, physical impulsivity, and emotional lability.

Duration of Mania: Because young people often show greater emotional lability than do adults, child or adolescent mania may not last for a full seven days. Rather, moods may alternate within the space of a day or over several days. Manic episodes of at least seven days are a defining quality for a diagnosis of bipolar disorder, according to the *DSM-IV*.[13] That said, lately research has suggested the need for new, specific criteria related to children and adolescents.

Manifestation of Mania: Children with mania exhibit symptoms that are limited by their developmental constraints. While an adult may take trips, get involved in grandiose schemes, and run up excessive credit-card debt, children often demonstrate behavioral problems such as academic failure, fighting, dangerous risk taking, or inappropriate sexual activity. The fact that some of these fall within the normal range of children's behavior increases the difficulty of diagnosis.[14]

The adolescent's demonstration of mania begins to take on greater similarity to that of adults but is still limited by the child's social and developmental boundaries. However, adolescents, more than children, may still exhibit psychotic symptoms, including mood-incongruent hallucinations, paranoia, and marked thought disorder; markedly labile moods, with mixed manic and depressive features; and severe deterioration in behavior.[15]

Children often lack the capacity to reflect on their emotional states and the language to describe their internal experiences. Self-awareness regarding emotional development follows a course of increasing complexity.[16] A child must first learn to recognize an emotion and the physical state that corresponds to it. He then learns to label his emotions with a vocabulary that takes on increasing complexity.

For example, he may initially only be able to say he feels "good" or "bad." Increased language development, an increased capacity to attend to his internal experiences, and feedback from others help him differentiate his emotions to include "sad," "mad," "happy," "jealous," and other feelings. At a more advanced level of emotional development, he may be able to identify mixed emotions—that is, feeling different ways about the same event. Children's immaturity in language and the capacity to self-reflect clearly interferes with their ability to fully participate in a diagnostic assessment.

Traditionally, both the clinical view and the general attitude of mental health professionals prevented the assignment of the diagnosis of bipolar disorder to a child. It is human nature to minimize personal discomfort. The tendency of

> *Children's immaturity in language and the capacity to self-reflect clearly interferes with their ability to fully participate in a diagnostic assessment.*

parents and even those in the mental health field was, and to a lesser degree still is, to regard the child's behavior as reflecting a quiet, pensive, or down mood and to ignore the severity of the symptoms. This tendency reflects an idealization of childhood that has hindered a more accurate assessment of the true clinical picture.

Likewise, professionals may dismiss mania in children and adolescents as indicative of the natural self-involvement expected of children and adolescents. Mental health professionals are hesitant to apply the diagnosis of bipolar disorder to children and adolescents because, as stated above, the symptoms do not match those of adults diagnosed with this disorder. The descriptions of disorders in *DSM-IV* do not correspond to the symptoms evidenced by children and adolescents, but adults who are "on the edge of *DSM-IV*" may be similarly overlooked and undertreated.

Most significantly, diagnosis is often a challenge because bipolar disorder is difficult to differentiate from other diagnoses that share symptoms.

DIFFERENTIAL DIAGNOSIS

The major challenge in diagnosing bipolar disorder in children and adolescents is determining whether or not a child has another disorder with similar symptoms, bipolar disorder alone, or a combination of diagnoses (comorbid, or occurring together). Bipolar disorders in children and adolescents are usually a comorbid condition.

Those diagnoses that are most often comorbid and/or difficult to differentiate include attention-deficit/hyperactivity disorder, conduct disorder, schizophrenia, borderline personality disorder, substance abuse, and sexual abuse. Additionally, diagnoses that can mask bipolar disorder but occur with less frequency include panic disorder, generalized anxiety disorder, obsessive-compulsive disorder, Tourette's syndrome, intermittent explosive disorder, reactive attachment disorder, and, in adolescents, posttraumatic stress disorder.[17, 18]

A diagnosis is based on a careful assessment of emotional, cognitive, and behavioral functioning. A detailed history is important for any diagnosis but especially when identifying bipolar illness in children and adolescents. Doctors also utilize psychological tests, urine drug screens, CAT scans of the head, and blood tests.

Attention-Deficit / Hyperactivity Disorder

Attention-deficit / hyperactivity disorder (ADHD) is often difficult to distinguish from mania because of the similarity in symptoms: impulsiveness, hyperactivity, distractibility, inattention, and irritability. Studies have indicated that many youths with bipolar disorder also have ADHD.[19] Conversely, at least 14 percent of children and adolescents with ADHD also have bipolar illness.[20] Since the cluster of symptoms are so similar, a diagnosis of ADHD is only reached after ruling out a mood disorder."[21] Otherwise, it may be suggested that the two are made in tandem.

One study suggests that pediatric bipolar disorder can best be differentiated from ADHD by the presence of grandiosity, elated mood, flight of ideas, hypersexuality, and decreased need for sleep.[22]

> *While bipolar disorder affects adults of both sexes equally, studies suggest that early onset of the illness occurs more frequently in males.*

Boys are more frequently diagnosed with ADHD than are girls. Similarly, while bipolar disorder affects adults of both sexes equally, studies suggest that early onset of the illness occurs more frequently in males.[23]

In general, the symptoms appear more intense and severe when bipolar disorder is comorbid with ADHD. When these two diagnoses are not comorbid, the symptoms of ADHD are evidenced by a chronic and persistent pattern of functioning; bipolar symptoms are more erratic and severe. Bipolar symptoms also reflect more severe difficulty in the regulation of affect (emotion), which may be reduced during periods of relative mood stability.

Important research continues to find methods to distinguish these two disorders and identify more readily when they are comorbid. A recent study suggests the Child Behavior Checklist (CBCL) can help to make this distinction when used in conjunction with other forms of assessment.[24] The purpose of this checklist is to assess competencies and problems of children and adolescents through ratings by observers. The checklist includes fifteen scales. Although the sample was relatively small, when parents rated their children, those with mania and ADHD had significantly higher ratings than those children with ADHD alone on the Withdrawn, Thought Problems, Delinquent Behavior, and Aggressive Behavior scales. In addition, they had higher ratings of comorbid depression, anxiety, and psychotic symptoms.[25]

Conduct Disorder

The hallmark symptoms of conduct-disordered children and adolescents are also evidenced by children and adolescents who have bipolar illness. These include aggression toward people or animals, destruction of property, deceitfulness or theft, and serious violations of rules. Both disorders involve difficulties with impulse control and behavioral regulation. According to some studies, 69 percent of youths diagnosed with bipolar disorder also evidence conduct disorder at some time.[26] Conduct disorder can occur prior to the onset of bipolar disorder and subsequent to the first episode.

The key focus of study in the differentiation of diagnosis is the presence of a repetitive and persistent pattern of identified behaviors (in the child or adolescent with a conduct disorder) versus more episodic or periodic symptoms (by the manic child or adolescent).

Unless the child or adolescent is also manic, those with conduct disorder consistently experience less anxiety about their behaviors and appear less perplexed and genuinely connected in their interpersonal relationships compared to those who are manic (except during acute mania). Children and adolescents who evidence conduct disorder show long-term patterns in their lack of genuine empathy for the pain of others. Bipolar-disordered children and adolescents (unless also diagnosed with conduct disorder) more typically express genuine remorse and guilt following incidents of aggression or the violation of personal and social standards. Such guilt and remorse may further compound depression in children and adolescents who have only bipolar illness.

> Bipolar-disordered children and adolescents (unless also diagnosed with conduct disorder) more typically express genuine remorse and guilt following incidents of aggression or the violation of personal and social standards.

Schizophrenia

Since adolescents with mania often have schizophrenic-like symptoms, it is difficult to distinguish an early onset of bipolar illness from the onset of schizophrenia in this age group. This is especially true when they exhibit hallucinations and delusions. Bipolar illness is more often accompanied by psychotic symptoms in children than it is in adults. The chaotic pattern of emotionality and behavior exhibited by children and adolescents with mixed states and rapid cycling also bears similarities to adult schizophrenia.

Psychosis used to be considered the defining symptom of schizophrenia, but a distinguishing feature for those with bipolar disorder is the presence of increasing mania prior to hallucinations and delusions, further complicating diagnosis.

Family history is an extremely important factor to consider in distinguishing between bipolar disorder and schizophrenia.

Borderline Personality Disorder

Key features of this diagnosis may include frantic efforts to avoid real or imagined abandonment; a pattern of unstable and intense interpersonal relationships characterized by alternating between extremes of idealization and devaluation; impulsivity that is potentially self-damaging; and recurrent suicidal behaviors, gestures, threats, or self-mutilating behavior. Borderline personality disorder can also entail affective instability owing to a marked reactivity of moods; chronic feelings of emptiness; intense anger or difficulty in controlling anger; and transient, stress-related paranoid ideation or severe dissociative symptoms.

Clearly, many of these symptoms are also part of the cluster of symptoms associated with bipolar illness. However, unless these conditions occur together, the distinguishing factor in borderline personality disorder is that these behaviors appear as part of the core personality and are pervasive and persistent. With bipolar candidates these behaviors may stand out in sharp contrast to a more stable ongoing personality.

Substance Abuse

A major distinction between those who demonstrate behaviors owing to substance abuse versus those diagnosed with bipolar illness is that the symptoms caused by substance abuse are more transient and fleeting. Such abuse may lead to euphoria, irritability, aggression, impulsivity, psychoses, or other symptoms similarly associated with child and adolescent bipolar illness. An accurate history, chemistry workup, and assessment over time are important in making this differentiation. Substance abuse is often a comorbid condition for adolescents with bipolar disorder. While substance abuse is less frequent in children, it should be emphasized that, like Danielle Steel's son Nick Traina, children may abuse over-the-counter medications.

Sexual Abuse

Children who have been sexually abused or have witnessed adult sexual behaviors often exhibit hypersexual behavior similar to that demonstrated by children with bipolar disorder. They may seem precociously preoccupied with thoughts and expressions of sexuality, demonstrate inappropriate sexual behavior, and engage in frequent self-stimulation including masturbation. A careful history and assessment over time are extremely important in making the differentiation between sexual abuse and bipolar disorder.

Differential diagnosis is a complex challenge that requires continued research to improve the accuracy of early diagnosis of bipolar disorder.

CAUSES OF EARLY-ONSET BIPOLAR DISORDER

A detailed discussion of theories regarding the etiology of adult bipolar disorder has been presented in a previous chapter. Some controversy exists concerning possible differences between the causes of early-onset versus late-onset bipolar disorder. For example, research indicates that prepubertal-onset bipolar illness is more likely associated with early aggressive hyperactivity, lithium resistance (a lack of response to lithium), and greater familial loading (frequency of the disorder in the family history).[27]

One family study of bipolar disorder I in adolescence found early-onset symptoms were linked to increased familial loading and lithium resistance.[28] Researchers are also exploring specific genetic factors that may lead to early-onset versus late-onset bipolar disorder.[29] Other studies suggest a high prevalence of alcoholism among parents of young people with mood disorders.[30]

> *Early diagnosis and prompt treatment for children suffering from mood disorders are essential because individuals with early onset of the disorder are at great risk for multiple episodes of depression throughout their lifetime.*

Certain medical factors may trigger bipolar illness in children and adolescents. These include oral steroids, certain street drugs, and neurological conditions such as strokes, multiple sclerosis, tumors, and epilepsy, all of which can cause symptoms that are similar to bipolar disorder.[31]

MEDICAL TREATMENT

Early diagnosis and prompt treatment for children suffering from mood disorders are essential because individuals with early onset of the disorder are at great risk for multiple episodes of depression throughout their lifetime. While children and adolescents with bipolar disorder are responsive to a variety of therapies, no single definitive treatment regimen is currently available for them. Therapies used include medication, psychotherapy, family therapy, and psychoeducation.

Medication Therapy

Medication therapy is an essential component of treatment for early-onset bipolar disorder. While adults with bipolar illness may have periods of low-level depression and hypomania, children and adolescents more consistently experience severe aspects of the illness. The intensity of their mania, depression, mixed episodes, and rapid cycling demands ongoing medication management.

Each of the medications discussed below has the potential to improve the conditions of bipolar illness; however, they also have a wide range of potential side effects. Regimens should only be determined by knowledgeable clinicians and with the full collaboration of parents. Doctors should discuss all side effects with parents, so that they are fully informed before making essential decisions and are alert to possible side effects while monitoring their child's treatment. Finally, it is important not to minimize or idealize the potential of medications to produce positive change.

Lithium: Lithium has been the most consistently effective medication in the treatment of adult bipolar disorder, and has been shown to help inhibit suicidal behavior. Approximately 80 percent of patients respond positively to lithium. That said, it is less effective for children and adolescents. There are also lower success rates in patients prone to rapid cycling.[32]

Dosage for children is similar to that for adults, and as with adults, blood levels must be carefully monitored to avoid lithium toxicity. Parents should be on the alert for possible signs of lithium toxicity, which include fatigue, sleepiness, confusion, hand tremor, intestinal distress, slurred speech, tremors of the lower jaw, and unsteady gait. Lithium may also cause weight gain and adolescent acne.

Nausea and vomiting are also early signs of lithium toxicity, as are mental confusion and loss of coordination. Patients who take lithium and suffer gastrointestinal illnesses resulting in vomiting or diarrhea can develop lithium toxicity from loss of sodium and potassium.

The effectiveness of lithium is usually evident within two weeks for mania and four to six weeks for depression. While long-term use of lithium with adults has not yielded any negative effects, there are few longitudinal studies on children using lithium.

Anticonvulsant Mood Stabilizers: In recent years, a number of anticonvulsant medications have been identified as effective treatments for acute mania and the prevention of bipolar episodes. Patients who do not respond to or who are intolerant of lithium may respond to these drugs alone or in combination with lithium. Since these anticonvulsant medications were found effective with rapid cycling and mixed mania, their usage with children has increased.[34] Depakote, Tegretol, Neurontin, Lamictal, Topamax, and Gabitril are most frequently prescribed for children, even though research of these drugs has concentrated more heavily on adults.[35]

Depakote can cause severe life-threatening liver toxicity, especially in children under ten years of age. Tegretol and Lamictal can lead to life-threatening skin rashes. Depakote may also be associated with weight gain and with increased testosterone levels in both male and female adolescents, so it is important that hormone levels are monitored.[36] While these are rare side effects, it is important to bring them to the attention of the doctor as early as possible.

ELECTROCONVULSIVE THERAPY FOR CHILDREN

Electroconvulsive therapy (ECT), which has undergone significant change and refinement over the years, has been found to be as effective a treatment for children and adolescents as it is for adults. Excellent results have been observed in some young people with severe depression, psychosis, suicidal ideation, and mania that are unresponsive to medication.

ECT in children is rarely used, however, and only in extreme cases, as when the child has failed to respond to all other known treatments.

Antipsychotic medications are used with hesitation in children, except in extreme cases of psychosis. In adults they've been used for psychotic symptoms such as hallucinations, bizarre thinking, and unusual movements. They have also been effective for mania and mixed bipolar disorder when psychotic symptoms are present. While each of these medications is associated with typical side effects, the newer atypical antipsychotic medications (developed since 1990) have fewer side effects. One of these atypical antipsychotic medications, Zyprexa, has been recently approved by the FDA for active mania.

Sedatives: This group of medications has been found to quiet people while diminishing anxiety and activity, and fostering a more normal sleep pattern. This is especially significant in light of studies indicating that normal sleep patterns greatly reduce the frequency of mania.

Antidepressants: Although antidepressants are invaluable in the treatment of unipolar depression, current research suggests they may actually be detrimental when treating children and adults for bipolar disorder during depressive episodes. Specifically, the administration of antidepressants during depressive episodes can trigger an attack of mania. This risk is much greater if the patient is not receiving a mood-stabilizing agent.

In one study of 120 children with bipolar disorder, more than 80 percent escalated into full-blown mania, psychosis, or aggressive behavior following the administration of antidepressant medications.[37] For this reason, they need to be used cautiously and with close monitoring.

Psychotherapy

Psychotherapy is essential to the effective treatment of child and adolescent bipolar disorder. Such therapy takes a number of forms, including individual therapy, group therapy, couples therapy, family therapy, and multiple-family therapy. Parents and patient may engage in any one of these treatments or in several treatments simultaneously.

Individual Therapy: Individual psychotherapy may be indicated for the child or adolescent with bipolar illness. A necessary prerequisite for such participation is that he is sufficiently stabilized to make use of such treatment. In the context of individual therapy, a child or adolescent is helped to explore his emotions and attitudes about his illness. He thereby develops an increased capacity to reflect on the details of his experience, so that he can become engaged as an observer of the course of his illness. He may similarly learn strategies for monitoring his behavior so as to maximize his capacity, in light of his illness, for recognizing depressive thoughts, irritability, anger, and other subjective experiences that accompany bipolar disorder. Individual therapy can also facilitate his compliance with medications, a major challenge in the treatment of bipolar disorder in both children and adults.

In one study of 120 children with bipolar disorder, more than 80 percent escalated into full-blown mania, psychosis, or aggressive behavior following the administration of antidepressant medications.

Individual therapy may be indicated for parents as well, to help each of them deal with the personal impact of the illness. This is especially recommended when a couple is simultaneously involved in couples therapy or when one partner is more severely affected by the child's illness.

Group Therapy: Children and adolescents in group therapy or a support group are given the opportunity to feel connected to others coping with the same challenge. As with individual treatment, such participation is only feasible when sufficient stabilization has been achieved.

Couples Therapy: In this form of psychotherapy, couples are encouraged to share their reactions to the intense demands of having a child with bipolar disorder. The relationship of couples with a special needs child is often extremely challenging. This is especially true when the special need involves bipolar disorder.

The chronic display of extremely difficult behavior demands constant attention and has a direct impact on all of the family resources and, indeed, on the stability of the marriage. Facing this challenge often causes parents to feel helpless, inadequate, and ashamed and, subsequently, to isolate themselves from others and each other. This is a time that calls for improved communication, sharing, and mutual support and nurturance. If the parents are to be effectively available to help their child, they need to be helped to be available to each other.

> *The chronic display of extremely difficult behavior demands constant attention and has a direct impact on all of the family resources and, indeed, on the stability of the marriage.*

Family Therapy: There may be times when the entire family, including the child with bipolar illness, will meet in special session. These periodic meetings help to foster candid communication, identify family strengths, and develop new ways of responding to this exceptional challenge. Family therapy is especially beneficial when siblings are involved. Participation by the child with bipolar disorder is suggested if he or she is emotionally available and can be an active participant in the process. Since this demands a level of stability and a capacity to hear potentially negative thoughts, such participation should be carefully evaluated.

Family-Focused Psychoeducation

As described in chapter 6, family-focused treatment (FFT) may be indicated to help the family develop new skills in communication, problem solving, and stress management.[38] Siblings and other caretakers can also be involved in such treatment in order to develop consistency in the approaches used.

FFT is a powerful tool in improving negative expressed emotion (EE). Research with bipolar disorder has identified negative EE—a critical attitude toward patients on the part of family members—as a crucial variable that can lead to a poor treatment outcome.[39] Addressing negative expressed emotion in family therapy and in FFT may have a significant impact on medication compliance, and foster appropriate sleep patterns and overall adherence to the treatment program.

All family members, including the child with bipolar disorder (when stable and of an appropriate age), benefit by learning cognitive behavioral and behavioral methods that can be used with children to help them increase self-control regarding attention, impulsiveness, and anger management. Families learn strategies to help them respond to the intense aggression that such children demonstrate.

Other issues addressed include recognition and management of symptoms, treatment approaches, criteria for hospitalization, and how to facilitate hospitalization, when necessary.

Multiple-Family Therapy

This form of therapy was first practiced with families of psychiatrically hospitalized patients. Therapists meet with many families of patients in a large group. This format allows for increased support by sharing general information and strategies to help families cope with bipolar disorder.

Parenting

Recent years have witnessed increased resources and specific guidelines for parents of children and adolescents with bipolar disorder. Many of these strategies evolved through research into ADHD, explosive personality disorder, Tourette's syndrome, obsessive-compulsive disorder, and Asperger's syndrome but are increasingly applied to children and adolescents with bipolar disorder.

These approaches involve providing structure, helping a child to enhance his capacity for emotional regulation, calming himself physically and emotionally, and increasing awareness of his internal states, including thoughts, emotions, sensations, and moods in general. Such interventions help the child develop increased resilience to stress in general, whether responding to unanticipated events or simple transitions throughout the day.

The Child and Adolescent Bipolar Foundation has identified an integration of these interventions as Therapeutic Parenting.[40] These include a range of recommendations to address irritability, impulsiveness, racing thoughts, attentional difficulties, and the variety of symptoms that correlate with depression and mania. These techniques help calm children when they are symptomatic and can help prevent and contain relapses. They emphasize the following:

1. Teaching children ways to calm themselves physically and mentally as they also increase their body awareness
2. Helping children anticipate and reduce stress
3. Improving communication skills with a focus on listening and monitoring feedback
4. Using music and sound, lighting, water, and massage to help children with waking, falling asleep, and relaxation
5. Helping children anticipate and manage the tension of transitions, whether related to a change of setting or a request to redirect attention
6. Providing children with routine structure and freedom within limits
7. Removing household objects that could potentially be harmful

A behavioral reward program is often extremely effective when used in conjunction with these approaches to help children and teens monitor their reactions and learn strategies in mood regulation. However, it is important to remember that such programs should only be initiated after stabilization of their moods has occurred.

Educational Needs

Children and teens coping with bipolar disorder require ongoing medical management. Both the illness and the medication they take can greatly impact their attendance, concentration, alertness, motivation, energy level, and overall capacity to respond to stress in the academic setting. Such variability may occur in a day, a week, or over the course of an entire year.

Children and adolescents with bipolar disorder are entitled to have special accommodations. These should be determined as part of a comprehensive collaborative effort by the parents, special educational staff, and other professionals who may be involved in treatment planning. Psychoeducational assessment is an essential requirement to help facilitate a plan that will meet the needs of the child. This plan is called an individual educational plan and contains a range of very specific recommendations to help a child maximize learning while coping with the disorder.

Finding Professional Help

Identifying a professional to help manage the treatment of child or adolescent can often be challenging. Ideally, you can find a child psychiatrist in your community who has experience treating bipolar illness. If not, seek an adult psychiatrist who has expertise in mood disorders and experience treating children and teens.

You may want to seek the primary assessment by an expert in the field and then have another physician help monitor treatment. A directory of doctors is listed on the Child and Adolescent Bipolar Foundation Web site (www.bpkids.org).

Additional Resources

When we wrote the first edition of this book, there was little information available for parents in terms of providing a comprehensive approach to parenting a child with bipolar disorder. Since that time, several books have been written that received praise for their sensitivity, practicality, and the breadth of information provided. These new titles and additional Web sites are all included in the Resources (page 333) and Bibliography (page 337).

Support Groups

While support groups are extremely helpful for adults with bipolar disorder, support groups for parents of children with bipolar disorder should be considered a necessary component of the treatment plan. Meeting and sharing with other parents who are also challenged by the trauma of this illness helps to provide knowledge and support while reducing the sense of isolation that parents often feel. Some groups focus on support or advocacy. Others serve both functions. You can find a support group by contacting your local mental health center, hospital social services, health-care professional organizations, the Child and Adolescent Bipolar Foundation (CABF), the Depression and Bipolar Support Alliance, or through Internet Web sites. The CABF offers free online parent support groups (see Resources, page 333).

> *While support groups are extremely helpful for adults with bipolar disorder, support groups for parents of children with bipolar disorder should be considered a necessary component of the treatment plan.*

NEW HOPE

In spite of this most complex and challenging disorder, new hope exists for parents and their children. Recent developments offer increased hope for earlier recognition, accurate diagnosis, and effective treatment and management of early-onset bipolar disorder. These developments include:

1. Increased awareness of early-onset bipolar disorder
2. New research regarding the medications most effective in the treatment of children and adolescents
3. The increased training and education of medical and mental health regarding diagnosis and treatment of an illness that, until recently, was rarely considered for children and adolescents
4. New forms of psychoeducation that promote stabilization
5. Mental health and professional organizations increasingly advocating for parity of mental health with physical health in insurance coverage
6. The Internet, which allows for the rapid access of information and facilitates communication among all people affected by bipolar illness and has enabled families (parents, children, and adolescents) to feel less isolated
7. Associations such as the CABF, which provide parents with a range of services, including education, support, and advocacy

The family with a child who has a bipolar illness is continually challenged, twenty-four hours a day, seven days a week. Initially, a major task is the differential diagnosis of bipolar disorder in children and teens. This is often made difficult by the fact that this diagnosis shares symptoms with other disorders, and it can also exist in combination with other disorders such as attention-deficit/hyperactivity disorder, conduct disorder, schizophrenia, borderline personality disorder, ADHD, and substance abuse and sexual abuse. A second major task is to find appropriate resources and treatment. Fortunately, the family is only one small part of a much larger community that can unite in a collaborative effort to help and support each other in meeting this challenge. In recent years, an expanding number of resources and increased knowledge offers new hope for all who are impacted by child and adolescent bipolar disorder.

CHAPTER 12

Living with People with Bipolar Disorder

What image do we portray to other people? If we could peer into a mirror and see our true reflection, could we accept what we see as truthful? Many of us might be surprised, and even shocked, to discover that our self-image is quite different from the image we project to others.

A quick glance in the mirror each morning gives us a surface impression, like the jacket cover of a book, but we cannot envision how others perceive us any more clearly than we can hear the tone of our own voice when we speak. Have you ever been startled by the way you sound on a tape recording of your voice? Moreover, everyone's perception is different because no two people view the same object or situation equally. The question remains, What is reality?

Each of us constructs a self-image, a defining personality that includes internal guidelines or standards by which we assess how to think, feel, and behave. If we are flexible in our guidelines, this permits a greater range for self-expression. A lack of guidelines or too much flexibility leaves us subject to whim and inherent confusion, both for ourselves and those observing us. More rigid guidelines, on the other hand, lead to great trepidation when coming close to the self-applied limits, and even greater anxiety, guilt, or shame if such guideposts are crossed.

Personal standards are based on a variety of factors that influence personality. These factors include genetic predisposition, messages one might have heard growing up, and modeling after mentors. In addition, occupation,

> *Our reactions to other people give us more insight into ourselves than into others. If we choose only to focus on the behavior of others, we will get to know how they behave. If we focus on how we are influenced by others and look still further inward, we will more clearly recognize our inner self.*

religion, gender, age, ethnicity, culture, and socioeconomic level all influence and provide a basis for the standards by which we live. For example, a teacher might expect to conform to certain guidelines that are acceptable within the parameters of her profession. People often follow standards of behavior based on their religion.

Public reaction to George Bush's parachute jump several years ago reflects a range of personal standards. Some reacted with strong annoyance, declaring that he should "act his age." Others applauded his efforts to redefine the parameters of how a senior could be spending time. Some watch movies of Robin Williams or Roberto Benigni and consider both actors "off the wall," while others are envious of their passion and energy.

Our reactions to other people give us more insight into ourselves than into others. If we choose to focus only on the behavior of others, we might scratch the surface, at best. But if we focus on how we are influenced by their behavior and look still further inward, we will more clearly recognize our inner self.

Witnessing the behavior of someone with bipolar disorder, particularly during severe manic or depressive episodes, forces us to visit the boundaries of our own personalities. While this may occur in the context of any relationship, the highs and lows of human emotion are especially apparent in a close relationship with someone who is bipolar.

> *Witnessing the behavior of someone with bipolar disorder forces us to visit the boundaries of our own personalities. While this may occur in the context of any relationship, the highs and lows of human emotion are especially apparent in a close relationship with someone who is bipolar.*

If people have conflicting feelings or are sensitive about their own spontaneity, they may experience heightened tension in a relationship with someone who is manic. For example, if your anxiety level escalates when you pursue a dream or feel uninhibited, you may experience tension in such a relationship and begin to question your guidelines. Other people, owing to their own uneasiness about attention-seeking behavior, may feel discomfort when observing aspects of flamboyant, manic behavior that elicit attention.

RECOGNIZING THE INNER SELF

Manic behavioral moods—grandiose and uninhibited thinking—may lead patients to the very brink of their own impulses until they are forced to confront and define themselves. Observers feel comfortable if certain manic behaviors resonate with their own—until a patient goes "too far." Most people can be objective in assessing when "too far" is clearly destructive. Even mild mania may be threatening, however, if observers perceive such behavior as beyond their own limits, dangerous, "bad," "not me," or if observers are fearful and somewhat anxious about their own dreams and hopes. Those unafflicted will similarly experience tension if mania stirs up their yearnings for spontaneity, especially if they are questioning their self-imposed limitations.

If you are an acquaintance of someone who is bipolar, it is easier to set limits and keep the relationship narrowly defined. If you are trying to maintain a deeper intimacy, however, you must expect some underlying tension. You may need to define specific guidelines for yourself regarding your relationship and how you will respond to extreme behaviors or emotions. If you don't set these guidelines, you may tend to react rather than act.

As in any relationship, the more prone we are to react without a real sense of choice, the more we feel overly influenced by the other person, which can lead to resentment. This is yet another reason to establish hard limits ahead of time if you're involved in an intimate relationship with someone who is bipolar. Communicating these guidelines out loud is secondary to establishing clear guidelines for yourself, because the person with bipolar illness may or may not be able to respect such limits, depending on the severity of symptoms.

If a friend or loved one suffers from severe depression, be forewarned that the impact of being around someone who is emotionally constricted can cause you grief. You may experience a mild sense of hopelessness and helplessness. Increased tension is possible, especially if a part of you shares a propensity to depressive moods. It is also possible that your relationship with a severely depressed loved one may bring your worst anxieties, self-doubts, and pessimism to light.

Although tension is a natural reaction, you may be less affected by someone's depression or

> *As in any relationship, the more prone we are to react without a real sense of choice, the more we feel overly influenced by the other person, which can lead to resentment.*

mania if you are comfortable and secure with yourself. You still feel empathy, but you don't feel threatened by the other person's state. Even so, it's still advised to set limits, both in terms of time spent together and the level of intimacy desired.

Always be prepared for a more intense and intimate relationship with someone who is bipolar. In the context of such intimacy, you will be confronted with a very different set of expectations. You may even feel pushed to the edge of your "defined" personality.

KNOW THYSELF

As mentioned earlier, our feelings toward others—our likes, dislikes, attractions, irritations, admiration, and our repulsion—tell us more about ourselves than about others. Our reactions inform us of our passions, hopes, needs, expectations, longings, anxieties, and fears. They represent an outward reflection of our inner selves.

It is especially important to "know thyself" if you are in a relationship with someone who has bipolar illness. Whether you are a spouse, parent, son or daughter, sibling, colleague, or friend, your relationship is bound to be a challenging one. It may lead to feelings of excitement and frustration, joy and anger, fear and resentment, a sense of contentment or a sense of dread. Within the relationship, you may feel strongly connected one moment and estranged another. Hopefully, most of the time you will feel trusted and accepted, but in rare instances, or during episodes, you should also expect to feel devalued and rejected. You may even experience that well-known stress response of "fight or flight": on one hand wanting to leave but on the other wanting to strike back. In the midst of all this, you are trying to sort out your guilt, your own needs, and the needs of your loved one.

> *Always be prepared for a more intense and intimate relationship with someone who is bipolar. In the context of such intimacy, you will be confronted with a very different set of expectations. You may even feel pushed to the very edge of your "defined" personality.*

Most relationships encompass many of these reactions and issues, but you may feel more vulnerable in a relationship with someone who has bipolar illness because of the unpredictable and intense nature of the disorder. While a sense of vulnerability may not necessarily arise during those weeks, months, or even years when the disorder is stabilized, it is likely to be triggered when your loved one is experiencing intense depression or mania. Knowing yourself is your best defense.

Becoming in tune with your feelings results from working toward a greater understanding of your own sensitivities to depression and mania. We all possess these predispositions. The uniqueness of your individual personality influences how you respond to these extremes of behavior. For some, depression may be a familiar feeling because of a propensity for depressed moods. Biology and family history, which may include manic or depressive episodes, trauma, or other negative experiences, contribute to these sensitivities. Even if you've grown up in a nurturing and positive environment (and are not reacting based on your own insecurities or unresolved issues), you may tend to adopt unconscious, universally held beliefs (e.g., the stigma regarding behavior associated with manic-depressive illness). These attitudes and sensitivities frequently surface when living with someone with bipolar illness.

While the maxim "know thyself" has in recent decades increasingly become a part of American culture, it is an especially important aspiration if you are in a relationship with someone who has bipolar illness.

By knowing yourself, you can more clearly see how your needs, fears, and expectations are impacted when confronted with depression or mania. Likewise, knowledge offers you a greater capacity to respond to and manage your reactions. You can more objectively assess your contribution to the relationship, react less intensely, and learn to recognize choices and make clear decisions. It is important to identify those aspects of the relationship over which you can exert some control and those over which you have none. If you prioritize your needs, it is fair to expect your partner to honor those that are most important to you.

Similarly, you need to examine your expectations of the relationship and determine which ones are realistic and which are unrealistic. With this knowledge, you can maintain a greater sense of stability while living with a person with bipolar illness. Without this knowledge, your relationship is more likely to arouse self-doubt and related internal and interpersonal friction.

In general, people tend to respond favorably to someone with low-level mania. The very traits that are symptomatic of hypomania—energy, drive, optimism, and lack of inhibitions—are also components of healthy, optimal living. In the presence of a person with hypomania, it is possible to feel more confident and energized, and inspired to take action as you strive toward the fulfillment of your own dreams. The qualities exhibited during mania are contagious and resonate with the part of ourselves that fosters trust. Leadership ability and creativity are exemplified characteristics of low-level mania (hypomania). It is this very energy that has inspired many artists and world leaders.

> *You need to examine your expectations of the relationship and determine which ones are realistic and which are unrealistic. Without this knowledge, your relationship is more likely to arouse self-doubt and related internal and interpersonal friction.*

How we react in a relationship with someone who has bipolar illness greatly depends on the context of that relationship as well as our own needs and expectations. Take, for example, a patient by the name of Mark who reported a gradual shift in his feelings toward his wife over a three-year period.

When Mark first met Rachel, she was a real estate agent, and he was immediately attracted to her gregariousness, high energy level, effervescent demeanor, and physical attractiveness. He reported that he felt "so alive" in her presence because she was "spontaneous, free spirited, and zany." Ironically, one year after their marriage, Mark's major complaint about Rachel was that she became "too outgoing, too gregarious, too free spirited, and too spontaneous." In the context of marriage, and partially as the result of his own anxieties and insecurities, Mark's needs and expectations of Rachel shifted. Although it is easy to place all of the blame on bipolar disorder, in actuality it is not uncommon for the very qualities that first attracted us to someone to end up repelling us.

Like Mark, people who are used to feeling "in control" find that even self-trust is more difficult in a close relationship with a manic individual. This could lead to severe tension and anxiety within

DENIAL AND ENABLING

Even a healthy partner may occasionally neglect to notice any signs of the stricken partner's illness. Consciously or unconsciously, it is possible to minimize, ignore, or even fail to see symptoms when in denial. We may even conspire with the afflicted by failing to acknowledge the illness and promoting the avoidance of treatment.

In studying alcoholism, researchers have termed this process enabling. This term is equally relevant to our understanding of bipolar relationships. The ultimate impact of such apparent neglect is that the individual with bipolar illness and the relationship suffer equal damage.

the relationship. In this context, strongly motivated people may feel threatened and take action to safeguard their own sense of security by stifling the first sign of manic behavior in the other person.

Author John Gray (*Men Are from Mars, Women Are from Venus*) suggests that men and women come from different places in approaching the needs and expectations of their relationships. Gray argues that women tend to focus a lot of emotional energy on maintaining harmony in their relationships and feel personally responsible for the results. Given this, if a well-informed bipolar woman overvalues her contribution to the relationship and insists on harmony at all cost, the relationship could actually become more challenging and stressful for the partner when problems arise. To know oneself, therefore, involves recognition of one's strengths, weaknesses, and limitations. We need to be realistic in our self-appraisal and in our ability to contribute to and influence the tone of a relationship.

SELF-ABSORPTION

In severe depression, the afflicted are self-absorbed and constricted in their thoughts, emotions, and behavior. They have little energy and must conserve whatever emotional resources do exist. As we have stated throughout this book, depression brings forth feelings of hopelessness and helplessness. Increased self-disparagement and a sense of futility,

> *People who are used to feeling "in control" find that even self-trust is more difficult in a close relationship with a manic individual.*

shame, and dread foster further self-preoccupation. When the intensity level and frequency of these thoughts and emotions take total control of their attention, depressed people are less available to listen to others, show empathy, or even interact with loved ones.

As we have seen in other chapters, people with extreme forms of mania are predisposed to self-absorption but are not marked by hopelessness and helplessness. On the contrary, extreme mania is punctuated by tremendous activity as well as thoughts that go in many different directions. In the extreme, self-absorption may involve distracting psychotic thoughts in which inner voices or delusions take the forefront of attention. People in this state may shun relationships that do not further their needs and dreams or view them as mere distractions.

Even low-level manic depressives tend to be self-absorbed. This is a challenge for friends and loved ones who want to understand and manage their own feelings about the illness but are blocked by the patient's reduced availability for interpersonal relationships.

If you are a friend or loved one of someone who suffers from bipolar illness, you may experience a deep sense of loss as the severity of symptoms increases. The dynamics of the relationship shift as the afflicted person becomes less available or responsive. Increasing self-absorption may produce such a shift in personality that you feel as though the person you loved is no longer there. This shift, and your sense of loss, may not be as intense when the depression or mania is at a mild level, but as their symptoms worsen, so will yours.

> *If you are a friend or loved one of someone who suffers from bipolar illness, you may experience a deep sense of loss as the severity of symptoms increases.*

While this loss is not comparable to losing someone to death, there are some similarities in the feelings involved.

If we first understand ourselves, we are then in a better place to manage our loss. The second step involves learning how to deal with this change.

A major goal in working with people with manic depression is to help them accept the reality of their illness. Those of us who have relationships with them need to learn how to manage our own part of the relationship constructively and to acknowledge and accept feelings we experience in reaction to their illness.

Whether we feel loss, resentment, frustration, or anxiety, only by identifying our reactions can we experience a greater understanding and control over them. For example, in our reaction to the loss associated with self-absorption, we might only recognize anger and not see the grief. Or we might personalize the situation and feel depressed over what we perceive to be our contribution to their behavior. It is also possible to turn on the "automatic pilot" and adopt the role of a parent rather than a caretaker. You may ruminate over what you perceive as personal weakness in your loved one or the fact that somehow your advice is no longer needed. Or you may worry about your loved one looking elsewhere for excitement and stimulation.

If you tune in to your self-talk, you might hear, "If only I say the right thing, then maybe he'll go for a medication assessment; if he cared for me more, he would be motivated to spend more time with me instead of on his many projects; I was too involved with my career and didn't pay enough attention to him." While any one of these comments may reflect some reality during the stable phase of the relationship, they are far less relevant when accounting for the reality of intense mania or depression.

In recent years, researchers have been exploring the role of attention-deficit disorder (ADD) in adults and how this disorder affects relationships. These studies provide an alternative view of self-absorption. As an illustration, here is the story of a couple whom Bernard Golden counseled several years ago.

Linda presented complaints that her husband, Peter, was constantly self-absorbed. She described him being late for appointments, not listening to her, and even forgetting her birthday for two consecutive years. In spite of numerous complaints, his continued self-absorption led her to feel that he no longer cared for her.

> *It is helpful to recognize that the self-absorption of your partner, colleague, or friend may not be a reaction to you but a reaction to bipolar illness.*

One view of Peter's lack of attention to Linda is that he was self-absorbed by his own needs, selfish, unable to be empathic with another human being, self-centered, and self-focused. Some might describe him as narcissistic. However, research now suggests that adults, like children, experience ADD. This information allowed Linda to consider a different expectation behind Peter's behavior, which she could then use to evaluate whether it was a genuine lack of caring or his heightened distractibility that made him unavailable to her.

In a parallel sense, it is helpful to recognize that the self-absorption of your partner, colleague, or friend may not be a reaction to you but a reaction to bipolar illness. Each person's availability also fluctuates based on their unique personality. Their true capacity to be available, empathetic, and caring is best reflected during stable moods. Moreover, we should acknowledge the presence of many other external and internal factors that may contribute to their capacity for intimacy. Gauging which part of a person's character or behavior may be due to bipolar illness as distinguished from their "normal" or baseline personality is difficult for all involved. If someone is narcissistic by nature, then being bipolar may only accentuate this characteristic.

COPING STRATEGIES

In addition to knowing yourself and understanding the dynamics of a relationship as affected by bipolar illness, you can further improve your sense of well-being and coping skills through stress management, creating your own support system, psychotherapy or counseling, psychoeducation, educating yourself about bipolar disorder, and developing a list of resources for information and services.

Stress Management

Whether you are a friend or a family member of someone with bipolar illness, you are likely experiencing stress. It may be in the form of tension in communication, a loss in the quality of the relationship, or difficulty being assertive. You may also experience stress related to role changes, the pressures of caretaking, financial pressure, stigma, lost income, and the emotional consequences of coping with someone in a depressed or manic state.

> *Maintaining balance in your life is difficult enough even during the best of times. Responding to a loved one who has bipolar illness can be all-consuming, especially during severe manic or depressive episodes.*

Stress management is essential when someone you love is ill. It should involve some of the guidelines that we generally associate with self-nurture but also focus on the specific stress of living with someone with bipolar. Techniques include learning new skills regarding time management, learning to care for the caretaker, physical relaxation strategies, maintaining your own life (friends, hobbies, your own activities), developing and practicing assertiveness skills, and maintaining healthy nutritional and physical well-being.

Maintaining balance in your life is difficult enough even during the best of times. Responding to a loved one who has bipolar illness can be all-consuming, especially during severe manic or depressive episodes. Whether you are concerned about suicidal potential in periods of intense depression, psychotic reactions to financial ruin, or legal involvement as fallout of severe mania, living with a bipolar adult draws on all of your energies and resources and can put the relationship to the test.

Attending to your needs is a priority for your own emotional balance and makes you more available to support your loved one. Although it's easier said than done during the more stressful periods, your own personal support system can be of great benefit in coping with this situation.

Create and Maintain a Personal Support System

Although you might be inclined to isolate yourself, maintaining ties with friends and relatives serves a variety of purposes, especially when you are experiencing a sense of loss. Maintaining contacts with people you genuinely trust offers you emotional support and an objective perspective when your own objectivity is damaged by the emotional strain. Support is also essential for your self-esteem, which can decrease in reaction to this challenge. People available to run errands and help out with chores can also be real lifesavers, especially during periods of exacerbation of symptoms. Don't underestimate the importance of such a support system which leaves you mentally and physically able.

Psychotherapy and Counseling

Whether you seek couples counseling, family therapy, or individual treatment, psychotherapy and counseling can provide not only greater understanding of how to live more constructively with a bipolar loved one but also how to better recognize, make sense of, and manage the wide range of reactions you will experience in this context.

Just as we suggest that you interview several psychiatrists regarding medication treatments, we strongly recommend that you interview several therapists for your own psychotherapy or counseling. Your major priorities should be the quality of the rapport as well as the experience a particular therapist has in addressing the issues you are facing.

Family-Focused Psychoeducation

Family-focused psychoeducation is another approach that shows much promise in helping relatives (parents or spouse) live with bipolar illness. While these programs were originally found to be highly successful family treatments for schizophrenia, they have now been adapted to help families cope with bipolar illness. The following assumptions can be made for both illnesses:[1]

1. An episode of a psychiatric disorder represents a severe environmental challenge to the family system.
2. In response to such episodes, families often become disorganized in ways that may inhibit the patient's recovery. Communication and problem-solving skills that were previously practiced are ignored during the period of acute illness, especially within families where tensions were previously present.
3. Family-focused psychoeducation can assist in achieving a new state of equilibrium.

Psychoeducation programs include educating the family unit about bipolar disorder, its signs and symptoms, and its etiology and treatment. Families are taught to learn communication skills (training in active listening, delivering positive and negative verbal feedback, and requesting changes in the behavior of the other family members) and problem-solving skills (identifying problems, generating, evaluating, and implementing solutions that help foster stabilization and may inhibit relapse.

> *Families who received family-focused psychoeducational therapy exhibit more positive interactional behavior, and patients have evidenced reductions in mood disorder symptoms when assessed one year after treatment.*

In part, these programs are based on research findings that intense emotional expression is associated with stressful patterns of interaction during the post-episode period. Expressed emotion refers to critical, hostile, or overinvolved attitudes that relatives maintain toward the family member with a psychiatric disorder. Families who received family-focused psychoeducational therapy exhibit more positive interactional behavior (specifically nonverbal behavior), and patients have evidenced reductions in mood disorder symptoms, when assessed one year after treatment. Research in this area continues to try to identify what skills are most effective with specific types of families.[2]

Education

Educating yourself about the illness is essential if you are going to live with a bipolar individual. As emphasized throughout this book, knowledge offers strength. Learning how to recognize symptoms, keep current of new medications, and develop awareness of support services and advocacy groups are all ways to educate yourself about mood disorders.

In addition to books that offer a clinical focus, reading biographies of people with bipolar disorder can lead you to a greater understanding of the illness through the personal disclosures and perspectives of the afflicted. Increasingly, those who live with bipolar adults are sharing their experiences in this manner. Reading other accounts can help restore your sense of connection and ease the isolation you may feel in responding to this illness.

Developing a List of Resources

Coping with a friend or loved one with bipolar illness requires a wide variety of resources. These may include educational groups, names of support agencies, books, or videotapes. Such resources have increased in recent years and offer invaluable aid in terms of information on available services and on dealing with every aspect of mood disorders.

Do research in your community to identify medical doctors who treat bipolar illness. Afterward, interview several to determine with whom you feel the most rapport. Inquire as to what percentage of their practice involves actual treatment of individuals with bipolar illness.

Since we have witnessed great advances in the treatment of mood disorders, your best choices of doctors are those who frequently treat this illness. These specialists will have the most up-to-date information about prescribing medications that might work best for each individual.

Bear in mind that close supervision of medical therapy is extremely important, particularly during the initial period of treatment. Frequent monitoring should involve face-to-face contact between the patient and the doctor to determine the effect of a specific drug and its dosage.

We strongly recommend careful research even if your loved one refuses treatment. If you wait for a crisis to occur before seeking help, it may be too late.

Your list of resources should include crisis assistance in the event your loved one needs medical attention or psychological help. While you may never require it, you will feel better prepared if you have these phone numbers on hand.

As part of your research, you may also want to inquire into the services that psychiatric facilities in your community provide for people with mood disorders. Learn which procedures are necessary to follow should you become so concerned that you need to commit your loved one to a psychiatric setting. Such agencies may provide support services in the form of education, self-help groups, and family therapy for both the healthy partners and family members, as well as those afflicted with the illness.

NANCY PROBES FOR ANSWERS

To understand how I, as a manic depressive, affect others living around me, I asked for candid responses. "Be honest," I urged. "This is a book about truth. I'm taking a hard look at myself—no pretenses permitted." The result has been an "out-of-body" experience for me, as I needed to step back and clinically reflect on the findings of my research without permitting emotion to dominate my thoughts.

Lois: Empathy and Unconditional Friendship

My friend Lois was somewhat hesitant because, as she honestly admitted, she felt uncertain about exploring such feelings.

"We've been friends for a long time, Nancy, but some things I feel uneasy about delving into. Over the years I have sometimes reacted positively and at other times negatively to various situations you've related to me. I carry these thoughts around with me while considering all aspects, both positive and negative. But regardless of how I personally feel about any one particular incident, what matters most is that our friendship is unconditional."

Although Lois internalizes a lot of what I confide in her, she also is forthright with her feelings and responses. If I happen to be at the height of a manic episode, she may defer saying something to me so as not to add fuel to the fire. When she feels that I'm in a good place to listen, she'll say, "I hear you, but I don't understand. I think you're making a mistake. I wish you'd reconsider."

"What I admire most is your willingness to accept criticism and your desire to change," said Lois. "You look for honesty in relationships, and I respect this. What's so reassuring is that we can level with each other without worrying about offending one another. This is what makes our friendship special."

I have known Lois for more than thirty years, since we were classmates in high school. As we matured, so has our friendship. We rec-

> *Lois is sensitive to my bipolar condition. She has never minimized it or ridiculed me for my actions, which at times I know can be difficult to deal with.*

ognize and accept each other's strengths and limitations, and from this has emerged a deep mutual respect and sisterly loyalty. Lois is sensitive to my bipolar condition. She has never minimized it or ridiculed me for my actions, which at times I know can be difficult to deal with. When I become too intense, she tells me about it.

Dianna: Setting Limits and Applying the Brakes

Frequently, Dianna Bolen, my coauthor on *Just as Much a Woman,* would caution me, "Slow down. Focus, Nancy. Focus!" Dianna described me as "charming and glowing with energy" but has often backed away when these very symptoms make her feel off-balance and uneasy.

While collaborating on our book, Dianna and I used to enjoy periodic get-togethers over a few glasses of wine as we talked business. We became personal friends and confidantes.

"When you describe an event, it's reflected both in your tone and rate of speech, as if something big is about to happen," said Dianna. "There's an aura of excitement around you, but as we sit for long periods I feel disjointed, somehow distant, like I'm viewing a special effects scene at a movie theater. I'm drawn into the drama, yet not fully a part." Dianna became edgy when I "rambled." She also commented about feeling "a twinge of sadness" although she did not understand why. "Is it me?" she asked herself, "or is it something about Nancy?"

During the drive home after one of our luncheon meetings, Dianna told me that her mind began to wander as she reflected on her afternoon experience. "I began with what I knew to be true," she mused, "that I am an outgoing, enthusiastic person with plenty of energy. But with you I felt kind of 'slow.'"

In time, Dianna began to grow weary of my apparent highs and lows, and likewise, I became increasingly disenchanted by what I considered her insensitivity to my affliction. The dilemma became more and more upsetting for me, and my agitation escalated further while my self-confidence temporarily eroded.

When we reached the final editing stages of *Just as Much a Woman,* our work pace quickened. As primary author and literary agent, I phoned Dianna more regularly during this period. Dianna's translation of my communications was "trivial details unrelated to the book." She felt that my messages carried a "sense of urgency" and that my points were sometimes "repetitive." I am accustomed to replying immediately to telephone messages, faxes, and e-mail correspondence. Dianna, on the other hand, gives herself a twenty-four-hour window for response. That works for her but annoys me. It seemed clear that Dianna and I had different ideas about what is "important." My manner of dealing was to wait an hour or two and if she didn't call or fax back, I sometimes repeated the message if I felt it was important and could not wait. "Is it possible," I thought, "that heightened tension has prompted Dianna to hold the relationship with me at bay by keeping it narrowly defined?" Apparently, she had begun to distance herself.

Finally, Dianna attempted to structure our conversations so they did not exceed ten to fifteen minutes. I found this restriction exasperating. "What has gotten into her?" I wondered. "Where is her flexibility? Isn't flexibility the name of the game? Since when does she have the right to place restrictions on me? How insulting!"

"What's your goal, Nancy?" Dianna would ask. Frequent clashes resulted because it is difficult and unnatural for me to talk "bottom line." I envisioned an imaginary time clock, and in order to get all my thoughts in I began to talk faster and faster.

Several months after Dianna and I had completed working on the book, she described her thoughts in a short personal essay: "Nancy is speaking louder and faster. Her voice is strident, the sweetness gone. How does she have time to breathe between words? She accuses me of being critical of her. I feel I am not being heard. In frustration, I put down the phone and walk away. When I return a few minutes later, Nancy is still talking; she did not even notice my absence.

"It's Tuesday afternoon and my answering machine is blinking to be played. My fax machine is spewing out pages sent by Nancy. I let out a sigh and ignore the faxes. I have received hundreds of faxes from Nancy at all hours of the day and night. Many times, there is no new information. Or I receive six faxes of the same form letter, each addressed to a different recipient. I despise the wastefulness. I resent the intrusiveness. I am angry."

> *Finally, Dianna attempted to structure our conversations so they did not exceed ten to fifteen minutes. I envisioned an imaginary time clock, and in order to get in all my thoughts I began to talk faster and faster.*

Stepping aside, I can now see how Dianna's frustration over this matter must have heated up to the point of actual boiling. But I, too, was at the brink of explosion. We are two strong-willed individuals who have different priorities and working styles that were just not meshing.

Over a period of months, our relationship eroded still further. While we continued professionally, we otherwise kept a comfortable distance. I wondered if this was another ending. Here I was again, experiencing heightened tension with a friend who was distancing, setting limits, and applying brakes.

Yuri: Visiting the Boundaries and Returning to Friendship

I had gone through that kind of distancing with Yuri, but we survived many endings and many new beginnings.

My relationship with Yuri has manifested extremes at every level because of the intimate quality of our friendship. Since he has observed me at close range during episodes of mania and severe depression, Yuri has been forced to visit the boundaries of his own personality. When Yuri feels threatened by the intensity of my mood swings, he slams on the brakes and takes off in flight. "I'm off to Australia," he'll announce. "Don't find me!" This sudden distancing leaves me bereft, exacerbating my already high level of anxiety, and I engage in irrational, sometimes dangerous, behavior.

Yuri and I had formed an intimate relationship of sorts as we struggled from 1982 to 1987 from both sides of the Iron Curtain for his freedom and right to exist. In response to my information gathering for this book on how my illness affected those around me, he said, "You know my answer. Of course it was difficult being with you during your mood swings. We struggled with it, and you resented me. When you'd question me with neon-bright emotional colors, the chances were high that your answer would be fortune-cookie style." By fortune-cookie style, he meant not the truth but what I wanted to hear.

"My answer is that any disorder is always superimposed on a personality," Yuri continued. "Nasty people with a mild case of flu can be hard to take. Nice people are loved even when they have a debilitating illness. So your illness has been less of a problem. You are free of malice. Our problems arose because of your tendency to manipulate, and I am particularly sensitive to any strong guiding hand. Still, I know that this is regarded as symptomatic of bipolar disorder. Manic-depressive illness not only presents a major challenge for those 'blessed' with it, but also for those of us around.

> *"When you'd question me with neon-bright emotional colors, the chances were high that your answer would be fortune-cookie style." By fortune-cookie style, Yuri meant not the truth but what I wanted to hear.*

"Friendship presumes respect, not just flattering words and empty comforting. But you couldn't accept it when I gave it to you straight. You got mad and I froze, retreating into my comfortable shell. But even the Berlin Wall has come down, so let's not reconstruct any more fences! Remember the dear past, and let's not risk another fight. We've come back to friendship."

Marty: Embracing Loss and Making Adjustments

The most important person in my life is my husband, Marty. "I'm very proud of you," Marty said recently. "I'm excited you're doing so well, and I know you're happy when you're writing. But I regret not spending much time together anymore. You're always working."

I know that living with me is not easy for Marty. If our marriage were not so strong, there have been many times over the years that it could have collapsed. It's difficult for him to relate to my passion. He doesn't understand that a writing task can't be put down as easily as an accounting problem. But many writers share my intensity toward writing. It may be less about my bipolar disorder and more about the nature of writing.

That said, the mania that surfaces during my periods of intense writing exacerbates my bipolar condition. It is especially challenging for Marty during these episodes.

"When I walk in the door from work, you are still in your office," said Marty. "You're either at the computer or on the telephone. We eat dinner late.

Afterwards, you fall asleep or go back to work. You're obsessed with work. Your work continues for hours, days, weeks, months, even years. It never stops. When you're not working, you talk about it, sometimes to the exclusion of everyone else in the room. You get so wrapped up in what you're saying that you lose sight of others wanting to speak. You eat, drink, and breathe your work, and you seldom quit before you're ready to collapse.

> *When I can't turn you off, I go into "overload." I tune out and don't hear anymore. It's very frustrating. Sometimes you'll ask me for an opinion, but you don't wait to hear my answer and you do what you want anyway.*
>
> —MARTY ROSENFELD

"When I can't turn you off, I go into 'overload.' I tune out and don't hear anymore. It's very frustrating. Sometimes you'll ask me for an opinion, but you don't wait to hear my answer and you do what you want anyway. You seem to pay more attention to other people than me."

It is clear that Marty experiences real stress and loneliness. His loss is real, and he longs to return to the earlier years of our marriage when life was much simpler. The adjustment for him has been twofold: dealing with the pain from all the stress I've put him through and the loneliness created by my absence.

Bernie: Empathic Without Feeling Threatened

Bernie instantly observed the mania in me at our initial meeting when I approached him about coauthoring this book. "I had eagerly looked forward to the meeting because I am attracted to people who exhibit excitement, energy, drive, and a certain lack of inhibition," said Bernie. "This affinity is part of my personality as well as a driving force behind my work with clients. I have experienced this positive feeling when observing people, both in personal relationships and in clinical settings, who evidence certain manic qualities. But I remained somewhat apprehensive about our getting together. In part, this concern was related to the daunting diagnosis of bipolar illness.

"Some patients learn to manage their illness extremely well, but others are completely taken over by it. I had a history of experience to fuel my apprehension.

"Although my real fear was in not wanting to maintain a clinical lens during our meeting, I didn't want to be swept away in the whirlwind of excitement that I know such energy can elicit from me. At the same time, I admit to having been more than a little excited after learning about your two successfully published books. Both personally and professionally, this reassured me of your ability to channel your energy constructively."

Our scheduled one-hour meeting lasted two hours because both of us were so engrossed. "You exuded so much energy," recalled Bernie, "and when you spoke, there was a sparkle in your eye as you communicated a clear passion about life and the desire for further enrichment. You demonstrated some expansiveness in gestures and were emotionally open."

When I described my book proposal and discussed past endeavors, Bernie recalled my exhibiting "great animation." He said, "As we shared, I experienced an internal dialogue which reflected my reactions to you and the surfacing of my personal issues regarding bipolar disorder."

Bernie found himself wondering if he would be able to keep up with me and meet our deadlines, especially when I boasted about getting by on a mere four hours of sleep for extended periods of time. He also wondered to what degree my potential for depressive or manic symptoms might interfere with and/or foster the progress of a joint project. Additionally, might he be persuaded from time to time, against his better judgment, to agree when he preferred to disagree?

"Gradually," said Bernie, "as the focus of our conversation shifted from professional to personal, I sensed a mutual understanding and genuine connection between us. We both knew intuitively that we were well matched and could complement each other in a one-to-one relationship."

Bernie recognized me as someone who had transformed a negative condition into a positive and meaningful life. He recognized my energy, drive, and lack of inhibition; and, appropriately, he paused. Might he be swept away in the "whirlwind of excitement" that he knew such energy could create? Should he apply the brakes? "I realized that it is at this junction that most of the turmoil arises for those who live with people with bipolar illness," said Bernie. "I stayed in this place for a moment, clarified my sensitivities and how I would address them, and moved on."

Bernie found a lot of correlation between his reactions and those of the other people I asked about their experience of me when relating to someone afflicted with this illness. "It is important that you know yourself," he said, "that you recognize the nature of manic and depressive symptoms, and that you are able to understand and recognize the interplay of these two polarized patterns of behavior."

> *It is equally important to remember that any disorder, as stated by Nancy's friend Yuri, is always superimposed on a personality; an individual with bipolar disorder still has a core personality throughout all phases of the illness.*

T hroughout this chapter, we have identified how individuals are impacted in relationships with those who have bipolar illness. We have shared personal examples and highlighted several key issues to help shed light on the nature of such relationships. While many of the inherent challenges parallel those of any relationship, bipolar illness may more severely affect intimacy at all levels.

It is equally important to remember that any disorder, as stated by Nancy's friend Yuri, is always superimposed on a personality; an individual with bipolar disorder still has a core personality throughout all phases of the illness. That personality has a history of values, attitudes, interests, and behaviors even though it is colored by depression or mania. This is true for both people in the relationship.

Those who responded to Nancy's request for feedback all refer to issues of personality and the influence of bipolar illness. These issues, however, are often difficult to separate. Nancy's friend Lois clearly focuses on personality when she says, "What I admire most is your willingness to accept criticism. You look for honesty in relationships." In contrast, Nancy alludes to the influence of bipolar illness: "If I happen to be at the height of a manic episode, [Lois] may defer saying something to me [until] she feels that I'm in a good place to listen."

It is human nature to include the internal standards by which we assess how to think, feel, and behave into our defining personalities. Similarly, we construct a defining image of those with whom we form relationships. We may develop expectations about how they should behave in general, as well as how they should respond to our expectations. When someone appears to move beyond the parameters that we have established as her "personality," we may be quick to say "it's not her." This is an inherent part of all relationships.

The impact of bipolar illness, however, challenges expectations and causes tension for both partners. It is this tension that leads to discussion or efforts to withdraw. These discussions can become less meaningful or productive when symptoms are exacerbated. Each partner may feel less understood and experience the other as insensitive. How you respond to this tension is an individual decision based on personality, expectations of the relationship, the level of intimacy, and the level of commitment.

Living with someone who is afflicted with bipolar disorder presents challenges that are both similar to and yet different from other relationships. Only by being aware of how our individual relationships are influenced by the illness can we make them more fulfilling. When we possess such awareness, we are better able to experience our relationship as one with an individual who has bipolar illness rather than as a relationship with a bipolar person. In this way, we can still feel connected and maintain both empathy and compassion.

CHAPTER 13

Compassion, Self-Compassion, and Bipolar Disorder

As a general guideline, compassion and self-compassion are key in responding to any major life challenge. It is as true for those living with bipolar disorder as it is for the lives they touch.

Compassion involves acknowledging that as humans we are all imperfect. It encompasses the recognition that each of us experiences various degrees of suffering as we respond to the challenges of living. Compassionate people embrace the desire to alleviate the pain of others, and translate this desire into action, behaving in ways to help reduce suffering.[1]

While Western culture provides some dialogue about the need for compassion, only in recent years have we begun to explore self-compassion, a concept that has been more thoroughly addressed in Eastern philosophy and religion. Self-compassion involves the same components of compassion but instead focuses on empathy, understanding, and caring that are self-directed.[2] Thus, we are self-compassionate when we can acknowledge our imperfections and suffering, maintain a desire to alleviate our pain, and act in ways to affect change in these regards. Self-compassion requires a nonjudgmental attitude toward imperfection that fosters the acknowledgment and acceptance of our flaws. Far from passive acceptance, however, genuine self-compassion moves us to act assertively to alleviate unnecessary suffering.

Every aspect of dealing with bipolar disorder demands compassion and self-compassion. This begins with the first recognition of symptoms and continues through stages of being diagnosed, engaging in treatment, and living with the disorder.

DIAGNOSIS

Making an accurate diagnosis of bipolar disorder is an act of compassion. Once made, this diagnosis has implications for treatment implementation; to seek and choose from the broad range of resources that might manage and reduce the suffering aroused by bipolar symptoms. And yet, far too often, attitudes of stigma interfere with an accurate diagnosis. Such stigma, rooted in fear and ignorance, can undermine all aspects of compassion in the diagnosis and treatment of bipolar disorder.

How any individual responds to such a diagnosis very much reflects a capacity for self-compassion. If, based on fear or ignorance, we maintain an attitude that the illness is a product of a weak character, or that the individual is flawed or inadequate, we fail to recognize and accept human imperfection and frailty. Certainly, this is a challenge, especially during a period of severe depression, a mood partially *defined* by feelings of imperfection and inadequacy. However, such an attitude reflects perfectionism regarding how one "should be," or despair over things we cannot control. Compassion and self-compassion drive us to responsibly take steps to exert control only over what we can control and to accept the things we cannot change.

As reflected throughout this book, we firmly believe that recognizing and acknowledging symptoms is a fundamental component of self-compassion and an initial step in effectively managing them.

TREATMENT COMPLIANCE

Treatment compliance—maintaining a medication regimen as well as psychotherapy—is a major challenge to effective management of bipolar disorder. The reasons for lack of compliance include the influence of stigma—that which is internalized as well as the concern for what others will think. Other obstacles to compliance include the enjoyable "highs" associated with mania, the fear that medications will stifle achievement, and the fear of losing one's identity.

Many individuals with bipolar disorder hold on to unrealistic expectations that they "should" be able to master the thoughts, emotions, and actions associated with this disorder without treatment. Certainly, those with bipolar disorder vary in their ability to manage the illness. The variation in the debilitating symptoms, individual resilience, support, and lifestyle allows some to manage their lives more effectively than others. However, the avoidance of treatment can also be viewed as a lack of compassion. Self-compassion involves practicing the same nurturance, care, and protective attitude that a loving parent would with her child.

Bernard Golden often asks his clients to imagine that a child has come to them with the symptoms they describe. "I help clients to envision the child sharing the details of their depression or mania, the experience of shame, guilt, inadequacy, or anxiety, which are associated with this disorder. I then inquire whether they would seek treatment for that child if they were the parent. In most cases, the response is, "Certainly! I would not want my child to have to suffer!" This response is truly an expression of deep-felt compassion. Yet all too often they fail to maintain this attitude in consideration of their own treatment.

DEALING WITH LOSS

The diagnosis of bipolar disorder can often challenge one's sense of identity. Many diagnosed with this illness report a sense of disbelief that they are unable to do things that were previously a normal part of their daily routine. Whether successfully fulfilling their duties in a work setting or maintaining meaningful relationships with friends and loved ones, the impact of this illness often leads them to experience a loss of identity. This is a valid fear that often inhibits seeking treatment. However, treated or untreated, the sudden onset of depression or mania is always disorienting, as it threatens the stability and continuity in one's sense of self. This experience alone may lead to perceived identity loss.

"I will be a different person if I take medication." This is a common misunderstanding expressed by clients with bipolar disorder. In reality, medication and psychotherapy actually help you become more of who you are and who you wish to become. In the context of treatment, you can develop increased control in your life to pursue what you hold meaningful. Adherence to treatment releases you from the chains of extreme emotions and incapacitating or expansive thoughts. It reflects self-compassion that supports truly following your own path in self-evolution.

Unfortunately, depression and mania both encompass a set of attitudes that reflect a lack of self-compassion. They often reflect an internalization of extremely high and unrealistic self-expectations, many of which are "super-human" in quality and clearly do not reflect the essential attitude of compassion: that being human means being imperfect. During depression, this lack of self-compassion is most revealed by thoughts of despair and inadequacy resulting in the paralysis to take action.

GRIEVING AND SELF-COMPASSION

Where there is loss, there is grieving, an essential aspect of self-compassion. Grieving involves a deep sense of sadness and an acknowledgment of the suffering surrounding loss. This grieving may best be described as "grieving the loss of the healthy self."[3] Most serious challenges are life-altering. So it is with bipolar illness. Some individuals with this illness experience a disruption in a career, financial ruin, or tremendous turmoil in a relationship owing to their illness. They must be encouraged to mourn over such loss within reason. At the same time, they need support to recognize their options, reduce their suffering, and continue working toward dreams, old as well as new.

Part of dealing with such experiences involves grieving and mourning what one "should" be or "could" have been. Yet those who overcome a physical or emotional handicap can recognize that such impairments are only a part of who they are. Whether adjusting to life after losing a limb, having a stroke, experiencing a chronic illness such as diabetes or AIDS, or experiencing mental illness, it is only when the individual can mourn and grieve his past sense of self that he can move on. Only then will he recognize his true identity and act assertively to nurture and support it.

This component of self-compassion needs to be embraced by individuals with bipolar illness, and emphasized by those who live with and treat them. Family members, friends, and health-care workers need to focus on this important aspect of grieving and the reality of loss if they are to genuinely support those with bipolar illness. In this way, compassion from others becomes internalized. It can be a powerful force that helps the grieving process move forward.

As described in chapter 6, those with bipolar disorder need validation of their loss and grieving, but at the same time they also need to be supported in identifying and pursuing change. Anyone who lives with and cares for individuals with bipolar disorder communicates compassion and encourages self-compassion by practicing these attitudes.

Descriptions of mental illnesses as "no-fault" disorders reflect this attitude. This emphasizes the lack of choice in developing bipolar illness but does not imply that patients refuse responsibility for their own care.[4]

This is especially important when dealing with someone in a depressed phase who is deeply enveloped by shame and hopelessness and who is emotionally challenged by the idea of responsibility and positive change. Bernard Golden describes a client he worked with early in his career who expressed this dilemma. "You have really helped me understand how this illness effects me. You do a good job of gently pushing me toward examining my choices and responsibly acting on my decisions. At the same time you have been there just to listen to and support me. However, in the last few weeks I feel you pushed me when I just needed a little more of that support." This person's request for compassion demonstrates sufficient self-compassion to articulate what he needed.

All too often we suffer because we chastise ourselves over insights we missed in the past. Hindsight, by definition, consists of new awareness gained following an action that offers alternative perspectives regarding that action. We help others practice compassion by encouraging them to be realistic regarding their hindsight.

It is through self-acceptance as part of self-compassion that transcendence becomes possible. The challenge of any physical injury, physical illness, or emotional disorder is to acknowledge and accept the limitations that may incur. This does not mean giving in to the crippling aspects of life's challenges. Rather, it calls for the openness to look for ways of living a satisfying and productive life in spite of them. This is what Dr. Fawcett refers to in chapter 14 when he describes being an "owner" of the illness; fully accepting it as part of your life but not defining who you are.

Many patients with bipolar illness describe intense anger at the diagnosis. This is a natural reaction. In fact, if channeled constructively, it can energize and motivate patients to take control of their lives. In contrast, dwelling on this anger can lead to passive acceptance and focusing on the illness as a major aspect of identity. Ultimately, this will only inhibit involvement in effective treatment. Similarly, anger based on shame and disappointment can lead to denial, avoidance, and minimizing of symptoms and consequently undermine the desire to seek treatment.

As with grieving and dealing with loss in general, transcendence does not occur at any given moment. Rather, it is a process that involves repeated moments of anger, sadness, and disappointment, followed by acceptance, self-nurturance, hope, reengaging in life, and seeking support when necessary, so as to continue on life's journey. During these moments, treatment and the validation of loved ones can further foster moving past the grieving process. Setbacks in managing bipolar disorder do occur, just as they may happen with regard to any chronic illness. This does not imply a failure to progress or weakness of character. Merely, it reflects the nature of the illness as well, as the challenge inherent in making significant life changes.

Even family and friends may interfere with this process and in effect set up barriers to the effective management of this illness. Some may view an attitude of self-compassion as a reflection of weakness. They may view acceptance of symptoms as giving in. According to this perspective, the depths of depression are merely signs of "laziness," "malingering," or a "lack of motivation." Yet these descriptions tell us nothing about their underlying meaning. Acceptance that stems from self-compassion means acknowledging that one is subject to severe variations in mood. Practicing compassion and self-compassion fosters the desire to reduce suffering that results from such mood swings.

THE SENSE OF EXPOSURE AND SELF-COMPASSION

Many individuals with bipolar illness resist diagnosis and treatment because they believe the diagnosis implies they are flawed. Unfortunately, the impact of bipolar illness is extremely difficult to hide. It is difficult, even at lower intensities, to mask behaviors that derive from racing thoughts or grandiosity, or feelings of inadequacy, hopelessness, and helplessness. Yet fear and ignorance conspire to further this attitude despite the urgent need for treatment.

Looking more closely at this attitude, we often find that many individuals with bipolar illness had feelings of inadequacy and not measuring up long before they were formerly diagnosed. Early experiences, combined with the impact of even subtle symptoms, contributed to this negative self-view. Difficulties in mood management, feeling significantly different than or not accepted by others, not understanding themselves, and feeling misunderstood are a few of the factors underlying this deep sense of inadequacy. For those experiencing this negative self-identity, being diagnosed is often validation of what they already believed. The diagnosis is now a public announcement of a very private experience of shame.

It is no surprise then that many who have mood disorders are reluctant to embrace their diagnosis. Imagine the trauma of making public a self-view you've desperately tried to hide, from others and yourself. The intensity of negative feelings in diagnoses derives in great part from reexperiencing past shame as it relates to feeling flawed.

Compassion from others and self-compassion are the antidote for this reaction. Viewing manifestations of symptoms as a human imperfection, recognizing and wanting to alleviate suffering related to the illness, and taking action to do so, depend on self-compassion and nonjudgment. More specifically, maintaining an attitude of nonjudgment reduces the paralysis of shame and the self-denigration that accompanies it. This then is part of the challenge for anyone living with bipolar illness; to be self-compassionate and consistently remind themselves that the illness just reflects one of many ways in which we are all imperfect.

SELF-COMPASSION AND MINDFULNESS MEDITATION

Much of psychotherapy involves fostering and practicing self-compassion. Through shared exploration and skills building, clients can better understand and manage how their attitudes and behaviors either sabotage or help them to live more productive lives. Additionally, they learn specific skills to alleviate symptoms that interfere with their life's journey. Mindfulness meditation is one strategy that truly nurtures an attitude of nonjudgment. This form of meditation has been found to be increasingly effective in mood management. It helps clients to develop a "decentered" relation to their negative thinking so as to prevent the escalation of such thoughts at times of potential relapse.[5] For this reason, we are including a detailed description of this approach as a valuable strategy to help practice self-compassion.

Much of our suffering is based on the meaning we attach to internal experiences. For example, we may have thoughts about our feelings, feelings about our thoughts, and thoughts and emotions regarding our sensations. You may have a depressive thought and immediately make a judgment about your entire character based on that thought. As such, your reaction only heightens your sense of hopelessness and helplessness. Or you may experience anxiety and become angry or anxious that you are experiencing anxiety. You may experience thinking you are inadequate to perform a specific task and immediately conclude you are inadequate as a person. More specifically related to bipolar disorder, you may think you are hopelessly flawed because of your illness merely because you are presently having depressive thoughts.

In each of these situations, much of your suffering and even the exacerbation of symptoms is aroused by your assessment of internal experiences. Coping with bipolar disorder involves being able to regulate moods, which are very much influenced by such assessments. It is what patients believe about their depressive thoughts or grandiose thoughts that either leads them to ignore or seek treatment. Similarly, what they conclude about their experiences of mood change determines whether they become increasingly depressed or accepting of typical difficulties of mood regulation. Mindfulness meditation offers an approach to reduce suffering by becoming less reactive to these inner experiences. By doing so, it promotes further self-understanding and more self-compassion.

There are many different forms of mindfulness meditation. Some are based in Buddhist religion and philosophy while others are Western adaptations. Though reviewing all of these is beyond the scope of this book, one form, Vipassana, reflects the key aspects of the practice and is most relevant for meeting the challenges of living with bipolar disorder.

Vipassana means "insight," having "a clear awareness of exactly what is happening as it happens."[6] This practice involves heightening awareness to internal experiences while at the same time reducing their potentially negative impact. Learning mindfulness meditation takes time, energy, determination, commitment, and resilience. Thus, it is most effective to practice it when stabilized rather than when actively depressed or manic. Through this practice it is possible to increase understanding that fosters internal flexibility, tolerance, and self-compassion.

Mindfulness meditation offers skills in self-awareness and mood regulation that can help alert you to the stressors that lead to relapse. Specifically, mindfulness meditation can help you recognize your thoughts and emotions and to feel more comfortable when experiencing them. Additionally, it offers an increased capacity to realize you do not have to act on or respond in any way to such internal experiences. Grandiose or depressive thoughts and feelings are seen for what they are—transitory internal experiences that can be ignored rather than obsessed over or acted on.

According to the Buddhist perspective, all of our inhibiting themes are a result of a compulsive "attachment" or aversion to people, things, or ideas.[7] Accordingly, we seek self-identity and meaning by becoming attached or overly invested in our thoughts and emotions as hard and fast definitions of who we are. We similarly become attached when we overly value the approval of others or narrowly define ourselves by job title or certain personality traits. In reality, however, who we are is fluid and forever evolving. You may have depressing or manic thoughts, but they can only define you if you overvalue and embrace them. In contrast, if you are able to view them as a narrow sample of the full spectrum of potential thoughts you could experience, you will become less reactive. Such thoughts lose their meaning when you are able to view their presence as transient and fleeting.

In several ways, this approach is significantly different than those already described as a part of cognitive behavioral therapy in chapter 5. Rather than dialoguing with or challenging thoughts, mindfulness meditation holds all mental events as transient and not a permanent part of your identity. It is when you observe them, let them go, and assertively choose not to attend to them that you will develop increased freedom to really connect with your reality.

The notion that all life is transient may at first appear to seem pessimistic and depressing. Yet only when we recognize the impermanency of life can it become meaningful. The recognition and reduction of intense compulsions then frees us to become more alive and in touch with life. It is from this realization that we develop choice and actually become energized, as we are no longer captive to our compulsive cravings or aversions.

The form of mindfulness meditation we present conveys some of the essential elements of the practice.[8]

MINDFUL MEDITATION EXERCISE

Find a quiet and relaxing place where you will not be disturbed. Sit on a cushion placed over a carpeted floor or on a comfortable chair. Try to sit up straight without making yourself uncomfortable. If sitting on the floor, cross your legs and place your hands in your lap, one over the other, palms facing up.

Focus on your breathing, specifically on a point at your nostrils where you actually sense the movement of inhaling and exhaling. While focusing on your breath, notice anything that disrupts your attention. Be sensitive to thoughts, sounds, images, or physical sensations you may experience while you are breathing. You may experience a variety of thoughts, including your plans for the evening, chores you need to attend to, the day's events, or your impatience with this exercise. You may experience a slight discomfort in your leg or an itch on your arm. Just notice these experiences without thinking about them. Gently redirect your attention to your breathing.

Ram Dass describes this process as seeing "your thoughts go by as if they were autumn leaves floating down a stream. The leaves drift by, being moved this way and that by the eddying water ... the leaves, the thoughts, float by, but keep your attention on the water itself."[9]

The emphasis is on viewing these experiences as transient, perceiving yourself as a "receiver" of such information but not as an "I" that has to attend to, fix, or become involved in any way with the experience. It is stepping back from each thought and with each return to the breath, emphasizing, "I do not have to respond to this."

Through practicing this process you learn at a deep level that thoughts and feelings do not define who you are. You will also learn that even suffering is transient, as you watch your reactions come and go. From the Buddhist perspective, this practice liberates us from making judgments about internal experiences. By practicing observation rather than response, you will become less critical and attached to such experiences. In the process you will become more human and compassionate, both with others and yourself.

As suggested by Thich Nhat Hanh, in *The Miracle of Mindfulness,* "To master our breath is to be in control of our bodies and minds. Each time we find ourselves dispersed and find it difficult to gain control of ourselves by different means, the method of watching the breath should always be used."[10]

Research shows that the consistent practice of meditation results in neurological changes associated with increased levels of alertness, relaxation, and attention control.[11] Most significant for those with bipolar disorder, mindfulness meditation has been shown to help foster mood regulation, especially as it relates to depression.[12] In effect, through practicing meditation you can increasingly experience certain levels of discomfort without exacerbating them by embracing judgmental thoughts. Mindfulness meditation helps you view such experiences as transitory events, not unlike clouds passing overhead. You can learn to experience them without feeling compelled to act on them.

We must reiterate that mindfulness meditation is just one of many strategies that can support the process of practicing self-compassion and compassion. Whatever you do to foster such compassion will invariably assist you in effectively managing the challenge of living with bipolar illness.

CHAPTER 14

Take Advantage of Support Groups

T he value of a support group is in the mutually helpful relationship that grows out of it—by helping others, you help yourself. These new friends, your fellow group members, can become a mainstay of support because you share something with everyone present: You all live with bipolar disorder. Your group becomes a forum for mutual acceptance, understanding, and self-discovery. A sense of camaraderie quickly develops.

Spending an evening with a group of strangers, all of whom have some type of mood disorder, may at first seem rather daunting. But as you become involved in discussion, you will feel buoyed by your new bond of support. Whereas you might feel very down on yourself (as people with any chronic illness often feel), if you continue with the group it should raise your self-confidence and help you feel improved. In the group, you have an opportunity to reach out to others and, in turn, accept their help. You will no longer feel alone with your problems; others have been there, too.

"Dealing Effectively with Depression and Manic-Depression," a brochure offered by the Depression and Bipolar Support Alliance, lists guidelines that form the foundation of effective recovery. Support groups throughout the country use this brochure. Here are the guidelines:

Hope: With good symptom management, it is possible to experience long periods of wellness.

Personal Responsibility: It is up to you, with the assistance of others, to take action to keep your moods stabilized.

Self-Advocacy: Become an effective advocate for yourself so you can access the services and treatment you need and make the life you want for yourself.

Education: Learn all that you can about depression and manic depression. This allows you to make good decisions about all aspects of your treatment and life.

Support: While working toward your wellness is up to you, the support of others is essential to maintaining your stability and enhancing the quality of your life.

Treatment for Bipolar Disorder: Treatment for bipolar disorder can be difficult. It is not easy to find a psychiatrist who can accurately diagnose and treat the condition, and it may be even more challenging to obtain insurance that will pay for the needed treatment, including prescribed medications. Nevertheless, good treatment is essential. Treatment can be further enhanced by participation in a support group.

PORTRAIT OF SUPPORT

Participation in a support group is no substitute for professional treatment, but it can help in ways beyond professional treatment and at minimum cost. Support groups are available in most locales. A variety of them exist, and frequently more than one type of group is available in any given region. As they vary in emphasis and "personality," depending on the type of group and the style of its leadership, you may feel more comfortable with one than another.

During the summer of 2006, Dr. Fawcett had the opportunity to speak with members of support groups in different parts of the country. During these one-on-one sessions it was clear that the members who received the greatest benefit from their experience were the ones who remained with their original support group the longest. He also learned about a whole universe of interconnecting support experiences from groups organized with national affiliations. Leaders of these affiliates are trained to help groups initiated by individuals with personal experience of bipolar disorder—an owner of the illness, a close relative of someone affected, groups with special purposes (like helping each other find employment), "spin-off" groups of several individuals who became acquainted through a larger support group and kept in touch by telephone and e-mail. These people became trusted friends who now support each other in decisions and confront one another if there are signs of a possible relapse.

Owner Versus Consumer

From speaking with these brave people who confront their illness on a daily basis Dr. Fawcett witnessed firsthand the "evolution" of support resources that respond to different preferences and needs throughout the lifetime of "the owner" of a condition.

"Notice how I use the unofficial neologism *owner* rather than the *official* term *consumer*," says Dr. Fawcett. "The term *consumer* reminds me of a marketing tool for selling a product, as if the person suffering from depression or bipolar disorder were the same as a consumer of automobiles, toothpaste, or beauty products. Yet not everyone with depression or bipolar disorder will qualify as an owner. To become an owner, you first must recognize and be willing to admit the following:

1. You have a problem.
2. Your problem needs addressing.

"In owning up to the condition, you are assuming the responsibility of being proactive to improve your own life. You 'own' the condition and commit to take full responsibility for getting help. Once you confront the 'Why me?' you arrive at the point of no longer wanting (or needing) to hide your bipolar condition. It is a fact of life, a position obtained through the experience of belonging to a support group. Now you can hold up your head and state with conviction:

> *I have bipolar disorder, it is part of who I am, but my identity is not limited to being bipolar. It's a medical problem that I have to deal with.*

"As human beings we all have limitations and struggles. In fact, we all are in the same lifeboat and doing our best to live meaningful lives, while trying to help others within our individual parameters. It is no different than any significant medical problem. You educate yourself, do whatever is necessary by obtaining the best possible help, and then try to move on with your life.

"In a state of depression, it is normal to want to withdraw from social contact. It is also difficult to get up the energy to attend a discussion involving a group of people, especially people who are basically strangers. Some feel ashamed when they are depressed, and the last thing they want to do is risk exposure—to themselves or to others. People often initially have trouble admitting they "are like that," or in the category of having "a mental illness" whether it's bipolar disorder, or some other condition."

Yet it is worth the effort. Discovering that many other people are struggling (or have struggled with) symptoms like yours can be reassuring. This allows you to obtain a level of understanding and support previously inaccessible. It is encouraging to hear the story of someone who experienced similar symptoms and suffered similar side effects and/or disappointments regarding their treatment. Personal success stories can give you the hope and reassurance necessary to buoy your own struggle, whereas someone who never had this experience cannot address it with as much conviction.

Depression and Bipolar Support Alliance

Although all support groups differ slightly in their approach, they also offer many similarities. One well-known and highly ubiquitous group available in many communities is the Depression and Bipolar Support Alliance (DBSA), a group that became a national organization in 1986 with headquarters in Chicago. DBSA, formerly known as the National Depressive and Manic Depressive Association (National DMDA), was started by two Chicago area patients, Rose Kurland and Marylyn Weiss, with the objective of providing support for people with depression and manic depressive illness (bipolar disorder). The National DMDA's primary efforts were initially focused on the elimination of stigma associated with mental illness. They aimed to accomplish their goal through public education, informing people that problems associated with mental illness are not caused by weak character or personal failure but illnesses like any other—including physical ailments like heart disease and diabetes—that require both medical treatment and coping skills. Eventually, this small core group extended to spouses and other relatives, until finally proliferating coast to coast to form a larger group that was capable of raising money and providing a hotline of information. The expanded group offered encouragement and written data about different types of treatment, further encouraging the formation of still more groups around the country until they ultimately attained national status in 1986. They then began to lobby for more extensive research and the fair treatment of patients with depression and bipolar disorder. Group members made very effective spokespersons before legislators and congressmen because they all suffered from the same illness and had survived by responding to treatment.

With the help and support of pharmaceutical companies and other sources, DBSA remains a valuable community resource that offers encouragement and information to local groups throughout the United States. Their educational materials provide guidance for patients who struggle daily with their illness, while encouraging them to stay hopeful and to maintain their dignity throughout the struggle for wellness. By their example and their strong presence in Washington, DBSA has made great inroads in their effort to combat stigma.

Support groups typically meet weekly at a local church, hospital, or public building. With advance permission of its members, Dr. Fawcett attended one such group in Santa Fe, New Mexico, in July 2006. The meeting was held at a Methodist church on a Tuesday evening. He asked the members what they felt was most helpful for each of them in attending the group. A common theme was the benefit of speaking with other people who had or were still going through the same symptoms and the opportunity to learn firsthand how they dealt with them. Members learned that they were not alone in what they were experiencing. Support, understanding, valuable information, and coping suggestions emerged from these sessions. DBSA meetings focus on all aspects of depression, manic and hypomanic episodes, the cycling from mania to depression, and helpful ways of coping. The group encourages the persistence of treatment while maintaining an objective eye on the limitations and benefits of any one method of treatment. As with any support group, the "personality" or tone of the group is established by the leader and its regular members. Although some groups may appeal more or less to different individuals, the groups are always supportive of new attendees.

Each meeting is guided by a group leader, usually someone who has been designated by the group's regular attendees. Most meetings are semistructured, and begin by going around the group for a brief "check-in." During this time, each member has the opportunity to discuss how the past week has been for him or her, which often elicits group discussion and input. Members are encouraged to express their thoughts freely and not hold back. Support groups offer a safe haven without fear of recrimination. After everyone has had the chance to speak, the group proceeds with a broader discussion of questions and ideas about treatment issues. Strict confidentiality, kindness, and support—rather than advice—remain strong group values. Members stand behind each other through personal crises, and they encourage one another to stay with treatment even if hoped-for results are not immediately attained. As a group, they might gently confront a fellow member who seems to be withdrawing or showing signs of relapse.

At the meeting that Dr. Fawcett attended in Santa Fe, eleven people showed up at the beginning and three others joined later. The group was led by Mary, whose sister suffered from major depression since childhood but remained undiagnosed until 1994. Although Mary's sister had participated in therapy, received antidepressant medications, and attended 12-step groups, her initial involvement stemmed from comorbid substance-abuse problems and not from depression. Ten years ago, she moved to Santa Fe to be near Mary but suffered a severe recurrence of depression after their mother's death in 2002. It took two years of treatment and the support of church and friends to lift her out of that depressed state. Mary's sister had felt desperate and isolated when she joined the group, but the support and connection of other people who had had the same illness gradually eased her suffering and helped her along the path to recovery.

> I still see the glass as half empty, and I get anxious, but the "quality" of my life is better.

Mary's sister said it is the *people* who have been crucial to her recovery. "Most important, I have emerged from focusing solely on myself and have learned to care for others. It is wonderful to give and not to just receive."

Marcel, a Ph.D. with bipolar II disorder and a two-year member of the group, announced he had a good week.

Sally called herself "the oldest living bipolar of the group." "We're here for one another—up or down, good or bad. It's that love and support you don't always get from your family." She described being in terrible financial straits and unable to work as a result of her illness. Sally was forced to sell her jewelry to pay for a place to stay until she could sufficiently recover and support herself. "I kept going and survived because of a couple handfuls of people. The group became my lifeline."

Sam recounted a history of major depression since the age of seventeen. He feels better now but still has difficulty in the morning and trouble initiating. He feels the group helped him feel less stigmatized by his illness. "I used to feel alone and often paranoid around people," said Sam.

Deedee told of having diagnosed herself as a teenager with bipolar I disorder but that her family physician had disagreed. She did not receive treatment for twenty years and said she was emerging from a prolonged mania. Deedee has attended DBSA groups for twelve years. "This is the only place I can get support." Loved ones feel burdened by Deedee's problem and can only stand to share so much.

Joseph, who lives with bipolar I depression, told of starting to drink at age thirteen. He needed electroconvulsive therapy for treatment but received none until five months ago. Prior to finding the group in Santa Fe, Joseph could not locate a source of support to unload his burden. Hearing firsthand stories from others is helpful for him.

As the wife of a man who suffers from depression, Nina discussed the painfully difficult past six months, in which she had witnessed her husband burst frequently into tears. Nina stated that she recognized the value of the group, but only from the vantage point of a patient, as she was present only to accompany her husband.

Inspiration from Recovered Patients

All fifteen people who attended the group facilitated by Mary, no matter what mood or state they were experiencing, expressed how group support had reduced their suffering by making them feel less alone, more accepted, and more hopeful. The experience of recovered attendees inspired them with a hope that neither medical nor psychological treatment could match. Although the benefits of a support group are no substitute for professional treatment, a support group can serve to enhance the treatment received during psychiatric and cognitive therapy.

National Alliance Against Mental Illness: At lunch with four members of the National Alliance Against Mental Illness (NAMI), the informality of the setting provided Dr. Fawcett the opportunity to inquire about the personal benefits of the group for themselves and others who live with a serious psychiatric illness. Marcia, who was chairperson of the local NAMI board, arranged the luncheon and attended with two other board members. A fourth member of our group, although he related closely to the others, maintained that he was attending *only* as an "independent."

NAMI was formed in the late 1970s by parents of patients who lived with a severe form of mental illness. The purpose of the group was to support each other in dealing with a loved one's illness, while advocating for better treatment and more research. These patients, most of whom were schizophrenic, were identified as "consumers." It now appears that the makeup of NAMI members has changed as the new generation of participants and leaders refer to themselves as "consumers."

Local NAMI groups traditionally meet bimonthly, with one meeting designated as an "informational" meeting where speakers provide up-to-date information on the diagnosis and treatment of various serious mental illnesses and/or issues related to "consumers" needs. The second monthly meeting, "Share and Care," is a support meeting led by a person trained for this role by NAMI. Both meetings are attended by consumers and their families. The guiding principles of the meeting are *acceptance* and the *ability to remain nonjudgmental* as members air their experiences. These presentations cannot be contradicted, and everyone in attendance is offered the same chance to speak. They know that whatever is said within the confines of the group is "safe" and remains in strict confidence.

SPITFIRE: Self-Protection First: Dr. Fawcett's lunchmates each talked about the positive effects that their participation in NAMI had on their illness. For example, they all experienced a sharp decrease of isolation and a shattering of imagined limits by their imposed illness. They emphasized the acceptance, nonjudgmental aspect of the group, the value of learning from the struggle of others firsthand, and the benefit of networking with people outside of the group. Yet they hastened to add that social contacts by telephone or e-mail from outside members had to be governed by the SPITFIRE principle: "self-protection first." This means that if any relationship becomes too negative for a particular party, to the degree that it threatens their very recovery, then that relationship should be promptly terminated. It can be done with a simple explanation that the person can no longer handle the relationship and, therefore, it must end before dragging them further into a state of depression. The principle that relationships should be mutually positive might be useful for relationships in general.

Fawcett asked the support consultants what they might suggest to a new attendee so the incoming member maximizes the positive effects of the "Share and Care" group, and in response they devised five guidelines:

1. *Focus* on your problem and what you want to accomplish.
2. *Listen* to others.
3. *Direct* your attention to the issue of caring.
4. *Persevere.* Know it may take several sessions to feel comfortable and benefited by attending the group. Try to attend a series of meetings regularly to permit you time to get to know the group and the individual participants.
5. *Don't monopolize.* Try not to monopolize the time since everyone needs an equal opportunity to express themselves. Listen before jumping in to speak.

People sometimes feel needy in a group, and they may even appear like "know-it-alls." "If you don't let this deter you as leader," said Marcia, "your group will usually deal with it in a gradual, compassionate way and things will balance out."

Dr. Fawcett's companions had all experienced severe problems and had done very well. All four had stayed with the group and had benefited greatly, by their own testimony. He could not help but feel admiration for their struggle and for what they had accomplished. It took persistence.

Persistence: Persistence is the only path to recovery, but it is a real challenge if your mental filter is distorting your outlook and keeps telling you, "This is not going to help, nothing will help." Well-meaning friends can further aggravate the situation by telling you, "Pull yourself together. Go out and jog. I do it when I'm depressed."

Networking and the Clubhouse Movement: One member of the NAMI group, John, was also actively involved in the local Santa Fe Clubhouse. Although Dr. Fawcett had not heard of it before, he was quite impressed with how excited John felt about his group. John explained how the group was dedicated to networking for the purpose of helping one another locate new jobs. Since many patients find that their illness interferes with job performance, networking is a very restorative activity. It has been shown in a study by the Harvard School of Public Health for the World Bank that depression is the fourth cause of disability throughout the world. It also was predicted that by 2020 depression would climb to the second cause of disability worldwide.[1] John described how his schizoaffective depressive condition precipitated his divorce and the loss of his capacity to work. In his descent, the local St. Elizabeth's Shelter for the homeless helped him to turn his life around. His treatment—the combination of psychiatry and cognitive therapy—and the NAMI group helped him stabilize his life. John now looks forward to his work with the Santa Fe Clubhouse, which is helping him recover his ability to enjoy a productive life. He described the clubhouse program as "people helping people," a peer-to-peer, psychosocial rehabilitation geared to reattaining a functioning productive life. John informed Dr. Fawcett that the clubhouse movement is also a national organization.

Daniel, the independent member of the group, talked about "spin-off" support groups that are formed by people who meet at formal groups like NAMI and how helpful these groups can be in providing needed support to progress in the face of self-doubt and lack of confidence that result from bipolar or depressive illness.

From Dr. Fawcett's four new companions, the presence of a support universe—a powerful movement driven by people determined to help themselves and their peers—holds real potential for people with mental illness, particularly those with the ability to participate and benefit over time.

Recovery, Inc.: Sara is a group leader at the Santa Fe Chapter of Recovery, Inc., one of the oldest support groups in the country. This mental health self-help program, based on Dr. Abraham A. Low's innovative and important work of 1937, operates as a nonprofit, nonsectarian organization that is completely member-managed. With more that 700 groups across the United States and around the world, members consist of people with depression, dysthymia, bipolar disorder, and all psychotic disorders including schizophrenia, anxiety, and obsessive-compulsive disorder. Recover, Inc., takes a "bottom-up" approach as contrasted with the "top-down" approach of DBSA and NAMI. The focus of DBSA and NAMI is on the illness, whatever leads to the symptoms of depression, anxiety, mood swings, and despair by utilizing support and education to help group members recover and cope with their symptoms and consequences of their illness. Recovery, Inc., is not illness focused, as diagnoses are not discussed. Dr. Low believed that illnesses that resulted from an accumulation of painful everyday experiences could be instrumental in helping patients help themselves. It is said that Dr. Low's approach of patients helping themselves was so radical in the late 1930s that he nearly lost his medical license when he formed the first recovery group. These groups, led by trained laypeople, deal with distressing life events and coping skills. Each group member is given approximately five minutes to describe his or her problem, and another ten minutes is allotted for the group's discussion about the specific problem. Storytelling is discouraged; rather, it is the situation that is to be described. This approach stems from the point of view that if everyday small situations are not skillfully handled, people can experience a spiraling down and ultimately arrive at a point where they no longer want to continue living. Mastering life's small problems is therefore the central focus.

The group uses "spotting" (Dr. Low's terminology) to help one another develop an understanding that they are experiencing a symptom-led response. Symptoms might be as "trivial" as not getting out of bed, not functioning, or having a panic attack while trying to make a decision. Catch phrases are learned to help people think more realistically about such a problem (e.g., "distressing but not dangerous" would be used to describe a panic attack). The focus is always on the specific event, not just feelings pertaining to the event.

The Recovery approach has been likened to current-day cognitive behavioral therapy but uses a vocabulary largely invented by Dr. Low. Although some of the wordage may seem antiquated, the overall approach continues to be helpful to many individuals.

Sara referred to the Recovery approach as "Zen for the Western mind" (the letting go of judgments). "It's an effort to break lifetime habits through retraining a lifelong dialogue with oneself." Group members are cautioned to be careful about the language of disease, and warned that it is for professionals only. They avoid going into detail about negative thoughts. Negative feelings are called fearful temper about yourself and angry temper about someone else.

What are some of the personal goals that might arise for a Recovery member?

1. *Retraining the brain* to take life tasks in small, manageable pieces.
2. *Identifying physical symptoms* that lead to unreal crazy thoughts and focusing on efforts to relax certain muscle groups that become tense in order to relieve distressing feelings.
3. *Having the courage to make a mistake.*
4. *Developing a sense of self-leadership* and recognizing your control over your behavior and your response to life challenges.

This description of the Recovery model is similar to a free peer cognitive group therapy process. Though not totally free, many support groups merely pass a hat around the table for contributions to pay for incidentals such as snacks at their meetings.

Similar Characteristics of Major Support Groups

Support groups promote closeness, a result of participants' opening up to each other and sharing both deep pleasures and profound pain. Members learn to trust one another. All group discussions remain confidential, and advice from fellow participants is taken seriously inasmuch as everyone present has "been there" (to hell and back), at least once.

The groups all share peer-to-peer qualities that offer support, experience in dealing with mental disorders, understanding, and nonjudgmental sharing of experiences with the intent to help each member overcome the isolation of dealing with their problems. The stories stimulate hope that whatever the problem, it can be overcome through appropriate treatment and persistence.

Group leaders are mostly laypeople, fellow patients who are in a recovery phase and have interpersonal skills and experience with a serious mental illness.

No fees should be expected, apart from small donations for incidentals and/or annual membership of a national group.

You might ask yourself why ill people would not avail themselves of a support group. Since groups vary "personality-wise," one may be more conducive to your needs than another. If you try one group and feel it does not suit your needs, try another. Never let a lack of confidence, or sense of shame, or the feeling that you "know it all," or the feeling of hopelessness prevent you from staying with a group long enough to be helpful. It's not just about what you learn in one session or how much or little help that you feel you received; it *is* about the relationship with peers who also are suffering. You do not want to be judged (a strong value of support groups), but neither can you be judgmental if you want to be open and receptive to the benefits that a peer group has to offer.

To be human is to have defects and to make mistakes, and we all are in the same lifeboat. By standing together, we—you and I—have the best chance for a meaningful life.

That said, support groups cannot substitute for treatment by a trained professional. Nearly all local support groups have a list of the most helpful mental health professionals in the community and which ones to avoid.

One final important characteristic shared by major support groups is humor. Although not mentioned by Dr. Fawcett's support member consultants, it was certainly a quality they all demonstrated. Humor for depressed, hopeless people? You bet! Gently teasing a member who repeats a mistake—like stopping medication—or joking about the hypocrisy of people outside the group who continually deny the reality of their condition is a natural way to react to the irony of illness itself. The humor that develops between peers in these groups is responsible for holding them together. Humor also helps us cope with what may seem like the unfairness of life and a lack of apparent empathy.

INDEPENDENT SELF-HELP GROUPS

Independent self-help groups, founded by individuals, are a creative response to a tragic and painful loss. One such group was initiated by Karin and Ed Cogswell, whose son Eric struggled with bipolar disorder and eventually committed suicide as a college freshman, in spite of ongoing treatment. Unfortunately, neither Eric nor his parents ever found a functioning support group for him to attend during the period he was receiving treatment. After Eric's death, Karin and Ed decided to set up a foundation in his memory and enlisted the cooperation of the Seacoast Mental Health Center in Portsmouth, New Hampshire. They now sponsor an annual educational conference on bipolar disorder for suicide prevention.

The Cogswells also wanted to make sure that a support group would always be available for someone in need, so they enlisted the help and trained leadership of Diane, a layperson from New Hampshire. Diane was a grandmother whose own marriage had ended in divorce as a result of her husband's severe bipolar disorder. Later, when she learned that her daughter was also suffering from bipolar disorder, she formed her own self-help group for patients and their loved ones. Diane follows procedures similar to the NAMI and DBSA groups, where attendees check in and each describe their last week, both troubles and triumphs, and follow with a general discussion. Diane feels the group has helped her cope with her daughter's illness and its resulting problems. She is heartened by the progress of her group members, and their success in breaking down isolation, buttressing low self-esteem, and promoting adherence to medication treatment. For the Cogswell family, setting up their foundation in cooperation with a treatment center was a very creative way to ensure that the support group would be stable and maintained over time. This alignment of interest can serve as a model that fosters stability and wide availability for support groups throughout the country.

Service Dogs

How about a service dog to give you unconditional love and support? Service dogs aren't only seeing-eye dogs for the blind. Take Del, for instance, and his dog, Schubert. A huge, cuddly, calm, affectionate, and very intelligent Bernese mountain dog, Schubert is a dog whom everyone falls in love with and wants to pet. Del even takes him to the hospital to visit patients with various stages of medical illness. Schubert also accompanies Del to restaurants where he seems indifferent to all food smells, preferring to nap behind Del's chair. Yet even as Del and Jan Fawcett were deep in conversation, Schubert remained ever alert to any possible need that his master might have. As a mental health service dog, fully trained and certified, Schubert is disciplined to lie next to a plate of food and won't even touch it if his master gets up and leaves the room.

It was not until Del received a master's degree in music and had signed with the Dallas Symphony Orchestra that he developed his first symptoms of bipolar disorder, a severe treatment-resistant depression. This exaggerated a self-image problem that stemmed from severe abuse as a child, which left him feeling "hideous" (Del has no physical deformities). Oftentimes he felt fearful of leaving home because of extreme self-consciousness about his appearance. Del found that having a dog as a companion not only motivated him to take the dog out for walks but also provided support when he was in stores and social situations. Even if he felt totally withdrawn, people approached him to relate to his dog and he found himself interacting with them and feeling slightly better. Of course, Schubert was always accepting and eager to be with Del. The landlord of Del's building strongly objected to his having a pet and sought to have him evicted, despite Del's plea that he needed his companion. It was suggested that Del take service dog training with Schubert, since the Americans with Disabilities Act requires all public places to accept the presence of certified service dogs. Unlike self-help groups, service dog training can be costly and requires hours with an expert trainer. Finally, a volunteer group at St. Vincent's Hospital and friends from the Unitarian Church got together and came up with the necessary funds to train Del and Schubert, who became students for about four months of intensive training. Now that Schubert sports his orange service dog vest, Del can take him into any public place and legally keep him in his apartment. Del is disabled and unable to perform because of his depression and medication side effects. Yet he does seem to be responding to medication and takes full advantage of both Recovery, Inc., and NAMI support groups. Always at his side is Schubert with his pervasive calmness, always alert to Del's mood and ready to assume the responsibility for his master's care—in addition to being his constant, appreciative friend. Although a well-trained pet with a good temperament might improve some patients, there is really no substitute for a service dog who is professionally trained to be ready with help and support.

CONSUMER BEWARE!

These days, sources of support and information are available to supplement the highly skilled treatment that remains a necessity for the treatment of bipolar, schizoaffective, and depressive conditions. Support group members can supply personal experience and information, but the Internet is loaded with information of all kinds about these illnesses. However, a few caveats should be kept in mind while pursuing third-party information:

The Internet: Much of the information available from individuals and on the Internet represents a particular point of view based on personal experience or belief. When you feel desperate to recover from an illness, particularly when you have not attained satisfactory results, there always are people out there happily waiting with advice for a whole range of motives. The information you receive may be geared to promote a certain belief system, or geared for the purpose of selling an untested and unscientifically verified approach. Even positively sincere and self-assured information you might obtain may be fallacious. Some Internet sites even urge people to stop their medication and take an alternative treatment that has nothing more than anecdotal support for its effectiveness. Even if a friend or relative swears by a given treatment, it is always important to remember that each patient responds differently to various treatments.

When things don't seem to be working out and you're fearful you may not recover, or feel hopeless about your treatment, you may be gullible to misleading information. A huge industry making fantastic claims lies in wait for those most desperate people willing to "do anything" to get better. All advice that you receive must be critically evaluated. Hundreds of people may offer untested guidance about some "new and more effective" treatment—usually based on personal testimony or on some alleged "cure" that helped a friend. Don't fall for it.

Unsubstantiated Literature: Don't trust a book written about a specific approach if the author stands to benefit financially from use of a particular product. Anyone can write anything they happen to believe and publish it in a book. Most effective treatments have been verified in scientific reports published in peer-reviewed medical journals. This means articles are subject to scrutiny by other scientists (who by nature are very critical) before they are published. Ask yourself: What are the qualifications of the person making the claim? Are they independent in their judgment, or do they stand to gain from your accepting their recommendation? Even treatments that are well studied in double-blind placebo controlled studies, with clear evidence of effectiveness, may not be helpful to an individual patient. The likelihood of some effective treatment, which is endorsed by only a handful of people, is very small. In fact, serious worsening may take place if it is substituted for even partially effective medications.

The Value of a Second Opinion: If you are not getting desirable results from your current treatment, seek a second opinion from an established expert in the field who is trained to treat your specific problem. A practicing clinician with solid skill and knowledge will never object to a patient's request for another opinion. Though your doctor might want you to wait until a new course of treatment is tried, an outstanding practitioner of medicine should welcome—if not make the first overture—toward a second opinion. Never settle for inflated claims or hearsay.

Support groups can enhance your efforts at recovery, and many such groups are now available in most areas. They also are cost effective. In this chapter we have reviewed a representative range of solid support groups, but there may be other suitable solutions that you may wish to investigate. For example, some patients may find 12-step programs very helpful, even though they usually focus on alcohol and substance abuse. It is worth your effort to check out every type of group before deciding which most closely fits your needs. Finally, always remember to give the group a chance by attending several meetings and getting to know at least some of the members before arriving at a final conclusion. For more information on how and where to find a support group in your area, see Resources on page 333.

CHAPTER 15

Questions and Answers Regarding Bipolar Disorder

1. What is the most significant message about bipolar disorder that I need to know?

Bipolar disorder is a serious medical disorder that involves impairment in emotions, thoughts, and behavior. It has the capacity to greatly interfere in daily functioning, including one's relationships, career, leisure, and overall well-being. Left untreated, it can result in suicide. However, it can effectively be managed. As with the management of any chronic illness, this requires acceptance, commitment, self-compassion, the support of others, and medication.

Effective management first requires recognizing and acknowledging the symptoms. Accurate diagnosis is essential in order to identify the appropriate treatment. This means an assessment by a certified mental health professional who has experience in the diagnosis and treatment of this disorder. Working in collaboration, you and your doctor can determine the most effective treatment for your specific needs. Identifying the specific medications and the proper dosage may take several treatments to determine.

Additionally, coping with a diagnosis of bipolar disorder involves experiencing a wide range of emotions. Hurt, sadness, anger, disappointment, frustration, and perhaps even hopelessness and despair are natural reactions when life doesn't turn out the way we expect it should. And yet, with the appropriate treatments and support, those with bipolar illness can learn to move beyond these immediate reactions toward a fulfilling and meaningful life that is not defined by their illness.

2. How do I respond to others who believe I am malingering in my attempts to take better care of myself?

Since bipolar patients function at different levels and vary in their pace of recovery, it is often difficult for people to see beyond their narrow conclusions that a family member or friend with this illness is merely being lazy, dependent, or unmotivated. It is similarly easy for those with bipolar disorder to internalize this attitude and, with guilt and shame, concur that they "should" be able to shake a depression or the obsessiveness or anxiety that often accompanies manic periods. However, for many with this disorder, this same guilt and shame only interferes with both seeking out and maintaining an appropriate treatment regimen, which are ultimately the only way to get better.

Words like *lazy* and *unmotivated* tell us nothing about what really interferes with functioning when facing the incapacitating symptoms of depression. Rather, it is the self-talk of despair and hopelessness, feelings of inadequacy, shame, and anxiety about confronting life's challenges, that inhibit attempts to focus and organize one's thoughts and actions. Such internal dialogue dilutes the will essential to overcoming emotional and physical inertia.

It is unfortunate, but the burden of informing others about the facts of bipolar disorder often falls on those who suffer with it. Ideally, friends and family should seek out understanding regarding this illness, but their fears and ignorance may prevent them from doing so. Similarly, self-doubts and mixed feelings about the diagnosis lead most of those who have it to justify their behavior and carry that burden of educating others.

We believe it is helpful for patients to guide loved ones in obtaining such information, but without getting caught up in defending or justifying their illness. Evidence increasingly mounts that when loved ones are informed, they can constitute a very powerful support system to help recognize and counter the escalation of symptoms, and also to ward off relapses.

3. How can I have hope when I have only been minimally helped by medications?

What we now know about bipolar disorder and the medications that help manage it have tremendously increased in recent years. The challenge of this disorder often requires numerous trials of different combinations and dosages of medications to offer the most effective treatment.

Individual biology and symptoms often vary to a great extent, making it difficult to determine the optimal regimen. At the same time, there is great variability in the training and experience of those who prescribe such medications. This makes it extremely important to work with a physician who has knowledge and experience with this particular illness.

In the short time since the original publication of this book, there have been significant changes in the use of medications and other treatments to help manage bipolar disorder. This progress fosters further hope in identifying more effective strategies to help manage this illness in the future.

4. I have extreme difficulty awakening in the morning. While I am thinking of resuming employment, I do not believe I can commit to actually being to work on time. What should I do?

Managing bipolar disorder involves trying to maintain a daily routine that addresses, medication, nutrition, and sleep as best as possible. Certainly, if you have not already done so, bring this symptom to the attention of your physician. He may suggest changes in your medications or reschedule the times you take them to remedy the situation.

Many bipolar individuals re-enter the work force on a part-time basis. Clearly, a part-time schedule is not possible for everyone. However, if you can manage it, it offers an opportunity to experience an increased level of confidence and mastery and a healthy reminder that bipolar disorder is not completely incapacitating. Additionally, you may seek a work environment in which you can openly share your concerns or one that offers a three-quarter-time position. Another option is to consider a position that involves working from your home. In recent years, there has been an increase in these types of opportunities.

5. What is helpful about psychotherapy that medication does not sufficiently address?

Medication is necessary to address the neuropsychophysiological activity that influences depression and mania, and the emotions and thoughts associated with bipolar disorder. Psychotherapy offers individuals understanding and skills in the management of these thoughts and emotions that can tremendously impact how one views and manages the illness. As such it also offers you approaches to help deal with negative attitudes and stigma.

The behavioral strategies learned in psychotherapy compliment the medications by helping you more effectively manage life stressors that have the potential to cause relapses.

Lastly, psychotherapy offers you education about how your specific patterns of thoughts, emotions, and behaviors interact with each other, and will help you better understand the interaction between aspects of your personality and bipolar disorder.

6. I am a twenty-five-year-old woman who has bipolar disorder. My mother had bipolar disorder. My younger brother does not evidence this disorder. My older sister seems to experience much anxiety but not the variety of symptoms I have. What are the chances of having children with this disorder?

Studies indicate that when both parents have bipolar disorder, the likelihood of having a child who evidences the disorder is 50 to 75 percent. In contrast, when only one parent has been diagnosed, that possibility decreases to 15 to 30 percent. However, these statistics only imply a disposition to the illness and not a prediction of whether the child will ever experience the symptoms.

7. What role does sleep have in my mood stability and vulnerability to either depression or mania?

Increasingly, studies show that disruptions in sleep patterns greatly impact the onset of symptoms associated with bipolar disorder. This reflects how our circadian rhythms impact our sense of well-being in general. More specifically, it reflects the sensitivity of those with this disorder to slight changes in routines that impact their body's stability.

In fact, studies show that changes in any routine—from one's work schedule, a workout schedule, travel, or other changes—may contribute to emotional instability. In our work with individuals with bipolar disorder, it is not uncommon to hear someone describe feeling exceptionally disoriented and anxious from staying up later than usual for a few nights, drinking more alcohol than usual, or significantly altering a daily routine related to work, leisure, or social activities. Such changes can be emotionally, and perhaps chemically, unsettling and can lead to a relapse of symptoms.

8. I experience intense difficulty transitioning from one activity to another especially when I experience hypomania. I become obsessed with a particular task and can't seem to stop working on it until I complete it. What can I do to address this compulsion?

Obsessions (repetitive thoughts regarding a particular issue) and compulsions (repetitive behaviors) are a common mania symptom but may also be attributed to a diagnosis that is distinct from that of bipolar disorder—one in which related symptoms only become more exacerbated owing to bipolar disorder.

There are a variety of skills that can be learned to gain increased control over them. These range from challenging self-talk (a major approach used in cognitive therapy), behavioral approaches such as breaking tasks down into smaller goals to increase a sense of accomplishment and closure, using a timer, or other monitoring techniques. The practice of mindful meditation can also help you observe and recognize these thoughts and urges without feeling like you have to respond to them. These strategies can be learned in workbooks (see Resources, page 333) or involvement in psychotherapy to provide more specific monitoring and feedback.

When these are extreme and persistent, certain medications can further reduce both obsessions and compulsions.

9. Taking medications makes me feel like I've failed somehow. How can I take them if I feel this way?

Clearly, there is much stigma regarding difficulties related to mental health. As described throughout our chapter on stigma, these stem from ignorance, fear, and a lack of compassion. This same stigma may be highly internalized and inform your own attitudes, especially when individuals who are important to us evidence such stigma in their words and actions. In part, such attitudes also stem from a primitive logic that says we "should" have complete control over our bodies and behavior. However, bipolar disorder is associated with a combination of biological factors that cannot be controlled without medications.

Not taking medications may help you to preserve an imaginary sense of control, but in reality without such medications you remain more vulnerable to the influences of emotions and thoughts associated with the phases of mania or depression. Such vulnerability will leave you weakened and passive as a result. On the other hand, medications will stabilize your thoughts and give you increased control over them.

A commitment to take medications may require tremendous courage and strength when others attach stigma to doing so.

10. I take medications and am involved in psychotherapy, both of which have been extremely helpful in my treatment. What would be the benefits of taking part in a support group?

While medications help address patients' moods and thinking, and psychotherapy can provide a variety of skills to impact them, support groups provide education, help participants experience a sense of empowerment as they take part in advocacy, and, above all, reduce the sense of isolation that's very challenging for individuals dealing with this disorder.

11. Why don't my medications work?

This is a common question on the minds of both patients (consumers-owners) and their loved ones. First, medications must be taken as prescribed to have a chance to be effective. Forgetting or deciding to skip doses will undermine any chance they have to be effective. However, it is not uncommon for medications to be ineffective and even to produce side effects even when taken correctly. Research studies tell us which medications may be useful for a given illness, but they do not yet tell us how an individual is going to respond to a given medication. Someday we may be able to use genetic testing to make these predictions, but those tests have not yet been developed. This means that your doctor has to use his experience and skill in deciding which medications will most likely help you. It may take even the best expert several trials to determine the most effective regimen. Do not give up. In some cases, a second opinion from an expert may help.

12. Why do medications cause side effects?

Medications are intended to target brain circuits, which affect certain aspects of mood or behavior such as depression, anxiety, agitation, and psychosis. Since medications are absorbed into and circulated by blood, they come into contact with the entire brain and body, and frequently affect other systems than intended. This creates unintended effects. Sometimes these are helpful or beneficial, but often they create a nuisance and make the medication more difficult to tolerate. Sometimes these side effects will decrease or disappear with time as the body adapts to them. Even with a very helpful medication, sometimes it is worthwhile to try another to reduce the severity of side effects, or change the prescribed dose. While there are many medications or combinations of medications that can help a given condition, it is a good strategy to try to put up with side effects for a while to give your body a chance to adapt (and to give the medication a chance to work) before giving up. Most side effects are distressing but not dangerous. Frequent communication with your doctor when you are starting a new regimen will help make the most of each treatment trial.

13. If one medication doesn't help, is it worthwhile to try another medication in the same class?

One of the most common classes of medication is SSRI (specific serotonin reuptake inhibitor). We have data that suggest if treatment with one SSRI doesn't work, a second trial of another SSRI will help 40 to 50 percent of the time. This is true with other classes of medication as well. People have specific response patterns, and different members of a class may have effects that we do not yet understand.

14. How long do I have to take a medication to know if it is working?

This depends on both the condition and the medication being used. In treating depression, a recent study showed that noting some improvement in the first two weeks bodes well for a positive response to treatment later. Of patients who went into full remission (a return to your usual self with few or any symptoms left), after only six weeks of treatment almost all noted lessened symptoms within two weeks. That said, about half of the patients that would attain remission within twelve weeks had noted early improvement, so it is possible to see drastic changes later even if initial results are subtle. Talk to your doctor about your progress and all changes in your condition to determine if you need to change your medications or regimen.

15. Can medications make me worse?

It is rare, but yes, some people will experience worsening of their condition after they start taking a new medication. If this is the case, you should contact the prescribing doctor immediately. If that is not possible, stop the medication and go to an emergency room if the worsening persists. Ordinarily, any doctor prescribing a new medication should be able to be reached in this situation.

16. What is a good working alliance?

To get the most out of treatment, you should establish a strong working alliance with your doctor. This means that the doctor should explain the expected benefits and likely negative effects to watch out for before you begin taking any new medication. The doctor should listen to your questions, doubts, and preferences and then explain why a certain course of treatment would likely be most beneficial to you. You can certainly ask your doctor about whatever medication you have heard about. A good clinician will respond to your question, but may advise another course of treatment while giving you a reason for this choice. This is good; you want your doctor to have an independent opinion based on his/her knowledge and experience, even if it doesn't coincide with your preference. With a good therapeutic alliance the two of you will work as a team to defeat your illness.

17. Are the latest medications always better?

New medications may offer a great advantage or they may be irrelevant to your specific situation. A competent physician will tell you if the latest medications are appropriate. Often an older and less commonly mentioned medication will have a greater success rate for your situation. The new is not always the true.

18. How can I improve interpersonal relationships when I frequently come on strong and sound like a runaway freight train?

It is important that you know yourself and that you can recognize the nature of manic and depressive symptoms. If you are able to understand and recognize the interplay of these two polarized patterns of behavior, you can learn to temper your behavior in the company of others. It takes discipline and the ability to maintain awareness.

19. How can I live a full and productive life with bipolar disorder?

By understanding and mastering the principles of a positive mental attitude, it is possible to transform a serious loss or human affliction, such as receiving a diagnosis of bipolar disorder, into a positive and meaningful life experience. The human mind is resilient and capable of reversing a negative situation despite its pain and cruelty. By learning how to live again, notwithstanding seemingly insurmountable obstacles, people can emerge stronger and more self-reliant, and with new goals and a new purpose in life.

Notes

CHAPTER I

1. Deborah Bullwinkel is the former program director of the National Depressive Manic-Depressive Association (National DMDA), the national organization that was cofounded by Jan Fawcett, M.D.
2. Sol Wachtler, *After the Madness: A Judge's Own Prison Memoir* (New York: Random House, 1997), 11.
3. Frazier Moore, "Hard Time in the Black Hole," *SouthCoast Today,* www.s-t.com/daily/01-98/01-05-98/c01ae100.htm.
4. Kathy Cronkite, *On the Edge of Darkness* (New York: Delta, 1995), 14.
5. Ibid.
6. Frazier, "Hard Time in the Black Hole."
7. Ibid.
8. Ibid.
9. Cronkite, *On the Edge of Darkness,* 13.
10. Ibid, 46.
11. Ibid, 72.
12. Ibid, 140.
13. Kay Redfield Jamison, *An Unquiet Mind* (New York: Vintage Books, 1996).
14. Cronkite, *On the Edge of Darkness,* 227.
15. Frederick K. Goodwin and Kay Redfield Jamison, *Manic-Depressive Illness* (New York: Oxford University Press, 1990).
16. Kay Redfield Jamison, *Night Falls Fast* (New York: Alfred A. Knopf, 1999).
17. Goodwin and Jamison, *Manic-Depressive Illness.*
18. Ibid.
19. "What It Would Really Take," *Time,* June 17, 1999, 54–55.
20. "Depression Confession," *Nation,* June 28, 1999, 10.
21. "Tipper Gore and Rosalynn Carter on America's Mental Health Crisis," *Psychology Today,* September–October, 1999, 31.
22. "What It Would Really Take."

CHAPTER 2

1. Frederick K. Goodwin and Kay Redfield Jamison, *Manic-Depressive Illness* (New York: Oxford University Press, 1990).
2. Demitri Papolos and Janice Papolos, *Overcoming Depression* (New York: HarperPerennial, 1997).
3. Goodwin and Jamison, *Manic-Depressive Illness.*
4. Ibid.

CHAPTER 3

1. Lewis A. Opler and Carol Bialkowski, *Prozac and Other Psychiatric Drugs:*

Everything You Need to Know (New York: Pocket Books, 1996).

2. The Gershon study is cited in A. Bertelsen, "A Danish Twin Study of Manic-Depressive Disorders," in M. Schou and E. Strömgren, eds., *Origin, Prevention and Treatment of Affective Disorders* (London: Academic Press, 1979), 227–239, and is summarized in Frederick K. Goodwin and Kay Redfield Jamison, *Manic-Depressive Illness* (New York: Oxford University Press, 1990).

3. E. Kringlen, "Twin Studies in Psychiatry," *Tidsskr Nor Laegeforen* 119, no. 22 (1999): 3322–3328.

4. Samuel H. Barondes, Introduction to "Report of the NIMH Genetics Workgroup," *Biological Psychiatry,* 45, no. 5 (1999): 559–602.

5. Ibid.

6. Steven H. Hyman, "Introduction to the Complex Genetics of Mental Disorders," *Biological Psychiatry* 45, no. 5 (1999): 518–521.

7. C. J. Murray and A. D. Lopez, "Global Mortality, Disability, and the Contribution of Risk Factors: Global Burden of Disease Study," *Lancet* 349, no. 9063 (1997): 1436–1442.

8. Nick Craddock, Michael C. O'Donovan, and Michael J. Owen, *Schizophrenia Bulletin* 32, no. 1 (2006): 9–16.

9. A. Caspi and Kenneth S. Kendler studies, *Archives of General Psychiatry* 58 (2001): 1005–1014.

10. E. S. Gershon, W. Berrettini, J. J. Nurnberger, et al., "Genetics of Affective Illness," in H. Y. Meltzer, ed. *The Third Generation of Progress* (New York: Raven Press, 1987), 481–491.

11. H. K. Manji, G. J. Moore, and G. Chen, "Lithium Up-Regulates the Cytoprotective Protein Bcl-2 in the CNS in Vivo: A Role for Neurotrophic and Neuroprotective Effects in Manic Depressive Illness," *Journal of Clinical Psychiatry* 61, suppl. 9 (2000): 82–96.

12. Robert Sapolsky, *Stress, the Aging Brain and the Mechanism of Neuron Death* (Cambridge: MIT Press, 1992). Another study was performed by Claire Rampon, Ya-Ping Tang, Joe Goodhouse, et al., "Enrichment Induces Structural Changes and Recovery from Non-Spatial Memory Deficits in CA1-NMDART-Knockout Mice," *Nature Neuroscience* 3 (2000): 238–244.

13. Hilary P. Blumberg, John H. Krystal, Ravi Bansal, et al., "Age, Rapid-Cycling, and Pharmacotherapy Effects on Ventral Prefrontal Cortex in Bipolar Disorder: A Cross-Sectional Study," *Biological Psychiatry* 59, no. 7 (2006): 611–618.

CHAPTER 4

1. L. Judd and H. S. Akiskal, "Depressive Episodes and Symptoms Dominate the Longitudinal Course of Bipolar Disorder." *Current Psychiatry Rep* 5, no. 6 (2003): 417–418.

2. National Depressive and Manic-Depressive Association, "Consensus Statement on the Undertreatment of Depression," *Journal of the American Medical Association* 277, no. 4 (1997): 333–40.

3. L. Tondo and R. J. Baldessarini, "Reduced Suicide Risk During Lithium Maintenance Treatment," *Journal of Clinical Psychiatry* 61, suppl. 9 (2000): 97–104.

4. L. Judd, H. S. Akiskal, "Depressive Episodes and Symptoms Dominate the Longitudinal Course of Bipolar Disorder."

5. Lewis A. Opler and Carol Bialkowski, *Prozac and Other Psychiatric Drugs: Everything You Need to Know* (New York: Pocket Books, 1996).

6. G. E. Simon et al., "Suicide Risk During Antidepressant Treatment," *American Journal of Psychiatry* 163 (2006): 41–47.

7. M. S. Bauer et al., "Prospective Study of Participants in the Systematic Treatment

Enhancement Program for Bipolar Disorder," *Journal of Clinical Psychiatry* 67, no. 1 (2006): 48–55.

8. Ibid.

9. Simon et al., "Suicide Risk During Antidepressant Treatment"; Bauer et al., "Prospective Study."

10. A. A. Nierenberg, T. Burt, et al., "Mania Associated with St. John's Wort," *Biological Psychiatry* 46, no. 12 (1999): 1717–1718.

11. Steven Bratman, *Beat Depression with St. John's Wort* (Roseville, CA: Prima Publishing, 1997).

12. R. M. Hirschfeld, L. Lewis, L. A. Vornik, "Perceptions and Impact of Bipolar Disorder: How Far Have We Really Come?: Results of the National Depressive and Manic-Depressive Association 2000 Survey of Individuals with Bipolar Disorder," *Journal of Clinical Psychiatry* 64, no. 2 (2003): 161–174.

CHAPTER 5

1. David D. Burns, *Feeling Good: Ten Days to Self-Esteem* (New York: Avon, 1992).

2. A. Beck, B. Shaw, and G. Emery, *Cognitive Therapy of Depression* (New York: Guilford Press, 1979).

3. Ibid.

4. Ibid.

5. Ibid.

6. David D. Burns, *Feeling Good: The New Mood Therapy* (New York: Avon, 1992).

7. Ibid.

8. A. Weissman, "The Dysfunctional Attitudes Scale: A Validation Study," *Dissertation Abstracts International* 40 (1979): 1389–1390.

9. Kay Redfield Jamison, *An Unquiet Mind* (New York: Vintage Books, 1996).

10. K. Dobson, *The Handbook of Cognitive Behavioral Therapies* (New York: Guilford Press, 1988).

11. T. D'Zurilla and M. Goldfried, "Problem Solving and Behavior Modification," *Journal*

of Abnormal Psychology 78, no. 1 (1971), cited in Dobson, *The Handbook of Cognitive Behavioral Therapies,* 107–126.

12. M. Goldfried and G. Davison, *Clinical Behavior Therapy* (New York: Holt, Rinehart and Winston, 1976).

13. R. Lazarus and S. Folman, *Stress, Appraisal and Coping* (New York: Springer, 1984).

14. Dobson, *The Handbook of Cognitive Behavioral Therapies.*

CHAPTER 6

1. Cory R. Newman et al., *Bipolar Disorder: A Cognitive Therapy Approach* (Washington, DC: American Psychological Association, 2002). Monica Ramirez Basco and A. John Rush, *Cognitive-Behavioral Therapy for Bipolar Disorder,* 2nd ed. (New York: Guilford Press, 2005).

2. Ibid., 2.

3. J. Scott et al., "A Pilot Study of Cognitive Therapy in Bipolar Disorders," *Psychological Medicine* 31, no. 3 (2001): 459–467.

4. D. H. Lam et al., "Cognitive Therapy for Bipolar Illness—A Pilot Study of Relapse Prevention," *Cognitive Therapy and Research* 24, no. 5 (2000): 503–520.

5. A. Perry, N. Tarrier, R. Morris, et al., "Randomized Controlled Trial of Efficacy of Teaching Patients with Bipolar Disorder to Identify Early Symptoms of Relapse and Obtain Treatment," *British Medical Journal* 16, no. 318 (1999): 149–153, cited in Basco and Rush, *Cognitive-Behavioral Therapy for Bipolar Disorder.*

6. Newman et al., *Bipolar Disorder: A Cognitive Therapy Approach.*

7. Basco and Rush, *Cognitive-Behavioral Therapy for Bipolar Disorder.*

8. Christopher R. Martell et al., *Depression in Context: Strategies for Guided Action* (New York: W. W. Norton, 2001).

9. Neil Jacobson et al., "Behavioral Activation Treatment for Depression: Returning to

Contextual Roots," *Clinical Psychology: Science and Practice* 8, no. 3 (2001): 255–270.

10. Sonia Dimidjian et al., *Behavioral Activation, Cognitive Therapy, and Antidepressant Medication in the Acute Treatment of Major Depression* (Ph.D. diss. University of Washington, 2005).

11. Michael E. Addis and Christopher R. Martell, *Overcoming Depression One Step at a Time* (Oakland, CA: New Harbinger, 2004).

12. Steven C. Hayes, "Acceptance and Commitment Therapy and the New Behavior Therapies," in *Mindfulness and Acceptance: Expanding the Cognitive-Behavioral Tradition,* ed. Steven C. Hayes, Victoria M. Follette, and Marsha M. Linehan (New York: Guilford Press, 2004), 1–29.

13. Ibid., 9.

14. Steven C. Hayes, *Get out of Your Mind and into Your Life* (Oakland, CA: New Harbinger, 2005).

15. Hayes, "Acceptance and Commitment Therapy and the New Behavior Therapies."

16. Steven C. Hayes, Kirk D. Strosahl, and Kelly G. Wilson, *Acceptance and Commitment Therapy: An Experiential Approach to Behavioral Change* (New York: Guilford Press, 1999).

17. Hayes, "Acceptance and Commitment Therapy and the New Behavior Therapies."

18. Addis and Martell, *Overcoming Depression One Step at a Time.*

19. Marsha M. Linehan, *Cognitive-Behavioral Treatment of Borderline Personality Disorder* (New York: Guilford Press, 1993).

20. Scott E. Spradlin, *Don't Let Your Emotions Run Your Life* (Oakland, CA: New Harbinger, 2003).

21. James P. McCullough Jr., *Treatment for Chronic Depression: Cognitive Behavioral Analysis System of Psychotherapy* (New York: Guilford Press, 2000).

22. James P. McCullough Jr., "Cognitive Behavioral Analysis System of

Psychotherapy for Depression," in *Handbook of Psychotherapy Integration,* ed. John C. Norcross and Marvin R. Goldfried (New York: Oxford, 2005), 281–298.

23. Ibid., 286.

24. J. Kabat-Zinn, *Full Catastrophe Living* (New York: Dell, 1990).

25. Edward S. Friedman et al., "Combining Cognitive Therapy and Medication for Mood Disorders," *Psychiatric Annals* 36, no. 5 (2006): 320–328.

26. Ellen Frank, *Treating Bipolar Disorder* (New York: Guilford Press, 2005).

27. Ibid., 23.

28. Ibid., 77.

29. Ellen Frank et al., "Two-Year Outcomes for Interpersonal and Social Rhythm Therapy in Individuals with Bipolar I Disorder," *Archives of General Psychiatry* 62, no. 9 (2005): 996–1004.

30. Zindel Segal et al., *Mindfulness-Based Cognitive Therapy for Depression: A New Approach to Preventing Relapse* (New York: Guilford Press, 2002).

31. Zindel Segal et al., "Mindfulness-Based Cognitive Therapy," in *Mindfulness and Acceptance: Expanding the Cognitive-Behavioral Tradition,* ed. Steven C. Hayes, Victoria M. Follette, and Marsha M. Linehan (New York: Guilford Press, 2004), 50.

32. John Teasdale et al., "Prevention of Relapse/Recurrence in Major Depression by Mindfulness-Based Cognitive Therapy," *Journal of Consulting and Clinical Psychology* 68, no. 4, (2000): 614–623.

33. Ibid.

34. S. H. Ma and J. D. Teasdale, "Mindfulness-Based Cognitive Therapy for Depression: Replication and Exploration of Differential Relapse Prevention Effects," *Journal of Consulting and Clinical Psychology* 72, no. 1 (2004): 31–40.

35. T. L. Simoneau and D. J. Miklowitz, "Expressed Emotion and Interactional Patterns in Families of Bipolar Patients,"

Journal of Abnormal Psychology 107, no. 3 (1998): 497–507.

36. Margaret M. Rea et al., "Family-Focused Treatment Versus Individual Treatment for Bipolar Disorder: Results of a Randomized Clinical Trial," *Journal of Consulting and Clinical Psychology* 71, no. 3 (2003): 482–492.

37. D. J. Miklowitz and M. J. Goldstein, *Bipolar Disorder: A Family-Focused Treatment Approach* (New York: Guilford Press, 1997).

38. D. J. Miklowitz et al., "A Randomized Study of Family-Focused Psychoeducation and Pharmacotherapy in the Outpatient Management of Bipolar Disorder," *Archives of General Psychiatry* 60, no. 9 (2003): 904–912.

CHAPTER 7

1. Richard C. W. Hall, Dennis E. Platt, and Ryan C. W. Hall, "Suicide Risk Assessment: A Review of Risk Factors for Suicide in 100 Patients Who Made Severe Suicide Attempts," *Psychosomatics* 40 (1999): 18–27.

2. In 1978, Jan Fawcett participated as a principal investigator in a fifteen-year collaborative study of suicide, National Institute of Mental Health. The study is still in progress. Initial results of this study were published in *American Journal of Psychiatry* 147 (1990): 1189–1194.

3. Eli Robins, *The Final Months* (New York: Oxford University Press, 1981).

4. R. W. Ettlinger and P. Flordh, "Attempted Suicide: Experience of 500 Cases at a General Hospital," *Acta Psychiatrica et Neurologica Scandinavica* 1955; 103 (suppl): 1–45; M. C. Tejedor et al., "Attempted Suicide: Repetition and Survival— Findings of a Follow-up Study," *Acta Psychiatrica Scandinavica* 100, no. 3 (1999): 205–211.

5. A. Roy, G. Rylander, and M. Sachiapone, "Genetics of Suicide. Family Studies and Molecular Genetics," *Annals of New York Academy of Sciences,* 29, no. 836 (1997): 135–157.

6. Jan Fawcett et al., "Time-Related Predictors of Suicide in Major Affective Disorder," *American Journal of Psychiatry,* 147 (1990): 1189–1194.

7. Ibid.

8. Michael Burlingame, *The Inner World of Abraham Lincoln* (Champaign: University of Illinois Press, 1994.)

9. M. S. Bauer, S. R. Wisniewski, L. B. Marangell, et al. Are Antidepressants Associated with New Onset Suicidality in Bipolar Disorder? A Prospective Study of Participants in the Systematic Treatment Enhancement Program for Bipolar Disorder. *J Clin Psychiatry* 63, no. 1 (2006): 48–55.

10. G. E. Simon, J. Savarino, S. Operskalski, P. S. Wang, "Suicide Risk During Antidepressant Treatment," *Am J Psychiatry* 163 (2006): 41–47.

11. F. Angst, H. H. Stassen, P. J. Clayton, J. Angst, "Mortality of Patients with Mood Disorders: Follow-up over 34–38 Years," *J Affective Disord* 68, no. 2–3 (2002): 167–181.

12. J. Angst, F. Angst, R. Gerber-Werder, A. Gamma, "Suicide in 406 Mood-Disorder Patients with and without Long-Term Medication: A 40–44 Years' Follow-up." *Archives of Suicide Research* 9, no. 3 (2005): 279–300.

13. R. J. Baldessarini, L. Tondo, P. Davis, et al., "Decreased Risk of Suicides and Suicide Attempts During Long-term Lithium Treatment: A Mea-analytic Review," *Bipolar Disorder* 8, no. 5, part 2 (2006): 625–639.

14. Hall et al., "Suicide Risk Assessment," 18–27.

CHAPTER 8

1. Paul Fink and Allan Tasman, *Stigma and Mental Illness* (Washington, DC: American Psychiatric Press, 1992).

2. Richard Chessick, *Intensive Psychotherapy* (New York: Jason Aronson, 1974).

3. E. Dodds, *The Greeks and the Irrational* (Boston: Beacon Press, 1957), cited in Fink and Tasman, *Stigma and Mental Illness.*

4. Fink and Tasman, *Stigma and Mental Illness.*

5. Michael Lewis, *Shame: The Exposed Self* (New York: Free Press, 1995).

6. Ibid.

7. Kathy Cronkite, *On the Edge of Darkness* (New York: Delta, 1995).

8. Ibid.

9. Ibid.

10. Ibid.

11. Lewis, *Shame.*

12. Martin E. P. Seligman, *Learned Optimism: How to Change Your Mind and Your Life* (New York: Pocket Books, 1998).

13. Lewis, *Shame.*

14. Susan Sontag, *Illness as Metaphor and AIDS and Its Metaphors* (New York: Peter Smith Publishing, 1995).

15. Ibid.

16. Ibid.

17. Harold S. Kushner, *How Good Do We Have to Be?* (New York: Little, Brown, 1997).

18. Patrick W. Corrigan, ed., *On the Stigma of Mental Illness: Practical Strategies for Research and Social Change* (Washington, DC: American Psychological Association, 2004).

19. Ibid.

20. Susan Stefan, *Hollow Promises: Employment Discrimination Against People with Mental Disabilities* (Washington, DC: American Psychological Association, 2002), 169.

21. Corrigan, *On the Stigma of Mental Illness.*

22. Susan G. Goldberg and Mary B. Killeen, "The Disclosure Conundrum: How People with Psychiatric Disabilities Navigate Employment," *Psychology, Public Policy, and Law* 11, no. 3 (2005): 463–500.

23. Stefan, *Hollow Promises.*

24. Amy C. Watson and Patrick W. Corrigan, "Challenging Public Stigma: A Targeted Approach," in Patrick W. Corrigan, *On the Stigma of Mental Illness: Practical Strategies for Research and Social Change* (Washington, DC: American Psychological Association, 2004), 281–295.

25. Ibid.

26. Irvin Esters et al., "Effects of a Unit of Instruction in Mental Health on Rural Adolescents' Conceptions of Mental Illness and Attitudes about Seeking Help," *Adolescence* 33, no. 130 (1998): 469–476.

27. Kathryn Foxhall, "APA Is Key to Anti-Stigma Campaign," *Monitor on Psychology* 31, no. 7 (2000).

CHAPTER 9

1. Martin E. P. Seligman, *Learned Optimism: How to Change Your Mind and Your Life* (New York: Pocket Books, 1998).

2. Ibid., 48.

3. Rollo May, *Existence* (New York: Basic Books, 1958).

4. Ibid.

5. Kay Redfield Jamison, *Touched with Fire* (New York: Free Press, 1994).

6. Ibid.

7. Shelley E. Taylor, *Positive Illusions* (New York: Basic Books, 1989).

8. Kay Redfield Jamison, *An Unquiet Mind* (New York: Vintage, 1995).

9. Mihaly Csikszentmihalyi, *Flow: The Psychology of Optimal Experience* (New York: HarperPerennial, 1991).

10. Ibid.

11. Jamison, *An Unquiet Mind.*

12. Ibid.

13. Seligman, *Learned Optimism.*

14. Daniel Goleman, *Emotional Intelligence* (New York: Bantam Books, 1995).

CHAPTER 10

1. Victor E. Frankl, *Man's Search for Ultimate Meaning* (New York: Insight Books, 1997).

2. Artemis P. Simopoulos and Jo Robinson, *The Omega Plan* (New York: HarperCollins, 1998).

3. Ibid.

4. Susan Musikanth, *Stress Matters* (Johannesburg, South Africa: William Waterman, 1996).

5. Susan Musikanth, *Depression Matters* (Johannesburg, South Africa: Delta Books, 1997).

6. Mary Ellen Copeland, *Living Without Depression and Manic Depression* (Oakland, CA: New Harbinger, 1994).

7. Julie A. Fast and John D. Preston, *Loving Someone with Bipolar Disorder: Understanding and Helping Your Partner* (Oakland, CA: New Harbinger, 2004).

8. Ada P. Kahn and Sheila Kimmel, *Empower Yourself: Every Woman's Guide to Self-Esteem* (New York: Avon Books, 1997).

9. Carl Jung, *The Undiscovered Self* (New York: Little, Brown, 1957).

10. Copeland, *Living Without Depression and Manic Depression.*

11. Kahn and Kimmel, *Empower Yourself.*

12. J. Krishnamurti, *Freedom from the Known* (New York: HarperCollins, 1969).

CHAPTER 11

1. J. McClellan and J. Werry, "Practice Parameters for the Assessment and Treatment of Children and Adolescents with Bipolar Illness," *Journal of the American Academy of Child and Adolescent Psychiatry* 36, no. 1 (1997): 138–157.

2. M. Hellander, executive director, Child and Adolescent Bipolar Foundation, personal communication, July 14, 1999.

3. Boris Birmaher et al., "Clinical Course of Children and Adolescents with Bipolar Spectrum Disorders," *Archives of General Psychiatry* 63, no. 2 (2006): 175–183.

4. B. Geller and J. Luby, "Child and Adolescent Bipolar Disorder: A Review of the Past Ten Years," *Journal of the American Academy of Child and Adolescent Psychiatry* 36, no. 9 (1997): 1168–1176.

5. Ibid.

6. D. Papolos and J. Papolos, *The Bipolar Child* (New York: Broadway Books, 1999).

7. Kay Redfield Jamison, *Night Falls Fast* (New York: Alfred A. Knopf, 1999), 48.

8. M. Strober et al., "Recovery and Relapse in Adolescents with Bipolar Illness: A Five-Year Naturalistic Study," *American Journal of the Academy of Child and Adolescent Psychiatry* 34, no. 6 (1995): 724–731.

9. Mani Pavuluri et al., "Pediatric Bipolar Disorder: A Review of the Past 10 Years," *Journal of the American Academy of Child and Adolescent Psychiatry* 44, no. 9 (2005): 846–871.

10. B. Birmaher et. al., "Clinical Course of Children and Adolescents with Bipolar Spectrum Disorders."

11. R. A. Kowatch et al., "Treatment Guidelines for the Treatment of Child and Adolescent Bipolar Disorder," *Journal of the American Academy of Child and Adolescent Psychiatry* 44, no. 3 (2005): 213–235.

12. McClellan and Werry, "Practice Parameters for the Assessment and Treatment of Children and Adolescents with Bipolar Illness," 138–157.

13. American Psychiatric Association, *Diagnostic and Statistical Manual of Mental Disorders,* 4th ed. (Washington, DC: American Psychiatric Association, 1994).

14. M. Bowring and M. Kovacs, "Difficulties in Diagnosing Manic Disorders in Children and Adolescents," *Journal of the American Academy of Child and Adolescent Psychiatry* 31, no. 4 (1992): 611–614.

15. Frederick K. Goodwin and Kay Redfield Jamison, *Manic-Depressive Illness* (New York: Oxford University Press, 1990).

16. C. Sarnii, *The Development of Emotional Competence* (New York: Guilford Press, 1999).

17. Boris Birmaher, *New Hope for Children and Teens with Bipolar Disorder* (New York: Three Rivers Press, 2004).

18. B. Geller and M. P. DelBello, *Bipolar Disorder in Childhood and Early Adolescence* (New York: Guilford Press, 2003).

19. R. Gittelman, S. Manuzza, and R. Shenker, "Hyperactive Boys Almost Grown Up," *Archives of General Psychiatry* 42, no. 10 (1985): 937–947.

20. J. Biederman et al., "Attention-Deficit Hyperactivity Disorder and Juvenile Mania: An Overlooked Comorbidity?" *Journal of the American Academy of Child and Adolescent Psychiatry* 35, no. 8 (1996): 997–1008.

21. C. Popper, "Diagnosing Bipolar vs. ADHD: A Pharmacological Point of View," *The Link* 13 (1996), cited in D. Papolos and J. Papolos, *The Bipolar Child.*

22. B. Geller et al., "Two-Year Prospective Follow-up of Children with a Prepubertal and Early Adolescent Bipolar Disorder Phenotype," *American Journal of Psychiatry* 159, no. 6 (2002): 927–933.

23. E. Costello, "Child Psychiatric Disorders and Their Correlates: A Primary Care Pediatric Sample," *Journal of the American Academy of Child and Adolescent Psychiatry* 8, no. 6 (1989): 851–855; Geller and DelBello, *Bipolar Disorder in Childhood and Early Adolescence.*

24. T. Achenbach, *The Child Behavior Checklist,* cited in J. Impara and B. Plake, *The Thirteenth Mental Measurement Yearbook* (Lincoln, NE: Buros Institute of Mental Measurements, 1998).

25. P. L. Hazell et al., "Confirmation that the Child Behavior Checklist Clinical Scales Discriminate Juvenile Mania from Attention Deficit Hyperactivity Disorder," *Journal of Pediatric Child Health* 35, no. 2 (1999): 199–203.

26. M. Kovacs and M. Pollock, "Bipolar Disorder and Co-morbid Conduct Disorder in Childhood and Adolescence," *Journal of the American Academy of Child and Adolescent Psychiatry* 34, no. 6 (1995): 715–723.

27. Papolos and Papolos, *The Bipolar Child.*

28. M. Strober et al., "A Family Study of Bipolar I Disorder in Adolescence: Early Onset of Symptoms Linked to Increased Familial Loading and Lithium Resistance," *Journal of Affective Disorders* 15, no. 3 (1988): 255–268.

29. M. Grigoroiu-Serbanescu et al., "Clinical Evidence for Genomic Imprinting in Bipolar I Disorder," *Acta Psychiatrica Scandinavica* 92, no. 5 (1995): 365–370.

30. Geller and Luby, "Child and Adolescent Bipolar Disorder," 1168–1176.

31. James Chandler, "Bipolar Affective Disorder (Manic Depressive Disorder) in Children and Adolescents" (2006), http://www.klis.com/chandler/pamphlet/bipolar/bipolarpamphlet.htm.

32. R. Baldessarini and L. Tondo, "Antisuicidal Effect of Lithium Treatment in Major Mood Disorders," in *The Harvard Medical School Guide to Suicide Assessment and Intervention,* ed. D. Jacobs (San Francisco: Jossey-Bass Publishers, 1998).

33. "Child and Adolescent Bipolar Disorder: An Update from the National Institute of Mental Health" (April 2000), http://www.nimh.nih.gov.

34. McClellan and Werry, "Practice Parameters for the Assessment and Treatment of Children and Adolescents with Bipolar Illness," 138–157.

35. Papolos and Papolos, *The Bipolar Child.*

36. Birmaher, *New Hope for Children and Teens with Bipolar Disorder.*

37. Papolos and Papolos, *The Bipolar Child.*

38. D. J. Miklowitz and J. M. Hooley, "Developing Family Psychoeducational

Treatments for Patients with Bipolar and Other Severe Psychiatric Disorders: A Pathway from Basic Research to Clinical Trials," *Journal of Marital and Family Therapy* 24 (1998): 419–435.

39. T. L. Simoneau and D. J. Miklowitz, "Expressed Emotion and Interactional Patterns in the Family of Bipolar Patients," *Journal of Abnormal Psychology* 107 (1998): 497–507.

40. Child and Adolescent Bipolar Foundation Web site, http://www.bpkids.org.

CHAPTER 12

1. D. J. Miklowitz and J. M. Hooley, "Developing Family Psychoeducational Treatments for Patients with Bipolar and Other Severe Psychiatric Disorders: A Pathway from Basic Research to Clinical Trials," *Journal of Marital and Family Therapy* 24 (1998): 419–435.

2. T. L. Simoneau and D. J. Miklowitz, "Expressed Emotion and Interactional Patterns in the Family of Bipolar Patients," *Journal of Abnormal Psychology* 107 (1998): 497–507.

CHAPTER 13

1. Kristen Neff, "Self-Compassion: An Alternative Way to Conceptualize and Measure Self-Attitudes" (paper presented at the American Psychological Association Conference, Atlanta, GA, 2005).

2. Ibid.

3. D. Miklowitz and E. Frank, "New Psychotherapies for Bipolar Disorders," in *Bipolar Disorders: Clinical Course and Outcome,* ed. J. F. Goldberg and M. Harrow (Washington, DC: American Psychiatric Press, 1999), 74.

4. C. Newman et. al., *Bipolar Disorder: A Cognitive Therapy Approach* (Washington, DC: American Psychological Association, 2002), 186.

5. Mark A. Lau and Shelley F. McMain, "Integrating Mindfulness Meditation with Cognitive and Behavioural Therapies: The Challenge of Combining Acceptance- and Change-Based Strategies," *Canadian Journal of Psychiatry* 50, no. 13 (2005): 863–869.

6. B. H. Gunaratana, *Mindfulness in Plain English* (Boston: Wisdom Publications, 2002).

7. The Dalai Lama, *An Open Heart: Practicing Compassion in Everyday Life* (Boston: Little, Brown 2001).

8. Ram Dass, *Journey of Awakening: A Meditator's Guidebook* (New York: Bantam, 1990).

9. Ibid., 45.

10. Thich Nhat Hanh, *The Miracle of Mindfulness* (Boston: Beacon, 1987), 20.

11. Steven C. Hayes, Victoria M. Follette, and Marsha M. Linehan, eds., *Mindfulness and Acceptance: Expanding the Cognitive-Behavioral Tradition* (New York: Guilford Press, 2004).

12. S. H. Ma and J. D. Teasdale, "Mindfulness-Based Cognitive Therapy for Depression: Replication and Exploration of Differential Relapse Prevention Effects," *Journal of Consulting and Clinical Psychology* 72 (2004): 31–40.

CHAPTER 14

1. Harvard Public Health, "Groundbreaking Global Burden of Disease Study Marks Anniversary," October 2006 http://www.hsph.harvard.edu/now/20061027/bdu.html.

Glossary

amygdala	Almond-sized group of cells which assign positive or negative emotional responses to experience.
anhedonia	Loss of ability to feel pleasure.
basal ganglia	An area of the brain known to control body movement; may have an effect on emotional responses.
bipolar disorder	Formerly known as manic-depressive illness; a mood disorder characterized by at least one episode of mania or hypomania.
cerebral cortex	The right and left hemispheres of the brain.
cingulate gyrus	Part of the limbic system, channels affect (emotions, feelings) and drive.
clinical depression	Depressed mood, low energy, loss of capacity for pleasure, changes in sleep and/or appetite lasting more than two weeks and causing impairment of work or social function.
cognitive therapy	Psychotherapy focusing on identifying distortions of thinking and challenging and replacing them with more realistic thoughts.
concordant	When referring to diseases in twins, both members of the twin pair are affected.
congenital	Being born with, genetically or during development in utero prior to birth.
cyclothymia	The mildest form of bipolar disorder, including numerous periods of hypomania and mild depression.

dementia	Severe impairment or loss of intellectual capacity and personality integration.
discordant	When referring to diseases in twins, affecting only one twin.
dizygotic (DZ) twins	Fraternal twins.
dysthymia	Depressive neurosis.
electroconvulsive therapy (ECT)	Commonly known as "shock therapy," works by transmitting weak currents through the brain to cause seizure while patient is anesthetized.
electroencephalogram (EEG)	Measures electrical brain wave frequencies.
etiology	Concerning the cause, or root of, an illness.
hippocampus	Folded area of the base of the brain in the temporal lobes, controlling short-term memory and conversion to long-term memory which involve intellectual and emotional responses.
hyperthymia	*See* cyclothymia.
hypomania	A mild form of mania that neither causes psychosis nor leads to hospitalization.
hypothalamus	A cluster of nerve cells that controls appetite, sexual responses, mood responses, and the pituitary gland.
limbic system	Near center of brain, composed of amygdala, cingulate gyrus, hippocampus, hypothalamus, pituitary gland.
lithium	A mood-stabilizing drug, used to treat the manic phase of bipolar disorder.
magnetic resonance imaging (MRI)	Scans that produce pictures of the body (including the brain) using magnetic fields and radio waves.
manic depression	*See* bipolar disorder.
monoamine oxidase inhibitors (MAOIs)	Tricyclic antidepressants.
monozygotic (MZ) twins	Identical twins.
neurotransmitter	A biochemical substance released by nerve endings which chemically transmit nerve impulses.
neurotropic substances	Substances that promote growth and repair of nerve tissue.
neutron	An electrically neutral atomic particle.

obsessive-compulsive disorder	Recurrent and intrusive thoughts and impulses (obsessions) and repetitive behaviors or mental acts (compulsions) causing discomfort that arises from anxiety/depression.
oligogenic inheritance	Inheritance owing to several genes.
pituitary gland	Major endocrine gland at the base of the brain, which controls growth and regulates hormonal stress.
Positron emission tomography (PET)	A means of measuring brain metabolism.
prefrontal (and frontal) lobes	Of the cerebral cortex, located behind the forehead, the center of human intelligence and individual personality.
psychosis	An extreme mental state, characterized by a seriously disorganized personality and reality impairment; may include auditory, visual, or tactile hallucinations or delusions.
rapid cycling	Four or more episodes (mania, hypomania, depression, mixed state) in a one-year period.
reuptake	A process of the inactivation of neurotransmitters (biochemical substances).
selective serotonin reuptake inhibitors (SSRIs)	Antidepressant medication that blocks the reabsorption of serotonin.
serotonin	A neurotransmitter (biochemical substance) released by nerve endings in the brain that is related to mood and anxiety states.
tricyclic antidepressants	The first discovered antidepressants; though still very effective, they cause more side effects and toxicity than SSRIs.
unidentified bright objects (UBOs)	Suspected (but unconfirmed) small vessel damage viewed light areas on MRI brain scans.
unipolar disorder	A mood disorder; recurrent bouts of depression without cyclic episodes of mania.

Resources

AMERICAN ASSOCIATION FOR GERIATRIC
    PSYCHIATRY
7910 Woodmont Ave.
Suite 11050
Bethesda, MD 20815
Phone: (301) 654-7850
Web site: www.aagpgpa.org

AMERICAN ASSOCIATION FOR MARRIAGE AND
    FAMILY THERAPY
1133 15th St. NW
Suite 300
Washington, DC 20005
Phone: (202) 452-0109
Web site: www.aamft.org

AMERICAN ASSOCIATION OF CHILD AND
    ADOLESCENT PSYCHIATRY
3615 Wisconsin Ave. NW
Washington, DC 20016
Phone: (202) 966-7300
Web site: www.aacap.org

AMERICAN ASSOCIATION OF SUICIDOLOGY
4201 Connecticut Ave. NW
Suite 408
Washington, DC 20008
Phone: (202) 237-2280

Fax: (202) 237-2282
Web site: www.suicidology.org

AMERICAN FOUNDATION FOR SUICIDE
    PREVENTION
120 Wall St.
22nd Floor
New York, NY 10005
Phone: (888) 333-2377
Fax: (212) 363-6237
Web site: www.afsp.org

AMERICAN PSYCHIATRIC ASSOCIATION
1400 K Street NW
Washington, DC 20005
Phone: (888) 357-7924
Web site: www.psych.org

AMERICAN PSYCHOLOGICAL ASSOCIATION
750 First Street NE
Washington, DC 20002
Phone: (202) 336-5700 or
(800) 374-3120
Web site: www.apa.org

ANXIETY DISORDERS ASSOCIATION
    OF AMERICA
11900 Parklawn Dr.
Suite 100

Rockville, MD 20852
Phone: (301) 231-9350
Fax: (301) 231-7392
Web site: www.adaa.org

BAZELON CENTER
1101 15th St. NW
Suite 1212
Washington, DC 20005
Phone: (202) 467-5730
Web site: www.bazelon.org

BIPOLAR CHILDREN NEWSLETTER
Web site: www.bpchildren.com

BIPOLAR DISORDERS PORTAL
Your Gateway to the Web
Web site: www.pendulum.org

BPSO PUBLIC PAGES
Web site: www.bpso.org

CENTERS FOR DISEASE CONTROL AND
    PREVENTION
National Center for Injury Prevention
    and Control
Web site: www.cdc.gov/ncipc

CHILD AND ADOLESCENT BIPOLAR
    FOUNDATION (CABF)
Phone: (847) 256-8525
Web sites: www.cabf.org;
    www.bpkids.org/site/PageServer

DEPRESSION AFTER DELIVERY
PO Box 1282
Morrisville, PA 19607
Phone: (800) 944-4773
Web site: www.infotrail.com

DEPRESSION AND BIPOLAR SUPPORT ALLIANCE
    (DBSA)
730 North Franklin St.
Suite 501
Chicago, IL 60610
Phone: (800) 826-3632

Fax: (312) 642-7243
Web site: www.dbsalliance.org

DEPRESSION AND RELATED AFFECTIVE
    DISORDERS ASSOCIATION (DRADA)
8201 Greensboro Dr.
Suite 300
McLean, VA 22102
Phone: (410) 583-2919; (703) 610-9026;
    888-288-1104
Web site: www.drada.org

HEALTH RESOURCES AND SERVICES
    ADMINISTRATION
Web site: www.hrsa.dhhs.gov

JUVENILE BIPOLAR RESEARCH FOUNDATION
    (JBRF)
Web site: www.bpchildresearch.org

MEN'S HEALTH NETWORK
PO Box 75972
Washington, DC 20013
Phone: (888) MEN-2-MEN
Web site:
    www.info@menshealthnetwork.org

NATIONAL ALLIANCE FOR RESEARCH ON
    SCHIZOPHRENIA AND DEPRESSION
60 Cutter Mill Rd.
Suite 404
Great Neck, NY 11021
Phone: (516) 829-0091
Fax: (516) 487-6930
Web site: www.narsad.org

NATIONAL ALLIANCE FOR THE MENTALLY ILL
2107 Wilson Blvd.
Suite 300
Arlington, VA 22201
Phone: (703) 524-7600; (800) 950-6264
Fax: (703) 524-9094
Web site: www.nami.org

NATIONAL ASSOCIATION OF SOCIAL
   WORKERS
750 First St. NE
Suite 700
Washington, DC 20002
Phone: (800) 638-8799
Web site: www.socialworkers.org

NATIONAL FOUNDATION FOR
Depressive Illness
PO Box 2257
New York, NY 10116
Phone: (800) 239-1265
Web site: www.depression.org

NATIONAL INSTITUTE OF MENTAL HEALTH
6001 Executive Blvd.
Bethesda, MD 20892
Phone: (800) 421-4211
Web site: www.nimh.nih.gov

NATIONAL INSTITUTE OF MENTAL HEALTH
   SUICIDE RESEARCH CONSORTIUM
Web site: http://www.nimh.nih.gov/

NATIONAL INSTITUTE ON ALCOHOL ABUSE
   AND ALCOHOLISM
6000 Executive Blvd.
Willco Bldg.
Bethesda, MD 20892
Web site: www.niaaa.nih.gov

NATIONAL INSTITUTE ON DRUG ABUSE
6001 Executive Blvd.
Bethesda, MD 20892
Phone: (800) 644-6432
Web site: www.nida.nih.gov

NATIONAL MENTAL HEALTH ASSOCIATION
1201 Prince St.
Alexandria, VA 22314
Phone: (800) 969-6642
Fax: (703) 684-5968
Web site: www.nmha.org

NATIONAL WOMEN'S HEALTH RESOURCE
   CENTER
120 Albany St.
Suite 820
New Brunswick, NJ 08901
Phone: (877) 986-9472; (732) 828-8575
Web site: www.healthywomen.org

OBSESSIVE-COMPULSIVE FOUNDATION
337 Notch Hill Rd.
North Branford, CT 06471
Phone: (203) 315-2190
Web site: www.ocfoundation.org

PARENTING BIPOLARS: A SURVIVAL GUIDE
   FOR PARENTS
Web sites: www.parentingbipolars.com;
   http://dmoz.org/Health/Mental_Health/
   Disorders/Mood/BipolarDisorder/
   Children_and_Teens/

SCREENING FOR MENTAL HEALTH, INC.
One Washington St.
Suite 304
Wellesley Hills, MA 02481
Phone: (800) 573-4433 (depression
   screening)
Fax: (781) 431-7447
Web site: www.nmisp.org

SEACOAST MENTAL HEALTH CENTER, INC.
1145 Sagamore Ave.
Portsmouth, NH 03801
Phone: (603) 431-6703
Web site: www.smhc-nh.org

SEXUAL FUNCTION HEALTH COUNCIL
American Foundation for Urologic Disease
300 West Pratt St.
Suite 401
Baltimore, MD 21201
Phone: (800) 242-2383
Web site: www.afud.org

Bibliography

Albom, Mitch. *Tuesdays with Morrie.* New York: Doubleday, 1997.

Bacon, Sir Francis. *Gateway to the Great Books.* Chicago: Britannica, 1963.

Beck, A., A. Rush, B. Shaw, et al. *Cognitive Therapy of Depression.* New York: Guilford Press, 1979.

Beitman, Bernard D. *Structure of Individual Psychotherapy.* New York: Guilford Press, 1987.

Birmaher, Boris. *New Hope for Children and Teens with Bipolar Disorder: Your Friendly Authoritative Guide to the Latest in Traditional and Complementary Solutions.* New York: Three Rivers Press, 2004.

Bowring, M., and M. Kovacs. "Difficulties in Diagnosing Manic Disorders in Children and Adolescents." *Journal of the American Academy of Child and Adolescent Psychiatry* 31, no. 4 (1992): 611–614.

Bratman, Steven. *The Alternative Medicine Ratings Guide.* Roseville, CA: Prima Publishing, 1998.

———. *Beat Depression with St. John's Wort.* Roseville, CA: Prima Publishing, 1997.

Burlingame, Michael. *The Inner World of Abraham Lincoln.* Champaign: University of Illinois Press, 1994.

Burns, David D. *Feeling Good: The New Mood Therapy.* New York: Avon Books, 1992.

———. *Feeling Good: Ten Days to Self-Esteem.* New York: William Morrow, 1993.

Carlson, Karen J., Stephanie A. Eisenstat, and Terra Ziporyn. *The Harvard Guide to Women's Health.* Cambridge, MA: Harvard University Press, 1996.

Carlson, Richard. *Don't Sweat the Small Stuff.* New York: Hyperion, 1997.

Chandler, James. www.drsoft.com/chandler/pamphlet/bipolar//bipolarpamphlet.htm

Clark, David M., and Christopher G. Fairburn. *Science and Practice of Cognitive Behavioral Therapy.* New York: Oxford University Press, 1997.

Copeland, Mary Ellen. *Living Without Depression and Manic Depression.* Oakland, CA: New Harbinger, 1994.

Costello, E. "Child Psychiatric Disorders and Their Correlates: A Primary Care Pediatric Sample." *Journal of the American Academy of Child and Adolescent Psychiatry* 28, no. 6 (1989): 851–855.

Cronkite, Kathy. *On the Edge of Darkness.* New York: Delta, 1995.

Csikszentmihalyi, Mihaly. *Flow: The Psychology*

of Optimal Experience. New York: Harper-Perennial, 1990.

Dobson, K. *The Handbook of Cognitive Therapies.* New York: Guilford Press, 1988.

Duke, Patty, and Gloria Hochman. *Brilliant Madness: Living with Manic-Depressive Illness.* New York: Bantam Books, 1992.

Esters, I., P. Cooker, and R. Ittenbach. "Effects on a Unit of Instruction in Mental Health on Rural Adolescents' Conceptions of Mental Illness and Attitudes About Seeking Help." *Adolescence* 33, no. 130 (1998): 469–476.

Ettlinger, R. W., and P. Flordh. "Attempted Suicide: Experience of 500 Cases at a General Hospital." *Acta Psychiatrica Neurologica Scandinavica* 103, suppl. (1955): 1–45.

Evans, Dwight L., and Linda Wasmer Andrews. *If Your Adolescent Has Depression or Bipolar Disorder: An Essential Resource for Parents.* New York: Oxford University Press, 2005.

Fawcett, Jan, W. A. Scheftner, L. Fogg, et al. "Time-Related Predictors of Suicide in Major Affective Disorder." *American Journal of Psychiatry* 147, no. 9 (1990): 1189–1194.

Feniger, Mani. *Journey from Anxiety to Freedom.* Rocklin, CA: Prima Publishing, 1997.

Foley, Denise, and Eileen Nechas. *Women's Encyclopedia of Health and Emotional Healing.* New York: Bantam Books, 1995.

Ford, Gillian. *Listening to Your Hormones.* Rocklin, CA: Prima Publishing, 1995.

Frank, Otto. *Anne Frank: The Diary of a Young Girl.* New York: Doubleday, 1995.

Frankl, Viktor E. *Man's Search for Meaning.* New York: Pocket Books, 1963.

———. *Man's Search for Ultimate Meaning.* Hagerstown, MD: Insight Books, 1997.

———. *Viktor Frankl Recollections: An Autobiography.* Hagerstown, MD: Insight Books, 1995.

Freud, Sigmund. *The Interpretation of Dreams.* New York: Avon Books, 1965.

Geller, B., and J. Luby. "Child and Adolescent Bipolar Disorder: A Review of the Past 10 Years." *Journal of the American Academy of Child and Adolescent Psychiatry* 36, no. 9 (1997): 1168–1176.

Gies, Miep. *Anne Frank Remembered.* New York: Simon and Schuster, 1987.

Gittelman, R., S. Manuzza, R. Shenker, et al. "Hyperactive Boys Almost Grown Up." *Archives of General Psychiatry* 42, no. 10 (1985): 937–947.

Goldfried, M., and G. Davison. *Clinical Behavior Therapy.* New York: Holt, Rinehart and Winston, 1976.

Goleman, Daniel. *Emotional Intelligence.* New York: Bantam Books, 1995.

Goodwin, Frederick K., and Tracey L. Irvin. "General Guidelines and Intricacies in the Treatment of Bipolar Disorder." Paper, annual meeting of the American Psychiatric Association, 1999, http://www.medscape.com.

Goodwin, Frederick K., and Kay Redfield Jamison. *Manic-Depressive Illness.* New York: Oxford University Press, 1990.

Gore, Tipper, and Rosalynn Carter. "On America's Mental Health Crisis." *Psychology Today,* September–October 1999, http://psychologytoday.com/articles/pto-19990901-000032.html.

Gray, John. *Men Are from Mars, Women Are from Venus.* New York: HarperCollins, 1992.

Grigoroiu-Serbanescu, M., P. J. Wickramaratne, S. E. Hodge, et al. "Genetic Anticipation and Imprinting in Bipolar 1 Illness." *British Journal of Psychiatry,* 170 (1997): 162–166.

Hall, Richard C. W., Dennis E. Platt, and Ryan C. W. Hall. "Suicide Risk Assessment: A Review of Risk Factors for Suicide in 100 Patients Who Made Severe Suicide Attempts." *Psychosomatics* 40 (1999): 18–27, http://psy.psychiatryonline.org/cgi/content/abstract/40/1/18.

Hazell, P. L., T. J. Lewin, V. J. Carr, et al. "Confirmation that the Child Behavior Checklist Clinical Scales Discriminate Juvenile Mania from

Attention Deficit Hyperactivity Disorder." *Journal of Pediatric Child Health* 35, no. 2 (1999): 199–203.

Hill, Napoleon, and W. Clement Stone. *Success Through a Positive Mental Attitude.* Chicago: Prentice-Hall, 1960.

Hite, Shere. *Women & Love.* New York: St. Martin's Press, 1987.

Jamison, Kay Redfield. *Night Falls Fast.* New York: Alfred A. Knopf, 1999.

———. *Touched with Fire.* New York: Free Press, 1994.

———. *An Unquiet Mind.* New York: Vintage Books, 1996.

Jong, Erica. *Fear of Fifty.* New York: HarperPaperbacks, 1995.

Jung, C. G. *The Undiscovered Self.* New York: Little, Brown, 1957.

Kahn, Ada P., *Stress A-Z: A Sourcebook for Facing Everyday Challenges.* New York: Facts on File,1998.

Kahn, Ada, and Linda Hughey Holt. *Midlife Health: A Woman's Practical Guide to Feeling Good.* New York: Avon Books, 1989.

Kahn, Ada, and Sheila Kimmel. *Empower Yourself: Every Woman's Guide to Self-Esteem.* New York: Avon Books, 1997.

Kierkegaard, Søren. *Philosophers of the Spirit.* London: Hodder and Stoughton, 1997.

Kovacs, M., and M. Pollock. "Bipolar Disorder and Co-morbid Conduct Disorder in Childhood and Adolescence." *Journal of the American Academy of Child and Adolescent Psychiatry* 34, no. 6 (1995): 715–723.

Kramer, Peter D. *Listening to Prozac.* New York: Penguin Books, 1994.

Krishnamurti, J. *Freedom from the Known.* New York: HarperCollins, 1969.

Kushner, Rabbi Harold S. *How Good Do We Have to Be?* New York: Little, Brown, 1996.

———. *When Bad Things Happen to Good People.* New York: Avon Books, 1983.

Lazarus, R. S., and S. Folkman. *Stress: Appraisal and Coping.* New York: Springer, 1984.

Lederman, Judith, and Candida Fink. *The Ups and Downs of Raising a Bipolar Child.* New York: Fireside, 2003.

Levi, Primo. *Survival in Auschwitz.* New York: Collier Books, 1961.

Lewis, Michael. *Shame: The Exposed Self.* New York: The Free Press, 1995.

Lynn, George. *Survival Strategies for Parenting Children with Bipolar Disorder: Innovative Parenting and Counseling Techniques for Helping Children with Bipolar Disorder and the Conditions That May Occur with It.* London: Jessica Kingsley, 2000.

Maclaine, Shirley. *Dance While You Can.* New York: Bantam Books, 1991.

———. *Dancing in the Light.* New York: Bantam Books, 1985.

———. *Going Within.* New York: Bantam Books, 1989.

———. *Out on a Limb.* New York: Bantam Books, 1983.

Masters, William H., Virginia E. Johnson, and Robert C. Kolodny. *Heterosexuality.* New York: HarperPerennial, 1992.

May, Rollo. *Existence.* New York: Basic Books, 1958.

McClellan, J., and J. Werry. "Practice Parameters for the Assessment and Treatment of Children and Adolescents with Bipolar Illness." *Journal of the American Academy of Child and Adolescent Psychiatry* 36 (1997): 138–157.

Müller, Melissa. *Anne Frank: The Biography.* New York: Metropolitan Books, 1998.

Muskianth, Dr. Susan. *Depression Matters.* Johannesburg, South Africa: Delta Books, 1997.

———. *Stress Matters.* Johannesburg: William Waterman Publications, 1996.

National Depressive and Manic-Depressive Association, "Consensus Statement on the Undertreatment of Depression." *Journal of the American Medical Association* 277, no. 4 (1997): 333–340.

Opler, Lewis A., and Carol Bialkowski. *Prozac and Other Psychiatric Drugs.* New York: Pocket Books, 1996.

Papolos, Demitri, and Janice Papolos. *The Bipolar Child.* New York: Broadway Books, 1999.

Papolos, Demitri, and Janice Papolos. *Bipolar Child: The Definitive and Reassuring Guide to Childhood's Most Misunderstood Disorder* (rev. and expanded ed.). New York: Broadway, 2002.

———. *Overcoming Depression.* New York: HarperPerennial, 1997.

Pinsky, Drew. *Restoring Intimacy: The Patient's Guide to Maintaining Relationships During Depression.* Chicago: The National Depressive and Manic-Depressive Association, 1999.

Pollitt, Kathy. "Depression Confession." *Nation,* June 28, 1999, 10.

Ratushinskaya, Irina. *No, I'm Not Afraid.* Newcastle upon Tyne, England: Bloodaxe Books, 1986.

Robins, Eli, G. E. Murphy, R. H. Wilkinson, et al. "Some Clinical Considerations in the Prevention of Suicide Based on a Study of 134 Successful Suicides." *American Journal of Public Health* 49 (1959): 888–899.

Rosenbaum, Jerrold F., M.D., and Steffany Fredman. "Medication Controversies in the Treatment of Bipolar Disorder." Paper, annual meeting of the American Psychiatric Association, 1999, http://www.medscape.com.

Rosenfeld, Nancy. *Just as Much a Woman.* Rocklin, CA: Prima Publishing, 1999.

———. *Unfinished Journey: From Tyranny to Freedom.* Lanham, MD: University Press of America, 1993.

Rothenberg, Robert E. *The New American Medical Dictionary and Health Manual.* New York: Signet Reference, 1992.

Roy, A., G. Rylander, and M. Sarchiapone. "Genetics of Suicide: Family Studies and Molecular Genetics." *Annals of New York Academy of Sciences* 29, no. 836 (1997): 135–157.

Sarnii, C. *The Development of Emotional Competence.* New York: Guilford Press, 1999.

Seligman, Martin E. P. *Learned Optimism.* New York: Pocket Books, 1998.

Sheehy, Gail. *Passages.* New York: Bantam Books, 1976.

———. *Pathfinders.* New York: Bantam Books, 1982.

———. *The Silent Passage: Menopause.* New York: Pocket Books, 1982.

Simopoulos, Artemis P., and Jo Robinson. *The Omega Plan.* New York: HarperCollins, 1998.

Singer, Cindy, and Sheryl Gurrentz. *If Your Child Is Bipolar: The Parent-to-Parent Guide to Living with and Loving a Bipolar Child.* London: Perspective, 2003.

Skog, Susan. *Embracing Our Essence: Spiritual Conversations with Prominent Women.* Deerfield Beach, FL: Health Communications, 1995.

Sontag, Susan. *Illness as Metaphor and AIDS and Its Metaphors.* New York: Doubleday, 1990.

Steel, Danielle. *His Bright Light.* New York: Delacorte Press, 1998.

Strober, M., W. Morrell, J. Burroughs, et al. "A Family Study of Bipolar I Disorder in Adolescence: Early Onset of Symptoms Linked to Increased Familial Loading and Lithium Resistance." *Journal of Affective Disorders* 15, no. 3 (1988): 255–268.

Strober, M., S. Schmidt-Lackner, R. Freeman, et al. "Recovery and Relapse in Adolescents with Bipolar Illness: A Five-Year Naturalistic Study." *Journal of the American Academy of Child and Adolescent Psychiatry* 34: 724–731.

Tarnopolsky, Yuri. *Memoirs of 1984.* Lanham, MD: University Press of America, 1993.

Taylor, Shelley E. *Positive Illusions.* New York: Basic Books, 1989.

Tejedor, M. C., A. Diaz, J. J. Castillon, et al. "Attempted Suicide: Repetition and Survival—Findings of a Follow-up Study." *Acta Psychiatrica Scandinavica* 100, no. 3 (1999): 205–211.

Torrey, E. Fuller, Ann E. Bowler, Edward H. Taylor, et al. *Schizophrenia and Manic-Depressive Disorder.* New York: Basic Books, 1994.

"The Uncounted Enemy: A Vietnam Deception." *CBS News Reports* (1982 documentary with Mike Wallace), http://www.s-t.com/daily/01-98/01-05-98/c01ae100.htm

Wachtler, Sol. *After the Madness: A Judge's Own Prison Memoir.* New York: Random House, 1992.

Weissmann, Arlene Nancy. "The Dysfunctional Attitudes Scale: A Validation Study." *Dissertation Abstracts International* (1979): 1389–1390.

"What It Would Really Take." *Time,* June 17, 1999, 54–55.

Wiesel, Elie. *Dawn.* New York: Avon Books, 1960.

———. *Les Juifs du Silence.* Paris: Editions du Seuil, 1966.

Wolpert, Dr. Edward Alan. *Manic Depressive Illness: History of a Syndrome.* New York: International Universities Press, 1977.

Index

Page numbers in *italics* refer to figures and tables.

About the Authors

JAN FAWCETT, M.D., professor of psychiatry at the University of New Mexico School of Medicine, shared the Falcone Prize for research in depression and suicide from the National Alliance for Research in Schizophrenia and Depression (NARSAD) in 2005 and is presently the principal investigator of the National Institute of Mental Health–funded study "Prevention of Recurrent Depression with Medication and Cognitive Therapy." Dr. Fawcett was the Stanley G. Harris Professor and chairman of psychiatry at Rush–Presbyterian–St. Luke's Medical Center, Chicago (1972–2002) and in 1992 was also appointed Grainger Director of the Rush Institute for Mental Well-Being. A graduate of Yale University Medical School, Dr. Fawcett received the 1999 Menninger Award for distinguished contributions to the field of mental health, and the 2000 Lifetime Research Award from the American Foundation for Suicide Prevention.

Among his many achievements, Fawcett has been a principal or coinvestigator on more than forty individual mental health research projects, including four funded grants. In 1986, he helped found the National Depressive and Manic-Depressive Association (National

DMDA), renamed Depression and Bipolar Support Alliance (DBSA). In 1987, Dr. Fawcett became the first recipient of the Jan Fawcett Humanitarian Award, an award established by National DMDA.

Dr. Jan Fawcett is the author of seven other books, including *Manic-Depressive Illness,* 2nd ed. (Oxford University Press, 2007), and the editor of *Psychiatric Annals.*

BERNARD GOLDEN, PH.D., has been a practicing psychologist for more than thirty years. He served on staff of a community mental health center and in psychiatric hospitals and was a former associate professor at the Illinois School of Professional Psychology. During these years he maintained a private practice, at which he now engages full-time.

Dr. Golden studied at the National Psychological Association for Psychoanalysis in New York and has worked extensively with children, adolescents, and adults. In 1994, Dr. Golden founded Anger Management Education to offer adults classes, workshops, and counseling on anger management. Through these programs he teaches a unique model for effectively understanding and managing anger in personal relationships, in the work setting, and in daily living. The programs are described on the Web site www.angermanagementeducation.com. This framework is presented in his book *Healthy Anger: How to Help Children and Teens Manage Their Anger* (Oxford University Press, 2003), which was translated into Polish (2005), Spanish (2006), and Japanese (2007). He also authored *Unlock Your Creative Genius* (Prometheus Books, 2006).

NANCY ROSENFELD is the author of two other books, *Unfinished Journey: From Tyranny to Freedom* (University Press of America, 1993), which details her fight to free a Soviet political prisoner, and *Just as Much a Woman: Your Personal Guide to Hysterectomy and Beyond* (Prima Publishing, 1999).

After suffering a nervous breakdown in 1988, Nancy was later diagnosed with bipolar disorder. She has spent nearly twenty years studying this illness to more fully understand and resolve her own issues.

In 1993, Nancy founded AAA Books Unlimited, a literary agency based in a suburb of Chicago. Today, the agency represents authors nationwide and worldwide in a variety of genres with a focus on medical and psychological self-help titles. Nancy also is a public speaker on mental health issues, with extensive radio and television experience. She resides in the Chicago area with her husband, Martin.

In this life-changing book, you'll find compassionate and informative methods to help manage bipolar disorder and develop the natural strengths, gifts, and skills that every child has to offer.

NEW HOPE FOR CHILDREN AND TEENS WITH BIPOLAR DISORDER

Your Friendly, Authoritative Guide to the Latest in Traditional and Complementary Solutions

$18.95 ($28.95 Canada)
ISBN 978-0-7615-2718-3